The Latino Big Bang in California

FIGURE 1. Justo Veytia y Valencia left Guadalajara to seek gold in California in February 1849. He kept a diary for the eighteen months of his adventures. This portrait was painted later in life, after his marriage in 1863. (Courtesy of Luis Jaime Veytia Orozco.)

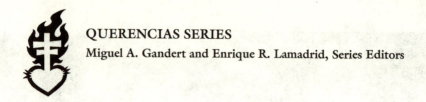

QUERENCIAS SERIES
Miguel A. Gandert and Enrique R. Lamadrid, Series Editors

Querencia is a popular term in the Spanish-speaking world that is used to express a deeply rooted love of place and people. This series promotes a transnational, humanistic, and creative vision of the US-Mexico borderlands based on all aspects of expressive culture, both material and intangible.

Also available in the Querencias Series:

The Poetics of Fire: Metaphors of Chile Eating in the Borderlands by Victor M. Valle

New Mexico's Moses: Reies López Tijerina and the Religious Origins of the Mexican American Civil Rights Movement by Ramón A. Gutiérrez

El Camino Real de California: From Ancient Pathways to Modern Byways by Joseph P. Sánchez

Chasing Dichos through Chimayó by Don J. Usner

Nación Genízara: Ethnogenesis, Place, and Identity in New Mexico edited by Moises Gonzales and Enrique R. Lamadrid

Querencia: Reflections on the New Mexico Homeland edited by Vanessa Fonseca-Chávez, Levi Romero, and Spencer R. Herrera

Imagine a City That Remembers: The Albuquerque Rephotography Project by Anthony Anella and Mark C. Childs

The Latino Christ in Art, Literature, and Liberation Theology by Michael R. Candelaria

Sisters in Blue / Hermanas de azul: Sor María de Ágreda Comes to New Mexico / Sor María de Ágreda viene a Nuevo México by Enrique R. Lamadrid and Anna M. Nogar

Aztlán: Essays on the Chicano Homeland, Revised and Expanded Edition edited by Francisco A. Lomelí, Rudolfo Anaya, and Enrique R. Lamadrid

For additional titles in the Querencias Series, please visit unmpress.com.

THE Latino Big Bang
IN California

The Diary of Justo Veytia,

a Mexican Forty-Niner

EDITED AND TRANSLATED BY
David E. Hayes-Bautista, Cynthia L. Chamberlin,
AND **Paul Bryan Gray**
EPILOGUE BY Luis Jaime Veytia Orozco

UNIVERSITY OF NEW MEXICO PRESS

ALBUQUERQUE

© 2023 by University of New Mexico Press
All rights reserved. Published 2023
Printed in the United States of America

First paperback printing 2025

ISBN 978-0-8263-6550-7 (cloth)
ISBN 978-0-8263-6814-0 (paper)
ISBN 978-0-8263-6551-4 (electronic)

Library of Congress Control Number: 2023943648

Founded in 1889, the University of New Mexico sits on the traditional homelands of the Pueblo of Sandia. The original peoples of New Mexico—Pueblo, Navajo, and Apache—since time immemorial have deep connections to the land and have made significant contributions to the broader community statewide. We honor the land itself and those who remain stewards of this land throughout the generations and also acknowledge our committed relationship to Indigenous peoples. We gratefully recognize our history.

Cover photographs courtesy of Wikimedia Commons and Bancroft Library at University of California, Berkeley.
Designed by Isaac Morris
Composed in Baskerville, Didot, and ITC Galliard

To the thousands of Latino '49ers and their children, who created the foundations of the bilingual, bicultural civil society of los Latinos de Estados Unidos during the California Gold Rush and US Civil War.

Latinos en Estados Unidos,
Ya casi somos una nación . . .
Pues todos somos hermanos
En un distinto país.

—Celia Cruz

Contents

PREFACE — xiii
ACKNOWLEDGMENTS — xvii

INTRODUCTION. The Latino Big Bang in California and Justo Veytia, a Mexican '49er — 1
David E. Hayes-Bautista
SPANISH TEXT OF JUSTO VEYTIA'S DIARY — 55
ENGLISH TRANSLATION OF JUSTO VEYTIA'S DIARY — 113
EPILOGUE. After Justo Veytia Returned to Mexico, 1850–2022 — 189
Luis Jaime Veytia Orozco

APPENDIX 1. Relative Population Composition Factors for San Francisco, Los Angeles, San Luis Obispo, and Tuolumne Counties and Combined Counties for 1850, 1860, and 1870 Censuses — 197
APPENDIX 2. Data to Estimate Latinos as Percent of California Population, 1860 and 1870 — 198
NOTES — 199
INDEX — 291

Preface

David E. Hayes-Bautista

On February 1, 1848, almost all of the 10,000 non-indigenous people in Alta California were Spanish-speaking citizens of the Republic of Mexico who lived their daily lives under Mexican civil institutions in a regional variant of Mexican society, identity, and culture. They were Mexicans in all senses of the term. In 2022, approximately 15.5 million people living in California call themselves Latinos or Hispanics or Mexican Americans or Chicanos or Central Americans or some other "Spanish origin."[1] By and large, they carry out their lives in both English and Spanish. They are not Mexicans in terms of citizenship, being primarily United States citizens or otherwise under US jurisdiction. They are proud to consider themselves Latinos.[2] What, when, why, and how did a regional variant of Mexican society, identity, and culture transform into the vibrant bilingual, bicultural civil society of los Latinos de Estados Unidos (US Latinos)?[3]

A sudden, forceful change in the mid-nineteenth century caused the transformation, which I like to call the Latino Big Bang. It wrenched Mexican citizens away from Mexico's society and institutions and placed them under US rule. It also shoehorned them not very comfortably into a US civil society whose Euro-American majority increasingly defined themselves and their institutions in white supremacist, and specifically Anglo-Saxonist, terms. The Latino Big Bang flared up on January 24, 1848, when the discovery of gold ignited the California Gold Rush. It blazed out ten days later, on February 2, when the Treaty of Guadalupe Hidalgo solidified the United States' conquest of Alta California.

This Big Bang created two aftereffects. The first was a Latino population explosion prompted by the discovery of gold. Hoping for riches, Latinos from Mexico, Central America, and South America flocked to California, inflating the Latino population by a factor of ten during the first decade of the Gold Rush. The second was a Latino constitutional earthquake when the Treaty of Guadalupe Hidalgo removed California from governance by the Mexican constitution, which had adopted racial equality in citizenship and the abolition of slavery, and placed it instead under the US constitution, which at the time enshrined principles of white supremacy in citizenship and the legal protection of slavery.

This book offers a rare window into this origin story of los Latinos de Estados Unidos in California. Justo Veytia, a Mexican '49er, came from Guadalajara to California to seek his fortune in the gold fields. He kept a diary of his eighteen-month sojourn, and through its pages we can witness the earliest years of this important social and cultural transformation.

A Note on Terminology

The Spanish-speaking population in California rocketed from 10,000 to more than 100,000 during the decades of the Gold Rush and American Civil War. It was a fluid mixture of native-born Californios and recently arrived immigrants from Mexico, Latin America (including Brazil), the Caribbean, and Spain, plus their children born in the United States. Faced with this robust heterogeneity, Spanish-language newspapers experimented with an array of ethnic terms to describe their readership. Some terms seemed too specific of one group and exclusive of others: *californios* (Californians),[4] *nativos californios* (native Californians),[5] *hijos del país* (native sons or children of the land),[6] *mexicanos residentes en California* (Mexicans living in California),[7] *sonorenses* (literally, people from the Mexican state of Sonora, but often used generally to mean recent Mexican immigrants),[8] or even *cholos* (a general despictive for lower-class Latinos).[9] Soon they came up with broader terms, some of which are still used today: *hispano-americanos* (Hispanic Americans),[10] *españoles* (Spanish speakers),[11] *hijos de las repúblicas hispano-americanas* (children of the Hispanic American republics),[12] and *raza latina* (Latino race).[13]

English-language newspapers, of course, had their own terms for Latinos. Some were more or less neutral, if not always accurate, such as applying the designation "Mexican" to any Latino, regardless of national origin,[14] or the English version of sonorense, "Sonoranian" (variants "Sonorian" and "Sonoran").[15] Others were openly derogatory: "greaser,"[16] "greaserita" (a female greaser),[17] "mongrel,"[18] and the like.

Given that Spanish-speaking newspapermen themselves struggled with this problem at the time, what terms should twenty-first-century scholars use to indicate collectively the people who made up this nineteenth-century population phenomenon?

The sudden acquisition of this exploding population in 1848 caught the 1850 census by surprise: while the census could provide instructions to the enumerators about how to carefully identify and enumerate Black and Indian populations, it had no ready-made category for the recently conquered mixed-race, Spanish-speaking populations in what are now California, Arizona, New Mexico, and Texas. While some members of these populations seemed clearly to be of African or Indian ancestry, others were not so easily identifiable, and this racial ambiguity caused problems for a census whose ethnic categories were based on the notion that people could be separated into races by a single drop of nonwhite blood. It would still do so during the 2020 census.

The debate about terminology continues in the twenty-first century: Latinx or Latine, Chicano, Nuyorican, Salvadoran American, and Chiricú (a portmanteau word combining Chicano, Puertorriqueño, and Cubano) are just a few modern terms. But in the interest of brevity and inclusivity, this book uses the terms *Latino* and *Hispanic* interchangeably, with a preference for Latino, to indicate members of a community whose daily life descends from three hundred years (approximately 1521–1821) of regional experiences of the Viceroyalties of New Spain (Mexico and Central America) and Peru (South America) and that currently exists under and participates in US institutions alongside the country's dominant English-speaking civil society. This community includes the experiences of American Indigenous peoples and the descendants of Africans and Asians as well as the descendants of Iberians and other Europeans.

The English-language press of the California Gold Rush used a number of terms to refer to the English-speaking population moving into California from the United States: Anglo Saxons,[19] Yankees,[20] white persons,[21] Americans,[22] Caucasians,[23] and even occasionally the rather pompous and inaccurate "Sons of the Pilgrims."[24] All these terms indicated the community descended from nearly 180 years (1607–1783) of regional experiences of colonies chartered by the British crown on the Atlantic coast of North America. As they arrived in California during the Gold Rush, these English speakers often still oriented themselves to that Atlantic coast. They left behind the "thickly settled states of the Atlantic" and journeyed west,[25] where they were pleasantly surprised on occasion to find "the staid matron and quiet maid of our own Atlantic States."[26] Their memories of home could be jogged by any number of small events, such as riding in an overcrowded omnibus to Mission Dolores, which evoked "memories of omnibus riding in the cities of the Atlantic."[27] Once they had made their fortune or else "busted out," they contemplated returning to "their homes in the Atlantic States."[28] Rather than try to distinguish between Celts, Anglo Saxons, Teutons, Franks, and Senegalese, however, this book refers to descendants of the British colonial experience on the Atlantic coast as Atlantic Americans, irrespective of race or ethnicity.

Acknowledgments

To provide historical context for Justo Veytia's diary, we have used both new and previously underused sources to present the experiences of Latinos during the California Gold Rush. The first such source is Veytia's diary itself, which to the best of our knowledge is the first diary of the Gold Rush written by a Mexican '49er to be published. The second source, previously little used by historians of California, is the Spanish-language newspapers published in the state during the Gold Rush and US Civil War. This qualitative source helps place Veytia's experience within a larger Latino narrative of those momentous events rather than trying to fit his experience into the already well-known Atlantic American narrative. The third is various quantitative sources, including US censuses for 1850, 1860, and 1870; birth, marriage, and death records from county recorders' offices in Los Angeles, San Luis Obispo, Santa Barbara, and Tuolumne Counties; lists of rancheros; and published lists of donors to the *Juntas Patrióticas Mejicanas* (Mexican Patriotic Assemblies) in 1862–1867. The census data was extracted by hand at the Center for the Study of Latino Health and Culture (CESLAC) at the David Geffen School of Medicine, UCLA, and entered into digital format for computer use, then analyzed for quality and completeness. Likewise, CESLAC staff hand-extracted from the Spanish-language newspapers 12,926 names and occasional personal information of the California donors to the Juntas Patrióticas Mejicanas and compiled lists of ranch owners from various published sources. The resulting data sets are available at CESLAC for those interested in digitized qualitative and quantitative data for the history of Latinos in Gold Rush and Civil War California.

Accordingly, this book is the product of the work of many people who mined and analyzed these data over years. They include Carlos Martinez,

Cecilia Cañadas, Juan Carlos Cornejo, Branden Jones, Gloria Meza, Sonia Hernández-Barrantes, Azucena Puerta-Díaz, Alejandra Martin, Karen Milian, M. Iya Kahramanian, Marta VanLandingham, Ernesto Medina, Jennifer Wei-Li, and Vivian Hsih. Further data on births were provided by Ted Gostin, a Los Angeles-area professional genealogist, who kindly augmented his published data for 1850 to 1859 with a hand tally for 1860–1869 from his unpublished data. Alejandra Osorio extracted key passages from the Spanish-language version of the minutes of the 1849 California Constitutional Convention.

Current members of CESLAC also assisted in many other ways. Through her administration of this project (and many others), both in person and remotely, Seira Santizo-Greenwood, CESLAC's chief of staff, kept the effort moving forward during the two years and more of the COVID-19 shutdown, ably assisted by project coordinator Adriana Valdez. Dr. Paul Hsu took time from his epidemiological interests to produce the maps of Justo Veytia's journeys and also constructed a robust system to manage the various types of data used in this project. Giselle Hernández produced the graphs. Laura Ochoa Jones translated into Spanish the footnotes to the transcription of Veytia's diary.

Profound thanks are also due to the Bancroft Library at the University of California, Berkeley, especially its Duplications and Permission Services; the Chicano Resource Center of the Los Angeles County Library system; Special Collections at the Charles E. Young Research Library, UCLA; Jennifer Lentz and Victoria Haindel of the UCLA Law Library; the Southern Regional Library Facility (SRLF) of the University of California; Special Collections at the University of Southern California Libraries; Alex Eloriaga at USC; the Lompoc Main Library; and Víctor Zúñiga, for design and technical assistance on one of the book's figures. This book could not have been made without them.

Heartfelt thanks go to Ramón Gutiérrez for steering this manuscript to the University of New Mexico Press; to Sonia Dickey, who functions marvelously as acquisitions editor there; and to Enrique Lamadrid for considering this book as part of the Querencias series. We would also like to thank our reviewers, John M. Nieto-Phillips and Anna Nogar, whose many suggestions made this manuscript stronger and more robust.

Cynthia L. Chamberlin would like to acknowledge the patience and moral support of her husband, Dr. Raymond V. Lavoie, during this

ACKNOWLEDGMENTS

years-long project; and her sister, Dr. Laurinda Chamberlin, for going out of her way to secure an important reference.

Paul Bryan Gray would like to acknowledge his wife, Felipa, for her patience throughout the work on this book.

Luis Jaime Veytia Orozco would like to acknowledge David E. and Teodocia Maria Hayes-Bautista for taking such interest in his great-grandfather's diary and in their efforts to make known to the public Justo Veytia's adventures in Alta California.

David E. Hayes-Bautista would like to acknowledge his wife, Teodocia Maria Hayes-Bautista, BSN, MPH, PhD, who gave of her time liberally while also heavily involved in graduate medical education at Adventist White Memorial Hospital; cousins Raúl and Ana Ofelia Bracamontes, who opened their house to him while he was conducting research in Guadalajara; cousins Dr. Hugo Wingartz and his wife, Patricia, who likewise hosted him while he was conducting research in Mexico City; and the Bluestone Lane coffee shop in Westwood, whose daily doses of double espresso fueled numerous iterations of this manuscript.

Introduction

The Latino Big Bang in California and Justo Veytia, a Mexican '49er

David E. Hayes-Bautista

The Latino Big Bang: Ten Fateful Days in 1848

On the morning of January 24, 1848, approximately 10,000 Spanish speakers residing in Alta California awoke and began going about their daily lives. The night before, they had been citizens of the Republic of Mexico, living their lives in a regional variant of Mexican society, language, and culture that had been developing in Alta California since 1769. But during the next ten days, what can be called the "Latino Big Bang" upended their existence, changing their way of life and even more so the lives of their children. By the end of this Latino Big Bang, they and their children were no longer citizens of the Republic of Mexico but were ambiguous, often second-class citizens of the United States. They and their children were no longer a small, agricultural population on the Mexican frontier; in the coming decades, their numbers would explode, and they would be catapulted into the mainstream of both Latin American and Atlantic American societies. They and their children would no longer live in a regional variant of Mexican society and culture but would become the first cohort of parents and children constructing a new form of daily life that endures into the twenty-first century: the bilingual, bicultural civil society of los Latinos de Estados Unidos (Latinos of the United States). Today, nearly 180 years after the Latino Big Bang, more than 15.5 million people living in California identify as Latinos—or Hispanics or Mexican Americans or Chicanos or Central Americans or some other "Spanish origin."[1] By and large, they carry out their lives in both English and Spanish. They are primarily US citizens or otherwise under US jurisdiction, but nonetheless they proudly consider themselves Latinos.[2]

This Latino Big Bang occurred during the ten days from January 24, 1848, when gold was discovered in California, to February 2, when the Treaty of Guadalupe Hidalgo took effect and California became part of the United States. The near-simultaneity and scale of these two events in 1848—the discovery of gold on January 24 and the implementation of the Treaty of Guadalupe Hidalgo on February 2—created a unique synergy. If gold had been discovered but California had stayed part of Mexico, the Gold Rush would have been a phenomenon of Mexican history, not US history. Had California become part of the United States without gold being discovered at the same time, it might have languished for decades as a distant, sparsely populated territory, exerting little influence either on the rest of the country or on Mexico and Latin America. But because the two events occurred so closely together, they jointly sparked the Latino Big Bang. This not only resulted in a Latino population explosion but also simultaneously subjected the rapidly expanding Latino population to a constitutional upheaval that seriously reduced many Latino residents' political agency. Life for Latinos in California would never again be what it had been before.

Latino Population Explosion

On January 24, 1848, James Marshall saw something glitter in the tailrace of the mill he was building in the foothills of California's Sierra Nevada. Reaching into the debris at the bottom of the tailrace, he scooped out flakes of gold. News of his find touched off the Gold Rush, and during the next decade "the world rushed in" to California.[3] And although this fact generally is given little coverage in histories of the Gold Rush, a good part of that world rushing in to California spoke Spanish.

In fact, "gold fever" infected California, Mexico, and then Central and South America early in 1848, nearly a year before it reached Atlantic Americans in 1849. Within weeks of Marshall's discovery, hundreds of Latinos living along the California coast journeyed inland, seeking gold. As 1848 went on, thousands more came, primarily from California, New Mexico, and northern Mexico. Tens of thousands poured in during the next decade from Mexico, Central America, South America, the Caribbean, Brazil, and Spain. The Latino population of California exploded, from approximately 10,000 in 1848 to around 100,000 by the beginning of the US Civil War. At over 1,000 percent growth in just over a decade, this truly was a population explosion.

INTRODUCTION

Constitutional Earthquake

Mexico's independence movement in the early nineteenth century was based on fundamental beliefs in racial equality in citizenship and the abolition of slavery. Nearly every other Latin American country also declared these principles of racial equality and abolition of slavery on achieving their independence from Spain. But just ten days after the discovery of gold in California, on February 2, 1848, the Treaty of Guadalupe Hidalgo took effect, and Alta California became US territory. The mixed-race Latinos pouring into California now were subject to the jurisdiction of the Constitution of the United States, which was based on a racial narrative that protected slavery where it existed and allowed states to deny full citizenship to nonwhites.

The Latino Big Bang

The Latino population explosion and the constitutional earthquake were two effects of the forceful change that took place during an eyewink of time, simultaneously increasing the Latino population while diverting it from the orbit of the Mexican Republic's racial narrative into that of the United States. A mere dozen years later, as the US Civil War began in 1861, this fundamental, cataclysmic change already had created a new normal for tens of thousands of Latinos in California, both immigrants and their US-born children, who in that space of time had successfully created a new, bilingual, bicultural civil society. The majority of them supported President Abraham Lincoln and the Union in the war against the slave states. A year later, they also supported democratically elected President Benito Juárez against the French, who invaded Mexico in 1862 to install a puppet emperor, Maximilian. Their support of freedom, equality, and democracy in both countries led to the creation of a new public holiday in the United States, the Cinco de Mayo.[4] The society that began in those ten days in 1848 continues to inform the daily lives of nearly 16 million Latinos living in California in the third decade of the twenty-first century.[5]

Justo Veytia, a Mexican '49er, left Guadalajara for California in 1849 to seek his fortune in the gold fields. He kept a diary of his eighteen-month sojourn, and through its pages we can see the earliest years of the social transformation caused by the Latino Big Bang.

Finding a Latino '49er in a Mexico City Bookstore

In the summer of 2006, however, as I walked down the Calle Madero in the Historic Zone of Mexico City, I knew nothing about the Latino Big Bang, Latino '49ers, Latino involvement in the US Civil War, or the origins of twenty-first-century Latino civil society in the United States. I was just going to one of my favorite bookstores. Yet the next hour introduced me to history I had never been aware of before.

The heavy door closed behind me, cutting off the noise of Mexico City. Don Enrique Flores Castillo, the owner of Librería Madero,[6] knew how much I enjoy discovery, so he let me go into the back of the shop, where his staff catalog new arrivals. As I ran my hand over a shelf of recently acquired books, it came to rest on a small, paper-bound book squeezed between taller companions, without any title on its spine. Its front cover read *Justo Veytia. Viaje a la Alta California, 1849–1850* (Justo Veytia. Voyage to Alta California, 1849–1850).

It was a facsimile publication of a manuscript, and I was struck by the beautiful penmanship. The first page of text read, in Spanish, "The Year 1849. February 9. Today I begin my diary, or the story of the events that occur on this journey I am going to make to Alta California." It was someone's diary of his experiences in the California Gold Rush. As a native Californian, I had heard about the Gold Rush all my life. I attended high school in a small town on the edge of the "Gold Country" in northern California. Throughout my adolescence, I heard tales of "argonauts" sailing around the Horn and '49ers trekking across the plains. But back then I had not heard there were any Spanish-speaking prospectors.

Skimming through the diary, I gathered that early in 1849, the writer, Justo Veytia, together with a group of friends and kinsmen, had traveled from Guadalajara to California. He recounted his journey to the Pacific coast through towns familiar to me from the times I have driven roughly the same route: Tequila, Tepic, and San Blas. There he boarded a Peruvian ship, the *Volante*, for San Francisco. From San Francisco, he went down the Peninsula in an ox cart to San José; across the Livermore Valley and through the Altamont Pass to French Camp, Stockton, and Sacramento; then north along the Sierra Nevada foothills to the Gold Country: Stanislaus, Agua Fría, and Los Melones. Later, he went back to the coast and south again, finding work with the José Arana family on their ranch in Santa Cruz.

I knew every one of the towns he mentioned. I had taken the SAT in

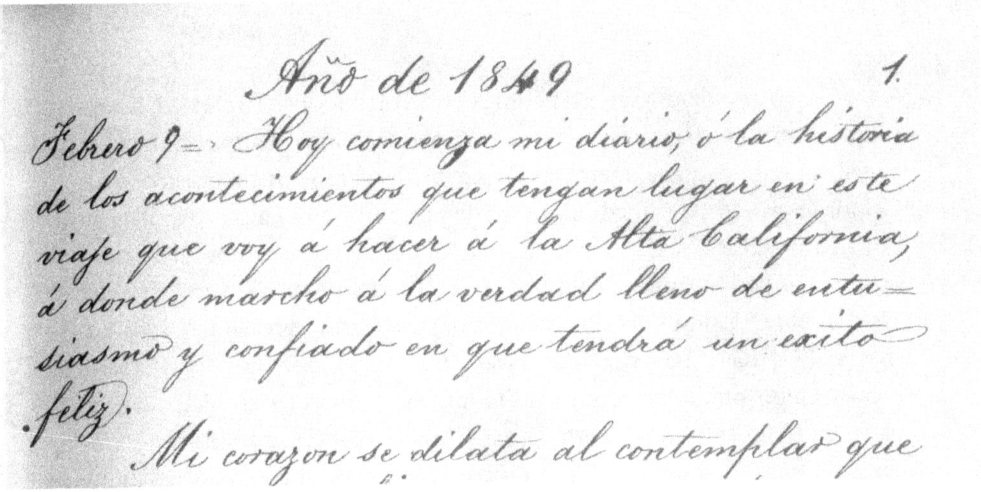

Año de 1849 1.

Febrero 9 = Hoy comienza mi diario, ó la historia de los acontecimientos que tengan lugar en este viaje que voy á hacer á la Alta California, á donde marcho á la verdad lleno de entusiasmo y confiado en que tendrá un exito feliz.

Mi corazon se dilata al contemplar que

FIGURE 2. The first page of his daughter's fair copy of Justo Veytia's diary: "February 9. Today I begin my diary, or the story of the events that occur on this journey I am going to make to Alta California, on which I truly do set forth filled with enthusiasm and confident that I will have happy success. My heart swells upon thinking that I am going to cross the sea; that I am going to learn about faraway lands, strange peoples, and different customs." (Courtesy of Luis Jaime Veytia Orozco.) Source: *Justo Veytia. Viaje a la Alta California, 1849–1850. Publicado por su nieto Salvador Veytia y Veytia, con una introducción por el Ing. Ricardo Lancaster-Jones,* facs. ed. (Guadalajara: privately printed, 1975), fol. 1r.

Sacramento, tried to learn to surf in the waters off Arana Gulch State Park in Santa Cruz, parked my motorcycle in San Francisco to attend classes at the University of California Medical Center, joined my in-laws on weekends at their house in San José. This Mexican '49er evidently had traveled very similar routes. It seemed Latinos, or at least one Latino, had taken part in the Gold Rush after all.

Latinos in California: Decline, Disengagement, and Disappearance?

In 1987, I published a book based on Latino demographic projections, predicting that by the year 2030 Latinos would comprise nearly half of California's population.[7] I was unprepared for the furious negative reactions to my demographic findings and conclusions. I received many rude comments—based on then-current perceptions of Latinos as mostly illegal immigrant gang members living on welfare—which insisted that California would be ruined beyond redemption by any Latino population growth, much less a Latino plurality. I sought to correct those false perceptions of Latinos in my 2004 book, *La Nueva California: Latinos in the Golden State*.[8] Using US Census data from 1940 through 2000, I showed that Latino daily behavior has always been very different from those too-common public perceptions. During the sixty years studied, Latino males in California consistently had the highest participation in the labor force. Latinos used welfare less, had stronger families, and established more businesses than any other ethnic group. In general, Latinos had fewer heart attacks, less cancer, and fewer strokes; and they lived nearly three years longer, on average, than any other ethnic group in the state, including non-Hispanic whites. Those whose perceptions of Latinos were formed primarily by English-language news broadcasts and talk radio apparently had no idea of any of this.

I chose to study behavioral patterns for the period 1940–2000 mostly because US Census data were available in digital form for those years, and I could analyze them using the SAS data analysis program. No data from censuses prior to 1940 were then available in electronic form; the data were locked up in microfilms of the original handwritten pages. As I finished the manuscript of *La Nueva California*, however, I began to wonder what Latino social life and behavior had been like before 1940, and if these unexpectedly strong social and health behaviors had been part of their daily life then, too.

Born, raised, and educated in California, I was taught in fourth grade (in 1954) the traditional narrative of Spanish speakers' part in the state's history. It went like this: A long time ago, Father Junipero Serra and missionaries from Spain built the missions and Christianized the Indian population. Then gold was discovered, and "the world rushed in" to California. I don't remember hearing in school about the Spanish-speaking population again after that.

My academic life from 1970 to about 2000 was spent exclusively in the world of health care, so I never had reason to question that fourth-grade historical narrative. While I was writing *La Nueva California*, however, curiosity awoke in me, and I could not get out of my head the question of what Latino life—work, welfare, families, businesses, and health—had been like in California prior to 1940. Eventually, I realized that while I knew when the Spanish missionaries had arrived, I had no idea when the Mexican population came to California, so I had no date *post quem* to anchor future research into the origins of the Latino behaviors I had documented. In short, I did not know the origin story of Latinos in California.

I needed to educate myself. I pulled out the California history books I had acquired since my undergraduate days at UC Berkeley and re-read them, this time with an eye to methodologies and sources. The books all agreed that when the United States took possession of California in 1848, some 7,000 to 10,000 Spanish-speaking persons called the newly acquired territory home. In an article published in 1940, Doris Marion Wright called this population, at the starting point of California's history as part of the United States, "almost unbelievably small"—although it was some 65 times larger than the 104 souls who founded Jamestown, which some historians treat as the starting point of the United States. Wright estimated that between 4,000 and 6,000 people came from Sonora, Mexico, to California's gold fields between 1848 and 1854, and worked there for some time. She assumed, though, that most of them then returned to Mexico and that, from that point on, immigration from Mexico "practically ceased" and "was no longer of any importance."[9] These numbers have been cited by subsequent historians, such as Richard L. Nostrand, who posited an even more rapid disappearance, suggesting that nearly all Mexican miners were gone by the summer of 1850, to avoid the Foreign Miners' Tax.[10]

But what happened to the "unbelievably small" number of Spanish speakers who remained in California? The title of Leonard Pitt's seminal 1966 work *The Decline of the Californios* summarizes the prevailing historical narrative. Pitt focuses on the swift, painful downward spiral of the land-owning Latino elite, who under US rule rapidly lost their lands, power, and influence.[11] Julian Samora and Patricia Vandel Simon also chronicled the sad fate of the formerly high-living rancheros, as they were "left to drift, aimless and poverty stricken."[12] Their disappearance was thought to have been so sudden and so complete that Leo Grebler, Joan W. Moore, and Ralph C. Guzman in 1970 termed the period between 1850 and 1900 the "extreme in demographic discontinuity between the Mexican and Anglo periods."[13] Arthur F. Corwin disparaged any attempt to show continuity in the Latino population in California between 1850 and 1910 as a "Brown Beret view of southwestern history."[14]

The prevailing opinion of historians of California, then, posited a steep decline in Latino numbers and influence during the Gold Rush, disengagement from larger Atlantic American society, and a disappearance that left virtually no trace. I call this the narrative of decline, disengagement, and disappearance. That was the narrative I learned in 1954, and it is still the prevailing school of thought about Latinos in nineteenth-century California.

Previous Hints of the Latino Big Bang

In 2001, my wife, Teodocia María, and I bought a weekend house in the small coast town of Lompoc in northern Santa Barbara County. I was familiar with California's central coast, for my family had moved from my hometown of Los Angeles to San Luis Obispo, just north of Lompoc, in 1953. As a child, I often clambered over the newly restored outbuildings of Mission La Purísima, and I read my father's copy of Richard Henry Dana's *Two Years Before the Mast* (1840), which describes vast ranchos in that area, populated by equally vast herds of cattle and worked by Spanish-speaking *vaqueros* (cowboys).[15] I grew up hearing about Santa Barbara's annual Old Spanish Days fiesta, celebrating life in mission days, before California became a US state in 1850.[16] While an undergraduate at UC Berkeley in the 1960s, I bought a book written and illustrated by the Uruguayan artist Jo Mora, *Californios. The Saga of the Hard-Riding Vaqueros, America's First Cowboys*, which was based on his experiences with Spanish-speaking cowboys in the Lompoc Valley in 1903.[17] Thanks to these youthful impressions, I had always assumed Spanish-speaking vaqueros were still working cattle on the ranchos around Lompoc until the early twentieth century.

Lompoc was established in 1874 by a group of Atlantic American temperance settlers, who purchased portions of Rancho La Purísima and Rancho Lompoc to found an alcohol-free community. Despite their efforts to escape demon rum, however, Lompoc became a wet town in 1888, and bars have been a lively part of its life since then. One weekend shortly after we moved into our weekend house in 2001, the Lompoc Museum announced a new exhibition: a photographic history of the town. At the time, 43 percent of the town's population was Latino—by the 2020 census, it would be 60.4 percent[18]—so I went to the exhibit expecting to see a history full of Latino faces in coastal California. Yet as I leafed through old photographs of grim-faced temperance settlers, their children, and their grandchildren, I was struck by the absence of Latinos. It didn't make sense. Certainly in 1874, and thereafter, the many cattle ranches around Lompoc were still operating. They would have needed scores, maybe hundreds, of vaqueros. Many of these presumably Spanish-speaking vaqueros would have had wives and children with them. Nonetheless, Latinos were completely absent from the museum's photographic history of Lompoc. Had all Latinos suddenly disappeared from the Lompoc Valley? If so, when had this happened? How could I reconcile the discrepancy between the total absence of Latinos in the Lompoc Museum's exhibition and Jo Mora's description of vibrant Spanish-speaking vaquero life in the same area in the early 1900s?

Reading that afternoon's issue of the local newspaper, I glanced at the masthead and saw that the *Lompoc Record* had been in publication since 1875. It might prove a source of clues about what had happened to the area's Latinos. So on another weekend, I visited the Lompoc Library and mounted volume 1, number 1 of the *Lompoc Record* on the microfilm reader—and suddenly began to read a history of Latinos in the Lompoc area from 1875 to 1889.

Don Estévan Quintán was congratulated in 1875 for erecting a two-story brick building for commercial use and a residence for himself in neighboring San Luis Obispo.[19] Edward Ruiz and Aloysia Valenzuela were married, as were Joseph Pico and Lugarda Calderón, by Father McNally on March 27, 1876.[20] Pedro Barreras, a native of Mexico and vaquero on the Rancho San Julián, died at age thirty-five in Lompoc in 1880.[21] Mr. A. Zapata opened up a hairdressing business inside Mrs. Webb's store.[22] In 1887, Dr. Ramón de la Cuesta died at his ranch in the neighboring Santa Ynez Valley; his obituary mentioned that he had been a '49er and had lived in northern Santa Barbara County since 1854.[23] In 1889, homesteader A. C. Bradford published his claim to his land, which was being contested by a Mr. Pleasant; Bradford cited as witnesses to his continuous residence and cultivation of the land four Latino neighbors from Santa Ynez: Francisco Corrales, Joaquin de la Cuesta, Vicente Carrillo, and Jesús Figueroa.[24] So not all Latinos had disappeared. At least a few had remained, mentioned in the *Lompoc Record*. But were there more than a handful? How could I find out about Latinos whom the local paper might have failed to notice?

I usually read two newspapers every morning, the English-language *Los Angeles Times* and the Spanish-language *La Opinión*, both published in Los Angeles. In general, Latinos appear infrequently in the pages of the *Los Angeles Times*; when they do, they are often depicted as criminals, gangbangers, undocumented immigrants, or single mothers living on welfare. But *La Opinión* reveals a parallel universe: Latino students are accepted into UCLA or Harvard, Latino businesses spring up and grow, community organizations offer services, musicians announce tours, Latino legislators debate the future of California. When appropriate, *La Opinión* does run gang and crime stories similar to those in the *Times*—but if I only read the *Times*, such stories would be nearly all I saw about Latinos. *La Opinión* gives a fuller, deeper picture. So it occurred to me that a similar bias in reporting probably characterized English-language papers during California's Gold Rush. Nonetheless, given that I had been able to find at least a few mentions of Latinos in the English-language *Lompoc Record*, perhaps I might find more in nineteenth-century Spanish-language papers—if there were any.

As it turned out, there were. I began collecting Spanish-language newspapers on microfilm, starting with *La Estrella de Los Angeles*, first published in 1851. It began as a single page in the English-language *Los Angeles Star* and soon grew to occupy two of the *Star*'s four pages. Other Los Angeles Spanish-language papers were *El Clamor Público* (1855–1859), *El Amigo del Pueblo* (1860–1862), *La Crónica* (1872–1892), *La Voz de la Justicia* (1876), *El Joven* (1877–1878), *El Aguacero* (1878), *El Éco de la Patria* (1878), and *La Reforma* (1878). In San Francisco, *El Éco del Pacífico* began in 1852 as an offshoot of the French-language *L'Écho du Pacifique*. It soon was joined by other Spanish-language papers, including *La Crónica* (1854–1855), *La Voz de Méjico* (1862–1866), *El Nuevo Mundo* (1864–1869), *La Voz de Chile y de las Repúblicas Hispano-americanas* (1867–1869), *La Voz del Nuevo Mundo* (1868–1884), *El Republicano* (1868–1869), *La Prensa Mexicana* (1868), *El Tiempo* (1869), *La Sociedad* (1869–1877), and *El Progreso* (1871).[25] While each editor had his opinion (in those days, nearly all newspaper editors and reporters were male), these newspapers did provide other points of view— pieces by self-appointed correspondents and letters to the editor—as well as legal announcements; advertisements; mentions of weddings, serenades, theater performances; and other snippets of Latino daily life.

I also combed California's English-language paper of record, the San Francisco *Alta California*, for mentions of Latinos, as advertisers, ship passengers, miners, defendants or witnesses in court, and so on. It soon became apparent that the disparity in how today's English-language papers and Spanish-language papers depict Latinos already existed in the mid-nineteenth century. The Spanish-language papers not only reported on many aspects of Latino life rarely mentioned in the English-language press, but they also showed an awareness of negative depictions of Latinos in the latter, and often explicitly reacted to them.

I also learned that a few Spanish-speaking miners wrote firsthand accounts of the Gold Rush around the same time Justo Veytia did. These included the Argentine Ramón Gil Navarro, the Chilean Vicente Pérez Rosales,[26] the Californios José María Amador and former California governor Juan Alvarado,[27] and Antonio F. Coronel, who originally arrived from Mexico in 1834, while California was still part of that country.[28]

As an undergraduate majoring in engineering in the 1960s, mainly I had learned quantitative skills. I then undertook graduate studies at the University of California Medical Center, San Francisco, in the early 1970s, specifically to learn qualitative research methods under Anselm Strauss and Barney Glaser, developers of a methodology known as "grounded theory."[29] I now use their methods, as modified by Kathy Charmaz into "constructivist grounded theory."[30] This approach consists of carefully reading source material, such as transcripts of interviews or focus groups, then breaking down the reported experience, as perceived and constructed by the participants, into component elements, in a process called "coding." I have used this methodology to see the Gold Rush and US Civil War through the eyes of contemporary Latinos, using nineteenth-century Spanish-language newspapers and memoirs as sources.

In "Mexicans in the California Mines, 1848–1853," Richard Henry Morefield used English-language newspapers as his main source. As a result, his article subscribes to the traditional narrative of decline, disengagement, and disappearance: a few Californios and Mexicans went to the mines in 1848, whence most were expelled in 1849. Those who remained were heavily taxed by the Foreign Miners' Tax in 1850 and, therefore, after a short period working as hired hands, left California by 1853, never to return.[31]

Yet Spanish-language sources tell a very different story about the Gold Rush: while Californios, Mexicans, and other Latinos sometimes were indeed hired hands working for others, they also discovered veins of ore; owned claims, even whole mines and mining districts; introduced mining techniques; and invested in mines. Mexican prospectors arrived in the Gold Country just weeks after James W. Marshall's discovery at Sutter's Mill, and they worked mines throughout the Gold Rush in California and the subsequent Comstock silver rush in Nevada, well into the Reconstruction Era (1849–1877).

Early in 1848, a Mexican from Sonora, known to twenty-first-century readers only by his nickname *El Chino*,[32] accompanied Antonio F. Coronel on his first trip to the Gold Country. El Chino brought from Mexico a reputation as a "famous prospector," and soon after arriving found a river-bank gold deposit that was so rich he simply scooped up gold with a hollowed-out cow's horn.[33] In 1849, Ramón Gil Navarro wrote that Latino miners, especially those from the Mexican state of Sonora, had a knack for finding claims from which "gold seemed to flow out in a stream."[34] An 1863 advertisement for the Copperage Mining Company touted one Lucas Palma as the *descubridor* (discoverer) of the mines of San José, Portales, Bella Vista, and Portezuelo.[35] That same year, Jesús Alcaraz discovered deposits of gold and silver along the Salinas River in Monterey County, where he staked a claim and opened a mine that was called *la mina de Zaragoza*, probably in honor of the recently deceased hero of the first battle of Puebla, Ignacio Zaragoza.[36] At Lone Pine, in the eastern Sierra Nevada, Pablo Flores and Blas Méndez established an entire mining district in 1866, later known as the "Mexican district."[37] In 1872, a letter in *La Crónica* related that three Latin-Yanquí brothers—Eduardo, Guillermo, and José Breck—and two unnamed friends had left Santa Barbara for the Najalayegua River, fifteen miles away, where they discovered a mercury mine and staked a claim. The article noted that the Breck brothers' father, William, was born in Boston in 1800 and came to Santa Barbara in 1837, where he married their mother, Francisca Antonia Ortega.[38]

English-language accounts of Latinos in the mines tended to be less detailed, generally referring to Latino miners anonymously, and often collectively, as "Mexicans," as in an 1849 *Alta California* account of a discovery in Tuolumne County: "Three Mexicans, however, near Wood's Camp, 1½ miles below, took out yesterday—(keep *your hat*) $2,200!!!" (emphasis in original).[39] A year later, the same newspaper reported that a thirteen-pound lump of gold was found "in the town of Sonora, by a Mexican."[40]

Latino ownership of mines and claims was widespread. In the summer of 1848, Antonio F. Coronel joined a party of thirty Latinos from Los Angeles composed of Californios, New Mexicans, and sonorenses,[41] who became some of the first prospectors in the gold fields. On arriving in the Stanislaus River area, they staked claims and began to work. Coronel said that one of them, a Californio from Santa Barbara called Valdés Chapanango, found so much gold on his first day there that he sold his claim to Lorenzo Soto from San Diego. After working the claim for a week and extracting fifty-two pounds of gold, Soto felt satisfied, and in turn sold the claim to some members of the Machado family from San Diego.[42] In 1863, a piece in *La Voz de Méjico* mentioned twenty or so mines on the Rancho Alisal in Monterey County, adding, "Me aseguran que . . . todas son propiedad de mejicanos, chilenos o hijos del pais" (They assure me that . . . all are the property of Mexicans, Chileans, or native sons).[43]

In 1851, "the company of Mexicans" that had claimed and worked the Carson Creek Vein were so successful that they hired "Townies" (i.e., Atlantic Americans) to undertake the hard labor.[44] One "Señor Garrilla" [Carrillo?] from Los Angeles sold his property in that town and invested the proceeds in a quartz mine in the southern mines. He then "admitted an American as a partner with him," who fraudulently sold the mine and absconded with the proceeds.[45] A Peruvian from Arequipa, José María Arias, discovered and worked a claim, then in 1851 "sold his interest for $6,000."[46] In 1873, Ventura Beltrán and his wife, co-owners of a mine named Guadalupe in Lone Pine, sold an 800-foot stretch of the claim to French Canadian immigrant Victor Beaudry for $7,000.[47]

Since the discovery of the Zacatecas silver veins in 1546,[48] the search for gold and silver drew miners north from Mexico City toward what one day would become the Southwest of the United States. The California Gold Rush was, in effect, another stop on this three-century northward movement of people looking for precious metals; and during it, Latinos brought mining technology and expertise developed in Mexico to California.

The *batea* was the staple of placer mining: a shallow bowl or pan—initially wooden, later made of metal—into which a miner placed small amounts of dirt. He (nearly all miners were male) then gently rinsed the dirt in running water, which carried off the lighter soil and, with luck, left the heavier gold flakes and nuggets at the bottom of the pan. The batea was so ubiquitous that even English-speakers used the Spanish word to refer to it. A correspondent from the Stanislaus Diggings, for instance, reported that he awoke one cold, windy morning in May to find "the water in my '*batea*' skimmed over with ice!"[49]

Mexicans also brought the technique of "dry washing" to mines where water was not readily available. An Atlantic American correspondent described his first experience watching an unnamed Mexican gradually tip a batea-load of earth onto a spread-out serape, "allowing the wind to carry off the fine dust," in a process similar to winnowing grain. The miner broke up clods of dirt with his hands and repeated the winnowing over and over, until he had a handful of dust remaining, which he then winnowed with his own breath, "leaving between three or four bills worth of gold."[50]

Mexican miners also brought the *arrastra* to California. A mule tethered to a central pole repeatedly dragged a heavy stone, or sometimes a heavy stone wheel, in a circle over gold-bearing quartz ore to crush it. This technique came to be used by Atlantic American miners as well, along with the Spanish term for it. In 1853, T. Dodge, one of the owners of new diggings near Curtisville, "employed no machinery than the rude Mexican *arrastra*."[51] By 1860, one Mr. Caldwell near Visalia owned and operated a number of arrastras to which miners brought their quartz ore for crushing.[52]

But not all Latinos participated personally "in the diggings"; some were investors. For instance, Antonio María Suñol, former mayor of San José, bought shares in the Guadalupe Mining Company in Santa Clara County. When J. D. Hoppe, president of the company, advertised in 1851 that all the stock would be sold, Suñol protested that his shares were not to be made available for sale to anyone.[53] In 1862, two new mines were discovered by Latinos in the Alisal district of Monterey County. The editor of *La Voz de Méjico* thought these mines would prove productive, because nearly all shares in them were held by *paisanos* ("fellow countrymen," i.e., Mexicans or those of Mexican descent).[54]

Many Latinos provided labor in mines owned by others. Some Latinos arriving by ship from Mexico and Central and South America in the summer of 1849 were recruited by Alexander Forbes to work in the New Almaden mercury mines south of San José. His advertisement offered *un trabajo productivo y tranquilo* (a productive and peaceful job) for *Hispano-Americanos de buena conducta* (Hispanic Americans of good conduct).[55] The job, however, was not always as uneventful as this sounds. In 1856, Anastacio Vargas, "a Mexican laborer" at the New Almaden mines, was descending a deep shaft in a bucket lowered by a horse-powered winch, when one of the horses shied, dislodging Vargas from the bucket. He fell "more than 100 feet on a mass of rocks at the bottom. He was killed instantly."[56] An 1859 accident at a mine in San Gabriel broke the legs of a Mexican named Santana, who was carried out on a litter by "his countrymen."[57] At the New Almaden mine in 1865, more than 600 Latino miners—*todos los de raza española* (all those of the Spanish-speaking race)—signed a protest at being ordered to buy all their goods only at the *tienda de raya* (company store) recently established by the mine's owners.[58]

The US Census: A Quantitative Record of the Latino Big Bang

Qualitative sources, especially Spanish-language newspapers, provide many anecdotes of Latinos in California during the Gold Rush, US Civil War, and Reconstruction. But these stories only give glimpses of Latino presence. I was not sure if the experiences of individual Latinos in newspaper accounts could be used to say anything accurate and useful about local Latino communities, much less Latino society as a whole, during this period. How many Latinos lived in California then? What were the population trends among them—was their population shrinking or growing? Were Latinos assimilating into non-Latino culture? Where could I find quantitative data that might answer these questions?

Throughout my academic career I have used census data as a foundation of my research. I also am aware of the difficulties the US Census has had since 1930 in defining, identifying, and counting Latinos. Because of my familiarity with Census methodology—sampling, questionnaire design, data cleanup and management—I served on an advisory committee to the Census on its first attempt to intentionally include "Hispanics," in the 1980 census, and made some critiques of their methodological decisions on terminology and operationalization.[59] So in using Census data in my research, I am mindful of its strengths and weaknesses.

Many US readers may remember, during the first months of the COVID-19 pandemic in 2020, receiving a short questionnaire from the US Census Bureau. The Census estimated that the average household could fill out this short form in ten minutes or less. Respondents had the option to fill out the actual form and return it by mail, dictate their responses over the telephone, or fill it out online. The form asked to know four apparently simple things about each person in the household: name, age, gender, and ethnicity-race. These data are used to draw the boundaries of congressional districts, among other purposes; and, except for the names of individuals, they are widely available to anyone.[60]

In addition to the short form sent to every household, the Census selects roughly one out of every hundred respondents to fill out a long form, which asks many more questions about income, education, employment, birthplace, home ownership, and so forth. These detailed data are called microdata and can be used to study specific demographic topics, such as how many Latina female physicians there are, how much they earn on average, and how many children they tend to have. For purposes of such quantitative study, this microdata must be extracted from the national data set by the use of software such as SAS or SPSS, which generally means that only those with programming skills have practical access to them. I have been mining these microdata for decades to learn more about the dynamics of the Latino population, both in California and in the United States as a whole.

As mentioned, in 2004 I published a book using this microdata to examine Latinos' patterns of work and family between 1940 and 2000. I began with 1940 largely because, at the time, that was the earliest year for which US Census data had been adapted from the original paper questionnaires to a digitized format (via old-school punch cards).

As I began to understand Latino life in California qualitatively through the pages of the newspapers in both Spanish and English, I realized that I could get quantitative data about how many Latinos there were in northern Santa Barbara County by consulting microfilmed original census returns from 1850 to 1870. The Census Bureau had microfilmed the original returns for California from 1850 onward and made them available for public inspection at a repository in Laguna Niguel, in Orange County.[61]

At the repository, I checked out the 1870 census microfilm roll that contained Santa Barbara County, mounted it in the microfilm reader, located the communities around Lompoc, and nearly fell out of my chair. Family after family, household after household, all with Hispanic names, popped up on the screen. Hispanic names populated these returns, organized into families and other kinds of household, with ages, places of birth, and even occupation. Many males' occupation was designated as "buccaro," which I realized was an English-speaking enumerator's way of writing *vaquero* phonetically. I had indeed discovered a data source to quantify the Latino population in Gold Rush and Civil War California.

Creating a Digital Data Set

In order to attempt any analysis, the data first had to be transferred from microfilm images of handwritten registers to a digital format. This meant that the research team at the UCLA Center for the Study of Latino Health and Culture (CESLAC) had to manually extract the data about Latinos and enter them into a computer program. The original census data, say for 1850, were organized by household, with the head of household listed first, usually followed by their partner (if any), then children (if any), then unrelated individuals, such as servants or boarders, who resided in the household. We extracted all data from any household that had at least one Latino living in it. If there were no Latinos in a household, we did not extract the data.

This, of course, prompted the first necessary question: Whom should we consider to be Latino? As the "Hispanic" identifier was not used until the 1980 census, how would we know who was Hispanic in the 1850 census? Before the 1980 census, Latinos were identified and postcoded after each decennial census was complete, by using three personal variables to identify them: Spanish surname, birthplace in a Hispanic country, or being Spanish speaking. The Census had developed a list of some 25,277 Spanish surnames, such as García, Rodríguez, Martínez, and so on, so we used essentially the same list.[62] We also used birthplace. With very few exceptions, someone born in Mexico or another Latin American country, but living in California at the time of the census, was coded as Latino. We also coded anyone born in California prior to 1850 as Latino, irrespective of surname, as they would have been born while it was still part of Mexico. Individuals born in California after 1850 would need to possess at least two variables to be counted as Latino: a Spanish surname and California birth.

We also modified this algorithm a bit. We included more Basque and Catalan surnames than the original US Census had, as these Iberian regions supplied a significant number of surnames common among California Latinos (e.g., Yorba, Serra).[63] Given the California tradition of blended Latin-Yanqui families, we also tracked particular apparently non-Latino family surnames, such as Dana, Hill, Branch, Watson, and Carson, and checked genealogical sources to determine whether such individuals were Latin-Yanquí descendants or Atlantic Americans.[64]

We quickly discovered that a number of errors had entered the original handwritten data when the census returns were filled out. Nearly all the census enumerators were English speakers, not Spanish speakers, with the result that frequently they were not able to capture and spell Spanish names very well. For example, the first name Refugio might be rendered as Rufufu or Rufufewoh.[65] Hispanic naming conventions were different from the familiar Atlantic American arrangement of first name, middle name, and last name. When faced with a multipart first name, such as María de Guadalupe, one nonplussed Atlantic American enumerator might write down only "Maria" as the individual's first name, while another might put down "Guadalupe" (often misspelled "Guadeloupe"), and a third might abbreviate the name as "Maria G." The Hispanic use of double surnames—paternal and maternal—also confused English speakers. Pablo de la Guerra y Noriega's surnames so puzzled English-speaking transcribers of the debates at the 1849 California Constitutional Convention that he was designated erroneously as "Mr. Noriego" throughout more than 400 pages of transcript.

The CESLAC team first extracted names exactly as they were written in the original census returns, misspellings and all. When team members were able to decipher these, they wrote a corrected version of the name in an adjoining column on the spreadsheet: e.g., after first extracting "Noriego" into one column, they then added the corrected version "de la Guerra y Noriega" in another.

The CESLAC team extracted the country of birth for every Latino in the census, as well as for non-Latino members of their households. One complication they encountered was that, at certain points during the mid-nineteenth century, some twenty-first-century countries had not yet formed. Italy and Germany, for example, did not come into existence as nations until the late 1860s or early 1870s. As a result, when asked for their birthplace, immigrants from those areas naturally told the enumerator the small polity or city-state of their origin, for example, Hamburg or Hesse-Kassel, rather than a country that did not yet exist (Germany). The converse case was of persons hailing from component states of a nineteenth-century empire that had not yet attained their modern independence, for example, Croatia in the Austro-Hungarian Empire. In their case, the enumerator often would put down "Austrian Empire" for a Croatian immigrant's birthplace. So after noting in one column the place of birth as originally recorded by the enumerator, the team then postcoded it in an adjoining column to conform with current national boundaries and designations.

Generation was also postcoded, using the following terminology:

- C = *Californio*. Persons of any ethnic background who regularly lived in California's regional variant of Mexican society before February 2, 1848. This included people born in California prior to 1848 and those who came to reside in California from another part of Mexico, Latin America, or Spain prior to 1848.
- L1 = *First-generation immigrants*. Persons born in Mexico, another Latin American country, or Spain who came to live in California after February 2, 1848.
- L2 = *Second-generation US-born*. Persons born in California after February 2, 1848, to either Californio or Latino first-generation immigrant parents.
- L3+ = *Third-generation-plus US-born*. Persons born in California after February 2, 1848, of Latino parents born in California or another US state, who also had Latino grandparents or even more distant ancestors born in Mexico, Latin America, or Spain. This included grandchildren and further descendants of Californios.

Technically, of course, Californio families were not immigrants. They never crossed the border; the border crossed them on February 2, 1848. After 1848, however, their experience was essentially similar to that of immigrants, that is, native Spanish speakers functioning in an increasingly English-speaking environment, under the jurisdiction of US national or state institutions.

How Big Was the Latino Big Bang?

San Luis Obispo County lies along the old Camino Real (now State Highway 101), roughly a third of the way between Los Angeles and San Francisco. During the Gold Rush, it was a refreshing stop on the journey to the gold fields after weeks traveling from northern Mexico through the scorching Sonora Desert. The coastal cool weather and green acres restored animals and humans alike to health before continuing their trek to the southern mines. In his memoir, Juan Francisco Dana remembered seeing "thousands" of *gambusinos* (prospectors) from northern Mexico travel past his father's adobe house (today's DANA Adobe & Cultural Center, California Historical Landmark No. 1033) on their way to the "gold diggings."[66]

San Luis Obispo was ranching country, boasting neither gold fields to attract the adventurous nor the urban life of San Francisco, San José, or Los Angeles to lure the cosmopolitan. But after the adventurous had "busted out" of the Gold Country and the cosmopolitan had tired of city life, some of them undertook a secondary migration to this coastal county, so it too experienced a version of the effects of the Latino Big Bang.

Table 1 shows how the county's Latino population changed during the first twenty years of California statehood. In 1850, two years after the discovery of gold, the Census enumerated the county's Latino population at a mere 293 individuals. By 1860, the enumerated population had grown to 1,189, and by 1870 it reached 1,645. These census numbers translate into explosive growth in the first decade after statehood and robust growth thereafter: a 305.8 percent growth rate from 1850 to 1860, and 38.4 percent from 1860 to 1870.

Table 1. San Luis Obispo County Population Enumerated in US Censuses of 1850, 1860, and 1870.

Year	Population	Percent Change per Decade
1850	293	—
1860	1,189	305.8%
1870	1,645	38.4%

Source: UCLA CESLAC extractions from microfilmed US Censuses for San Luis Obispo County for 1850, 1860, and 1870.

For comparison, table 2 shows the growth of the total US population from 2000 to 2020. In the first decade, the US population grew from 281.4 million to 308.8 million, a 9.7 percent growth rate. In the following decade, it grew to 331.5 million, a 7.4 percent growth rate.

Table 2. United States Population Enumerated in US Censuses of 2000, 2010, and 2020.

Year	Population (millions)	Percent Change over Decade
2000	281.4	—
2010	308.8	9.7%
2020	331.5	7.4%

Source: UCLA CESLAC, Decennial Census of Population and Housing by Decades, https://www.census.gov/programs-surveys/decennial-census/decade.html.

Census Undercounts

During the 2020 census, if a household failed to fill out and return its questionnaire, an enumerator made as many as six personal visits to the household's address to obtain the desired information. After all these efforts to count the nation's population, the 2020 census reported that there were 62.1 million Latinos in the United States.[67] But to double-check its numbers, the Census then conducted a Post-Enumeration Survey, using independent external records (e.g., tax payments, Social Security numbers, Medicare enrollment), to evaluate how large an undercount might have occurred. Ideally, everyone who had paid taxes should appear in the 2020 Census enumeration. Yet, to its dismay, the Census Bureau discovered it had undercounted the Hispanic population by 4.99 percent. As many as 3.1 million Latinos had been left out of the 2020 count.[68]

This undercount in 2020 was anything but a new phenomenon. The US Census has grappled with the uncertain quality of its data for decades, including during the Gold Rush. In 1878, Francis Walker, superintendent of the 1870 census, declared that, thanks to understaffing, untrained personnel, unclear instructions, and other reasons, the censuses of 1850, 1860, and 1870 were "loaded with bad statistics. There are statistics in the census of 1870 . . . where some of the results are false to the extent of one half. They had to be published *then*, because the law called for it; but I took the liberty of branding them as untrustworthy."[69]

In 1850, there were no income tax, Social Security, or Medicare records against which to check the census returns when estimating potential Latino undercount. But two external independent data sources have survived the past 170 years, by means of which the Latino undercount during the Gold Rush decades can be at least roughly estimated.

The poor quality of those decades' census data is exposed via an 1850 list of rancheros in San Luis Obispo County. By that time, there were approximately thirty-four ranchos in the county.[70] The number is approximate because some ranchos straddled county lines and others were joined together or split apart over the years due to inheritance or sale, with the dates of these changes not always clearly recorded. Ownership of these thirty-four ranchos was claimed by as many as forty-six rancheros at the time of the 1850 census, as some ranchos were owned by two or more individuals. Thirty of the ranchos had been granted by the Mexican government during the tumultuous 1840s, and four during the late 1830s, so these titles were not burdened by centuries of ownership. Mexican land grants required owners to maintain residence and make improvements on the terrain. As a result, before statehood ownership was generally stable; rancheros were not likely to pick up and move on a moment's notice.

Yet despite their stability and high social profile, only sixteen of the forty-six owners can be definitely identified in the 1850 census. In other words, only one-third of the high profile, stable, comparatively wealthy rancheros were counted in the census. Two-thirds, somehow, were not. One can only imagine how much more underrepresented the working-class vaqueros and other laborers may have been.

A uniquely high-quality external data source exists by which to check the accuracy of the 1860 and 1870 censuses: the contribution lists of the San Luis Obispo County Junta Patriótica Mejicana for the period July 1862 through August 1864. In the giddy aftermath of the unexpected victory of Mexican troops over the French invaders at the first Battle of Puebla, fought on May 5, 1862, Latinos in California, Nevada, and Oregon formed the first regional network of Latino political organizations, the *Juntas Patrióticas Mejicanas* (Mexican Patriotic Assemblies). Their purpose was to support Mexico's President Juárez, both politically and financially, in his efforts to expel the French, and to give political support as well to US President Lincoln in his fight against the Confederacy.[71]

Typically, a local junta met every month to sing patriotic songs in both Spanish and English and listen to fiery speeches about the threats to freedom, racial equality, and democracy posed by a possible French or Confederate victory. Then members donated what money they could manage, which was sent to the Junta Central (Central Assembly) in San Francisco to be forwarded to the Mexican capital. To give public recognition to their efforts, lists of the donors' names were published in at least one of San Francisco's two Spanish-language newspapers as they came in from the local juntas.

CESLAC researchers collected the published lists, extracted the donors' names and whatever identifying information that was included—for example, were they Mexican, Central American, Californio, Chilean, and so on. This arrived at a total of 12,926 unduplicated names in all the lists published for California.[72] This number forms the floor for any tally. Yet not all lists submitted were published, as evidenced by the complaints of local juntas in letters to the editors about not being publicly credited for

LISTA

☞ De donativos patrióticos para auxiliar al *Ejército de Oriente* en México.

Suscricion de San Luis Obispo.

MES DE NOVIEMBRE.

Valentin Mancilla.............$	5 00
Juan Cappe.......	2 50
José Maria Muñoz................	2 50
José Maria Orduño.......	2 50
Pascual Moto....................	2 00
Valerio de Lama.................	2 00
Félix Figueroa...................	2 00
Joaquin Estrada.................	2 00
Mariano Bonilla..................	2 00
Lascano y hermano.............	2 00
Refugio Cervantes...............	2 00
Joaquin Almada.................	2 00
A. L. Cervantes.................	2 00
Navor Tapia.....................	1 00

FIGURE 3. A portion of the *junta patriótica mejicana* donation list from San Luis Obispo for November 1862, provides evidence of Census undercounts. For example, Joaquin Estrada appears on nine such donation lists between 1862 and 1864, and he also appears in both the 1860 and 1870 censuses for San Luis Obispo County; Félix Figueroa appears on fourteen junta donation lists but does not appear in either the 1860 or 1870 census. (UCLA CESLAC.) Source: "LISTA De donativos patrióticos para auxiliar al *Ejercito de Oriente* en México," *La Voz de Méjico,* November 22, 1862, 2.

their efforts. Nor did all published lists survive, as the surviving runs of the two newspapers are not complete. For example, the now-extant run of *El Nuevo Mundo*, which began publication in 1864, is missing nearly all issues from April 20, 1866, to May 29, 1868; only two issues survive from those two years, both from July 1867. Sporadic lacuna exist in *La Voz de Méjico*'s extant run as well.

Despite these shortcomings, the junta donation lists are valuable because they were generated of, by, and for Latinos, providing an internally derived listing of one stratum of Latino males. According to the lists that were published and survived, 173 adults in San Luis Obispo County, nearly all male, donated to their local Junta Patriótica Mexicana—again, to simplify calculation, all members are presumed to have been male. In doing so, they had to publicly pledge their political support to both Juárez and Lincoln, and generally they tried to donate the equivalent of one day's wages per month for the duration of the two wars, the US Civil War and French Intervention in Mexico. Obviously, not everyone could have, or would have, made such public commitments.

When we cross-checked the names on the junta lists with the names on the 1860 census returns for the county, the undercount became more apparent. Only 36 of the 173 donors appear in the census returns. This means only one-fifth of the junta members (20.8 percent) were represented in the census. As the junta donors' lists were created about halfway between the two censuses of 1860 and 1870, the names were also checked against the 1870 census. The undercount persisted: 37 of the 173 donors appeared, a scant improvement to nearly one-fourth of all donors (21.4 percent).

Table 3 provides an estimate of the undercount of Latinos in the two censuses, ranging from one-third of mostly male rancheros in 1850, to a quarter to one-fifth of the mostly male junta donors in 1860 and 1870. In other words, about two-thirds to four-fifths of adult Latino males whose existence is documented were not counted in the census. It is a reasonable assumption that the undercount among Latino adult males not on the ranchero or junta lists was at least of a similar order of magnitude. To simplify calculation in table 3, we have presumed all rancheros to be male, although one or two women are also known to have owned ranchos in the county. Because these two particular lists are about 90 percent male, we have here treated female rancheros and junta members as if they were males, assigning them the same composition factor as males.[73]

Table 3. Underrepresentation of Adult Males in List of Rancheros (1850) and Junta Patriótica Subscription Lists (1860 and 1870) Compared to Same Males Enumerated in US Censuses.

Year	External Record	Number in Record	Number Counted in Census	Underrepresentation Fraction
1850	Rancheros	46	15	1/3 (32.6%)
1860	Junta list	173	34	1/5 (19.7%)
1870	Junta list	173	37	1/4 (21.4%)

Source: UCLA CESLAC extractions of junta patriótica lists published in *La Voz de Méjico* and *El Nuevo Mundo*, 1862–1867.

The ranchero and junta patriótica lists help to estimate the undercount of Latino adult males but say nothing of Latino children and adult women. Fortunately, the census data provide the microdata needed to estimate the number of women and children. The census data is more representative of the composition of the population than the nearly all-male ranchero and junta patriótica lists, so the relative proportion of adult females per adult male, as well as the relative number of children per adult male, can be derived. Table 4 summarizes the relative proportions of children and adult females to adult males.

INTRODUCTION

Table 4. Relative Ratio of Latina Adult Women and Latino Children to One Latino Adult Male in San Luis Obispo County, 1850, 1860, and 1870.

Year	Adult Males	Adult Females	Children	Relative Composition Ratio
1850				
N=	61	47	182	
Ratio	1.00	0.73	2.83	4.56
1860				
N=	374	204	611	
Ratio	1.00	0.55	1.63	3.18
1870				
N=	461	266	918	
Ratio	1.00	0.58	2.00	3.58

Source: UCLA CESLAC calculations.

For example, the 1850 census counted 61 adult male Latinos, 47 adult females, and 182 children in San Luis Obispo County. So for every adult male Latino (1.0), there were 0.73 adult females and 2.83 children. Adding these relative ratios together produces a "relative composition factor" of 4.56 for 1850. Multiplying the number of adult males by this composition factor of 4.56 then yields an estimate of the total Latino population, men, women, and children. The relative composition changed in the 1860 and 1870 censuses, so those composition factors are also listed.

Now the total Latino population in San Luis Obispo County for the period from 1850 to 1870 can be estimated far more accurately. We used the following equation to estimate total population number:

$$\frac{(adult\ males)}{(underrepresentation\ fraction)} \times (composition\ factor) = estimated\ total$$

If in 1850 there were 46 adult Latino males, the underrepresentation fraction was one-third, and the relative composition factor was 4.56, plugging in the numbers results in:

$$\frac{46}{\frac{1}{3}} \times 4.56 = 629\ Latinos$$

Our figure of 629 total Latinos is nearly twice the figure of 293 yielded by the census that year.

Using different underrepresentation fraction assumptions creates a range of population estimates: low, middle, and high estimates. If the underrepresentation fraction among males was only one-half, we get a low estimate (420 total). We can then use estimates of one-third (ranchero fraction in 1850), one-fourth (the junta fraction in 1870), and one-fifth (the junta fraction in 1860) to create midrange and high estimates of the Latino population. Table 5 lays out the data for these differing population estimates, based on varying assumptions of the underrepresentation fraction for the 1850 census. Depending upon the underrepresentation fraction used, the total estimate varies from a low of 420 total Latinos to a high of 1,049.

Table 5. Latino Population Estimates for San Luis Obispo County, 1850, under Different Latino Underrepresentation Fractions.

Rancheros	Underrepresentation Fraction	Relative Composition Ratio	Population Estimates
46	1/2	4.56	420
46	1/3	4.56	629
46	1/4	4.56	839
46	1/5	4.56	1,049

Source: UCLA CESLAC calculations.

We performed similar calculations for 1860 and 1870, shifting the adult male figure from total rancheros to the total junta membership and modifying the relative composition factor to reflect changes in the relative composition for each census. (See appendix A for data for San Luis Obispo County.) Figure 4 provides a summary of these calculations. The solid line at the bottom shows total Latino population, as represented in the censuses from 1850 to 1870. The line above it with the hollow circle symbol shows the estimate for an underrepresentation fraction of one-half. The line above, that with the X symbol, shows the estimate for an underrepresentation factor of one-third. The line with the triangle symbol is the estimate for an underrepresentation factor of one-quarter; and the line above that, with the hollow square symbol, is the estimate for an underrepresentation factor of one-fifth.

The original, flawed census population totals already showed explosive growth in the Latino population of San Luis Obispo County. CESLAC's postenumeration evaluations, which factors in various potential levels of census undercount, all show vastly more explosive growth of the Latino population during the period studied.

INTRODUCTION 27

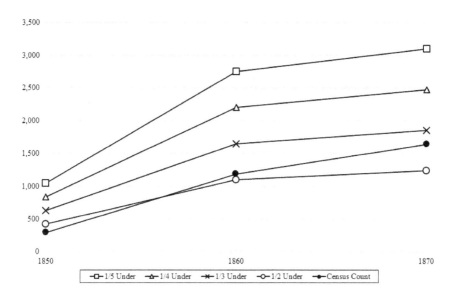

FIGURE 4. Total Latino Population Estimates Under Various Levels of Male Underrepresentation Fraction: San Luis Obispo County, 1850, 1860, and 1870. (UCLA CESLAC.)

CESLAC also did similar calculations, using junta donation lists, for three other counties in California, each with a different socioeconomic and national-origin profile. Los Angeles County was more urban than San Luis Obispo, even in the mid-nineteenth century, with a Californio-dominant population. San Francisco County was by far the most urbanized in the state and had a Latino immigrant-dominant population. Tuolumne County's economy in those decades was focused on mining, and its population, like San Francisco's, was dominated by Latino immigrants. See appendix A for relevant data.

This research enables CESLAC to provide initial estimates of the total Latino population of the state of California during the Gold Rush and Civil War (appendix B). Because San Francisco County's microdata sheets were lost,[74] and because Tuolumne County did not have a significant number of rancheros, relative composition ratios and estimate populations for these two counties could not be calculated for 1850. These estimates begin in 1848, with the thus far generally accepted figure of a population of around 10,000 Latinos in California.

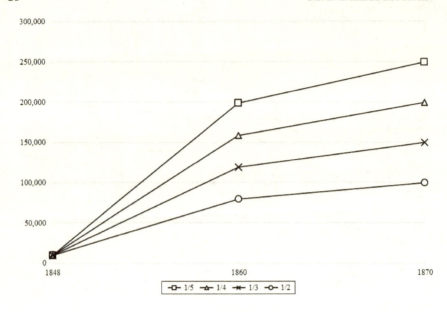

FIGURE 5. Estimated Latino Population in California, 1848, 1860, and 1870, per Various Underrepresentation Fractions. (UCLA CESLAC.)

CESLAC's examination of published donation lists of the juntas patrióticas, dated largely between August 1862 and May 1866, yields 12,926 junta members in California during that period.[75] Using the equation given above, the low estimate, at an underrepresentation fraction of one-half, would result in an estimate of a total Latino population of 79,366 in 1860 and 99,789 for 1870. The high estimate, using a one-fifth underrepresentation fraction, results in 198,967 in 1860 and 249,472 in 1870. Figure 5 shows different Latino population estimates according to various underrepresentation fractions.

As these new calculations show, during the Gold Rush, the state's Latino population exploded, from around 10,000 to around 100,000. After the initial Gold Rush explosion, the Latino population's growth was slower in the decade from 1860 to 1870. Nonetheless, by way of comparison, its growth was still twice that of overall US population growth between 2010 and 2020. We can continue making fine adjustments to the data and to our assumptions, but the overall picture is clear: the traditional narrative of Latino population disappearance in California is not substantiated by any reliable data. Latinos did not disappear; they multiplied.

INTRODUCTION

The Myth of Latino Disappearance from California

As early as 1852, the trope of Latino disappearance was already appearing in English-language newspapers, when an article in the San Francisco *Alta California* proclaimed the growth of the "Anglo Saxon, the French, the German and the Italian" populations, "while the old Californian [Latino] and the Indian are withering away."[76] Some historians claim "the lure of intermarriage" into the Atlantic American population as one reason for this presumed Latino disappearance.[77] This modern theory presumes that intermarriage between Atlantic Americans and Latinos was a way for the latter to be accepted into white society, not vice-versa, and therefore inevitably would lead to both a cultural and a physical "bleaching out" of the Latino population.[78]

Some historians cite anecdotal comments about Latino disappearance such as the one in the *Alta California* as if they were firm population-based evidence. Yet there is at least one data source that can be used to test these anecdotal conclusions about Latino disappearance through intermarriage: the archive of marriage licenses filed with the Los Angeles County Recorder's Office. Prior to statehood in 1850, marriage in California was a purely religious sacrament, performed and recorded by the local parish.[79] With the change in constitutional and legal structure in 1850, marriage became a civil event as well and, accordingly, was documented by County Recorders.

Using the same algorithm to identify Latinos in this civil marriage data as in the census data, CESLAC's research team manually inspected every marriage record extant at the County Recorder's Office. If one or both of the couple were Latino, the team extracted all data in the record. The amount and quality of these data, however, did prove somewhat variable. Initially, during the 1850s and 1860s, the Recorder's Office took down minimal information, usually just the names of the bride, the groom, and the officiant. Due to this paucity of information, endogamous and exogamous married couples could not be identified with much confidence in these decades. Nevertheless, during this two-decade period of data paucity, 1851 to 1873, there was one anomalous period—June 1858 to March 1860—when, for unknown reasons, the Recorder's Office chose to include the ages and birthplaces of both bride and groom. This allowed us to make some observations about intermarriage for that nearly two-year period.

During that period, 106 couples having at least one Latino partner registered their marriages. As seen in figure 6, about 75 percent of the

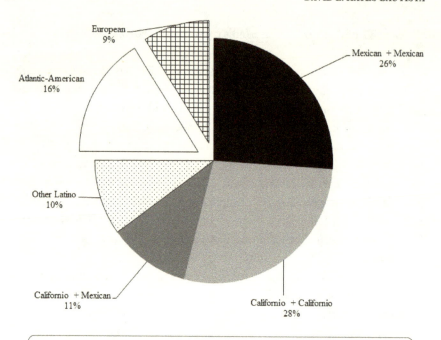

FIGURE 6. Latino Marriages, Endogamous and Exogamous, Los Angeles County, June 1858–January 1862. (UCLA CESLAC.)

marriages were endogamous (Latino married to Latina) and roughly 75 percent were exogamous.

The most common pairings were endogamous: a Californio married to another Californio (28 percent of all Latino marriages),[80] a Mexican immigrant married to a Mexican immigrant (26 percent), a Californio married to a Mexican immigrant (11 percent), and all other Latino-Latina pairings (e.g., a Californio married to a New Mexican, 10 percent). Exogamous marriages between a Latino and a non-Latino were rarer: 16 percent involved a Latino married to an Atlantic American and 9 percent a Latino married to a European immigrant.

These data are interesting, but their generalizability might be questioned, given the brief time period concerned. A study currently under peer review provides Los Angeles County marriage data from the period 1851–1910, with data on birthplace noted for nearly all marriage partners from 1873 on. A few individual records during this latter period do not contain complete data, but those are exceptions, probably due to

INTRODUCTION

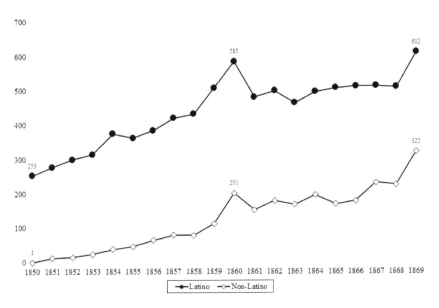

FIGURE 7. Latino and Atlantic American Births, Los Angeles County, 1850–1869. (UCLA CESLAC.) Source: Graph is based on data supplied by Ted Gostin, *Southern California Vital Records* (Los Angeles: Generations Press, 2001); and data for 1860–1869, commissioned by CESLAC, compiled by Gostin from materials prepared for his yet unpublished second volume of *Southern California Vital Records, Los Angeles and Orange Counties, 1860–1869.*

contemporary clerical error. The data from 1858–1860 presented in figure 6, therefore, are validated by the data from 1873 to 1910, during which time Latino marriages in Los Angeles County were also from about two-thirds to about three-quarters endogamous.[81] Given that between two-thirds and three-quarters of Latinos married other Latinos, obviously they could not have been disappearing via intermarriage with non-Latinos.

Given the large influx of immigrants from Mexico, Latin America, and Spain during the Gold Rush, many of whom settled and formed families in California, it should not be surprising to see a concomitant dramatic increase in Latino births. Figure 7 shows that this was exactly what happened. Between 1851 and 1869, the number of Latino births in Los Angeles County nearly tripled. Atlantic American births also grew but by 1869 still comprised only about a third of all births in the county.

A Latino population explosion, endogamous Latino marriages, and a Latino baby boom all indicate a sudden, rapid growth of California's Latino population during the Gold Rush and US Civil War. This population explosion via both immigration and natural increase is statistical proof that not only did Latinos not disappear from California during this period, as some historians have imagined, but instead their numbers actually increased dramatically.

Constitutional Earthquake

As noted above, the Mexican Republic's constitution was based on principles of racial equality and abolition of slavery.[82] Accordingly, nearly a full generation of male Californios grew up able to vote and hold office—and all Latinos, male or female, could conduct business and marry freely—regardless of their racial background. But these principles of freedom and male suffrage for all races were upended ten days after the discovery of gold in California, when the Treaty of Guadalupe Hidalgo took effect on February 2, 1848. California was abruptly removed from the rule of Mexican law and subjected to the United States Constitution, which at the time was based on principles of white supremacy and the legal protection of slavery.

A documentary record of this constitutional earthquake exists in the minutes of the California Constitutional Convention of 1849. These were printed in both English and Spanish, and a comparison of the two versions reveals the different constitutional experiences and expectations of the Spanish-dominant Latino delegates and the English-speaking Atlantic American delegates.

Problems of proper translation of US legal terms recur in the Spanish-language version of the minutes, as the translator, William E. P. Hartnell, strove to communicate concepts from the English and US common law tradition that did not exist in the Spanish and Mexican civil law tradition.[83] In addition, entire days of debate inexplicably were omitted from the official, printed Spanish-language version that Latinos had to rely on, which was issued by a different publisher in 1851, a year after the English-language version.

The US Racial Binary

In the minds of most of the Atlantic American delegates, human beings were divided naturally into a mutually exclusive binary of two groups: the "white race" and the "inferior races."[84] According to this perspective, English-speaking members of the "white race" in the United States were "the most energetic and adventurous of the modern races," as opposed to the so-called inferior races,[85] composed of Indians, Blacks, and their descendants.[86] Various negative characteristics were imputed to the latter: "They are idle in their habits, difficult to be governed . . . thriftless, and uneducated."[87] Consequently, one of the most important goals of these delegates at the California Constitutional Convention of 1849 was to make the new state a suitable home for white people, which in practice would mean legally excluding or disenfranchising all persons of color.[88]

In the California of 1849, this perception of wholesale racial inferiority could be made to encompass the majority of the Latino population. For example, it would include 96 percent of the pobladores who had settled Los Angeles in 1781 and all their descendants. The 1781 settlers were Indians, Blacks, mestizos, mulattos, and other mixed-race individuals with nearly every possible combination of ancestry from the Americas, the Iberian Peninsula, Africa, and Asia.[89] In 1834, Bostonian Richard Henry Dana visited Alta California and subsequently described a spectrum of racial mixture in the population, from a few individuals of "pure Spanish blood" to the large majority who were of various "dark and muddy" shades, including quadroons and octoroons, "until you come to the pure Indian."[90] In the run-up to the Mexican-American War, US Secretary of State James Buchanan disdainfully described Mexico's population as comprised of "Spaniards, Indians and negroes, blended together in every variety."[91]

Who Gets to Vote?

For the Atlantic American delegates who viewed California's population through the lens of this racial binary of superior whites and inferior nonwhites, the Treaty of Guadalupe Hidalgo's stipulation that racially mixed former citizens of Mexico in the territories transferred to the United States could become US citizens raised the uncomfortable possibility that nonwhite men night be able to vote and run for elected office.[92] But those delegates had not far to look for an argument for keeping these new mixed-race US citizens from voting: the pre–Civil War doctrine of states' rights.[93]

Under the terms of the treaty between the federal governments of Mexico and the United States, former Mexican citizens in the transferred territories would become de facto citizens of the United States by simply not leaving those territories. But at that time, US citizenship did not automatically confer the right to vote or run for office.[94] Rather, under the doctrine of states' rights, each state could determine in its own constitution which socioeconomic characteristics qualified a person to vote in that state. In accordance with this line of thinking, the constitution of the new state of California potentially could stipulate that only adult white males could vote, as the constitutions of many other US states then did.[95] According to the binary racial logic espoused by many of the Atlantic American delegates, therefore, any adult "white" males who previously had been Mexican citizens would be eligible to vote under California's new state constitution, but nonwhite former Mexican citizens—Indians, Africans, and their descendants—would not, even though they were still technically US citizens.[96]

The proposed limitation of the vote to adult white males, however, evoked strong reactions from the Latino delegates. Hoping to explain their reaction to more recently arrived Atlantic Americans among the delegates, New York–born Edward Gilbert, founder and first editor of the San Francisco *Alta California*, informed them that what was meant by the word "white" was generally not understood in Mexican California, although it was well understood in the United States.[97] Latino delegate from Santa Barbara Pablo de la Guerra y Noriega demanded, through the convention's interpreter, that "it should be perfectly understood in the first place what is the true signification of the word 'white.'" He then remonstrated that although many citizens in California had received from nature a dark complexion, nonetheless they had the right to vote, and some held even the highest public offices. He saw no reason to strip them of these rights merely because they had not been born with paler skins.[98]

De la Guerra's questioning of white privilege evidently unnerved some proponents of the binary racial narrative. Southern slave owner William Gwin asked, in some disbelief, if Indians and Blacks had the right to vote under Mexican law.[99] De la Guerra replied that no race of men in Mexico was deprived of the right to vote. Gwin prodded at this strange idea of nonwhites having political agency, asking if Indians were actually considered citizens of the Mexican Republic. Not only were they citizens, de la Guerra replied, but some of the most eminent men of the republic were Indians.[100]

The debate over race and the right to suffrage continued on subsequent days. Monterey delegate Missouri-born Lewis Dent objected that if the new California constitution were to give *all* adult male former citizens of Mexico the franchise, a Black Mexican would not only have the right to vote—he might even aspire to become governor of the state![101] To avoid such an unthinkable prospect, Atlantic American delegates discussed how the vote in California could be limited to adult "white" males. Gwin cited the precedent of Louisiana, which had a large mixed-race population comparable to California's, but whose state constitution specified that only "free white males" had the vote.[102] Texas's constitution was even more specific, also stipulating who did not: all Africans, all descendants of Africans, and the vast majority of Indians who did not pay taxes.[103]

Yet de la Guerra's question still had not been answered. What, exactly, did his Atlantic American colleagues mean by the word "white"? New York–born Scott Sherwood, a delegate from Sacramento, opened a racial Pandora's box by admitting that the term "white" was not as clear-cut as many Atlantic Americans fondly imagined. Many Spaniards, Frenchmen, and Italians tended to have darker skin tones than "the Anglo-Saxon race," yet were considered "white men" and therefore had the vote.[104] White supremacist delegates had to try a different tactic. Although they could not themselves satisfactorily define what a "white man" was, Kentucky-born Robert Semple declared that using that term was good enough, because the issue had been "sufficiently" argued and litigated since the founding of the United States, and the courts would know who was "white" and who was not. It could safely be left to them to decide which former Mexican citizens might qualify as voters and which would not. Rather sarcastically, Gilbert retorted that although the term "white" might be understood by the courts, it should be spelled out in the state constitution nonetheless, so ordinary citizens would not have to go to court to find out what it meant.[105]

In the closing days of the convention, New Jersey–born delegate Thomas Lloyd Vermeule summarized the decision on voting rights: even though under Mexican law Indians, Africans, and their descendants had

had the right to vote, the new California constitution must deny it to them, in "unavoidable conformity to American principles."[106] So a Latino man's race, and thereby his eligibility as a voter, was to be decided henceforth by a judge and jury, both of which would be comprised only of "white" men.[107]

Slavery and Negrophobia

The abolition of slavery in Mexico early in the nineteenth century was based on moral and legal repudiation of human bondage. Enslaved Blacks from the United States who reached Mexican territory automatically became free, and both Mexican government officials and ordinary Mexicans resisted, sometimes with force, attempts by white slavecatchers to return them to US territory and to bondage.[108]

The potential expansion of slavery into newly conquered territory had been a major controversy in the United States during the prosecution of the Mexican-American War, with Northern states generally opposed to such expansion and Southern states generally eager for it. The signing of the Treaty of Guadalupe Hidalgo in 1848 prompted the rise of a new political party, the Free Soil Party, whose main goal was to stop the growth of slavery. This short-lived political party (1848–1854) tried to bring together different factions who were debating how, and why, to stop slavery's spread. Eric Foner identifies a number of these Free Soil strategies,[109] and at least four of them were debated at the California Constitutional Convention in 1849. Early in the debate, the delegates voted unanimously not to allow the institution of slavery in California. Yet the reasons they voted to prohibit slavery varied widely, from moral repugnance at slavery to an overt "negrophobia" that hoped to prohibit any Black presence in California at all.

The moral stance against slavery was that it was simply wrong and should not be allowed to spread. Adherents of this view generally also held that free Black men should enjoy all the rights of citizenship, including the vote. Drawing upon the Mexican moral stance on slavery, delegate José Carrillo, then mayor of Los Angeles, declared that Latinos in southern California were as firmly opposed to the idea of introducing slavery into the state as anyone.[110] New York–born Kimball H. Dimmick pointed out the contradiction that European immigrants could become US citizens and vote, whereas Blacks, born and educated in the United States, who spoke English and followed American customs, nonetheless were denied full citizenship.[111]

Others who opposed introducing slavery, however, sought merely to protect the incomes of white male workers. Kentuckian J. M. Jones declared his opinion that California's mines were populated by respectable, intelligent, educated, talented (white) men, any of whom could have qualified as delegates to the Constitutional Convention. But these white paragons would rather leave California than dig for gold alongside Black men.[112] Ohio-born Oliver M. Wozencraft thought the arrival of Southern capitalists with large, enslaved labor forces working without pay would undercut and outproduce white yeoman miners, driving them from the Gold Country. But prohibiting slavery in California would ensure that white men could make a living and the state, in consequence, would prosper.[113]

Many Atlantic American delegates' opposition to slavery was motivated by negrophobia. They feared that slaveowners, after enriching themselves through the labor of their bondsmen, would then leave the state, abandoning any further responsibility for their slaves by manumitting them and leaving them behind in California. These delegates assumed, without evidence, that such freedmen would be unaccustomed to fending for themselves and therefore would turn to crime or become habitual beggars. Keeping slavery out of California in the first place, this group declared, would avoid these social ills. It is obvious from the language used in their arguments, however, that fear of any Black presence in the state, based on racial stereotypes, was what really animated their opposition to slavery.[114]

A fourth group was even more overtly negrophobic. They opposed the entry even of Blacks who were already free, on the grounds of their presumed inherent racial dysfunctionality, as well as the threat they allegedly posed to white workers' wages. New York–born Henry A. Tefft described free Blacks as immoral, vice-ridden, brutish, and depraved.[115] Wozencraft opined that free Black people were one of the greatest evils that could afflict a free (i.e., white) society.[116] Kentuckian Morton McCarver labeled any free Black population lazy, lawless, improvident, ignorant, and detrimental to the state's prosperity.[117] They argued that any presence of free Blacks, as well as enslaved ones, would degrade whites' earning power and consequently their social status.[118] Not only should free Blacks be forbidden to enter California, but any enslaved Blacks manumitted there should have to leave the state very soon after gaining their freedom, as was the case in many Southern states.[119]

Latinos Stand Their Constitutional Ground

This constitutional earthquake jolted Latinos out of the Mexican legal framework of racial equality and abolition of slavery, into the US framework of white supremacy and legal protection for slavery. But Latinos were not mere passive victims of this upheaval, as the minutes of the California Constitutional Convention show. Although the constitutional ground had moved beneath them, Latino delegates exercised political agency to preserve as much of the values of freedom and equality as could endure in the new environment.

The final draft of the 1849 state constitution, Article II, Section 1, declared that only white male citizens of the United States, including those who previously had been citizens of Mexico, would have the vote. Yet thanks to an amendment argued into being by Pablo de la Guerra of Santa Barbara, it was allowed that some full-blooded Indian men someday might be able to vote, given special legislative approval.[120] So the door to at least some nonwhite suffrage was kept open in the new constitution, even if only a crack.

By unanimous vote, slavery was not allowed in California. Although the negrophobic element wanted to go further and prohibit the entry of free Blacks into the state, the convention decided that such a provision was not an appropriate part of a state constitution. They left it as a topic for the new legislature to consider. Negrophobes at the convention kept pressing for a specific request that the new legislature address this anti-Black measure during its first session. Dimmick countered that the citizens of his district, San José—at the time, a majority Latino community—did not approve of the proposed restrictions on the entry of free Blacks into California.[121] Three separate motions were made during the convention to explicitly direct the future legislature to pass such bills. The first two motions failed, with the Latino delegates unanimously opposed. The third motion also went down to defeat, with all but one Latino delegate opposing it.[122]

Married women's right to own property independently of their husbands stemmed from medieval Castilian legal tradition, which had been continued in Mexican law after independence. Married Latinas in California legally owned land, houses, and businesses in their own right, and also half the couple's community property. This was in contrast to the English and US common law tradition of coverture, which, with very few exceptions, placed a married woman and all her property under the sole control of her husband.[123] Despite dire predictions by some Atlantic American delegates that allowing married women to be economically independent would literally result in the end of Western civilization, ultimately Latino legal tradition prevailed, and the new constitution stipulated, "All property, both real and personal, of the wife, owned or claimed by marriage, and that acquired afterwards by gift, devise or descent, shall be her separate property."[124] This eventually led, in the twentieth century, to the adoption of marital community property laws in many US states, as well as for federal tax purposes throughout the country as a whole.[125]

During the convention, Latino delegates insisted that if the laws and regulations of the new state were not available in the Spanish language, Spanish speakers would not be able to abide by them. Due to their persistence, the final draft of the constitution stipulated that "all laws, decrees, regulations, and provisions, which from their nature require publication, shall be published in English and Spanish,"[126] making California officially a bilingual state until a revised constitution was adopted in 1879.

The Latino Big Bang: Sudden, Forceful Change

Before the Latino Big Bang, the 10,000 or so Spanish speakers in California had lived their lives in a regional variant of Mexican society, culture, and identity, under a constitution and institutions based on principles of racial equality in citizenship and the abolition of slavery. Afterward, they suddenly found themselves under the jurisdiction of the United States, whose constitution and institutions were based on white supremacy and the legal protection of slavery.

The Gold Rush resulted in a Latino population explosion, a tenfold growth in a single decade. But this rapidly expanding population now lived under institutions that could be quite hostile and was increasingly surrounded by a similarly expanding white, Atlantic American civil society, much of which displayed hostile attitudes toward people of color.

Nonetheless, the Latino population continued to form families, raise children, worship, participate in the economy, and create community, albeit now under conditions not entirely of their choosing or under their control. They learned English, but also continued to speak Spanish. And as they did all these normal, everyday things, they began to create the bilingual, bicultural civil society of los Latinos de Estados Unidos. Over the next 170 years, multiple subsequent waves of immigration, followed by respective waves of births, would join this Latino civil society.

Justo Veytia and the Latino Big Bang

My discovery of Justo Veytia's diary precipitated the conception of a new theoretical model that provides a new, fact-based narrative of Latino life in the US state of California. This model begins with the origin story of the state's bilingual, bicultural Latinos. From January 24 to February 2, 1848, a mere ten days initiated a sudden, forceful change that shook California's Spanish-speaking world, causing a regional variant of Mexican civil society to begin transforming into a new, bilingual, bicultural civil society, that of Latinos living in the United States. Mexican '49er Justo Veytia was an eyewitness to its early days.

He was no sociologist or anthropologist, merely a rather hapless young middle-class Mexican man who kept a diary of his misadventures. He was not conceptualizing the origin story he witnessed. Indeed, he seems to have been largely unaware he was witnessing one. Yet he recorded a good deal about Latino daily life, starting just twelve months after the Latino Big Bang, and interestingly, he already tended, in 1849–1850, to view Californios not as fellow Mexicans recently subjected to US rule but rather as belonging to a separate society or culture.[127] In so doing, he unwittingly described some of the foundations being laid for the society of los Latinos de Estados Unidos that still inform the "habits of the heart" of more than 15 million Latinos living in California in the early twenty-first century.[128]

Generations earlier, between 1769 and 1781, the Spanish Crown recruited poor, starved-out small farmers from Sonora and Sinaloa in Mexico to go settle in Alta California, thereby establishing Spain's claim to the region in the face of colonial expansion by rival European powers. These humble settlers were racially mixed, of Indian, African, European, and Asian heritages. After Mexico became independent from Spain, the Mexican president in 1834 authorized José María Híjar and José María Padrés to recruit a group of educated professionals from Mexico City and Guadalajara—physicians, teachers, craftsmen, and printers—to reinforce the small, mostly pastoral settlements in Alta California.[129] These Híjar-Padrés colonists included José Arana, originally a maker of gunpowder and fireworks; his wife, Feliciana Alderete; and their children, José Jr., Felipe, Marcos, and Florencia.[130] On his way through the San Joaquin Valley to the gold fields, Justo Veytia met members of the Arana family, describing José Arana senior as "a Mexican who came here with the Colony of 1834 . . . 14 years ago as a settler." He made friends with José Arana's son, Felipe—aged thirty to Veytia's twenty-seven when they met in 1849—who had grown up in California since the age of fifteen.[131] During part of his time in California, Veytia traveled with or worked for the Arana family, whose members had been part of the regional variant of Mexican society, identity, and culture prior to the Latino Big Bang.

Initially filled with enthusiasm and confidence and dreaming of golden riches, Veytia left his comfortable home in Guadalajara on February 9, 1849, and joined the early wave of Spanish-speaking gold seekers. On April 1, 1849, aboard the *Volante*, he passed through the Golden Gate into San Francisco Bay. At last he was in the "much-desired Harbor of the Land of Gold," eager to try his luck, although he acknowledged, "Who knows but that it all might be in vain, with no reward. . . . We shall see."[132] Spanish speakers from all over the Americas, likewise hoping to strike gold, arrived by land and sea for the next decade and more, up to the outbreak of the US Civil War. The welcome they received was decidedly mixed. While California's Spanish-speaking residents, like the Aranas, were generally friendly, most English-speaking immigrants were not. The latter soon formed a majority in the government of the new state and legislated accordingly.

The constitutional earthquake of 1848 imposed a new government on California's population, one which sought to deny citizenship to persons of African and Native American descent. At the 1849 California Constitutional Convention, San Joaquin delegate Thomas L. Vermeule, a veteran of the Mexican-American War, recognized the military conquest of California by the United States: "Sir, this land of California was acquired to the American people—how? . . . It was acquired by military occupation." Citing that authority, he maintained that "unavoidable conformity to American principles restricts from the right of suffrage numbers of Indians, descendants of Africans &c., whom it is asserted possessed that right under the Mexican supremacy," as under US law the franchise was limited to adult white males only.[133] California's former regional variant of Mexican society and culture in many ways was now under hostile rule.

When the new California State Legislature met for the first time in

1850, Senator Thomas Jefferson Green of San José decried the ongoing "[im]migration overwhelming in number and dangerous in character" of "the worst population" from Mexico, South America, Australia, and the South Pacific in response to the Gold Rush. The remedy he proposed came to be known as the Foreign Miners' Tax, which intended to levy twenty dollars per month on non-US citizens for the privilege of working a claim or mine.[134] As a dollar a day was a working man's average wage in 1850, this was a tax of 60–70 percent on income. Along with many other Latino immigrants, however, Justo Veytia had no intention of allowing this new law to stop him panning for gold. He wrote in his diary, "We're all right, though; we already see how we will avoid paying this tax."[135] He and his companions knew of a loophole: the Treaty of Guadalupe Hidalgo had granted US citizenship to the conquered Californios in 1848, which officially exempted them from the tax. So Veytia and his fellow Mexicans pretended to be Californios and continued their operations without further bother. Spanish-speaking '49ers used this and other strategies to resist the new government's attempts to discriminate against them, including economic boycotts, armed resistance, and withdrawal to isolated diggings far away from tax collectors.[136]

Californios born before 1850 technically did not immigrate from a foreign country into California; they were born into a California that was then still part of Mexican civil society. But their experience after 1848, suddenly subjected to a population, language, culture, and sometimes hostile state institutions not their own, was equivalent to that faced by immigrants. Their children, who grew up during the Gold Rush and US Civil War, were therefore in an equivalent situation to that of children of immigrants, whom today's demographic terminology calls the "second generation," their immigrant parents being the "first generation." While working for the Arana family in Santa Cruz in the fall of 1849, Justo Veytia encountered some of these children. He grumbled in his diary, of his friend Felipe Arana's two little boys, "They gave us headaches day and night."[137] Little Epifanio Genovevo Arana and José Ygnacio Arana, born in Santa Cruz in 1847 and 1848 respectively, belonged to the first cohort of second-generation Latino children born in California after statehood.[138] They would grow up part and parcel of the new bilingual, bicultural Latino society.

Bilingual, Bicultural Latino Civil Society

After "busting out" more than once in the gold fields, as so many fellow miners did, Veytia returned to Mexico in August 1850, penniless and deeply disappointed. It is worth noting that he went home on a steamship, probably the *Panama* of the Pacific Mail Steamship Company. Travel and commerce between the new US state and the Spanish-speaking Americas had already become so important that, having come to California on a specially chartered sailing ship in 1849, he could go back to Mexico a year later aboard a steamship that was part of a regular line. Most of the steamship's 400 passengers leaving California, though, were Atlantic Americans returning to the eastern states. Although the traditional narrative has hordes of Atlantic Americans replacing conveniently disappearing Latinos in California during this period, the exodus of Atlantic American '49ers was itself considerable, at one point reportedly numbering more than 2,200 in one day. From the English-speaking viewpoint, their departure left "considerable of a vacuum" in California.[139] Nonetheless, a substantial core of English-speaking Atlantic American population stayed in the state, even after many failed prospectors went back East. In similar fashion, a substantial new Spanish-speaking population remained in California long after Veytia's departure.

Tens of thousands, in fact, stayed and continued habits of the heart familiar to them from Mexican civil society. Yet at the same time, they absorbed aspects of the new culture. Some of their children attended Spanish-language or bilingual schools,[140] but many others went to English-language schools and soon demonstrated proficiency in that language.[141] Growing up bilingual, these children, to the chagrin of their Spanish-dominant elders, casually mixed words and phrases from the two languages on a daily basis, for instance creating the word "marketa" out of the English word "market" when speaking of what Spanish speakers called a *mercado*.[142] California's Latinos ate foods from both cultures, downing pancakes, French bread, and plum pudding in addition to tortillas, while still drinking traditional toasted corn-flour *atole* or spicing their dishes with *chilipiquín*, made from dried chili peppers.[143]

While continuing to observe Día de Muertos, California's Latinos started celebrating Thanksgiving as well.[144] They also quickly took to the Fourth of July. A Santa Cruz correspondent of the English-language

Alta California noted in 1852 that the "Spanish population" of his town, "with good will," joined in the celebration of "the national anniversary of their adopted [country]."[145] In 1853, two young "Mexican boys," who showed "such a deep interest in our Anniversary," celebrated the Fourth of July so enthusiastically with firecrackers "in a dangerous place" in fire-prone San Francisco that they were arrested, then released with a warning.[146] To commemorate the Fourth of July in Los Angeles in 1855, *El Clamor Público*'s editor, Francisco P. Ramírez, provided his readers with a Spanish translation of the Declaration of Independence, beginning "Cuando, en el curso de los eventos humanos."[147] California's Latinos showed patriotism toward their new country in other ways as well. When the Women's Society of Mount Vernon asked residents of California for funds to help purchase and preserve George Washington's home, Joaquín Carrillo of San Luis Obispo and Pablo de la Guerra of Santa Barbara publicly supported the request.[148]

California became a crossroads between Mexico, Latin America, and the United States, and still is. Thanks to the Gold Rush economic boom, the exploding Latino population in California enjoyed not-inconsiderable incomes, which made it a desirable market, particularly for high-end goods and services from Mexico and Latin America. Musical performers added California to their tours through Mexico and Latin America. After a three-year stint in Valparaiso and other South American cities, "actress and danseuse" Aurelia Dimler came to San Francisco in 1853, "to begin a career in our State."[149] A few months later, a theatrical troupe arrived and put on a play by the Spanish playwright Zorrilla, *Los dos Virreyes* (The Two Viceroys), for which effort "Doña [Leonarda] Garivay and Señor [Rafael] Guerrero" were singled out for special mention by a local theater critic.[150] Throughout the ensuing 170 years, musicians and actors based in Mexico and South America have continued to tour California.

Printed materials from around the Spanish-speaking world found new markets in California's Latino civil society. In 1854, the bookstore Librería Española in San Francisco advertised a stock of more than 3,000 books on hand, including collections of dramas by Zorrilla, Calderon de la Barca, and Quevedo, as well as a book on the event that helped produce the Latino Big Bang, *Guerra entre Mejico i los Estados Unidos* (War Between Mexico and the United States). To keep Latinos abreast of events around the Spanish-speaking world, the Libreria Española also offered "Periodicos españoles por cada vapor de Nueva York, Mejico, Havana, Chile i Peru, etc."

(Spanish-language newspapers by every steamship, from New York, Mexico City, Havana, Chile, and Peru, etc.). To round out its offerings, the Libreria also carried sheet music: "Canciones mejicanas i españolas, Polkas i Galopas modernas, etc. Metodos para piano i canto, solfeos, etc." (Mexican and Spanish songs, modern polkas and galops, etc., piano and voice methods, scales, etc.).[151]

During the 1850s and 1860s, moreover, California also became a haven for political refugees from Mexico and Latin America, which brought political figures, journalists, writers, academics, and labor leaders to the state. This tradition continues in the twenty-first century.[152]

While Latinos continued to celebrate Mexican Independence Day on September 16, the holiday took on new meanings for Latinos of Mexican decent born in California. In his Mexican Independence Day editorial in Los Angeles's *El Clamor Público* in 1856, Francisco P. Ramírez reminded fellow Latinos that, by virtue of the Treaty of Guadalupe Hidalgo, they were now citizens of the United States and had every right "to take an active part in public affairs," including voting for candidates who would defend Latino interests.[153] Even after a decade of state-sanctioned discrimination, squatterism, and occasional lynching, Ramírez optimistically urged his readers to seek the promise of the United States, a future that would provide equality and justice for all: "We are Californio by birth, and American by adoption. The shield of liberty and of law will defend us against threats and insults."[154]

Latino Civil Society and the US Civil War

When the US Civil War began in 1861, most Californios, now citizens of the United States, supported the Union against the Confederacy. So did their children born in the US state of California, as well as many of the post-1848 Spanish-speaking immigrants from Mexico, Central America, South America, and the Caribbean. They did so despite their presence having been contested by hostile state actions for more than a decade: the Foreign Miners' Tax, the Land Act, the "Greaser Act," toleration of squatterism, the invective of the American Know-Nothing party, the US Supreme Court's Dred Scott decision and its implications for non-whites. When Napoleon III invaded Mexico just a year later to install a puppet monarch, and seriously considered making an alliance with the

Confederate rebels, many of California's Latinos also rallied in support of Mexico's democratically elected president, Benito Juárez. For them, the two causes were effectively one. California's Latinos paraded with the flags of both the United States and Mexico on the Fourth of July and on September 16. The sang the "Star Spangled Banner" and the Mexican national anthem, followed by popular songs like "Home, Sweet Home" and "Adios, Mamá Carlota." They listened to patriotic speeches in English and Spanish that urged them to support Lincoln against the Confederacy and Juárez against the French invaders. Some Latino men joined the US Army to fight the Confederacy; others joined the Mexican army fighting the French.[155] In only thirteen years, these Latinos had created something new: the bilingual, bicultural civil society of los Latinos de Estados Unidos.[156]

This new generation of bilingual, bicultural Latinos founded businesses and participated in politics. Far from shrinking from contact with Atlantic American culture and institutions, they engaged with the larger society around them, especially the second generation and their descendants. Thanks to their support for the Union, Latinos held positions of honor in Fourth of July parades and in 1865 walked in funeral processions mourning Lincoln's assassination. During Reconstruction, the second generation regularly did business with Atlantic Americans and engaged in social activities with them as well, such as tug-of-war competitions, outings to the beach, and the creation of Spanish-speaking chapters of fraternal organizations like the Ancient Order of Foresters.[157] A significant minority of each group married spouses from the other. The growing Latino population expanded geographically, moving into new communities, such as Lompoc. The society they created persists in the twenty-first century, and nearly 40 percent of modern California's population is a part of it today.

Veytia's diary provides an eyewitness account of the early days of these developments. This is the real story of Latinos in California history—not one of decline and disappearance, but one of engagement, empowerment, and expansion. The Latino Big Bang started the transformation of a regional variant of Mexican society into the bilingual, bicultural civil society of los Latinos de Estados Unidos. The origin story recounted above is supported by hard data from contemporary sources, not the fuzzy ex post facto myths repeated to generations of California schoolchildren.

Epilogue: The Experience of a Memory

At the Librería Madero, I paid Don Enrique 200 pesos—about $16 at 2006's exchange rates—for Justo Veytia's diary, then went down the street to the bar of the Casa de Azulejos. I sat down there and devoured it in one sitting. As I closed the cover on the last page, I knew that I had to share this diary with the world, the first known diary of the Gold Rush written by a Mexican '49er.

But if I was going to publish an English translation for an academic audience, I needed to find who currently held the rights to this intellectual property. Examining the volume for clues as to its provenance, I realized that what I had was not Veytia's original manuscript, but a privately printed facsimile of what looked like a fair copy made of the original. The book's brief introduction by Ricardo Lancaster Jones informed me that this facsimile had been privately published in 1975 by Justo Veytia's grandson, Salvador Veytia y Veytia, who held the rights to the diary, and who in that year was living in Guadalajara. I searched online for "Justo Veytia," and within a few days I was able to get in touch with his great-grandson, Luis Jaime Veytia Orozco of Guadalajara, Salvador's son, who now held the rights to the diary. As I was already scheduled to make a trip to Guadalajara, I arranged to meet him there.

When I first met him in Guadalajara in 2007, I had in my mind that we were meeting simply for the purpose of securing the rights to translate and publish his great-grandfather's diary. Over a long lunch, however, Veytia Orozco shared stories and anecdotes about Don Justo and his diary that had been passed down in his family. It turned out that Justo Veytia had not lived long enough to share his journey to California with his children and grandchildren. But his diary survived him, and it became one of the few fixed points on which subsequent generations could build family memories of his bittersweet journey.

As Veytia Orozco shared the family anecdotes, he also was sharing those family memories as they had been shaped and transmitted for more than 150 years. Matilde Veytia y Reyes, Don Justo's daughter by his wife, Mercedes Reyes y Delgado, was a small child when her father died in 1870. How much of him could a five-year-old girl have remembered? At some point, she obviously had access to his original diary, but he was not there anymore to elucidate names and terms or correct her interpretation of his (possibly difficult) handwriting. It may be that other family members shared their memories of Don Justo with her, but there is no way to know for sure if they did.

She shared family stories of Don Justo with her son, Salvador Veytia y Veytia, who in turn shared his experience of Matilde's memories with Luis Jaime Veytia Orozco when the latter was a young boy. Veytia Orozco recalled, "I heard so much about Justo that he sometimes seemed present," even though the two had never met.

In speaking of Don Justo or his daughter Doña Matilde, Veytia Orozco unconsciously revealed that he was creating his own memories, as he prefaced his thoughts about Matilde and Justo with phrases such as "I imagine that . . . ," "It seems to me that . . . ," "I have to think that . . . ." The Veytia family's interactions with their ancestor's diary reveal that their experiences of his memory are, in a way, as much a part of his Gold Rush journey as the translation and annotation herein presented. As such, they, too, needed to be part of any publication.

In 2013, my wife, María, an experienced qualitative interviewer, had Luis Jaime Veytia Orozco dictate anecdotes about his grandmother and great-grandfather. This dictation is the basis for his "Epilogue," which describes some of the experiences of the Veytia family after Justo's return from Alta California. Herself a child immigrant from Mexico, María is thoroughly bilingual and understands the mores of social interaction among urban, educated Mexicans—she would be called *bien educada*, if not *niña bien*.[158] Working from a prepared list of prompts to reach different areas of his experienced memories, she knew when and how to ask him to go into specific incidents in more detail.

These digitally recorded interviews then were transcribed in their original Spanish. The transcriptions became the primary source material for preparing the epilogue. The first step was to sift through the interviews and assemble a coherent narrative storyline, using Veytia Orozco's own words. This edited version then was provided to him for review and further editing. Once he had approved the Spanish language narrative derived from his interviews, we translated it into English.

After his return to Guadalajara in 1850, disillusioned by his failures in in the gold fields, Justo Veytia dedicated himself to more mundane and practical business as a store owner rather than seeking sudden, fabulous wealth by prospecting for gold. In 1863, he married Mercedes Reyes Delgado.

FIGURE 8. Portrait of Mercedes Reyes y Delgado de Veytia. Born in 1831, she married Justo Veytia y Valencia in 1863, and died in 1865 after giving birth to their only child, Matilde. (Courtesy of Luis Jaime Veytia Orozco.)

Two years later, she gave birth to their only child, Matilde Veytia Reyes. Mercedes died the same year Matilde was born, possibly in giving birth to her, although no information as to her cause of death is available. Justo Veytia himself died when Matilde was about five, and the child was placed in the girls' section of the Hospicio Cabañas, then an orphanage and school, and now a UNESCO World Heritage site and museum in Guadalajara.

One of the few of her father's possessions she kept, or which was kept for her while she lived in the Hospicio Cabañas, was the original manuscript of his diary. As an adult, Matilde left the orphanage and in 1890 married a cousin, Luis Veytia Villaseñor; Salvador Veytia y Veytia was one of their sons; and Luis Jaime Veytia Orozco is their grandson. At some point after her marriage, Matilde copied out her father's manuscript in her own fine handwriting, producing the version whose facsimile I found at the Librería Madero.[159] What became of the original diary after she made the fair copy is not known. Nor is it clear why Matilde copied it, although the number of times she miscopied words—for example, *enfarrar* for *enyesar* (fol. 18r.), *hule* for *tule* (fol. 26v.), and so on—suggests that perhaps her father's handwriting was poor to begin with or that his original diary had been damaged in the interim, either of which would have been reason to make a new copy.

A transcription of Justo Veytia's diary was published in 2000, without the Veytia family's permission, by the Universidad Nacional Autónoma de Mexico (UNAM), in its series Papeles de Familias (Family Papers).[160] We have used the authorized facsimile of Matilde Veytia's fair copy published in 1975 as the basis of the present translation, although we have occasionally consulted the unauthorized edition of 2000 for purposes of comparison.

Justo Veytia's diary, serendipitously encountered on the shelves of the Librería Madero, provided the spark needed to organize the demographic data that CESLAC's research team had been collecting. What emerged from the study of that data and of contemporary narrative sources such as Justo's diary and Spanish-language newspapers, was not the old, invalid narrative of decline, disengagement, and disappearance, but a story of empowerment, engagement, and expansion for Latinos in California and beyond.

FIGURE 9. Portrait of Matilde Veytia y Reyes de Veytia in 1953, when she was about eighty-eight years old. Only child of Justo Veytia and Mercedes Reyes, she was orphaned in 1870 and raised in the Hospicio Cabañas in Guadalajara. She married a cousin, Luis Veytia Villaseñor, in 1890. Her fair copy of her father's diary, made at an unknown date after her marriage, is the source of the present translation. (Courtesy of Luis Jaime Veytia Orozco.)

My Traveling Companions

I have spent the past ten years and more with three traveling companions. Together we have retraced Justo Veytia's journey from Guadalajara to California and back. I have had the pleasure of working with Cynthia L. Chamberlin since the 1990s, when we were involved in a years-long project studying the meeting of scientific and medical cultures that began in 1492, when Mesoamerica and Europe first came into sustained contact during the Columbian exchange. We met when she was part of a team translating previously unpublished writings by a sixteenth-century Spanish physician who meticulously described plants and minerals used in traditional Mesoamerican healing. *The Mexican Treasury: The Writings of Dr. Francisco Hernández*, edited by the late Simon Varey, was published by Stanford University Press in 2002. Earlier, she was cotranslator of *A Synoptic Edition of the Log of Columbus's First Voyage* (Turnhout, Belgium, 1999). She is the historian, translator, and editor at CESLAC and has transcribed and translated the bulk of Justo Veytia's diary, as well as supplying many of the footnotes to the text. She is my coauthor of several articles about the history of Latinos in California and a bilingual book for popular audiences about the Cinco de Mayo holiday's origins in California, as well as of "Women's Business: *Las Juntas Patrióticas de Señoras* and Latina Women in Public Life in California, 1850–2014," an exhibit at the California Museum, Sacramento, in May 2014, and of "¡Somos UCLA! (And Always Have Been): Three Latina Alumnæ of the Los Angeles State Normal School," a traveling exhibit originally meant to premiere in March 2020.[161] Her current research interests are the history of Latina women in nineteenth-century southern California and crime and society in nineteenth-century Los Angeles.[162]

In addition to running a successful law practice, Paul Bryan Gray—Don Pablo, to all who work with him—is a published historian of nineteenth-century California. In 2001, he received the Donald H. Pflueger Award for distinguished research and writing from the Historical Society of Southern California for his book *Forster vs. Pico: The Struggle for Rancho Santa Margarita*.[163] His recent biography *A Clamor for Equality: The Emergence and Exile of Californio Activist Francisco P. Ramírez* narrates the life of an extraordinary nineteenth-century Spanish-language editor and politician in California, whose newspapers were among those providing information used in this volume.[164] I had the honor of serving with Don Pablo on the Board of Directors of the Historical Society of Southern California in 2016–2107.

Luis Jaime Veytia Orozco is thoroughly in love with his native town of Guadalajara. He once said, "Pues siento un cariño muy profundo por todo lo que significa la ciudad. No es como un mueble, sino como costumbres, como relaciones, como la gente" (Well, I feel a very deep love for everything that this city means. But it is not like piece of furniture; rather, it is made out of customs, relationships, the people). In addition to providing the Veytia family's history subsequent to Don Justo's return to Mexico, he describes in his epilogue how his own work on an exhibit of sacred art from towns in the state of Jalisco led to the restoration and renovation of the Hospicio Cabañas, where his grandmother Matilde Veytia grew up.

Spanish Text of Justo Veytia's Diary

Año de 1849

[1r.] Febrero 9 = Hoy comienzo mi diario, ó la historia de los acontecimientos que tengan lugar en este viaje que voy á la Alta California, á donde marcho á la verdad lleno de entusiasmo y confiado en que tendrá un exito feliz.

Mi corazon se dilata al contemplar que voy á atravesar los mares: que voy á conocer paises lejanos: diferentes gentes y diversas costumbres; que sufriré ciertamente muchas finalidades y me veré espuesto á mil peligros, pero que al fin seré premiado de todo esto, con un porvenir pronto y brillante, al q[u]e es preciso para alcanzarlo pasar por todos estos escollos y dificultades, en que se cifre el principal merito cuando se acometen aventuras de éste género; aventuras que tienen no se que atractivo para mi por lo romantico y novelesco y cuya consideracion en vez de arredrarme me anima y ecsaspera mas y mas mis deseos de conocer el mundo y probar fortuna lejos de mi pais. Yré pues; la fortuna coronará mis esfuerzos y pronto volveré á mi patria, al lado de mi familia y en su seno disfrutaré tranquilamente [1v.] el premio de mis fatigas.

Hoy paramos en Amatitan,[1] que es un pueblo pequeño situado entre cerros, sus calles son mal distribuidas: tiene algunas tabernas ó fabricas de vino mescal, una atarjea en la playa de donde se proveen de agua los habitantes y un mal meson.

Antes de llegar, poco mas allá de la Venta se ven pendientes de una viga colocada horisontalmente sobre otras dos verticales, los cadáveros de tres ajusticiados colgados del cuello. Su aspecto es horroroso y causa pavor: sus miembros medio desecados ya, por el calor del sol y carcomidos en partes, presentan á la vista un esqueleto forrado de una piel tirante y gracienta que brilla al sol como se estuviese barnizada. Sobre una tabla blanqueada que esta arriba se lee el sig[uien]te lema: "Asi castiga la ley al ladron y al asesino."

10. .... Pasamos por Tequila, poblacion bonita: calles rectas y empedradas, con sus aceras, edificios razonables y aspecto alegre.[2]

Llegamos á Santo Tomas, haciendo de beneficio de platas, y taberna de vino mescal. La maquinaria toda, es movida por el agua [2r.] un pequeño chorro hace andar seis tahonas y el mortero á un tiempo: es bonita y digna de verse.[3]

El camino es pedregoso hasta Mochitiltic, en donde paramos; hay buen meson con sus portales al campo.[4]

11. ... Hoy pasamos por Yxtlan, pueblo pequeño é insignificante.[5] Antes de llegar á el, está la hermosa barranca de Mochitiltic: larga y profunda, con sus desfiladeros pendientes y en parte pedregosos, pues una gran parte del camino está abierto á tajo en la falda de la montaña bella, é imponente formando calzadas.

La vista de esta barranca es hermosa y romantica. Las altas cumbres de los cerros encarpados y llenos de quebradas: las inmensas profundidades en cuyo fondo corre mansamente un riachuelo con su margen cubierta de arboles diferentes: sirve de asilo á multitud de aves de un hermoso plumaje, como urracas, pericos y otras varias. Todo presenta una vista magestuosa, pero particularmente al despertar la aurora, cuando los primeros rayos del sol penetran en aquellas profundidades, deslisandose por entre el follage de los arboles y yendo á reflec– [2v.] tarse en las cristalinas aguas del arroyuelo que serpentea mansamente en aquel lecho de perpetuo verdor.

Llegamos á Ahuacatlán, pueblo pequeño, con sus portales en la plaza, meson é Yglesia.[6]

Por la noche hubo un fandango en el estremo de uno de los portales de la plaza. La iluminacion era una vela colocada en la pared, que daba luz solamente á la mitad de la concurrencia, sentada en el suelo: los bailadores zapateaban al son discordante de una guitarra, y todo ello presentaba un aspecto mas bien fastidioso que divertido.

12. .... Pasamos por Santa Ysabel, que es una rancheria en donde almorzamos y seguimos el camino cubierto en gran parte de inmensas arboledas y monte en los cerros muy espeso y verde, formando vistas y paisajes muy bonitos.

El volcan del Ceboruco, está en este camino y forma una montaña de peñascos fundidos hacinados, unos sobre otros, que parecen de fierro[7]; esto hace á esta parte del camino muy pedregoso hasta llegar á San Leonel, que es un pueblecillo insignificante y de mesquina apariencia, con una que otra casa, una mala Capilla y meso con tres cuartos y portal al Campo.[8]

[3r.] 13. . . . . . . Llegamos por la mañana á Tepic, ciudad grande y bien situada en una gran esplanada regada por varias vertientes.[9]

Sus calles son rectas y anchas, y las mayor parte de sus edificios bajos: dos Yglesias en que no hay nada[10] notable, y otra Yglesita ó Capilla á estramuros de la ciudad, llamada la Santa Cruz, por tener esta figura la vegetacion encerrada en el estrecho recinto de cuatro paredes sin techo pegadas á la Yglecia, y comunicadas con esta, por medio de una puerta con reja por donde se ve.[11]

El suelo es sumamente húmedo y la temperatura muy desigual. En un mismo dia se esperimentan los estremos de frio y de calor, que hace subir ó bajar el termometro 10 ú 11 grados.[12]

La mayor parte de las casas, tienen las salas á la calle, donde se sientan á coser las señoras, viendose en todas las mas, la hamaca, que tanto sirve en el Verano para refescar y aun duermen en ellas por la noche.

Se nota bastante lujo particularmente en muebles de Casas, pues casi todos por pobres que sean, tienen sus sillas finas, sofaes, catres con cortinas, tocadores y vidrieras en las ventanas.

Parece que hay bastante inmoralidad [3v.] en las costumbres y mucha prostitucion.

La plaza está circundada de corpulentos fresnos, que tejiendo sus ramos espesas forman una sombra en toda la circunferencia sobre los canapeses de piedra que tienen para sentarse.

Una fuente que está en medio de la plaza prové [sic] de agua á una parte de la poblacion, pues la otra la trae de los vetientes inmediatos.

Tres portales y el frente de la Yglesia, forman el cuadro de esta plaza, en que tambien hay mercado los domingos. Hay otro mercado razonable en una plazuela y algunos portales en el centro de la Ciudad.

Tiene una alameda en la orilla, junto á la garita de San Blas. Está cercada por un lado con un balaustrado de madera, asegurado en pilares de ladrillo enjarrados con mezcla, sobre pretiles de los mismo. Está plantada de árboles formando calles, de los cuales la mayor parte son naranjos pequeños entre los que hay multitud de rosales y flores del Norte sembrados en cuadros. En fin, es aspecto de la Ciudad es alegre aunque en cielo es muchas veces nebuloso, sobre todo por las tardes á causa de su inmediacion á la costa.

[4r.] Dia 14.

Hoy sali con un mozo para San Blas, haber si alla se consiguen nuestros pasages con mas facilidad.[13]

Camine hasta el rancho de Navarrete.[14]

Dia 15.

Llegue al Puerto cosa de las diez de la mañana, habiendo salido tan demadrugada [sic] que caminé grande parte de la noche por una senda formada entre el monte.

Fui luego á ver á Don Carlos Tapia[15] con quien crei conseguir los pasages en el mismo buque donde tenia Puga ajustado los suyos,[16] pero este me dijo que Fernandez Peral estaba encargado de arreglar los pasages de ese buque[17] por lo que inmediatamente fuí á verme con él[;] consegui solamente uno y vendiendome toda la lisonja me dijo que por pura amistad me costaria doscientos pesos y que me conseguiria otro en el "Republicano," buque que salia el mismo dia que el "Volante." Por fin hasta en la noche me avisó que estaba conseguido el otro pasage en [4v.] ciento noventa pesos.

Por tantas dificultades que se presentaban para conseguir trasporte y por que los dos buques salian en un mismo dia, resolví tomarlos aunque con gran pesar por ser preciso ir separado de Ygnacio, pues no se pudo conseguir cambiar el pasage de un buque á otro.

Se me dijo pues que para el dia 26 de este, debiamos estar en San Blas sin falta ninguna, pues otro dia se hacian los buques á la vela.

Entregué en la casa de Perez la carga de Puga y la nuestra para que la embarcaran[18] y me fui á posar á un jacalito que está en la orilla, en donde me dieron una amaca [sic] para que me acostara y me librara de las pulgas; pero á los mosquitos no me les escapé.

Dia 16. de Feb[rer]o.

Me volví para Tepic.

Llegué á las once de la mañana á Navarrete en donde almorcé y me dijeron que por el camino de los palos Marias,[19] llegada á Tepic como á [5r.] las siete de la noche, tome el consejo y segui.

Camino mucho mas malo que el otro: mas cubierto de arboles y mas pedregoso.

Al comenzar á subir una cuesta se nos oscurecio completamente: ni uno ni otro sabiamos el camino: la noche estaba tan tenebrosa y la barranca que comenzamos á bajar, tan profunda, segun se observaba por el ruido de los arboles, que crei no haber pasado con bien, pero quiso Dios que despues de haber andado como dos horas en tinieblas y en various precipisios sin que nos sucediera nada, llegamos á un jacalito de sacate cosa de las nueve y media.

Recordé á los caseros para que me vendieran algo para cenar; pues mi estomago se hallaba con bastante apetito por no haber tomado nada desde las once de la mañana. Consegui que me dieran un plato de frijoles cocidos algo frios y unas tortillas que los comi con buena gana. Tambien me vendieron unos ma– [5v.] nojos de hoja y un poco de maiz que el mozo echó á las bestias que llevabamos.

Concluida [sic] estas operaciones me decidé á acostarme en el corredorito de la casa que estaba lleno de pulgas, gorupos y chinchis, pues aunque me ofrecieron los dos caseros que pasara á la pieza, no quise incomodarlos, pues deseaba no dormirme mucho para salir los mas temprano que pudiera.

Dia 17.
Llegué á Tepic á las ocho de la mañana.
Los pormenores del camino y la impresion que me causó la vista del mar, cuando vuelvo á S^n Blas para embarcarme los esplicaré, por ahora me ocuparé en divertirme en el Carnaval, que hay bastante alboroto.

[6r.] 17, 18 y 19 = Domingo, Lunes y Martes de Carnaval.

En estos dias y particularmente el ultimo, Tepic es una Ciudad de locos y payazos. Desde que oscurece comienza el movimiento que no cesa en toda la noche. Centenares de personas de ambos secsos (de la clase baja) recorren las calles con grande alboroto y griteria, con sus caras enharinadas y cantando en discordantes coros al son de un tamboril ó pandero la tonada de los papaquiz.[20]

Cuantas personas encuentran al paso, llevan su untada de harina, sean quienes fueren. Las señoras tambien acompañadas de algunos jovenes hacen lo mismo aunque sin tanta bulla, entrandose á las casas de las personas conocidas y no conocidas, sociedad y portales para untar á todo el que encuentran.

De aqui siguen regularmente los bailes que duran hasta el amanecer, y en los que animados de la alegria mas desordenada y cubiertos con sus antifaces caras de harina, cometen las mayores locuras.

Hasta el martes me habia escapado de caer en manos de las untadoras; pero esta misma noche estabamos parados Ygnacio [6v.] y yo en la puerta de una tienda á donde soliamos concurrir en union de otros tapatios á oir tocar y cantar á un joven truhan que nos divertia con sus canciones, cuando la tempestad trono sobre nosotros.[21]

Estabamos solos por que los otros contertulianos andaban en la bola y sin entrar en ella, quise sin embargo ver lo que pasaba en las calles. En efecto: á poco rato una gran turba pasó por allí con grade [sic] alboroto: la esperamos sin huir creyendo estar alli á cubierto de su audacia, pero nos engañamos. Ynunda la calle aquella multitud sedienta de placer, buscando victimas para saciar su loco gusto. Se agolpan á las puertas de la tienda á la que penetraron cuatro mugeres rabiosas con sus caras enharinadas medio desgreñadas sus cabezas y ademan furioso. Una de ellas entra donde estaba el dependiente, y lo unta sin la menor oposicion de su parte. Tres se dirijen á Ygnacio como furias, empeñando grandes porciones de harina que tratan de untarle en la cara. El las rechazó á empujones, y se hizo de una puerta que daba á la sala y por donde quiso entrar para escaparse, pero en vano por que estaba cerrada. Las mugeres viendo que no [7r.] podian tan facilmente untarle, le arrojaron desde lejos grandes puñados de harina que cayeron en su cara y vestido, y despues aprovechando el momento en que se limpiaba los ojos, llegaron y lo untaron á su antojo. . . . .

Durante un pequeño intervalo, entre su primer resistencia y el primer puñado de harina que le arrojaron, una voz femenil mas compasiva que la otras "no le echen" dijo, "que le echan á perder su vestido." Cien veces á un tiempo se levantaron desaprobando aquella compasion y pidiendo á grandes gritos que lo untaran, quedando á merced de aquellas harpias bañado de harina de los pies á la cabeza.

Yo saltando el mostrador y echandome encima un candil con aceite habia huido, pero no por eso me escapé. Me seguian los hombres, y como corria por terreno desconocido y la noche estaba oscura, iba en peligro de caer, por lo que juzgue mejor pararme á pie firme con mi navaja en la mano á esperar á tres gandules que asusados por aquella multitud me acosaban. Viendo que estaba armado se contuvieron; pero antes de retroceder me echaron me echaron [sic] mi buena despolvereada de harina y corrieron.

[7v.] Como habia huido sin saber por donde, me estravie al querer volver á la casa y tuve que dar mil vueltas y revueltas para encontrarla.

Asi terminó para nosotros el carnaval de Tepic, cuyo bautismo de harina si lo hubiesemos recibido de otra mano, tal vez lo habriamos dado por bien empleado.

Nuestros paisanos dieron algun escándalo con motivo de algunas pendencias que hubo entre ellos y los tepiqueños y particularmente con un estrangero.[22]

22 — — Hoy salio para S[a]n Blas, nuestro compañero Puga, con quien debiámos haber ido juntos para embarcarnos; pero la cosa se arreglo de otro modo y nos quedamos esperando otro pasage mas comodo.

Esta misma noche celebráron varios tapatios una junta en la casa de Julian Romero; en la cual se acordó que se nombraran dos individuos de entre nosotros, para que ajustaran los pasajes de todos los asociados, ó contrataran un buque por entero, segun lo hallaran mas conveniente quedando todos obligados á no separarnos de la compañia, ni tomar pasajes en particular, pues de no haber para todos, no lo [8r.] no lo [*sic*] habria para ninguno.[23]

Los comisionados fuéron D.n Andres Gonzalez y Julian Romero, asociados con Canitrot.[24]

25. Hasta hoy nada de particular: los comisionados han salido para S.n Blas á ver un buque que está en el Puerto.

26. Hoy muy demañana [*sic*] recibimos un propio de Fernandez Peral, que nos envio con una carta en que nos dice marchemos al momento á tomar los pasajes que yo habia ajustado, pues de lo contrario tendriamos que pagar falso pasage. Marchamos luego y caminamos hasta llegar al rancho de Navarrete.

Gran parte del camino está cubierta de árboles y entre la yerva hay multitud de güinas y otros insectos perjudiciales y apesar de la sombra, esperimentamos en todo el, un calor exesivo.

27. Salimos muy demadrugada [*sic*] y caminamos en medio de la oscuridad mas densa, por un camino formado entre un monte de corpulentos y espesos árboles que formando una calle se prolonga á alguna distancia. Llegamos al Puerto de S.n Blas á las 8 de la mañana.

[8v.] El mar se ve desde un cerrito que domina la poblacion.

Un espectáculo nuevo para mi se presentó á mi vista en aquel momento. Aquel inmenso mar que se pierde en el horizonte, donde parece juntarse con el Cielo: sus aguas entonces quietas y socegadas, sobre las que flotan algunas embarcaciones: todo en fin es grandioso, magnifico é imponente, y á su vista el animo se siente naturalmente inclinado á dar gracias al autor de tanta grandeza.

Bajamos al Puerto, cuya escasa poblacion habita en Jacales, formados de varas clavadas en el suelo, cubiertas con barro y techadas con palma que los naturales llaman palapa.

Dos ó tres casas solamente hay de terrado, que es la Aduana y particulares.

El calor es exesivo y el mosquito abundante. Estuvimos este dia y al anochecer nos embarcamos en una Lancha para ir á bordo. Entretanto dimos algunos paseos por la playa, y nos bañamos en la orilla del mar.

Afortunadamente para nosotros, el Bergantin "Republicano," en que debia haber ido uno [9r.] de los dos, se habia hecho ya á la vela,[25] y logramos conseguir pasage para los dos en el "Volante," Bergantin Peruano, que aun estaba allí, y en el que yo no habia podido conseguir antes si no un solo pasage por lo que habia tomado el otro en el "Republicano" que habia salido ya.[26]

Los dos pasages nos costaron 350$ que nos salió mejor, pues yendo separados nos habria costado 390$.

Como dije antes: nos embarcamos en una lancha y fuimos donde estaba fondeado el buque.

Subimos por la escala ya de noche: estaba ya á bordo del barco: de otra cosa nueva para mi, y mucho mas para mi estomago, que luego que sintió el balancé, aunque lento, no pudo guardar mas lo que tenia y lo hizo salir por mi boca: primer mareo.

El Bergantin es del porte de 400 toneladas, tendra de largo unas 30 varas ó mas, y cosa de unas 6 varas de ancho.[27]

Contiene como 1500 tercios en la bodega,[28] 8 puercos gordos, y 8 carneros vivos y ciento y tantas gallinas encerradas en gallineros á manera de jaulas, atados á los bordos de la popa. [9v.] Su tripulacion se componia de cosa de 15 hombres y el numero de pasajeros asciende á 130.

El entrepuente ó antecamara en que veniamos Ygnacio y yo, era pieza cuadrada y tan baja que era necesario andar agachado.

Los camarotes ó dormitorios estan dispuestos en toda la circunferencia en forma de cajones sobre el suelo.

La escasa luz que recibe este aposento, es por un abujero abierto en el techo (ó cubierta) de poco mas de una vara en cuadro; y que llaman escotilla.

Una mesa de cedro larga y chaparra, colocada en medio del aposento, servia al mismo tiempo de escalera para salir arriba, para comer de dia y para dormir de noche.

La descripcion de lo restante del buque, seria á mas de muy larga, poco inteligible para quien no conoce embarcaciones, y no puede formarse una idea esacta de su mecanismo.

Marzo 1ro/1849— Hoy por la mañana levamos áncla y nos hicimos á la vela con un ligero viento.

Al grito del Capitan que mandaba la [10r.] maniobra parado sobre la popa; los marineros enrollaban compasadamente la larga cadena del áncla sobre un torno ó malacate, entonando al mismo tiempo un cantico triste y peculiar á ellos: otros echaban al viento las anchas velas que se desplegaban poco á poco á proporcion que los hombres halaban los cables, haciendo rechinar las garruchas, sobre que giraban. Otro en fin parado enfrente de la brújula, tenia en sus manos la rueda del timon para gobernar el barco.....[29]

La maniobra se concluyó; el viento infló las velas y el buque comenzó á alejarse insenciblemente de tierra. Entonces diriji mi adios á aquella tierra que dejaba para no volver á ver ¿hasta cuando? tal vez nunca! ... Esta consideracion y otras muchas me atormentaron oprimiendo terriblemente mi corazon; pero las esperanzas de un pronto y feliz regreso, me reanimaron y dieron valor, sofocando por un momento aquel pesar, aquel tal vez secreto presentimiento de fatalidades futuras, haciendome aguardar un porvenir halagüeño y feliz.

Marzo[30] 15 — — — Quince dias han pasado! pero ¡que dias! ¡Dios mio! de sufrimiento, de agonia!

[10v.] La gran debilidad y postracion en que me hallado ocacionada por el terrible mareo, me tenian en un estado de aturdimiento y de malestar indefinible.

La mayor parte de mis compañeros de viaje, estaban en el mismo ó peor estado que yo. No se v[e]ia por todas partes sino el estripito que hacian al deponer el estomago: quejas, lamentos é imprecaciones contra la navegacion.

El interior del entrepuente ofrecia escenas lastimosas y los continuos diálogos á que todo esto daba lugar, causaban risa en medio de las penas que uno sufria.

—Fulano ¿que dices? se preguntaban con voz desfallecida. ¿Si hubieramos sabido esto, habriamos venido?

—¡Que capaz![31] respondia el otro, (sacando fuerzas de su misma debilidad para dar á su voz alguna energia y aire de firmeza) me hubiera venido por tierra aun cuando supiera que iba á hacer un ano [*sic*] en el camino y que tenia que esponerme á perecer á manos de los barbaros á cada momento: siquiera tendria para vever [*sic*] agua buena y no estaria continuamente vomitando lo que como.[32]

—Maldito sea el "Volante" y la hora que pensé embarcarme, decia otro. Si yo he sabido los trabajos [11r.] que se pasan aqui, maldito si vengo, aun cuando supiera que venia a cargar el oro ya encostalado.

—¿Quieren Oro? pues tengan oro, esclamaba otro, dando á su voz sepulcral el acento de la mas amarga ironia.

¡Ah Oro! cuanto cuestas! murmuraba alguno con acento moribundo.

Estos y otros coloquios semejantes mezclados con lamentos, imprecaciones y desvergüenzas, pasaban en la antecamara y particularmente de noche en que todos estaban alli.

Por la mañana se renovaban estas conversaciones, acompanadas [*sic*] de gritos desaforados é imprecaciones dictadas por el hambre.

Venga el atole!!! ¿A que hora nos daran de desayunar? ¿Querran matarnos de hambre? Dennos aunque sea una galleta, decian otros.

Cuando bajaba el tarro con el atole, cien cuerpos se rebullian en sus camarotes sacando la cabeza, unos; otros arrastrandose lentamente hacia la mesa, y todos alargando la mano para que les dieran, formando una griteria de = á mi = á mi = á mi = que aturdian, al infeliz que tomaba á su cargo repartirlo.

Los que no estaban mareados salian sobre [11v.] cubierta temprano, é interceptaban el caldero de atole antes de bajar á la antecamara, tomando apresuradamente, unas dos ó tres tasas ó lo que podian, de lo que resultaba que muchas veces no alcansaba para los de abajo y algunos se quedaban sin desayunar: igual escena se repetia en la comida.

Cuando el Sol alumbraba, comenzaban á salir, uno á uno por la boca de la escotilla, arrebufados en sus frasadas: macilentos, desgreñados, palidos y cadavericos: parece que un sepulcro se abria y los muertos se levantaban de el.

Se dirijian con paso vacilante á los bordes del buque, á deponer el estomago, ó á sentarse tristente en alguna parte.

Ya hoy afortunadamente los mareados son pocos y los semblantes van recobrando su natural color con la vuelta del apetito y la ausencia de la enfermedad.

En este intervalo de tiempo hemos tenido algunas calmas y algunos malos temporales.

Al segundo dia de navegacion divisamos las Yslas Marias que son pequeñas,[33] y al tercero ó cuarto, perdimos de vista la peña blanca, que se ve desde tierra, y es una masa de piedra emblan– [12r.] quesida por las suciedades de los pajaros y aves marinas, y que elevandose sobre el mar brilla con el Sol como si fuese de mármol.

Una noche de calma, encontramos una barca y otro dia una lancha.[34]

Vimos tambien á lo lejos alguna ballenas que serpenteando sobre las aguas, elevaban grandes chorros de ellas en forma de abanicos, espumosa y trasparente como de plata y cristal.[35]

Multitud de peces dorados se veian al rededor del buque; entre ellos algunos muy grandes.

Un dia pescaron uno que se sirvió en la mesa de la cámara y tenía un gusto esquisito.[36]

Hasta alguna distancia de tierra, siguieron al buque gran numero de gaviotas: aves de color ceniciento, del tamaño de un gavilan que se mantienen con los desperdicios de la cocina.[37]

En medio del amonadamiento en que me hallaba, no podia menos de tener presente aniversarios de ciertos dias.

El de S[a]n Juan de Dios ¡Cuantos recuerdos me traia á la memoria[!], gratos al par que tristes por considerar mi presente con mi pasada situacion un año antes. Ese dia en que en medio del bullicio y alegria de aquella hermosa Gua– [12v.] dalajara, paseaba en la concurrida calle de S[a]n Juan de Dios,[38] en compañia de mis amigos disfrutando del contento general que reinaba en todo ese dia. ¡Cuantas comparaciones no se hicieron y cuantos antojos y apetitos no se suscitaron entre mis compañeros! y tambien cuantas maldiciones á la suerte por no poder satisfacerlos.

Un acontecimiento que llamó la atencion de todos los pasajeros, tuvo lugar en uno de estos dias. Como existia una especie de rivalidad entre los pasajeros de la Camara y los de la Antecamara, por que aquellos se les daba mejor trato que á estos, estalló una especie de sedicion para que se nos diese de comer mejor: un dia uno de los companeros [*sic*] instigado por otro, asaltó, de chanza ó deveras [*sic*], un plato de carne con papas que el criado llevava á la mesa. Este atentado produjo su efecto, y fué que viniese primero uno de los pasajeros á reclamarlo desde arriba, con palabras bastante injuriosas y que algunos le contestaron.

Entre tanto el quiso habiendo bajado por la escotilla, circulaba de mano en mano, tomando cada uno apresuradamente lo que podia: [13r.] pero derrepente [*sic*] vino otro pasajero, bajó furioso insultando á todos por aquello y en particular al que habia ejecutado el robo, desafiandole para que subiesen á batirse sobre cubierta.

El lance era comprometido, y la menor imprudencia de parte de alguno, podia haber producido efectos funestisimos. Afortunadamente se tomó el partido mas prudente y razonable que en semejante caso[39] podia adoptar, que fué callar; haste [*sic*] que por la interpretacion de algunas personas de respeto,[40] los animos se calmaron y aun se dió una satisfaccion á los pasajeros de la antecamara, por aquel insulto tan generalmente dirijido y no merecido de todos.

27. Han pasado doce dias mas: dias de continuo malestar con sus intervalos de alivio, y de hambre tambien con sus intervalos de mal comer.

¡Cuantos dias sin desayuno ni almuerzo! y hasta sin comida! y cuantos sacrificios tambien para pasarla cuando nos la daban!

Por la mañana, un mal atole de arroz, ó de pinole: crudo ó quemado y hecho por supuesto con agua corrompida, mas á proposito en verdad para vomitar que para alimento.

Por almuerzo frijoles, con arroz o carne salada [13v.] o papas, y por comida lo mismo; esto es cuando lo habia y sin mas cena.

En los primeros dias sirvieron para desayuno cafe y té; pero como lo hacian con agua salada, muy pronto ya no hubo quien lo quisiera tomar, pues solo de oirlo nombrar se revolvia el estomago.

Dias peores no espero pasarlos en la prision mas mala del mundo.

Dicen que pasado mañana veremos tierra: Dios lo quiera.

En estos doce dias no ha habido nada de particular, sino un paseo que dieron dos ballenatos al rededor del buque, y un fuerte Norte que nos sopló ayer y antes de ayer, en que las olas del mar embrabecido, se alzaban como montañas, llegando á pasar algunas veces por sobre cubierta.

Hoy ha amanecido el dia, hermoso y despejado, precedido por una noche quieta y limpia, en que la Luna nueva brillaba en el puro azul de un Cielo sembrado de estrellas.

El viento frigidisimo é insufrible que ha reinado en todos estos dias, se ha moderado ya un poco y el Cielo antes nebuloso y triste, empieza á despejarse.

28 y 29 = Una cruel borrasca nos afligió en [**14r.**] estos dos dias y nos puso en gran peligro.

Llegamos al estremo de quitar las velas y poner el buque á la capa: es decir, amarrar el timon y abandonarlo á su propia defensa.[41]

El aspecto que presentaba el mar era horroroso. Las olas se levantaban como grandes montañas que chispeaban vivamente, arrojando bramidos sordos y continuados.

El buque oscilaba fuertemente en las ondas hasta ponerse casi de lado, y las olas pasaban sobre el á cada momento bañando la cubierta.

30. Desde Este dia fué mas tranquilo y quieto. Desde por la mañana se nos anunció que para las dos de la tarde se veria tierra: en efecto para esta hora divisamos un promontorio á lo lejos formado de varios picos blanquecinos que sobresalian en las aguas.[42]

La sensacion de placer que esperimentamos fué grande, y mucho mas al anochecer del si[guien]te 31 que pasando la bocana del Puerto echamos per fin el ancla.

Este acto se celebró con grandes demostraciones de alegria.

Reunidos en el entrepuente muchos de los compañeros, cantabamos en coro al compaz [**14v.**] de una guitarra, y humedeciendo frecuentemente la garganta con vino, que se sacó de la bodega.

Abril 1°.—Al romper el dia levamos el ancla y comenzamos á entrar en el Puerto.

El aspecto risueño y pintoresco que ofrece con sus rancherias y casitas de madera, que parecen pendientes de la Colina verde y hermosa, reaniman el animo abatido y causa un sentimiento de esperanzas y temores.

A cosa de las diez de la mañana fondeamos en la bahia, donde ondeaban magestuosamente como **40** embarcaciones mayores y menores.

Cerca de nosotros flameaba arrogantemente la bandera de un Bergantín de guerra peruano de 16 cañones. Luego vino el Capitan á visitar al nuestro, segun la costumbre de los marinos.

Despues vino el Capitan del Puerto á la visita del buque, y despues otras personas que tenian, ó creian tener, á bordo de este, amigos ó conocidos, entre ellos José María Ybarra primo mio.[43] Grande fué el gusto que esperimentamos al verlo; y mucho mas cuando nos presentó dos hermosas tortas de pan fresco, un queso de flandes, y una botella de vino. Este refuerzo nos pareció bajado de los Cielos, [**15r.**] por que nuestro apetito era atroz y la galleta nos tenia fastidiados.

Devoramos con ancia el pan y queso en compañia de otros amigos despues que se fué Ybarra, y luego subimos arriba para contemplar el puerto, las embarcaciones y los botes que bogando á remo hacia los buques ofrecian á los pasajeros trasportarlos á tierra.

Teniamos á la vista por fin el tan deseado Puerto del pais del Oro objeto de tantas esperanzas.[44] Habiamos terminado aquel viaje por mar, tan penoso y de eterna memoria. Ybamos á seguir la comenzada cadena de aventuras y á sufrir acaso mayores privaciones y quien sabe si estas en vano, sin ninguna recompensa. . . . .veremos.

Estamos aguardando con ancia el poder saltar á tierra.

4 = Hoy por la mañana me embarqué en un bote y fui á tierra en compañia de Ygnacio y Games.[45]

El caserio se estiende á lo largo de la playa, formando á veces calles, grupos y casas diseminadas acá y alla: todas de madera y con sus techos de caballete; algunas con portal, y todas con vidrios en las ventanas, construidas con arte y gracia y pintadas de varios colores. [15v.] Hay ademas multitud de tiendas de campaña de los transeuntes que van para los Placeres.[46]

El movimiento es grande y en todo el dia no cesa. Gentes á pie, hombres y carros cargados, van y vienen á la playa en donde se esta desembarcando continuamente carga de los buques.

Casi toda la poblacion es de Americanos, algunos estrangeros y muy pocos Californios.[47]

Hay buenos almacenes, y casas de comercio bien surtidas, pero todo lo mas, caro, particularm[en]te los viveres.

En los hoteles cuesta 2 á 3 $ comer, otro tanto almorzar y no muy bien servido.[48]

Lo que mas vale, es el trabajo personal; pero para obtener mayores ventajas en esto, es necesario poseer el ingles, por ser la lengua que se habla casi esclusivamente.

Mugeres hay muy pocas y los hombres lo hacen todo.

Nosotros este dia compramos un botecito de Sardinas, una torta de pan y nos fuimos á sentar entre unos arbustos á comer. Luego que concluimos, fuimos á la playa en donde tomamos un bote para ir á bordo.

6 = Hoy fuimos á tierra y pasamos la noche en una especie de gruta formada entre la arena con [16r.] ramas y que nos cedió Pepe.[49]

Yo mismo conduje á ella mi equipage y silla, cargandolas sobre mi espalda, pues aqui nadie se avergüenza de ninguna clase de trabajo por que todos se ven precisados á hacerlo y ademos nada es notable.[50]

20 = Hasta hoy nada ha habido de particular. Pasamos 5 ó 6 dias bajo la gruta, sufriendo el frio é incomodidades consiguientes á su estrechez,[51] y otros tantos bajo una especie de hato ó cobertera formada con mantas, hasta ayer que concluimos una tienda de Campaña y la colocamos aqui mismo.

La mayor parte de este tiempo, lo pasó Ygn[aci]o postrado con un par de sacotillos en una nalga que no lo desaban menear.

El sitio en que estamos es pintoresco y digno de ocupar el pincel de algun pintor.

A nuestra espalda se eleva un paredon tajado en la arena, de que está formada una colina cubierta toda de arbustos.

Al abrigo de este paredon, habia muchas casas de campaña ó chozas, formadas con apilleras de tercios, sabanas, palos ó pedazos de tabla, colocadas sin orden ninguno, y en donde vivian gentes [16v.] que iban y venian de los Placeres; por consig[uien]te, todas eran efimeras é improvisadas en el lugar, en que muchas veces en una semana se levantaban 5 ó 6 de diversas formas y tamaños.

El terreno es pura arena, entre la que se encuentran multitud de pequeñas conchas y caracoles, lo que indica que á pesar de estar alto, ha estado en algun tiempo cubierto por las aguas del mar.

Al lado derecho está la casa de un comerciante rico: Al Norte la poblacion y al Oriente el mar.[52]

Nos alternabamos los cuatro compañeros (con Ybarra) para todos los quehaceres precisos, como cocinar, traer agua, leña del monte d[ic]ho, siendo de Pepe Puga el mas flojo y atenido á que otro lo desempeñara.

21. Hoy vino una carreta que compramos en 50$ y 4 bueyes que costaron 350$.

La cargamos con 5 ó 6 tercios de viveres y ántes de haber caminado 12 pasos se habia quebrado el eje; tal era el estado en que estaba toda ella. Fue necesario al momento buscar un palo á proposito, para reponerlo; pero no se encontró sino de pino y por 8$. La necesidad nos hizo comprarlo y nos pusimos luego á labrarlo; [17r.] pero no pudo quedar concluido este dia.

22. Hoy domingo concluimos el eje, cargamos la carreta y nos pusimos en camino para la Mision de Dolores, pueblo distante una legua del Puerto.

Empleamos todo el dia para llegar, por que el camino es tan arenoso que las ruedas se enterraban mas de una cuarta y los bueyes no podian y particularm[en]te en algunas subidas en donde era preciso aligerarles el peso,[53] quitando tercios que llevavamos á la espalda.

El camino lo hice por supuesto á pie, calzado con unos guarachis [sic]; llevaba pantalonera y paltó de pañete.[54]

Esta primer fatiga me fué sumamente penosa, tanto por lo malo del camino como por lo ardiente de los rayos del Sol que reverberaban en la arena.

Al ponerse el Sol, llegamos á la Mision y descargamos en una especie de plaza que forma las Casas y cercados.

Alli se rompio la caja de la escopeta de Ygn[aci]o que la paso una rueda de la carreta.

Hicimos lumbre y pusimos á cocer frijoles; asamos carne y cenamos con una sola tortilla [17v.] de harina que se pudo conseguir unicamente, pues no hubo pan.[55]

Alli mismo dormimos Ygn[aci]o y yo, sobre unas mantas y tapados con otras para librarnos del rocio.

23. = Hoy por la mañana me fui con los mozos y la carreta á traer otro viaje,[56] é Ygn[aci]o se quedó á cuidar la carga, hacer unas estacas para la carreta y hacer de comer, que se redujo á frijoles cocidos, por que no hubo pan, manteca, ni nada mas.

Llegamos con la carreta á las 3 de la tarde, comimos; Ygn[aci]o se fue al Puerto á arreglar lo que quedaba para el último viaje que debe venir mañana.

Como á las 2 de la tarde llegaron todos con la carreta[57]; comimos cecina cocida y frijoles lo mismo y dormimos en un corredor.

Ya es tiempo de hacer una descripcion de la Mision en que estamos.[58]

Es una rancheria con honores de Pueblo. Al entrar, viniendo del Puerto, hay dos ó tres semi-manzanas de casas de adove [sic] techadas de teja y en su mayor parte arruinadas (á la derecha).

A la izquierda una ó dos manzanas tambien y algunos corrales.

[18r.] Al frente se estiende un corredor de pilares de madera, techado de teja, terminado por un lado con un alto cuyo balcon tiene barandal de madera, si á esto puede llamarse tres ó cuatro palos encajados y cayendose, y por el otro con la Yglesia que es tambien de adove [sic] y techada de teja.

Su frontispicio es de columnas pegadas á la pared á la altura de la puerta, rematadas por capiteles y cornisas.

Sobre estos pilares hay otros que llegan hasta contra las tejas y entre ellos tres campanas que se repican por fuera con unos cordeles y quedan como embustidas en la pared.

Todo el edificio está sin blanquear y aun sin enfarrar.[59]

El interior ofrece un contraste bastante singular. Es una especie de galera,[60] large y oscura, sin pinturas ni adornos en las paredes blanqueadas solamente.

A la izquierda un cuartito que sirve de bautisterio pintado y decente; á a derecha un confesonario y alla á lo último el altar mayor, dorado á la antigua, pero decente y con una buena imagen de la Purisima Concepcion.

Cerca de el á derecha é izquierda otros dos altares bastante feos.

El pavimiento hasta la mitad de la Yglesia [18v.] es de tablas sueltas y la otra mitad hasta la puerta sin nada.

En el portal de afuera hay una vivienda contigua en que está el Cura, y las otras que le siguen y forman el todo de la casa de la Mision son en las que habitan el Alcalde y otros dos ó tres particulares.[61]

El temperamento es lo mismo que el del Puerto ventoso y frio.

Los habitantes son todos del pais sin mezcla de Americanos que ocupan tan solo el Puerto.[62]

Hay entre ellos algunos indios medio civilizados y que tienen un tipo singular:—Tez cobrija mas ó menos oscura tirando en algunos á negra; cara redonda; nariz pequeña y un poco chata; ojos chicos y vivos; carrillos muy prominentes y cabello negro y lasio, que llevan muy largo y asegurado al rededor de la cabeza, con un pañuelo, mascada ó banda, encarnada ó amarilla con que se adornan. No usan sombrero y lo demas del vestido es pantalon chaqueta ó paltó, ó algunos pura camisa.[63]

Salimos hoy con nuestra carreta á los 4 de la tarde, de la Mision, y caminamos poco mas de una legua por que los bueyes no perdieron con la carreta en una pequeña subida en donde nos fué preciso [19r.] quedarnos.

Nos guarecimos un poco del terrible viento que hacia con el lienzo de la tienda junto á la carreta; pusimos lumbre, hicimos chocolate y nos tendimos á dormir sobre el sacate verde, despues de haberlo tomado.[64]

26. = Hoy fuimos á un ranchito inmediato á conseguir de cualquiera manera otra yunta de bueyes para poder seguir nuestro camino. A duras penas logramos que el viejo ranchero nos los alquilara despues de haber ido á dejar lavando á su muger en un arroyo á donde la llevó en un carreton.

Con la ayuda de ellos pasamos todas las subidas incomodas que habia en este camino, donde nos acompañó el viejo ranchero; nosotros le dabamos sus tragos de mescal frecuentemente para que no se llevase tan pronto sus bueyes y de este modo nos ayudó bastante y no nos quizo cobrar nada. Sin embargo le regalamos una botella de mescal y un lapicero, de todo lo cual quedó muy agradecido.

Caminamos otro poco hasta donde pudieron los bueyes; me quedé yo alli con la Carreta y Ygn[aci]o y Puga siguieron hasta el Rancho de Burebure [*sic*] á ver si conseguian bueyes.[65]

Puse lumbre[,] hice chocolate, lo tome y me acoste á [19v.] dormir sobre mis chaparreras y sin resguardarme nada del viento fuertisimo que hacia y habia ademas, bastantes ciento-pieses.

Este dia caminamos por campos alfombrados de flores amarillas matizadas con blancas y girasoles; presentando vistas muy hermosas y dando á conocer, ser terrenos muy fertiles.

27. Salimos por la mañana con una yunta de bueyes que compramos en 120$ y llegamos hasta el rancho donde se quedaron Ygn[aci]o y Puga la noche anterior, hasta en la tarde que continuamos nuestra marcha.

Llegamos ya puesto el Sol á una arboleda á donde nos quedamos á dormir medio cubiertos con el lienzo de la tienda puesta en la Carreta.

Hicimos fuego para cocer atole de pinole y azar carne que cenamos, disponiendo para el dia siguiente un hermoso anzar que habia cazado Ygn[aci]o.

28. Despues de habernos desayunado atole y chocolate, estubimos esperando á los mozos que fueron á buscar los bueyes y vinieron bastante tarde por que se habian ido lejos; uncimos y seguimos caminando hasta en la tarde que paramos en un rancho que llaman San Francisquito muy cansados y asoleados.[66]

29. Caminamos este dia sin contratiempo nin– [20r.] guno hasta las 4 de la tarde, hora en que se nos quebró el eje de la Carreta al pasar un zanjon, distante todavia como una legua del rancho de Cantua.[67]

Fue necesario que fuera Ygn[aci]o á la casa de un negrito que le llaman Portugues, cerca del rancho á pedir una carreta prestada para trasportar la carga cerca de la casa. Nos la prestaron y en ella mudamos la carga hasta allí, á donde llegamos ya de noche, por habernos detenido en dos malos pasos en que con mucho trabajo subieron los bueyes. Paramos en la orilla de un arroyo cubierto de arboles en sus margenes, en donde dormimos como las noches anteriores.

30 = Pusimos la tienda de Campaña y fuimos Ygnacio y yo al rio, á lavar la ropa sucia que teniamos. Empleamos todo el dia en esto y en cazar algunas perdices que comimos juntamente con un hermoso ánzar.[68]

Mayo 1º Hoy le toco cocinar á Ygnacio; nos dieron leche en el rancho de Cantua é hizo atole de pinole con ella.

Vino la familia del rancho á visitarnos á nuestra tienda; las obsequiamos con chocolate, dulces y otras frioleras de que quedaron muy agradecidas, y despues tambien nos regalaron ellas [20v.] queso, budin, carne con chile, y con arroz, gallina y tortillas de harina. Nos relacionamos bastante con toda la gente del rancho y conseguimos allí mismo por 5 pesos, un eje con una rueda para componer el de nuestra carreta.

De todos los ranchos por donde hemos pasado, este es el mas considerable y en que se ve alguna mas laboriosidad; pues todos los mas son pequeños, algunos de una casa ó pieza hecha de madera con muy pocos habitantes y muy perezozos. No trabajan ni cultivan la tierra, sino es para sembrar una ó media fanega de trigo.[69] Viven del producto de la cria de ganado y de la leche que venden. En este hay algunas casas de madera; un molino de harina y una órdeña de 16 Vacas.

Dia 2. Trabajamos hoy en avenir el eje y alistar nuestras cosas para salir mañana.

Dos Yankes [sic] marineros desertores de una fragata de guerra, que se nos reunieron en el camino hace dos dias, se fueron hoy con otros camaradas suyos que pasaron por aqui. En la noche estando ya acostados volvió uno de ellos, pidiendo á señas que lo dejásemos dormir dentro de la tienda. Como esta venida fué á deshora, creimos que podria [21r.] ser en compañia de otros y con malas intenciones; pero no fué asi, por que aquel se acostó y al dia siguiente vino tambien su compañero, arrepentido sin duda de habernos dejado, por los trabajos que pasarian, solos, sin provisiones y sin abrigo para dormir.

3. Hoy cazó Ygn[aci]o 7 perdices y una guilota,[70] gordas como unos pollos; las guizó con una salsa que improvisó y que á todos nos gustó. Comimos tambien un buen arroz con leche, y unos frijoles refritos que hice yo. Esta

comida para nuestra posicion era opipara, pues dificilmente volveremos á gustar estos mánjares deliciosos y servidos aun en la mesa de los grandes.

Cosa de las 4 de la tarde uncimos los bueyes y caminamos con nuestra carreta hasta ya puesto el Sol; llegamos á otro rancho llamado el Agua Caliente donde pusimos la tienda y dormimos.[71]

4. Hoy llegamos al rancho de San Antonio donde dormimos despues de haber comido carne fresca.[72]

5. Caminamos hoy hasta las 4 de la tarde y paramos á la entrada de una cañada formada por cerros cubiertos de pastos pero sin arboles.

El rancho de las positas, por donde pasamos hoy, es el último que se encuentra en este camino.[73]

Segun lo que he observado hasta aqui los modales y costumbres de los Californios, son sencillos pero al mismo tiempo chocantes para nosotros. Fanfarrones, groseros, perezozos y nada industriosos, merced á la riqueza del pais, á la abundancia del ganado y á lo reducido de los alimentos, pues la carne es el principal de ellos. Gustan del juego, y la embriaguez, y aunque algunos son hospitalarios los mas son interesados y no hacen ni dan nada de valde. Esto es diametralmente opuesto á lo que sucedia antiguamente en las Misiones, segun dicen, pues en tiempo en que no se conocia la riqueza metalica del pais, un estrangero podia viajar en todo California y permanecer en un lugar ó casa el tiempo que quisiese sin tener que gastar un peso.[74]

Hay en todos los ranchos algunos indios bautisados en las antiguas Misiones, y son lo mismo que los que describi antes.

La Mision de San José por donde pasamos ayer y de que me habia olvidado hacer mencion, está poco mas ó menos que la de Dolores en ruinas; la Yglesia es un poco mejor y en la poblacion hay algunas huertas de peras, manzanas y perones; pero no se encuentran viveres ni provisiones de ninguna clase.

[22r.] 6. . . . . Caminamos hoy cerca de 4 leguas por un camino formado entre una cordillera de montañas sin mas vejetacion que un pequeño pasto en unas partes y en otras musgo y despues como otras dos leguas por una llanada inmensa y arida. Paramos junto á una lagunita en donde nos sopló desde en la tarde un terrible viento.[75]

El camino fue penoso por lo fuerte del Sol y la sed, pues no traimos ni una gota de agua, ni la encontramos en todo el camino, ni hallamos ninguna sombra en todo el. A la que daba un peñasco me senté á escribir los acontecimientos del dia de ayer.

¡Cuantos pensamientos y cuantas reflecciones á la vista de aquellos campos: de aquel camino de felicidad ó de desgracia. . . . . !⁷⁶

Ahora es la noche, y bajo la tienda de campaña estoy á la luz de una vela escribiendo estas lineas. El viento muge fuertemente, y sus voces inspiran á mi imaginacion ideas tristes y melancolicas. Los rayos de la luna que brilla en medio del Cielo resbalando suavemente sobre las aguas de la laguna pasan á veces por entre el tule en donde duermen socegadamente el pato, el ánzar y la rana! ¡todo duerme, solo yo velo! Mi fantacia acalorada me presenta sin cesar, imagenes [22v.] ya risueñas ya fatales.

Mis deseos son encontrarme en el Placer para decidir mi suerte; ya me figuro entre mi familia y mis amigos. ¡Quiza llegará tiempo en que esto se verifique y sea de una manera favorable y halagüena!

7. Dia de trabajos. Caminamos lo restante del llano hasta llegar á uno de los brazos del rio de San Joaquin.⁷⁷

Desde poco antes de llegar fue preciso descalzarnos de pie á pierna por lo fangoso del piso. En la orilla descargamos la carreta que se pasó sola despues y la carga se pasó parte en una mula y parte en hombros.

Héteme aqui desnudo, y metido en el agua hasta el estómago y cargado con mi tercio para pasarlo al otro lado. Con el primero que pasó Ygn[aci]o, que era la ropa de dormir, se resvaló al salir cayó en el agua y lo mojó, pero al fin despues de haber concluido estas fatigas descansamos un rato bajo la sombra de un arbol donde comimos. Volvimos á cargar en la tarde y caminamos hasta la orilla de otra lagunita inmediata en donde nos quedamos á dormir.

8. . . . . Estoy á la margen del rio San Joaquin. [23r.] Despues de haber mudado los mas importante de la carga en cuatro mulas que nos alquiló un Sonorense,⁷⁸ cargamos de las estacas de la carreta las maletas y demas cosas livianas. Caminamos como una legua por charcos y atascaderos de los cuales en algunos nos daba el agua al pecho. Por supuesto veniamos enteram[en]te desnudos por no mojar la ropa.

Otras varias gentes á pie y á caballo seguian el mismo camino que nosotros y en el mismo traje Adánico. = Era curiosa esta escena, grotesca y ridicula al mismo tiempo: ver pasar gentes de diversos colores solas ó arreando y desatollando á cada paso del lodo las bestias que llevavan siendo esto general nadie notaba lo inocente de la traja, ni havian caso del ¿que diran?

¡Ah Oro cuanto cuestas! ¡Cuantos padecimientos se tienen que sufrir para adquirirte! y ¿te adquiriré . . . ?[79]

9. A la orilla de una lagunita cuyas aguas quietas reflejan la luz de la luna que se levanta magestuosam[en]te sobre el horizonte, estoy bajo la carreta cubierto con el lienso de la tienda, descansando de las fatigas del dia que han sido escesivas.

Al medio dia pasamos el rio en una gran balsa, pelida por una cuerda, lar carga, bueyes y Carreta. Despues tuvimos que meternos en el agua helada [23v.] hasta la garganta á desatorar aquella de un palo donde se habia atorado.

Luego fue necesario mudar de alli la carga á otro lugar seco, teniendo que pasar un atascadero medio cubierto con ramas y en donde inevitable caia uno á cada paso aun sin carga. De alli á poco mas delante, sobre una red que pusimos de las estacas de la carreta y en tres viajes por no poder pasarla toda sin mojarla en otros dos zanjones con agua que habia en el camino.

Concluimos ya de noche, por lo que apenas hubo tiempo de hacer chocolate que cenamos para entregarnos al descanso tan necesario en esta vez.

Cansado, enlodado, espinado y raspado, no me sostenia otra cosa en medio de todos estos males, que la esperanza y la idea de un porvenir pronto y feliz.

11. A la sombra de un frondosa encina, en medio de una selva espesa y acaso habitada en otro tiempo por salvajes, me encuentro escribiendo estas lineas. ¡Que escena tan animada para ser descrita por un poeta!

El Sol va á llegar á la mitad de su carrera en un dia quieto y sosegado! Todo calla y no se escucha mas ruido que el ligero murmullo que forman las hójas de los arboles suavemente [24r.] mecidas por el viento, semejando al ruido lejano de un torrente.

Las aves parecan [*sic*] gozarse en la hermosura de este bosque formado por la mano del Criador. Cantan á porfia saltando alegres en las ramas de los arboles. El zanate chilla; los gorriones gorgean; la tortola y la perdiz arruyan y cantan[80]; otros mil pajarillos trinan de diversos modos saludando con sus cantos le vuelta de la alegre Primavera, y formando un concierto poetico y encantador. Pero sobre todas esta avecillas inocentes é incautas que cantan descuidadas se mece una que oscilando en los vientos y estacionandose en ellos á veces asecha su presa y el momento oportuno de de [*sic*] lanzarse sobre ella: este es el raptor halcon.

Asi las desgracias y fatalidades vienen al hombre descuidado, cayendo sobre el como el halcon sobre su presa.

Ayer 10, desputes de haber pasado en un bote la lagunita á cuya orilla paramos, pasamos los bueyes á vado y despues la carreta tirada con sogas.

Cuando todo estuvo del otro lado cargamos de nuevo y caminamos con un Sol ardiente, cosa de tres leguas hasta las cuatro de la tarde, hora en que llegamos á esta punto, conocido con el nombre de campo de los Franceses.[81] Hoy no hemos podido salir de aqui por aguardar al compañero que fue á Stokton [*sic*] distante [**24v.**] poco de aqui á ver si han venido algunos viveres pertenecientes á nosotros.[82]

Estoy rodeado de hombres dormidos y su vista comunica no se que gravedad á mis párpados que se me caen. Me siento fuertemente impelido á imitarlos y los esfuerzos que hago por repeler á Morfeo son inutiles. . . .[83]

Mis ideas se obfuscan; mis facultades se entorpecen; todo lo que hace poco me parecia poetico y encantador, ahora me es indiferente; todos los sonidos que antes á mi oido formaban un harmonia, no son sino un ruido confuso que el viento se lleva en sus alas . . . . . . la cabeza se me cae . . . . los ojos se cierran por fin . . . . y mis manos no pudiendo ya sostener el lapiz entre sus dedos . . . . los dejan caer flojamente . . . .[84]

13 [*sic*][85]. . . . . El Sol se levanta radiante en el horizonte dorando con sus rayos las copas de las gigantes encinas de una hermosa selva alfombrada de verde y hermoso pasto; una ligera niebla producida de la evaparacion del abundante rocio que durante la noche ha caido, se levanta humeante formando una nube diafana por entre los troncos de los arboles. Por medio de esta floresta lleva sus aguas quietas y cristalinas un riachuelo [**25r.**] silencioso. A su margen se ve la escena siguiente:

Cerca de un sitio donde está una carreta metida en el agua se ven various tercios diseminados por el suelo. Mas allá puesto á una hoguera, various hombres haciendo desayuno y otros tomandolo. Otro reclinado sobre la yerba y con la vista fija en un arbusto de cuyas ramas penden algunas piezas de ropa mojada. Sentado sobre un cajon se ve otro cuyo pantalon desgarrado, cae sobre un zapato roto y mal guarecido con un guarache. Tiene un papel en la mano y escribe en el sobre otro cajon donde se ven algunos posillos sucios de chocolate y una vela de cera hecha pedazos . . . .[86]

Dormimos anoche al descubierto pues apenas hubo tiempo para tomar chocolate y descansar de las fatigas de la tarde que fueron muchas; despues de haver caminado como 4 leguas para llegar aqui y cuyo rio teniamos que pasar.

Luego que comimos pusimos manos á la obra, adoptando para ello el sig[uien]te modo ó industria por ser la unica de que se puede hechar mano en circunstancias presentes.

Pusimos una red de las puntas de las estacas de la carreta; sobre ella echabamos 3 ó 4 tercios y los pasabamos llevando entre dos hombres (Ygn[aci]o y Rico) **[25v.]** sostenidas las ruedas de uno y otro lado para por la orilla opuesta. Facil en concebir el trabajo que nos costaria semejante empresa: subir y bajar los tercios á la carreta y andar (por supuesto desnudos) metidos en una agua helada hasta el cuello yendo y viniendo sufriendo de la cintura y de la multitud de mosquitos y zancudos quo nos picaban en todo el cuerpo cuando saliamos.[87] Al cabo de dos horas de este ir y venir concluimos ya de noche rendidos de fatiga y cubiertos de ronchas que daban una insufrible comezon; pero en fin, dicen que mañana entraremos al Placer; que llegamos al termino deseado de este viaje de penas donde debe comenzar otra epoca de brillante porvenir. Veremos si mis esperanzas me quedan fallidas y mis trabajos son ó no compensados.

13. . . . . Hoy permanecimos aqui todo el dia por habersenos extraviado una yunta de bueyes y ser preciso buscarlos.

Este sitio ó arroyo es conocido con el nombre de las Calaveras.[88]

14. Hoy por fin salieron, quedandome yo con un amigo, hijo de un mejicano, que vino aqui en la Colonia el año de 1834,[89] á buscar los bueyes que no ha parecido aun.—Como este mejicano, sus hijos **[26r.]** y otros vienen juntos con nosotros, ó nosotros con ellos hace 3 ó 4 dias y como traen tambien Carretas, bueyes, vacas y caballos sueltos que van arreando, pareceme un pueblo errante que camina por estos inmensos deciertos buseando [*sic*] pastos para sus ganados.[90]

Caminamos todo el dia por un largo bosque donde hay multitud de zancudos que no cesan de picar. No pudimos hallar los bueyes y nos fuimos á alcanzar á los compañeros que los encontramos parados cerca de un rio donde nos quedamos. ¡Ganancia anticipada!

15. Hoy antes de salir fue preciso curarme de las ronchas que tenia en el ano ocasionadas por la yedra (planta caustico) que me hace mucho y hay bastante aqui.[91] Como hacia tiempo que no montaba á caballo y ayer que buscamos los bueyes corrimos mucho, se me rosaron ó inflamaron las ronchas.

La medicina que me apliqué, fue agua caliente; alli meti á un bosquesito; culimpinado y á calzon quitado, recibia de mano de Ygn[aci]o baños de agua caliente que me daba con un trapo y como estaba con todo el nalgatorio de fuera no me dejaban de picar ni un instante los zancudos. Acabada la operacion salimos y caminamos cosa de 5 leguas.

A la luz de una hoguera: en medio de una selva decierta, sombria y pavorosa, donde me parece [26v.] ver salir á cada momento una numerosa nacion de salvajes; regada por un rio, cuyas heladas aguas bajan de las montañas nevadas, me encuentro escribiendo estas lineas.

A la orilla opuesta del rio se ven dos cabañas habitadas por Yndios que ahora se han retirado.

Por todos estos bosques hay multitud de berrendos y buras de enorme tamaño y caballada alzada que los naturales del pais llaman mesteña.[92]

16 . . . . . . Anduvimos hoy poco por ser el camino incomodo, pues todo es lomas cubiertas de malezas muy crecidas entre las que hay algunas yerbas aromaticas, que esparcian un olor suave y agradable al romperse bajo las ruedas de las carretas. Seguimos toda la vega del rio, que llaman de los Moquelamos en donde hicimos la primera <u>tentadura</u> ó ensayo,[93] con tierra sacada de la orilla; produjo oro muy menudo y poco y determinamos pasar mañana el rio, para ir á cualquiera otro de los Placeres inmediatos.

17 . . . . Pasamos el rio en un bote de hule que hay y las Carretas solas tirandolas con un cable.[94] Concluimos ya tarde, por lo que nos quedamos alli á pasar la noche; al otro dia se representaba la escena siguiente:

18 . . . . Era un dia nebuloso y triste. A la [27r.] margen de un rio, en la pendiente de una Colina veianse dos carretas; no lejos de ellas dos grandes hogueras encendidas y en torno de ellas muchos hombre teniendo en sus manos diversas piezas de ropa que secaban al fuego.—Hombre, decia uno ¿como te fue? malisimamente contestaba el otro ¿no ves que no me quedó seco ni la camisa? y tu ¿hasta á que hora sentiste el aguacero? hasta que ya me corria el agua por debajo ¿no ves las armas como estan? Pues yo decia otro secando unos zapatos, luego que desperté quize componerme

de modo de no mojarme tanto, pero me sentí echo [*sic*] una sopa y me quedé quieto por que consideré que seria peor moverme.

Por estos dialogos se vendrá en conocimiento que durante la noche una fuerte lluvia nos habia empapado, sin dejarnos nada seco en el cuerpo.

Salimos algo tarde por aquella detencion y caminamos poco por montañas formadas de piedras calcinadas y rocallas de diversos colores. A nuestro transito encontramos algunos indios de ambos secsos [*sic*], que juntaban algunas yerbas y raices con que se alimentan. Las mugeres iban adornadas algunas con collares de conchas y abalorios vestidas con enaguas y cubierto el pecho con una especie de schal [*sic*][95] de lana muy tosco ó una frazadita [27v.] y a la espalda un canasto en forma de cuvo terminado en punta, formado de varas y un tule delgado y fuerte en que juntan las semillas y raices.

Al llegar á la orilla de un arroyo donde paramos, vimos algunos indios muchachos de una rancheria inmediata vestidos de diferentes modos. Unos con camisas de lana encarnadas, otros con uniformes militares que han comprado á los que pasan y los mas con vestidos comunes, pantalones camisas y bandas viejas y nuevas; pero todos sin sombrero y con una hilacha, paño ó mascada encarnada en la cabeza.

19. . . . . Hoy fuimos conducidos por un Yndio en traje de Capitan á un arroyo á donde nos dijo que habia mucho oro. En efecto habia allí algunos Yndios que sacaban algo metidos en el agua; pero no habia pastos para los animales y los compañeros piensan ir á otra parte.

Cambiamos arroz y carne seca por oro á los Yndios de aqui; que todos traen vestido, pero que se echa de ver su antigua habitud á la desnudez por el modo con que lo llevan y por el ningun cuidado que les da los vean desnudos.[96]

Ygn[aci]o y yo fuimos á dormir en compañia de otros dos [28r.] á la orilla opuesta del rio; sirviendo de puerta á un corral donde se encerraron los bueyes; tanto como por no tener con que taparla, como por cuidarlos esa noche.

Al acostarme no daba yo un sigarro por mi cabeza que creia iba á amanecer aplastada por las pesuñas de los bueyes; pero gracias á Dios nada me sucedió y estoy sano y salvo y dispuesto á seguir el hilo de mis aventuras placenteras hasta que San Juan baje el dedo.[97]

20. . . . . Estivimos [*sic*][98] hoy todo el dia haciendo ensayos que no dieron

ningun resultado satisfactorio; por lo que determinamos retrodecer á otro punto inmediato que dicen es mejor y hay pasto bueno para los animales.

21. . . . Caminamos como tres leguas hasta una Cañadita donde nos establecimos para trabajar.

22. . . . . Los resultados no han correspondido á las esperanzas: trabajamos toda la mañana y parte de la tarde y apenas sacamos 3 adarmes de oro.[99] Nuestra poca inteligencia en el arte de lavar, influyó demasiado en los resultados por que algunos de los compañeros sacaron mas que nosotros.[100] Resolvimos hacer una maquinita para lavar,[101] por que en batea se ocupa mas tiempo y se pierde oro cuando no se sabe manejar.

25. . . . Tres dias han pasado, que empleamos en construir una especie de lavadero con las tablas de los cajones que desbaratamos. Hoy en la tarde la pro– [28v.] bamos lavando tierra; el resultado fue bueno en cuanto á la maquina y malo en cuanto á la tierra de que apenas se sacó 2 pesos de oro de 6 arrobas.[102]

Yo me vi ayer bastante malo de una especie de fiebre; pero con un cordial sudorifico que me ministró Ygn[aci]o anoche amanecé hoy casi bueno.[103] Esta enfermedad fue sin duda á consecuencia de las mojadas de pies y el fuerte sol que comienza ya á abrazarnos.

28. . . . . Hasta hoy todos los ensayos y trabajos que hemos hecho, nos han producido el mismo resultado, por lo que determinamos buscar otro lugar mejor. Al efecto levantamos el campo la mañana de este dia y emprendimos nuestra marcha hacia el interior de la Sierra, en donde tuvimos trabajos infinitos para pasar con las carretas por algunos puntos. Andando por montañas ásperas y pedregosas teniamos á cada momento que ayudar á los bueyes en las subidas, con sogas, ó para detener la carreta que no se volteara en algunas partes, ó para desatorarla á cada paso, quitando peñascos ó tumbando arboles, aquijoneando [sic] y animando sin cesas [sic] con gritos á los bueyes.[104]

El dia concluyó y la noche nos encontró todavia en estas fatigas. Por fortuna la luna derramaba una hermosa claridad y con su ayuda llegamos como á las 8 á la margen de un arroyo, y bajo un frondoso arbol pusimos lumbre é hicimos atole de piñole que tomamos por unico alimento todo el dia despues del desayuno que fué café con leche.

Junio 7 . . . . . . Nada de particular ha acaecido en los dias que han pasado. Hace tres ó cuatro he estado yendo con otros á trabajar á una Cañada distante del campo como una legua, y volviendo por la noche á comer. Muy poco ó ningun provecho he sacado de esto y mis fatigas han sido inutiles.

¡Cuantas veces al ver lo infructuoso de mis trabajos, casi pierdo la esperanza y me desaliento, haciendome entonces mi situacion sumamente pesada.

¡Oh suerte adversa! ¿no cambiaras algun dia? ¿siempre me has de atormentar?

¡Este dia! ¡Dia de Corpus![105] ¡oh! este ha sido de angustia y tormentos para mi! El recuerdo de aniversarios de hoy han caido sobre mi memoria destrozadores é implacables! Las comparaciones de mi pasada con mi presente situacion, se agolpan tambien á mi imaginacion haciendo sumamente tormentosa y desdichada mi posicion. En efecto, la diferencia es inmensa y mi corazon se oprime al contemplarla. Por que ¿como podrá ser lo mismo vivir uno en su pais, entre su familia y amigos sin tanto afan para subsistir, desfrutando los goces y comodidades domesticas y las [29v.] ventajas que ofrece la sociedad, á vivir en un pais estrangero, remoto y en medio de una Serrania decierta, sujeto á un trabajo duro y penoso, y espuesto á mil peligros? ¿Será lo mismo la vida del comerciante que la del operario? ¿Andar destras del mostrador de una tienda que en el campo, con la barra en la mano, cavando la tierra al rigor del Sol, ó metido de pies en el agua?[106] ¿Comer á cierta hora alimentos variados y sabrosos, á comer solamente carne salada, arroz y frijoles con galleta dura ó tortilla de harina y todo esto preparado por uno mismo?[107] ¿Lo mismo en fin dormir bajo de techo y cama mullida, que dormir en el suelo sin otro abrigo que una tienda de campaña y no siempre? ¿Y esta diferencia por que? ¿por que se dejó aquella vida grata y pacifica y se tomó esta agitada penosa y llena de peligros? Por buscar el Oro. El oro que creiamos encontrar tan facilmente; pero que no hemos visto aun y ¿lo veremos? Quien sabe!

11 . . . . . . Hoy levantamos el campo y nos internamos hacia el Norte hasta un sitio no muy distante de las cumbres de las montañas designadas en el Mapa con el nombre de Nevosas,[108] á donde fue antes de ayer en compañia de Arana á ver un placer que nos pareció mas rico segun los que vimos.[109]

Anduvimos todo el dia por un camino escabroso [30r.] y dificil y llegamos ya tarde, bastante cansados, estropeados, y mojados por una lluvia que nos comenzó á caer desde poco antes de llegar y fue arreciando progresivamente, sin dejarnos poner la tienda de campaña.

Esperando que se quitara, estabamos metidos debajo de unos ramajos [*sic*][110] que muy poco nos resistian hasta que viendo que era tarde y no cesaba[.] Puga puso por unica vez la tienda donde ya nos guarecimos mejor y nos dormimos <u>sin cenar</u>.[111]

12. Hoy fui con otros compañeros á cortar madera para hacer un corral en donde encerrar los bueyes y caballos y librarlos de este modo de la rapacidad de una tribu de Yndios ladrones (como todos) que capitaneados por Polo su gefe hacen sus incursiones nocturnas á estos placeres para robar Caballada.[112]

14 . . . "En tal altura vale un peso una asadura."

El autor de este refran que es un mejicano que vino hace 14 años de colono aqui,[113] vendió hoy á otro hombre <u>ocho plumas</u> de una gallina que le queda de las que trajo por <u>tres pesos</u> que le pagaron en oro[114]; necesitandolas el que las compró para curar un macho segun dijo. . . . [115] Lo que es el Placer! Hay muchos que pagan algunas cosas (por la escaces) á un precio escesivo; y otros que cambian el oro que sacan por plata hasta 5 pesos la onza, cuando tienen necesidad de pesos para jugar; siendo este un [**30v.**] vicio muy comun en los Placeres, en donde juegan hasta los que jamas habian visto baraja.

Volví á ver ayer las labores de los gambucinos que trabajan aqui; todos sacan oro y algunos han llegado á sacar hasta dos libras en un dia. En vista de esto determinamos quedarnos á trabajar aqui.

18. . . . Hemos trabajado, pero como la mala suerte nos persigue á donde quiera que vamos, no hemos sacado nada y nuestras esperanzas han quedado enteramente desvanecidas. Abrimos una gran labor y de la tierra mejor que lavamos <u>dos Carretadas</u>, no sacamos mas de <u>cuatro pesos</u>.[116] Lo que es la mala suerte vuelvo á decir: trabajar sin fruto en donde casi todos lo obtienen y cavar precisamente en el lugar en donde nada hay aunque todas las reglas tengan de ello. y ¿que remedio para esto? Nada mas, que paciencia y barajar. . . .[117]

21. . . . . Hoy salia á trabajar con uno de los compañeros á un placer distante como una legua; subí en las ancas de su caballo[118]; tomé la barra en una mano y la batea en la otra y al tiempo de hacer andar el caballo, ó por que se asustó ó lo pico, dió un fuerte reparo que me aventó como tres

varas y cae de espaldas.[119] Me levante luego sin sentir nada; pero á poco, ya no alcanzaba resuello de las dolencias tan fuertes que sentia en la espalda.

[31r.] 25. . . . . Hace dos dias que he podido trabajar y en los que he sacado cosa de 14 pesos de oro.

Hoy ya muy tarde, llegó Arana del Sacramento,[120] que fué en comp[añ]ia de Ygnacio á comprar algunos viveres que nos faltaban, preguntando "si no habia llegado, que habia salido mucho antes de él." Me sorprendió bastante esta pregunta, por que luego crei que Ygn[aci]o se habia extraviado del camino y estaba espuesto á perecer en manos de los salvajes y me dispuse para marchar á buscarlo otro dia temprano.

26. . . . . Habriamos andado ya media legua Arana y yo cuando lo encontrámos que venia con sus dos bestias cargadas de viveres.

Por ciertas super[s]ticiones de Arana de que Ygn[aci]o se burló, no quiso salir ese dia; é Ygn[aci]o cargo sus bestias y se puso en camino solo. Habia andado poco, cuando perdió el camino; quiso tomar el rumbo pero no le fué posible por que caminaba por lomas asperas, llenas de veredas y tenia que ir ya de un lado ya de otro á echar las bestias que se separaban. Despues de cuatro horas de andar por aquella Sierra, sin ver mas que uno que otro Yndio desnudo y negros [sic] como un tizon; volvió al mismo <u>sitio de donde habia salido por la mañana</u>.[121] Volvió á andar por el, incierto y casi seguro de volverse á extraviar; de facto asi sucedió. Volvió á errarlo, y á [31v.] veces creia haberlo encontrado y daba gracias á Dios pero pronto su ilusion se desvanecia viendo que la senda que seguia iba á perderse en la pendiente de una montaña ó en la profundidad de una Cañada.

Ya al oscurecer determinó buscar donde hubiera pasto y agua para los animales y quedarse á pasar la noche; pero sin querer fué á dar á una rancheria de Yndios de donde ya no pudo retroceder por que las bestias estaban muy cansadas.

Se puso en manos de la Providencia y descargo entre ellos mismos.

Para complacerlos y captarse la benebolencia [sic] de ellos, les dió un puñado de galleta y otro de harina, con que hicieron luego tortillas y le dieron.

Despues de de haber estado un rato entre ello, se retiró á acostarse bajo el arbol donde tenia la carga con bastante temor de que lo robaran por matarlo, pero gracias al Cielo nada le sucedió.

Al dia sig[uien]te no parecian las bestias que fue á traer un indio; él no podia ir á buscarlas y rogó al capitan que las trajera. Fué, pero solam[en]te una trajo, diciendo que la otra no parecia. A repetidas instancias trajo la otra. Luego ensilló y cargo ayudado de ellos. Despues de emplear muchas [**32r.**] promeses y súplicas, consiguio con el capitan, (dándole un par de Zapatos) que lo condujese al camino para el placer á donde afortunadam[en]te sabia por haber ido ya otras veces alli á comprar viveres y habia visto las Carretas que llevamos. Para todo lo cual se habia hecho entender por señas, pues poco sabia español.[122]

Siguió pues el capitan acompañado de otros Yndios armados con su arco y flechas, pasando lomas, cañadas y arroyos, llegaron al camino carretero, en donde se pararon y no quisieron acompanarlo [*sic*] mas. Le pidieron galleta que les dió y continuó solo su camino, hasta poco andar que lo encontramos.

Julio 3. . . . . Hoy levantamos el campo para salir hacia fuera; la suerte ha manifestado hasta aqui contraria y vamos aun á perseguirla.

Caminamos poco hasta la orilla de un arroyo.

5. . . . Ayer no caminamos por aguardar á los compañeros que se detuvieron para hacer un eje nuevo á su carreta.

Hoy se fue Ygn[aci]o en comp[añi]a de Marcos Arana para arroyo seco,[123] con el objeto de recojer alla diez pesos que le debian y ver á D[o]n Ricardo Jones, para ver si conseguia colocacion para los dos en la empresa [**32v.**] de la campana de busear.[124]

Yo me vine con la Carreta; aqui fue donde los trabajos se me aumentaron, pues solo Rico y yo cuidabamos de desatorar la Carreta y de arrear los bueyes, por que Puga de nada nos servia. Con esta fatiga: subiendo lomas y pasando atascaderos,[125] se nos cayó un tercio con cosa de dos a[rroba]s[126] de harina, una barra que nos regalo un amigo y otros frioleras, que no supimos donde y por supuesto se quedaron perdidas.

Ygn[aci]o llegó ya tarde sin haber encontrado á Jones. Fue por lana y volvió tresquilado, pues perdió en el camino objetos de duplicado valor que los 10$ que fue á cobrar. ¡paciencia!

¡Cuantas veces he deseado al ver la diversidad de nuestra suerte volver á mi patria, no ya con las arrobas de oro que ántes de venir me proponia recojer y que tan facil me parecia en mi loco entusiasmo y en los jardines de viento que mi acalorada fantacia me presentaba, sino en el estado en que estoy, aunque pobre con salud[127]; pero no me es posible es necesario trabajar para conseguirlo; es preciso seguir el hilo de hierro de mi suerte, á ver si tiene algun pedaso dorado aunque sea al fin. Es necesario por último sobreponerse á [33r.] la adversidad; tener valor y constancia y ver si á fuerza de trabajo, llegamos á vencer esta suerte en todo este año ó la muerte nos corta los pasos, impidiendose volver á nuestra patria de cualquier manera.

6. Hoy salieron para Stokton [*sic*] á comprar algunos viveres que nos faltan, Ygn[aci]o y Puga, en compañia de los Aranas que van para S[an]ta Cruz que es donde viven.[128] Las simpatias que mutuamente habiamos contraido durante el tiempo que permanecimos reunidos, nos hizo estrañar su comp[añi]a como era natural.

S[eñ]or Rico y yo nos quedamos bajo de un arbol junto á una rancheria de Yndios para cuidar los bueyes que nos quedaban y la carreta con algunos viveres. En esta rancheria conseguí un arco con sus flechas y un surron de sorra [*sic*] para guardarlos,[129] por una batea que no valia un tlaco,[130] y por lo que no habia podido conseguir antes ni por 10$ en dinero.

Ya que no llevo oro, llevaré siquiera estas armas.

9. . . . Hoy volvieron Ygnacio y Puga.

10. . . . . Cargamos la carreta y los caballos y nos dirijimos hacia la margen derecha del Rio de Moquélamos,[131] cuyas aguas van bajando y dejando secas sus orillas de donde se saca algun oro. Llegamos; y creo que de aqui no daremos un paso mas con la malde– [33v.] cida carreta; estoy enfadado de andar peregrinando y deceo establecerme en alguna parte, que aunque sea poco lo que saque, al cabo de dos ó tres meses tendré con que trasportarme á mi pais: á Guadalaj[ar]a entre mi familia y amigos; ¡Oh! estos son mis constantes deseos y mi corazon oprimido no anhela ya otra cosa.

18. . . . . Ocho dias han pasado de los cuales solo los 5 últimos he empleado, por haber tenido que cuidar y buscar bueyes y caballos. Parece que la suerte cansada de atormentarnos y vencida quiza por la constancia nos concede al fin alguna gracia; parece que comienza á sonrreirme deponiendo su antiguo rigor, pues he visto ya como catorce pesos de oro sacados por mi en un dia.

Hoy al medio dia salí en compañia de Puga, por que convine con Ygn[aci]o en que el se quedara con Rico y yo acompaña á Puga diciendole que me voy con él á Guad[alajar]a, pero no es asi, pues solo lo acompañaré hasta S[a]n Fran[cis]co en obsequio de su familia, pues se está volviendo loco y es incapaz de caminar solo por tan cobarde y el mozo que le quedaba ya no quiso seguirlo.[132]

Caminamos como cuatro leguas con una bestia cargada y las otras dos ensilladas y nos quedamos á la orilla del rio Moquélamos.[133]

Voy tam– [34r.] bien á S[a]n Fran[cis]co con el objeto de ver á un amigo que me ofreció proporcionarnos una manera mas descansada de ganar el dinero viajando con fruta de las Misiones, para lo que cuenta él con recursos en el pais.[134] Llevó una carta para la madre de Ygn[aci]o para entregarsela á Puga cuando se valla.

19.. Hoy ya muy tarde llegamos á Stokton [*sic*], sin mas novedad que haber caminado como siempre (á pie) por que el caballo en que yo vengo apenas puede con la silla.

23 . . . . . . Hoy llegamos á S[a]n José y por conocimiento de un tepiqueño con quien nos juntamos desde que salimos de Stokton [*sic*], paramos en un corredor de una casa que tiene alquilada Wester [*sic*], sobrino de Forbes,[135] para vender sus efectos mejicanos.

Agosto 4. Doce dias han pasado ya de permanecia en S[a]n José, los cuales he empleado en armar unas sillas de montar que me pagó Forbes á dos pesos cada una.[136] Con este auxilio, compré ayer una yegua bruta en tres onzas de oro, pues un caballo manso no lo podria conseguir ni por cien pesos. Mañana saldré para S[a]n Fran[cis]co á ver á Arana.

6 . . . . Volvi de S[a]n Fran[cis]co sin haber encontrado al amigo que buscaba ¡viaje perdido! pero sirvió por que le di buena caminada á la maldita yegua que reparo bastante conmigo dos veces y que afortunadamente no me tumbo.

[34v.] Mañana ¡que diferencia! Puga sale con direccion á S[a]n Fran[cis]co en donde debe embarcarse para S[a]n Blas para retornar á Guadalajara. ¡Dichoso él, que va á tener la satisfaccion de estrechar entre sus brazos á su amada familia! A mi no me es dado disfrutar aun de este placer. ¿Como seria posible, sin recursos y en situacion en que tengo probabilidad de adquirirlos?[137] ¿Abandonaria la empresa cuando considero indemnizar por los menos lo que he gastado en este viaje? no: no me es posible.

Con tres meses mas que permanezca donde dejé á Ygn[aci]o quedaré desengañado y mi cuerpo trabajado lo suficiente para no estrañar el trabajo por mucho tiempo; por que el trabajo del gambuceo es duro y doblemente penoso por lo fuerte del Sol de esta estacion.[138] Tener que estar todo el dia cavando la tierra y metido en el agua á lavarla para obtener unos cuantos granos del deseado Oro, por quien he venido tan lejos: por quien he sufrido tanto y sufriré todavia . . . . . .[139] Yo salgo tambien mañana para distincto rumbo: para el Placer á donde tengo que hacer cinco dias de camino: solo, en una bestia bruta: en donde no se encuentra mas de una poblacion (Stokton [sic]) en donde hay muchos osos y otros animales y en fin sin mas bastimento, que unas argenitas con galleta, azucar[,] tee y una ollita de hoja de lata para cocerlo. No puedo llevar otra cosa, por que aumento el bulto y voy espuesto á [35r.] que me tire la yegua en en Camino. La Divina Providencia me acompaña y confio en que nada me sucederá.

11. . . . . Hoy en la tarde llegué donde está Ygnacio, sin que me hubiera sucedido nada, pues aunque hace dos dias que reparo la yegua conmigo, me afiance bien y gusto Dios que no me tumbara. En la misma noche soné [sic] que me habia tumbado y arrastrado. ¡Cosa estraña en mi! por que rara vez sueño; pero tal era el miedo que me infundia el animal.

12 . . . . Hace como 15 dias que estaban dando de comer á un Americano á quien dejo aquí su compañero (que tenia una canoa) solo[,] enfermo y abandonado, y aunque tiene segun dice un rancho en Napa,[140] aqui de nada le sirve, tanto por estar distante, como por no tener á nadie de su parte. Hacia como 3 dias que no tomaba alimento, pues aunque tenia galleta no la podia comer, cuando lo vieron Ygn[aci]o y Rico por la primera vez le llevaron de comer. Apenas podia moverse por la hinchazon de piernas que tenia á consecuencia de la gota. El abrigo que tenia contra la intemperie, era una enramada donde apenas cabia y que en realidad de nada le servia. Como ya habia llegado yo y teniamos bestia, se le trajo un caballo que tenia en un rancho inmediato y que no habia podido hallar quien se lo trajese. Se lo [35v.] ensillamos, alistamos y ayudamos á montar lo que hizo aunque con mucho trabajo para irse á un rancho de donde debe conducirse para su casa. Parece que fue muy agradecido de nosotros, y tanto mas debe estarlo, cuanto que los beneficios que recibió no fueron de mano de sus paisanos, sino de mejicano: de un enemigo se puede decir[141]; pero en el estado en que estaba este pobre hombre no se debia atender á su origen sino á la humanidad; debia socorrersele aun cuando hubiese sido un enemigo personal: hacer bien en fin sin ver quien era segun el mandato del Señor.[142]

13. . . . . Hoy por la mañana nos avisó un negro que el Americano se habia quedado anoche en el campo por no poder caminar mas. Como seguramente necesitaba de auxilios, resolvió Ygnacio ir ayudarle (en caso que él pudiese) á montar á caballo y acompañarlo hasta el rancho. Lo acompañó hasta dejarlo en el rancho distante como tres leguas, despues de haberlo ayudado á subir dos ó tres veces que se apeo en el camino; volvió ya muy tarde sin mas novedad que dos ampollas en los pies.[143]

14. . . . . Anoche me vi atacado de un fuerte dolor de costado; pero afortunadamente Ygnacio se acordó haber oido decir que los pajosos de Caballo quemados y apagados en el agua eran buenos, bebiendo esta, me la dió y amanecé muy aliviado.

[36r.] 24 . . . . Diez dias han pasado sin que ocurra cosa notable. Yo sané á los dos dias,[144] pero S[eñor] Rico se ha puesto muy malo de unas fuertes calenturas.

Hoy fue dia de regalo para nosotros, por que tuvimos carne fresca y manteca (de vaca) cosas de que careciamos hacia ya muchos dias por que no habia quien vendiera. Tomamos un buen puchero y buen asado que fortaleció nuestro debil estomago alimentado tan solo por varios dias con arroz y frijoles, ambas cosas nomas [*sic*] cocidas, con tortillas de harina.

25. . . . . Aunque estoy fastidiado de todo lo que me rodea, y la naturaleza en mi presente situacion muy poco ó ningun encanto ofrece á mis sentidos cansados y embotados en fuerza de tantas impresiones, hay sin embargo ocasiones que el animo se siente naturalm[en]te inclinado ó por mejor decir arrostrado á la contemplacion y á mirar cosas al traves de ese velo fantastico y divino que se llama Poesia. Tal ha pasado en mi esta vez y la escena siguiente habia hecho alguna impresion en mi mente; mas no me habia ocupado de ella hasta ahora por reunirse otras circunstancias.

¡Era la noche! ¡pero que noche! serena y sosegada! Los dulces céfiros, pasando con suavidad, refrescaban el ambiente haciendo deliciosa la temperatura.

[36v.] La naciente Luna derramaba su apacible claridad al declinar sobre el puro azul de un Cielo recamado de Estrellas. En medio del silencio, oiase tan solo el murmullo de las aguas del rio que serpenteando en espumosas ondas por entre los peñascos, formaban una especie de cadencia misteriosa son el continuo chillido de las Chicharras y el monotono y compasado canto de las ranas. . . . .¹⁴⁵ Este silencio era interrumpido de tiempo en tiempo, por el ruido que hacian las botellas al chocarse, los gritos de alegria y los cantos en coro de una cuadrilla de sonorenses que trabajaban en la rivera opuesta, y cuyas armonias llevando el viento en sus alas iban al cabo á confundirse con este concierto de la naturaleza . . . . . .

En tanto nosotros bajo nuestra carpa, yaciamos acostados con la cabeza atada (por dolernos á todos) contemplando silenciosos esta escena magestuosa é interesante á la verdad, pero triste para nosotros por pasar tan lejos de nuestra patria.

El torpe vuelo del murcielago y otras aves nocturnas que se agitaban en torno de nosotros, venia á aumentar el horror de nuestra situacion y á amilanar el animo, dispuesto siempre en tales circunstancias á la supersticion y á deducir funestos presagios y fatales agüeros de las cosas mas sencillas . . . . . . .¹⁴⁶ [37r.] Al fin: con el sueño, los cantos y ruido bacanal cesó; . . . . todo volvió á quedar en paz; y el grave y solemne silencio de esta noche ya no fue turbado por la voz de ningun ser humano . . . . . .

27. . . . Hoy salimos del Placer con intencion de permanecer dos meses en S[a]n José, á donde vamos. Vendimos los viveres y herramientas que habia, por lo que nos dieron para desembarasarnos de estorbos. Nuestra salida fue ya tarde, por que la yegua que teniamos para trasportar nuestro equipage, reparó con la carga luego que se la echamos, la tiró é hizo pedazos la silla. Fue necesario buscar quien quisiera cambiarla por una bestia mansa que no hiciera lo mismo; lo que al fin conseguimos despues de mucho trabajo y dando una onza de oro mas, por un Caballo muy flaco y matado; pero era preciso y caminamos con el.

29. . . . Stokton [*sic*]. Hoy llegamos á este punto donde tuvimos la fortuna de comprar por una onza, una Yegua fuerte y sana que lleve la carga, por que el infeliz rosinante ápenas pudo llegar con ella.¹⁴⁷ Mañana continuaremos nuestra marcha para S[a]n José á donde vamos á buscar otra manera de subsistir: otro genero de vida menos espuesto á enfermedades y otra clase de aventuras.

[37v.] A Dios Placer!—A Dios! quiza para siempre pues no espero volver á ti: á ti que tan mal has pagado mis trabajos, y tan crueles desengaños me has ofrecido; á ti que reduciste tus dones á un átomo de mis esperanzas y que quiza me habrias quitado el unico y verdadero que poseo que es la salud. A Dios. . . . . A Dios . . . . . .

Setiembre 3. Hoy llegamos á S[a]n José con solo la yegua, pues el rosinante se nos atorsono en el camino; no lo pudimos levantar y tuvimos á bien dejarlo tirado. ¡Otra ganancia de cuatro onzas!

Es increible lo mucho que ha aumentado esta poblacion en tan pocos dias que dejé de verla; aunque las casas estan esparcidas acá y alla, unas de adove, otras de madera y muchas de lienzo. Debe crecer rapidam[en]te por el gran movimiento que hay. Todos los dias entran gentes y todos los dias se levantan nuevas casas.

Como no tuvimos donde alojarnos dormimos arrimados á la pared de una casa donde nos dieron licencia.

Mañana salgo para S[an]ta Cruz que dista de aqui once leguas por la Sierra (segun me han dicho) para ver á Arana en quien tengo mis antiguas esperanzas y por quien fué en vano hasta S[a]n Fran[cis]co; [38r.] cuando vuelva, veremos á que nos dedicamos ó en que emprendamos que nos produzca algo.

8 . . . . . . Hoy volvi de S[an]ta Cruz, ¡Que viaje tan penoso! Sali de S[a]n José de tarde y me quedé al pie de la Sierra en un ranchito que hay alli[148]; otro dia temprano, despues de haberme desayunado, ensillé; me informé bien del camino y monté para seguir. Todo el dia caminé por una vereda infernal; todas las subidas á pie para que no se me cansara la bestia. Al fin despues de tantos trabajos, llegué á la Mision al oscurecer,[149] donde encontré á los Aranas que me manifestaron mucho aprecio y me hicieron hospedar en su casa.

Me detuve un dia para arreglar con D[o]n Felipe Arana el modo de trabajar en la Sierra para hacer tajamanil. Me ha asegurado que es muy facil, escasea bastante y se puede ganar una onza en el dia. El se comprometió á ir en compañia de nosotros. Tambien me han dicho que se puede aprovechar una oportunidad de rentar un aserredero[150]; resolvi pues ir por Ygn[aci]o para volver á trabajar, veremos si tambien es juntar Oro con palas.[151]

Ayer muy temprano sali, para alcanzar á llegar al rancho donde me quedé el dia que sali de este pueblo,[152] pues no hay ningun otro en todo el camino; pero no fué asi, por que la Yegua antes de medio camino se empezo á cansar; me apie luego y la eche por delante; anduve como dos leguas [38v.] y ya no puedo dar un paso la infeliz Yegua, seguram[en]te por que no la dejaron cenar otras bestias que estaban alli. Ya el Sol se habia metido y distaba todavia como dos leguas y media del rancho; por mas que hice ya no pude hacerla andar; yo la acariciaba, la maldecia, la azotaba. En fin la desensille un rato para que se refrescara, volvi á ensillarla, pero siempre no pudo andar ya. Determiné cargar en mis espaldas las chaparreras y la ropa de dormir é irme hasta el rancho, dejando la Yegua amarrada donde hubiera pasto, y la silla escondida; pero considerando que ya era de noche y estaba tan lejos, podria estraviar el camino, desbarrancarme ó encontrarme con algun Oso (que abundan tanto en esa Sierra y de los que habia visto muchos rastros) que me hiciera anicos [sic], asi es que, despues de que amarré bien la Yegua y escondí la silla, traje una olla de agua de un arroyo inmediato, puse lumbre, calente el bastimento que me dió Arana, lo cené y me puse en manos de la Providencia, acostandome bajo un arbol, sin mas arma que una navaja. Me acababa de acostar, cuando comenzaron á ahullar los lobos y los collotes en las profunidades de las barrancas,[153] resonando fuertemente en mis oidos que me hacian estremecer; pero al fin el sueño mio vino á poner en quietud mi espiritu, hasta el amanecer que desperté sano y salvo sin poderlo creer aun viendolo.

[39r.] Con el descanso que tuvo en la noche la Yegua, ya pudo llevar la silla hasta S[a]n José á donde llegué hoy despues de medio dia.

11. . . . . Sigue la peregrinacion. Parece que somos descendientes del pueblo hebreo y que nuestro destino es andar errantes fuera de nuestra patria. Hoy volvimos á empreder [sic] nuestro camino á pie y arreando á nuestra humilde rosinante que nos hace favor de conducir sobre sus flacos lomos un baul y una maleta con ropa de dormir. Sigamos pues, la mano invisible de nuestro travieso destino que nos guia de aventura en aventura hasta parar ¿á donde? no lo se; caminemos y lo sabremos.

14. Hoy por la mañana, despues de caminar dos dias llegamos á la Mision de S[an]ta Cruz. Paramos en la casa de Arana que dista como un cuarto de legua de la Mision. La familia es muy afable y parece mas civilizada que todos los Californios, que en lo general son intratables.[154] Llegamos en ayunas por que los coyotes nos comieron el pan la noche anterior, en el paraje donde dormimos; y con esta van dos por que en otra tambien nos comieron la carne de junto á la cabecera.

22 . . . . Es la mañana nebulosa y triste; los rayos del Sol esparandose á veces por entre las [39v.] nubes y penetrando por el inmenso follaje de los gigantescos pinavetes ó palos colorados,[155] cuyas copas parecen perderse en las nubes, suelen bajar hasta el fondo de una gran cañada cubierta en toda

su estencion de estos y otros muchos arboles y por medio de la cual corre mansamente un arroyuelo de frias y sabrosas aguas. Cerca de este se eleva una tienda de campaña que sirve de abrigo a cuatro hombres que hacen tajamanil. Estos somos nosotros; ayer tarde llegamos y nos establecimos aqui para trabajar, despues de haber conseguido con mucha dificultad algunas herramientas prestadas para comenzar el trabajo. Este sitio dista como dos leguas de la Mision á donde vamos á proveernos de los viveres necesarios.

29. . . . . . Hasta hoy casi nada hemos echo, por que perdimos el tiempo en trozar un arbol caido que de nada sirvió por que no raja bien. Trabajamos por supuesto bajo la direccion de D[o]n Felipe Arana (q[u]e es el maestro) y que creo sabe tanto somo yo. Ademas hemos estado haciendo unos bancos para desarmar el tajamanil y alistando todas las herramientas.

30 . . . . . . Dia de funcion: Ayer venimos á la Mision, para ver la funcion que se celebra á S[a]n Miguel patrono de ella. Asistí á la Misa que la celebró el Padre con toda la solemnidad posible en la arruinada Yglesia del [40r.] pueblo. La orquesta se componia de unos cuantos Yndios que cantaban acompañados de violines, triangulos, tambor y tambora, formando un estruendo que casi igualaba al de un cañoncito que disparaban afuera de tiempo en tiempo.[156] Concurrió á ella toda la aristocracia de la poblacion y las inmediaciones, y luego que salieron se dirijieron á la plaza en donde habia dos toros encerrados para lidiarles. Esta era de palos rajados, tan mal puestos y debiles que el toro podia salir por donde quisiese, y los palcos para los espectadores se reducian á una especie de balcon medio caido de una casa inmediata y al tejado de otra en donde habia algunas mujeres que se agarraban de el para no rebalarse.

Trajeron el primer toro; lo tumbaron y cortaron la mitad de los cuernos y luego que lo soltaron se salió levantando los palos del cerco por un lado.

Trajeron el otro; toreado y experimentado, que no avanzaba un paso sino era á golpe seguro. Cuantos caballos se le pusieron por delante, probaron el suave contacto de sus hastas, y cuantos indios ebrios entraron los rotó como si fuesen conejos, dejando á uno medio muerto. Por fin lo echaron fuera reservando los otros tres para el segundo espectáculo de en la tarde, el cual no se verificó por que se salieron de la plaza.

[40v.] Por la noche el baile. Comenzó desde en la tarde en una salita estrecha. Vaya bailes celébres y en que el modo de sacar á bailar á las Señoras es de los mas cortes, fino y medido que se puede dar. El hombre palmotea las manos á la Señorita que quiere para compañera, ó le sacude en frente una mascada ó pañuelo; ninguna se rehusa y se para luego á bailar. Esto lo hacen al compas de violines que tañen los sones mas fastidiosos que en mi vida he oido.

De esta manera son la mayor parte de los bailes en California, á escepcion de uno que otro que hacen en S[a]n José, Monterrey ú otros puntos mas poblados, en donde la concurrencia de estrangeros hace que esté la gente un poco mas civilizada.[157]

Asi terminó el dia de la fiesta mayor que tiene S[an]ta Cruz, en el que por supuesto para aumentar la solemnidad, hubo la suficiente embriagues, gritos y demas cosas consiguientes.

Octubre 1ro ... Hoy en la tarde, ya casi puesto el Sol, volvimos á la cañada donde trabajamos. Como era tarde y la niebla que se levantaba era muy espesa, muy pronto oscureció y nos perdimos en el laberinto de veredas que hay por entre muchas lomas.

Anduvimos mucho tiempo errando á la ventura, hasta que cansados de tanto subir y bajar infructuosamente [41r.] resolvimos quedarnos bajo de un arbol hasta que amaneciera para buscar el camino. Asi lo hicimos y pasamos alli la noche envueltos en nuestras frazadas que afortunadamente llevavamos, (unica cama) pero muertos de hambre por que mal habiamos desayunado, no comido y por consiguiente tampoco cenado.

Vaya una mala noche, pero paciencia: pues estamos en California á donde hemos venido á recoger el Oro con palas.

A la mañana del siguiente dia 2, continuamos nuestra [...][158]; encontramos pronto el camino y llegamos á nuestra casa sin encontrar mas novedad que algunos pedasos de carne menos en el palo donde estaba[159]; segun el rastro que vimos, los siempre comedidos coyotes, fueron los que nos hicieron favor de ayudarnos á consumir los viveres.

6. ¡Es la noche! lobrega y pavorosa![160] la espesa niebla que cubre la tierra contribuye á aumentar la oscuridad y el horror de la noche tenebrosa. La debil claridad de los Cielos, solo dejase ver en parte por el inmenso follaje del espeso bosque y á lo largo de la estrecha senda de la cañada, distinguese ápenas por entre las sombras los mas inmediatos troncos de los robustos y gigantes arboles, que la cubren como inmensas columnas de un vasto templo. [41v.] Todo lo que me rodea es espantoso y los sonidos que hieren

mis sonidos son tambien pavorosos. El siniestro canto del Tecolote y otras aves estrañas: el continuo chillido de una multitud de insectos que viven entre la yerva: los sordos bramidos de las irritadas olas del mar: todo en fin se reune á dar á esta noche el aspecto mas horrible y fatal.—Junto a la tienda de campaña ardé una pequeña hoguera y adentro á la luz de una vela escribo esta escena que contemplo.

10. . . . Anteayer volví de S[a]n José con un serrote que fui á comprar. Muy diferente fue el viaje, pues en lugar de llevar la pobre Yegua flaca, llevé un Caballo de Arana muy bueno y en poco mas de medio dia me puse en S[a]n José.

Ayer nos ocuparmos en amolarlo y trabarlo; mas como no quedó bueno, fué necesario llevarlo á un herrero á la Mision para que lo dejase listo. Ygn[aci]o se le dió esta comision y cargo con el; lo compusieron y se volvió. A la vuelta le cayó una fuerte lluvia, pero dió por bien empleada esta mojada, tanto por que quedo bueno el serrote, como por que fué portador de una buena nueva; digo buena por que nos volvia á la paz y tranquilidad de que antes gozabamos, sin los dos muchachos que tenia la muger de D[o]n Felipe que se habia ido alli á vivir con su marido y que nos que- [42r.] daban la cabeza todo el dia y toda la noche. Hoy se nos quitó esta guerra por que Marcos su hermano mandó decir con Ygnacio que se iba a Monterrey y dejaba la casa sola si no iban á cuidarla, y tuvo ella que irse con sus malditos muchachos.[161]

Noviembre 10. Hace poco mas de ocho dias está lloviendo y parece que ya se han declarado las aguas.[162]

La lluvia es continuada con muy pocas intermitencias, pues en todo este tiempo ápenas ha habido un dia limpio y despejado, único en que hemos podido trabajar. Hoy amanecio lloviendo y estabamos en la tienda cuando recibimos un recado de la S[eño]ra dueña del Rancho inmediato[163]: decia que fuesemos á su casa á pasar lo fuerte del aguacero y que llevasemos consigo las cosas que quisiesemos para que no se mojasen. Por un equivoco del mensajero creimos que era un llamado espreso, tal vez para algun convite ó para algun negocio. Nos pusimos en Camino hacia el citado rancho, distante como un cuarto de legua; cuando llegamos teniamos los pies lle– [42v.] nos de lodo y el vestido algo mojado.

Por las primeras palabras de la Senora [sic] conocimos que habian tergiversado el recado y habiamos ido inutilmente pero ya estabamos allí, y no tenia remedio. Nos pusieron para sentarnos unos banquitos sumamente bajas y luego mandó traer un gran sarten lleno de brazas que cólocó á nuestros pies para que nos calentasemos, segun dijo. ¿A quien se le ocurre hacer secar el calzado mojado, puesto en los pies á fuerza de fuego? Solo á esta gente. La prudencia exigia callar y sufrir aunque conociamos que nos dañaba aquello; pero es la costumbre del pais; es persona á quien le debemos cariño y favores, y no habia mas que complacerla, pues de lo contrario habria creido que se le desairaba.

Todo el dia llovio y todo el dia estuvimos alli con el bracero á los pies. En la tarde cuando nos despedimos para volvernos, las piernas me dolian y estaba[n] entumecido[s] por haber esatdo tanto tiempo sentado, el cual empleamos despues de almorzar en jugar baraja con algunas personas de la familia.

[43r.] Volvimos pues á mojarnos los pies despues de calientes (cosa muy provechosa) pero en fin nos quitamos de la tortura en que estabamos con el aciento y junto á la lumbre.

Dia 29. Hoy vamos á salir de la Sierra. Hace como ocho dias concluimos el palo que atabamos trabajando y que produjo 18 mil tajamaniles los cuales no hemos vendido aun por que no se ha encontrado marchante [*sic*].

Ya es tiempo de hacer una reseña de la clase de vida que durante nuestra permanencia aqui hemos tenido.

Ya he dicho antes, que este lugar dista de la Mision dos leguas, y á donde teniamos que ir cada 6 ú 8 dias á provernos de los viveres necesarios. Facil es concebir lo penoso de estos viajes y mucho mas en la presente estacion.

Como no teniamos aqui bestia ninguna, era forzoso traer á cuestas, la harina, azucar, velas y los demas viveres que teniamos que llevar y que atravesar de este modo, lomas empinadas, arroyos y pantanos. Al salir de la cañada esta el rancho de la Señora dueña de ella y de quien hemos recibido como he dicho bastante cariño y favor, pues á mas de habernos permitida [43v.] trabajar alli sin estipendio ninguno por la madera, siempre que pasamos por su casa nos hace almorzar ó comer y nos carga con legumbres que nos regala de su huerta. Le hizo Ygn[aci]o una cama que le mandó hacer, sin cobrarle nada por supuesto, para recompensarle de alguna manera una parte de sus favores.

Todo este tiempo vivimos bajo una tienda de campaña que nos prestó un amigo, la cual no nos libertaba enteramente del agua cuando llovia por que se pasaba bastante. Junto al tronco de un arbol hicimos cocina, en la que nos alternabamos los tres compañeros, pues Arana hace mas de un mes dejó de trabajar con nosotros so[bre] pretesto de enfermedad. Muchas veces volviamos de la Mision ya de noche y algunas de ellas yo solo. Entonses figurabame uno de esos personajes misteriosos que pintan las novelas, habitantes de las selvas, y que á veces se les mira al ausilio de las últimas luces del crepusculo vespertino, caminar con paso grave y mesurado y en actitud meditabunda, á lo largo de una tortuosa senda y perderse luego con ella entre la espesura del bosque.

Diciembre 6. El dia 30 del pasado sali– [**44r.**] mos de S[an]ta Cruz para S[a]n Fran[cis]co á donde venimos con el objeto de recojer algunas cosas que habiamos dejado cuando estuvimos aquí y de que pagabamos 4$ cada mes por almacenage y por ver si lograbamos vender el tajamanil que teniamos en S[an]ta Cruz.

Paramos en la Mision de Dolores en la casa de un paisano,[164] de donde ivamos á pie á S[a]n Fran[cis]co.

En el trascurso de este viaje tuve algunos trabajos que solia distraer la alegre prespectiva [*sic*] del camino, que corre por toda la costa sin apartarle de la orilla del mar, el cual presenta ecsenas [*sic*] variadas y magestuosas. El bramido continuo de las irritadas ondas que chocando contra las peñas, las carcome y las destruye, formando en algunas partes, arcos-paredes ó piramides que se mantienen aisladas en medio de las aguas, son atacadas sin cesar por las olas que se estrellan[165] y gimiendo contra ellas, caen espumosas y blancas cual si fuesen de plata.[166] Jamas habia visto un horizonte tan bello, cual se presento á mi vista el primer dia.[167] El Sol parecia hundirse en las aguas, y sus rayos moribundos reflejandose en la [**44v.**] atmosfera la daban un tinte de purpura brillante y este inmenso horisonte, esta bobeda en el fondo de la cual creia yo ver aparecer á su grande Autor rodeado de toda su gloria, se perdia en la inmensidad del espacio en donde la vista estaviada [*sic*] vagaba de un lado á otro sin poder apartarse de aquel cuadro grandioso y magnifico.[168]

Este dia caminé á pie un rato, llevando Arana mi silla en las ancas de su caballo, pues encontramos á un amigo de él que nos fletó un caballo en 5$ para llegar á un rancho donde tenia sus bestias que distaria quince leguas y en donde me debia prestar una de las suyas. Ygn[aci]o salio á pie un dia antes para el mismo rancho donde teniamos la Yegua y en la que se fue[169] en pelo hasta S[a]n Fran[cis]co.

Dos dias fueron los mas penosos en esta expedicion.[170] El segundo dia de camino tiene uno que pasar por la playa muy cerca del agua y esto solo se puede hacer cuando la mar está baja y el dia que pasamos estaba bastante picada. Tanto Arana como yo ignorabamos el camino; ási es, que cuando entramos á la playa se nos figuró que estaba bueno pues cuan– [45r.] do la ola venia muy grande á penas llegaba á la pesuña de los Caballos.[171] Asi caminariamos cosa de 300 varas habiendo tenido dos pasos muy malos por unas peñas, cuando la mar muy irritada comenzó á bañarnos hasta la calza de la silla. No hallabamos que partido tomar, pues retroceder era evidente el peligro por que las peñas ya estaban tapadas y no podiamos ver las abras que tenia, de modo que decidimos seguir adelante para buscar algun paso por donde poder subir, pues las olas nos tenian repechados contra un paredon bastante alto. Seguimos pues y caminamos cosa de 200 v[ara]s hasta que hallamos una vereda por donde subir y luego que nos pusimos en salvo nos desnudamos completam[en]te para poner á secar nuestra ropa, pues por tres veces nos voltearon las olas con todo y caballos que fue necesario apearnos y sacarlos estirando.[172] Salimos á las diez de la mañana y luego que concluimos de tender la ropa y sillas, nos sentamos encueros [*sic*] sobre el sacate para almorzar el bastimento que llevabamos tambien echo una sopa. Este dia llegamos al rancho donde alcanzamos á Ygn[aci]o y remudamos para salir otro dia juntos, pero no fué asi, por que Ygn[aci]o se fue delante con otros tres compañeros y yo salí despues con Arana. La bestia que [45v.] me prestó fué un macho bastante gordo y algo regego. Como á tres leguas leguas [*sic*] de camino sele antojó á mi compañero hacerle ruido al macho con las armas de montar[173]; este se asustó y echo á correr con todas ganas; yo quise sujetarlo, pero viendo que era imposible y que las riendas estaban sumam[en]te debiles, me tiré á pie y lo deje ir. Arana que no se habia quedado muy lejos inmediatamente fue á seguirlo diciendome que "en ese mismo punto lo esperase para no extraviarnos." La paciencia se me acababa y el hambre me aflijia, pero era preciso aguardar allí, pues no estaba muy seguro de acertar al rancho donde habiamos salido y esto seria peor. Luego que oscureció, perdí del todo la esperanza de que volviera ese dia, de modo que procuré acomodarme lo mejor que pude, poniendo debajo mis chaparreras que habia tirado el macho; el paragua que me dejó Arana para que no le estorbase, lo coloqué al lado del viento que hacia muy fuerte, amarrandolo con mi banda de unas yerbas que habia allí; puse mi sombrero de cabecera y me envolvi con dos sarapes que me habia dejado el comp[añer]o para librarme de la lluvia menuda que comenzó á caer luego que oscurecio, la que se quitó pronto. Habria pasado una hora despues de haberme acostado cuando oí gritos de mi [**46r.**] compañero que me buscaba á los que contesté inmediatam[en]te.

Pareciame haber vido la voz de un Angel que me hablaba, tanto fue el gusto que recibí por que ya no pasaria solo la noche espuesto á que algun Oso me hiciera añicos. Llegó por fin con otras dos bestias, pues las que traiamos las dejó cansadas por haber corrido lo mas del dia. Determinamos no seguir adelante por no esponer á perdernos pues la noche estaba tenebrosa.

Al otro dia que nos levantamos blanqueaba el sarape que teniamos encima por la fuerte nevada que habia caido en la madrugada. Este dia alcanzamos á los demas compañeros.

Dia 9. Hoy se nos perdio el Oro que nos quedaba en una bolsita que yo traia en la de la chaqueta [*sic*][174]; esta la puse junto á la cabecera, anoche cuando me acosté que fue cerca de la puerta y ahora que me levante ya no estaba en el sitio donde la habia puesto. Como hay varias gentes en la casa no se pudo averiguar que de los que salieron por la mañana la tomó. Desgracia mas—paciencia ya que nuestro destino es padecer.

Dia 27. Mañana vamos á salir para S[an]ta Cruz, á pie y con la maleta á la espalda. Haré una [**46v.**] reseña de los trabajos y padecimientos que durante nuestra permanencia hemos tenido aqui.

Fin á traer las bestias que habiamos enviado á cuidar al rancho de Sanchez,[175] pues que ya perdido el Oro no nos quedaba mas recurso que marcharnos cuanto antes. Las busqué en compañia del que las llevó; no pude hallarlas, por lo que sospechamos que este las habria dejado en otra parte ó las habria vendido pues era hombre de no muy buena conducta, y á mas iba ebrio cuando las llevó. Fue preciso ecsijirlo para que las entregase, y se fue á buscarlas, quedando nosotros pie á tierra sin medio real que gastar y yo sin sombrero, por que el dia que salí á buscar las bestias me tomó en el camino un viento tan fuerte que se llevó mi sombrero á larga distancia que no era facil alcanzarlo pues corria mas que yo, á esto se agrega los granizos tan grandes y tupidos que no me dejaban ver. En el rancho me prestaron uno para poder volver á la mision el que mantuve dos dias mientras Ygn[aci]o consiguio dinero en S[a]n Fran[cis]co y me compró uno.—En tales circunstancias, con pocas esperanzas de recobrar nuestras bestias y sin recursos para subsistir, pensamos irnos por agua para lo que habiamos visto un buque que salia para S[an]ta Cruz. En este querian que pagasemos el pa– [47r.] sage adelantado; pero casualmente el sobre cargo era conocido de Arana y habiamos convenido en que lo pagariamos en S[an]ta Cruz. Teniamos ya entregadas las sillas de montar y alguna ropa para que se embarcasen y esperabamos que al dia siguiente nos iriamos á bordo del Malek Adel que salia ese dia segun nos habia dicho.[176]

Todos los dias veniamos por la mañana á S[a]n Fran[cis]co y volviamos por la noche á la Mision á la casa donde dormiamos. Ese dia se quedaron Ygn[aci]o y Arana en S[a]n Fran[cis]co confiados en que al dia siguiente saldrian y yo me volví para la Mision, pues habiamos convenido en que me quedaria para tener razon de las bestias y buscar algun destino para poder subsistir mientras permanecia aqui. Tres ó cuatro dias pasaron, quedandose los dos compañeros á dormir en S[a]n Fran[cis]co á donde yo iva á verlos todas las dias y me volvia por la tarde á la Mision, hasta que el último sucedió el acontecim[ien]to siguiente.

Era la madrugada del dia de la Navidad de Jesuscristo [sic]; todo estaba en silencio: todos dormian á escepcion de algunos que reunidos en el Hotel de Parker House, asistian á la cena publica que se dio en honor de esta festividad. Duraba aun la embriaguez y los gritos que resona– [47v.] ban en toda la casa. De súbito se alza una voz que llena de espanto á todos los convidados: ¡fuego! gritan y la voz corre de boca en boca; el festin para todos aterrados se precipitan por las escaleras hacia la calle; todo el mundo se pone luego en movimiento; entre tanto el fuego cunde de casa en casa (todas de madera) y llega cerca de donde estaban Ygn[aci]o y Arana, durmiendo en un cuartito que un Sonorense les habia permitido pasar alli la noche;[177] las voces y carreras los despiertan y oyendo que el fuego venia cerca, se levanto Ygn[aci]o precipitado creyendo que estaria mucho mas cerca y se puso solam[en]te su Chaqueta, tomó su sarape y atraveso las calles llenas de lodo corriendo hacia las lomas. Cuando quiso volver á salvar la ropa, la multitud de gente que inunda la plaza no lo dejan y lo llevan de un lado á otro; entretanto el incendio cunde con voracidad y ya viene cerca de[l] cuarto donde dormian; vuelve pues á tomar su primera resolucion corriendo hacia las lomas para escaparse creyendo que llevarian gente á apagar.[178]

Cuando llegaba yo de la Mision á San Fran[cis]co comenzaba á asomar el Sol y sus rayos se oscurecian por los torrentes de humo negro y espeso que se levantaban en medio de las llamas. [48r.] Esto era horroroso: volavan tablas, trapos y otros objetos impelidos por la polvora que se ardia, y las pipas de aguardiente que se inflamaban, reventaban con horrible estrepito cual si fuese pieza de artilleria.[179] Nada podia contener la voracidad de aquel fuego que cundia á gran priesa consumiendo una tras otra las casas que iba invadiendo, á pesar de que no hacia viento. Los dueños de ellas y muchos que les ayudaban se empeñanaban en salvar al menos los objetos de mas valor y manuales, arrojandolos por las puertas, ventanas y balcones á la calle, al lodo; de allí los tomaban otros y los amontonaban en medio de la Plaza, y otros muchos aprovechandose del desorden y la confusion robaron todo cuanto pudieron.

Veianse hileras de hombres prolongados hasta el mar pasando de mano en mano valdes llenos de agua que arrojaban para atajar el fuego; otros con hachas golpeaban terriblemente las casas por el pie, mientras que various con cuerdas procuraban derribarlas tirando de ellas.[180] Otros en fin tendian multitud de frazadas mojadas para que el fuego no cundiese, hasta que al cabo, de mas de dos horas de esfuerzos, lograron (ausiliados tambien con una bomba) atajar el incendio, [48v.] que consumio casi toda la manzana que era bastante grande. Cuando el fuego ya se apagó me acerqué á la plaza poco á poco; no se veia sino montones de cenizas donde poco antes existian inmensos almacenes de comercio y magnificos Hoteles; ni señal quedó siquiera del cuartito donde dormian.

La perdida la han calculado algunos en dos millones de pesos y otros la hacen ascender mucho mas. Despues de un rato de estar en la plaza, encontré á Arana quien me dijo que Ygn[aci]o habia echado á correr, no sabia para donde y que él volvio despues que habia salido del cuarto y habia salvado la ropa que dejaron. Estaba bastante inquieto por que no encontraba á Ygn[aci]o hasta que al fin lo vi aparecer en una orilla de la plaza que venia de las lomas desde donde habia observado la escena, segun me dijo despues.[181]

No teniendo ya donde dormir esa noche y las siguientes, tuvieron que volverse con migo á la Mision á la casa donde estavamos antes, pues el buque no salia todavia; los encargados para recibir los pasages, los estaban aplazando continuamente y no podian tener ya seguridad ninguna del dia de la partida. Mientras, nosotros estabamos sufriendo mil penurias y necesida– [49r.] des; los recursos se nos habian agotado completamente; no teniamos medio alguno de subsistencia, por que los amigos y paisanos con quien contabamos, nos habian echo [*sic*] ya varios préstamos y no teniamos á quien ocupar, ni en que ocuparnos nosotros para ganar alguna cosa. Algunos dias pasabamos sin comer por la falta de numerario contentandonos con tomar una taza de café. En fin aburridos por la tardanza del buque y desesperados de nuestra situacion, resolvimos volver á S[an]ta Cruz á pie habiendo dejado antes las sillas y ropa para que vayan allá en el buque, por no poderlas llevar nosotros, y cargando á la espalda solamente lo muy preciso para dormir.

Diré algo aunque sea de paso de San Francisco, de esta nueva Roma, poblada de hombres entre los cuales solo se ve una que otra muger. Su crecimiento es rapido; todos los dias se levantan casas y se establecen nuevos Hoteles y Almacenes; la poblacion es bastante grande ya y el paisaje que ofrece la ciudad vista desde algun punto dominante es alegre y variado. A pesar de ser el piso muy desigual (pues todos son lomas) las calles estan ordenadas y el ca– **[49v.]** serio se estiende á lo largo de la playa donde hay porcion de edificios fundados dentro del agua y un gran muelle para el embarque y desembarque de los efectos en los buques á mas de otros dos ó tres mas pequeños. El Puerto esta cubierto de embarcaciones cuyos mástiles reunidos, semejan á un bosque de pinos en el invierno, presentando á la vista aquel grupo de palos desnudos en medio de las aguas.[182] El comercio es muy activo y el trafico no cesa; multitud de carros corren por las calles todo el dia trasportando efectos de los muelles á los almacenes y de estos á otros; la gente no para de andar á pie y á caballo á pesar del mucho lodo que hay en las calles y de lo frecuente que son las lluvias en este tiempo. En fin todo es movimiento y las principales ocupaciones de los habitantes (casi todos americanos) son el comercio y el juego.

Enero 1° de 1850. Hoy amanecí ya en S[an]ta Cruz; anoche llegué muy estropado y molido por el cansancio y la fatiga.

Salimos de la Mision de Dolores, á pie como he dicho y con la maleta al hombro, sin mas resfuerzo que 4 p[eso]s que nos prestó un paisano de Tepic, á quien le dejé **[50r.]** mi sable.

Llegamos ese dia al rancho de Sanchez distante 7 leguas, donde tuvimos la fortuna de encontrar al dia siguiente una de las Yeguas que se nos habian perdido; esto fue ya un gran alivio, pues en ella llevamos las maletas y nos alternabamos á montar á ratos p[ar]a descansar. Al dia siguiente llegamos á otro rancho donde encontramos otra Yegua que la dejamos allí mismo recomendada [*sic*] para que la entregasen en el rancho donde antes estaba.[183] Al tercero hallamos las demas bestias que habian vuelto á la querencia, y al cuarto caminamos en ellas en pelo hasta llegar aqui que fue á media noche.

Tuvimos grandes trabajos por lo malo del camino: la mucha agua que hay en todo el y la necesidad que teniamos muchas veces de caminar por la orilla del mar irritado algunas veces y atravesar esteros, en uno de los cuales se vio Ygn[aci]o en peligro con el agua hasta el cuello é impelido fuertemente por las olas, pero afortunadam[en]te salio sin novedad y ya pudimos pasar con mas seguridad.

Por último, espiró el año de 49: año de penas, de trabajos y fatigas inutiles: año de fa– [50v] talidades y desgracias y que aun en sus ultimos dias hizo sus postreros y mas terribles esfuerzos[184] por abatirme, y que ya espirante me asestó sus mas desesperados golpes para dejarme una memoria eterna de su nombre y un recuerdo indeleble de todos mis padecimientos y particularmente de los últimos. ¿El joven que le ha sucedido, el año de 50, será tan impio como su antecesor? ¿Se habra sucedido para continuar la lista de mis penas? ó ¿apiadado acaso de ellas se mostrará mas benébolo, acordandome algun bien? Veremos. La esperanza y las ilusiones que son las que alimentan al hombre y particularlmente á los jovenes, me sostienen aun, haciendome aguardar algo favorable y ver el reverso de esta medalla cuyo amberso [*sic*] ha sido hasta ahora de desdichas.

Enero 31. Un mes ha pasado: mes de inaccion y de espantoso letargo. ¡Ah! con que lentitud ha pasado este tiempo y que amargas han sido sus horas! Cuantos sufrimientos morales he tenido y como se han visto abatidas mis pasiones: mi orgullo y mi amor propio! ¡Encontrarme sin ningun recurso y tener que vivir á espensas de un amigo, de quien recibiamos [51r.] doblemente el favor por hallarse en situacion muy semejante á la nuestra! ¡Oh miseria, cuan dura eres, y á cuantas humillaciones, baldones, y desprecios espones á tus victimas! Nadie puede conocerte hasta que no te pruebe y hasta no apurar hasta las heces tu amargo caliz! ¡Cuantas veces! ¡oh cuantas, rogué fervientemente á Dios me diese tan solo resignacion para poder sobrellevar mis penas y tolerar con paciencia mi infortunio! ¡Oh religion Santa! en aquellos momentos sentia aliviarse mi corazon del gran peso que le oprimia y me consideraba con el suficiente valor para sobrepujar á la adversidad y aguardar tranquilo los altos designios de la Providencia confiado en que no me desampararia! ¡Que cierto es que el hombre se olvida de su Dios mientras vive en la abundancia, en la prosperidad y los deleites y solo recurre á él en los momentos de amargura desesperada y cuando ya no puede esperar nada de los hombres! Entonces nos acordamos que profesamos una religion Santa y consoladera y nos acojemos á ella como única tabla de salvacion! Ninguno queda burlado cuando ruega con el corazon, y yo no [51v.] lo he sido esta vez, pues que la Providencia me ha proporcionado al fin con el trabajo medios de subsistencia.

Un acontecimiento desgraciado influyó indirectam[en]te en provecho nuestro. Una casa se incendió hace pocos dias en la playa, y con este motivo nos compraron tajamanil para reponerla, que aunque á precio muy bajo pero fué ya un recurso. A esto se agrega el valor de 1.500 tablas de 4 pies que contratamos para la misma á 35 p[eso]s mil y que harémos en la misma cañada donde hicimos el tajamanil, tan luego como el tiempo nos deje pues no cesa de llover.

Febrero 3. Hoy nos fuimos á la cañada para comenzar mañana el trabajo.

Dia 18. Hoy salimos del monte por haber concluido ya las tablas, tumbado un arbol y echo otras 1.500 tablas mas que nos mandaron hacer. En todo este tiempo nuestra comida se redujo á frijoles por no haber podido conseguir carne ni otra cosa; pero al fin los comiamos cuando teniamos gana y en la cantidad que queriamos, sin estar atenidos á nadie y con libertad sobre todo. Afortunadamente en todo este tiempo no llovio, por consiguiente no tuvimos que perder tiempo. Volvemos á la casa [52r.] de Arana á nuestras antiguas penas.

Marzo 7. Mañana voy á comenzar un nuevo trabajo. D[o]n José Arana, Marcos y yo, hemos echo un contrato con unos Americanos en un molino de acerrar,[185] de acarrear 200 trozas por 300$. El primero pone bueyes y aperos y persibirá la mitad, y Marcos y yo, el trabajo personal, por lo que nos tocará una cuarta parte deduciendo 12 r[eale]s diarios que pagamos á un mozo que nos ayude.[186] Dicen que se arrastraran de 15 á 20 trozas diarias; veremos, peor es estar ocioso.

Abril 30. ¡Por último! ¡hasta que quiso Dios! 54 dias han pasado ya durantes los cuales me entretenia en lo siguiente: Algunos dias que el mozo estaba malo me levantaba temprano y luego me iba á juntar los bueyes á pie y volvia á la casa para unsirlos, lleno de agua hasta la rodilla por el rocio que caia y el sacate que estaba grande; luego nos ivamos para el molino que distaba como una legua; pasabamos los bueyes por un arroyo que atravesaba el camino y nosotros ibamos á pasar por un palo que se habia caido en la orilla del rio que nos servia de puente. Las trozas teniamos que bajarlas por unas laderas muy empinadas y bastante estorbadas por los árboles y despues las arrastrabamos dos cuadras en lo parejo, que sera lo que dista el molino. Ya se podra conocer lo dificil que seria bajarlas y[187] [**52v.**] lo espuesto, pues á esto se agrega que tres yuntas de bueyes eran nuevos y mañosos y solo una teniamos de mansos. No habiamos perdido irnos por no haber concluido el contrato de las trozas, en el cual ahora que liquidamos cuentas salí malisimamente, por que despues de haber perdido algunos dias á causa de la lluvia y muchos mas por causa de los empresarios, estos no han pagado mas de la mitad de lo que deben, y se fueron para S[a]n Francisco, diciendo que <u>poco tiempo</u> vuelven á pagar lo demas.[188] De esto, segun el convenio que teniamos y deducido lo que pagamos al mozo, todo lo que percibí fueron 30$ ¡gran cosa! Con esto, el importe de 3.500 tajamaniles que nos quedaban y que vendimos á <u>4 p[eso]s millar</u> y diez pesos que nos pagaron por la tableta que hicimos á Arana, vamos á salir mañana para los Placeres, pagando antes unos picos que debemos. Nuestras proviciones para el camino, son sumamente limitadas por que vamos muy incomodas, Ygn[aci]o en una Yegua <u>en pelo</u> sentado solamente en una especie de albardon que formará con frazadas[189]; tendrá gran trabajo para llevar su maleta y arguenas con los trastes de cocina. Yo en otra Yegua que le cambie á Arana por 4 mil tajamaniles y cuya montura se reduce á un fus– [**53r.**] te viejo que no tiene mas cuero que el que con que esta forrado, formando las arriones y estribas de unos pedazos de coyundas, teniendo que llevar mi maleta de ropa, dos bateas y una barra, pero que se ha de hacer, paciencia, pues la silla se perdió. Esta y la ropa que habiamos recojido en San Francisco y que debia venir en el Malek Adel, no la he vuelto á ver por que aunque el buque vino despues y estuvo mas de un dia descargando en la playa, nuestras cosas no salieron, ni otras muchas que aun quedaban por desembarcar, por que al tercer dia hizo un mal temporal y levando áncla se salio para otros puntos á donde iba y no lo he vuelto á ver ni á tener noticia de su paradero.[190]

Ygnacio en todo este tiempo se ocupó en hacer una cama, una mesa y componer dos relojes de sala en la casa de Arana y otras obras de carpinteria que hizo á la S[eño]ra dueña de la cañada quien por toda recompensa le regalo un par de bateas de valor de 8$ y un saquito de pinole de trigo y tres quesos que llevaremos para comer en el camino.[191] Facil es concebir los deseos que tengo de salir á probar de nuevo fortuna en los Placeres.

En la larga escena de aventuras que he tenido en S[an]ta Cruz, la suerte me ha sido [**53v.**] siempre contraria, pues todas han sido adversas. Todas pueden reducirse á tres epocas principales: la primera = Tajamanilero = haber trabajado tanto tiempo esperando vender el fruto de mi trabajo á un precio que indemnizase tantas fatigas y privaciones: esperanzas burladas. La segunda el Viaje á S[a]n Francisco: perdida de oro y bestias; penurias y calamidades consig[uien]tes. La tercera á tiempos de inaccion y á otros de algun trabajo recompensado cual se dice comunmente como al perro con la comida: ó aquel en recompensa de esta que es lo mismo. He aqui que todo ha sido trabajos, penalidades y miserias durante el tiempo de mi mansion en Santa Cruz. ¿Podré tener una memoria grata de esta malhadada Mision, en donde no he tenido sino sufrimientos fisicos y morales? No: las impresiones desagradables que han echo en mi esta série de acontecimientos desgraciados, las tendré siempre presentes y haran epoca en mi vida.

Mayo 9. Hoy llegamos al Placer conocido con el nombre de "las Mariposas,"[192] sin accidente ninguno en el camino que lo hicimos con felicidad. Despues de haber atravesado el inmenso Valle de San Jose [sic], pasamos el rio de S[a]n Joaquin, luego el de la [54r.] Merced y nos internamos en la Sierra hasta llegar á este punto que está al Sur de los otros Placeres conocidos hasta hoy y situados todos en las montañas nevosas [sic].[193] Hay aqui mucha gente, bastante comercio, partidas de juego villar y plaza donde trabajan unos maromeros mejicanos, todo en carpas de lienzo y algunas de morillos ó de piedras pegadas con lodo.[194] La mayor parte de los gambucinos sacan muy poco, por lo que vamos á otra cañada inmediata llamada Agua fria.[195]

Dia 12. Manana [sic] saldremos de aqui en comp[añ]ia de D[o]n Juan Smith y sus hermanos,[196] con quienes nos reunimos en el camino, hacia un punto atras poco distante del rio de la Merced, por que aqui no hay casi nada. Muy poco ó nada sacan la gente que hay; nuestros ensayos no han dado ningun resultado y ademas ya no hay donde abrir labor por que todo está trabajado. En estos dias se ha dado una ley para que todo estrangero que trabaje en los Placeres, pague 20 pesos cada mes y adelantados; bien estamos: ya veremos como nos escapamos de este pago.[197]

Dia 15. Ayer llegamos á este arroyo donde hay una gran rancheria de Yndios que viven á su margen bajo enrramadas. Se preparan á recibir á un Ca– [54v.] pitan de otra rancheria á quien han convidado para que venga á comer Ciervo, pues creo que es el tiempo mas á proposito para la caza de este animal. Comenzaremos hoy á trabajar en el gambuceo y veremos como nos pinta. La necesidad nos aflije y el hambre nos ha acosado bastante en estos dos últimos dias, en que no hemos tenido para alimentarnos sino un poco de pinole que nos quedaba; nuestro bolsillo se agotó completamente y no tuvimos con que provernos de los viveres necesarios: paciencia ¡que se ha de hacer!

Dia 19. Estoy á la margen izquierda del rio de la Merced, bajo la sombra apetecida de una frondosa cucina que me pone á cubierta de los rayos del Sol del medio dia. ¡Oh que vida tan agitada y llena de aventuras! ¿hasta cuando teminará? Heme aqui fugitivo puede decirse, en union de mis compañeros y sin saber todavia que partido tomar. Anoche hemos salido de donde estabamos y caminado una parte de la noche con el ausilio de la luna, huyendo de dos enemigos que nos amagaban á un tiempo: el uno era el fuego que cundia á gran priesa hacia donde nosotros estabamos, consumiendo el pasto [55r.] seco en una grande estension de terreno y cuyo incendio avivaba el viento. El otro eran [*sic*][198] los Yndios que reunidos en gran número y animados por la embriaguez, daban terribles alaridos y amenazaban á un Californio que vendia viveres y aguardiente, de arrojarlo de aquel lugar; siendo causa de todo él mismo por haberles fiado y sobre todo por haberles vendido licor. Salimos pues por determinacion de los compañeros que nos aseguraron ser muchos los Yndios que habian visto al pasar por la rancheria y que sus intensiones para con todos los que habiamos alli eran muy deprobadas, esponiendo ademas los pocos medios de defensa con que contábamos en caso de ataque. Los seguimos tomando un camino por donde no nos viesen, lo que no sucedio y llegamos á un sitio distante como legua y media donde dormimos.[199] Queriamos volver hoy á[200] ver si habia sucedido algo; pero como ya estabamos cerca del rio, á donde está la familia de los Smiths, seguimos con ellos hasta aqui. = En los dias que trabajamos alli sacamos lo suficiente para mantenernos y ademas un sobrante de cosa de una onza.

Dia 21. Hoy salgo para Estanislao[201] en compa- [55v.] ñia de D[o]n Antonio Smith[202] con el objeto de ver allá á Ybarra mi primo que tiene casa de com[erci]o para informarme del estado en que estan las cosas,[203] tanto de choque entre Americano[s] y estrangeros con motivo de la ley sobre pensiones, á los mineros estrangeros, como por ver si se consigue alguna colocacion ú otro empleo en que poder ganar algo para irnos. Aqui no se ha sacado casi nada; solo un rato trabaje ayer y saqué 6 r[eale]s. [L]os Americanos luego prohibieron trabajar alli; mas ahora ya no en razon de que la gente que habemos aqui, hemos dicho que somos Californios.[204]

Dia 24. Antes de ayer llegué á la Ciudad de Estanislao que esta bastante poblada con algunas casas de madera, adove y las mas de lienzo. Pare en casa de Ybarra mi primo, quien tiene en compañia de otro una cantina y ocho mesas de juego que alquilan por las noches. Ha tomado mucho empeño en que me quede, para lo que me ha ofrecido que la comp[añ]ia pondra el dinero y yo tallaré por lo que me tocará una tercera parte. Veremos si me la saco por el juego. Hoy se vuelve Smith para el rio de la Merced,[205] con quien le mando á Ygnacio las dos Yeguas y una carta diciendole que dentro [56r.] de doce dias lo espero en esta.

Junio 18.
    Veinticinco dias he pasado en mi oficio de taur [*sic*],[206] en los que solamente ganaria cincuenta y tantos pesos de los que me tocaron cosa de diez y ocho, habiendome quedado libre para buscar otro destino; digo libre por que ayer tuvieron los socios un compromiso de 500$ y hubo necesidad de que dispusieran del fondo de la partida, el que creo no volveran á reunir ya. El que haya sido taur conocerá los malos ratos que me hacia pasar el juego en las alternativas de <u>ganar</u> y <u>perder</u>.[207]
    Ygnacio aun no viene; lo esperaré ocho dias é iré mientras á las cañadas inmediatas á gambucear, para no estar de ocioso y ver si algo se saca y si en este tiempo no viniere iré á buscarlo al rio de la Merced en compañia de Silvano Valencia que ha ofrecido acompañarme para determinar lo que debemos hacer.[208]

Dia 29. Manana [*sic*] salgo en compañia de otros dos para un placer que llaman de los Melones,[209] con mi ropa de dormir y un costalito de bastimento [56v.] á cuestas. Dista seis leguas; me dicen que está bueno y que se podrá sacar una onza diaria. Aqui no he sacado casi nada.

Julio 12.
    Hoy volvi de mi expedicion sin que me hubiera ocurrido nada particular. Todo el Oro que me sobró fuera de los gasto [*sic*], es el valor de 20$ los que preste hoy a un amigo.

Dia 25.
    ¡Por último! hasta que voy á salir para mi pais! á mi pais donde siempre anhelo volver! Volveré, pero no con el gusto que poco mas de un año ha me figuraba por mediar estas circunstancias. 1ra: por estar mi salud

sumamente quebrantada, a causa de una fuerte inflamacion que hace once dias me comenzó y en la que me ví un gran peligro de perder la vida.

Estuve ocho dias en cama, sufriendo á mas de las dolencias, un calor ecsesivo, pues la casa es de lienzo y el Sol que se esperimenta en estos meses es ardoroso.

El Doctor Rodgers (Americano) quien despues de Dios me salvó la vida,[210] con sus medicinas y eficaz asistencia, me ha dicho que salga de [57r.] aqui los mas pronto que pueda, pues si recaigo tal vez ya no habra remedio por que mi naturaleza está muy estenuada; que él sale mañana mismo para Guadalajara y me ofrece acompañarme para lo que me pueda suceder en el Camino. 2da por dejar á Ygnacio mi verdadero amigo, sin saber donde ni como estara y 3ra por volver á mi pais, no solo con [sic][211] las riquezas que mi ilusion forjaba, sino que ni aun mi salud que habia recobrado ya, y con lo que estaba muy conforme, volvi á perder de nuevo. Mañana saldré pues en comp[añ]ia del Doctor en la diligencia que corre hasta Stokton [sic] y cuyo asiento me ha costado 25$.

Dia 30. Ayer luego que llegué á S[a]n Fran[cis]co fui á ver si conseguia pasaje en el Vapor que sale para S[a]n Blas el dia 1º y me encontré con que ya todos estaban vendidos; afortunadamente encontre á Ygnacio Tapia que tenia comprados dos para él y su hermano y dos para sus mozos; me vendió uno de un mozo por 100$ y á este le compró otro en un buque de vela por 35$.[212]

El Doctor no consiguió dos pasages que necesitaba en el Vapor por lo que los[213] ajustó en un buque de vela y saldrá despues. Mucho siento [57v.] que no nos vallamos juntos pero siquiera voy acompañado con unos paisanos y amigos.

El dia que sali de Estanislao llegué á Stokton [sic] en la noche y me aloje en un Hotel que me asistieron muy bien; me estuve dos dias para esperar el vapor que corre á S[a]n Francisco. Todavia no he sanado por que no se me acaban de quitar los ardores de estomago. Por D[o]n Roque Delgado que se dirije á Mazatlan he parado en un cuartito de un amigo suyo que no está muy distante del muelle y que no me cuesta nada.[214]

Agosto 2.

Hasta ayer por la tarde salí de S[a]n Francisco, trayendo á bordo mi maleta desde antes de medio dia para asegurarme de un buen campo antes que otros vinieran, pues me tocó dormir sobre cubierta por que los pasages de la antecamara valen 200$.

Salí por último de California; pasamos la bocana del Puerto y perdimos de vista á S[a]n Fran[cis]co. Mi corazon entonces lo agitaban diversas sensaciones, y mi imaginacion la ocupaban tambien diversas ideas que en otra época semejante, cuando perdia de vista [58r.] á S[a]n Blas para venir á California. ¡Que diferencia! Entonces me traian las iluciones y las esperanzas; ahora me llevan los fatales desengaños y la costosa esperiencia; la fuerza en fin de una amarga y terrible realidad.

Dia 6.

Hoy dia de mi Santo para felicitarme me han robado de mi cabecera, un reloj de plata que me regalo Pepe. Como he dicho, vengo durmiendo sobre cubierta, seguramente algun curioso vio donde lo puse anoche y me velo el sueño. Cuando desperté, me levanté precipitado recojiendo mi ropa para que no me la mojaran, pues ya venian echando valdes de agua para lavar el buque. Luego eche menos el reloj y empese á preguntar á varios; unos me decian que no sabian quien lo tomaria y los mas que son Americanos, no me respondian, ó por que no me querian contestar ó por que no me entendian. Quise hablarle al Capitan para que se hiciera un registro, pero me dijeron que era necesario interprete y no sé que otras cosas, y que en mas de 400 pasageros que hay, y que mañana debemos llegar á Mazatlan donde desembarcaran muchos [58v.] es muy dificil que se pueda averiguar[215]; asi es que á mi pesar me conforme en perderlo y no llegar á mi casa con alguno de los dos que traia, pues otro de oro que me dio tambien Pepe en 9 se lo empeñe al Doctor Rodgers en 100$ para pagar mi pasage.[216] El se quedó en S[a]n Fran[cis]co y tal vez, no lo veré nunca.

Dia 9. Hoy por la mañana llegamos á S[a]n Blas y á poco rato salté á tierra: á aquella tierra tan deseada y á cuya vista mi corazon palpitaba con fuerza dentro del seno; pero ¿era de alegria? yo no lo se ¿era de tristeza? tal vez ¿no voy á ver á mi familia, á mis amigos? ¿por que pues hay una mezcla de alegria y tristeza? ¿por que razon predomina esta? no lo sé tampoco; pero será tal vez por que en vez de los bienes de fortuna que pensaba traer, no me acompaña sino la historia de mis padecimientos y desgracias y el tormento de un costoso desengaño. Esto es muy triste á la verdad retornar al seno de mi familia y sin poderlos aliviar ó darles lo que deseo ¡oh! esto es un doble padecimiento.[217]

Como á las 5 de la tarde, saldré para Tepic [**59r.**] en comp[añ]ia de los Tapias, en unas mulas que hemos fletado.

Dia 13. Hace tres dias que llegamos á Tepic y paramos en el Meson de S[a]n José no hemos podido salir por que se nos dificultaban bestias baratas, hasta hoy las conseguimos ya, y creo que para mañana seguiremos nuestro camino.

Yo compré una silla de montar en cuatro pesos con lo poco que me sobraba y con diez pesos que me prestó Tapia compré un Caballo bastante flaco; pero creo que me llegara.

Dia 18.

Hoy á las diez y media de la mañana llegué á Guadalajara; á proporcion que me acercaba á ella y que percibia mas clara y distintamente sus torres y sus edificios mi corazon se comprimia de tristeza. ¡Cuando en otros tiempos, despues de una corta ausencia me cansaba la vista de esta Ciudad á mi vuelta, un gozo inesplicable[!]

Estaban saliendo de la misa de diez de Santuario cuando llegue y encontré á toda mi familia buenos, solo Tula la encontré con una fuerte palpitacion que ni aun podia hablarme; esto lo causó seguramente mi llegada tan repenti- [**59v.**] na despues de una ausencia de poco mas de diez y ocho meses.

Fin.
Guadalajara Año de 1850
J. V.

Ygnacio llegó á esta, hasta el 19 de Mayo de 1851.

English Translation of Justo Veytia's Diary

[fol. 1r.]

The Year 1849

February 9.
   Today I begin my diary, or the story of the events that occur on this journey I am going to make to Alta California, on which I truly do set forth filled with enthusiasm and confident that I will have happy success.
   My heart swells upon thinking that I am going to cross the sea; that I am going to learn about faraway lands, strange peoples, and different customs; that certainly I will endure many hardships and find myself exposed to a thousand dangers; but that, in the end, I will be rewarded for all this with a sudden brilliant future. In order to achieve this, it is necessary to get through all these dangers and difficulties. The chiefest merit accrues when adventures of this sort are undertaken: adventures that have I don't know what attraction for me, in their romantic and novelesque qualities. The consideration of them, instead of frightening me, encourages me and further goads my desires to learn about the world and to try my luck outside my own country. So I will go. Good fortune will crown my efforts, and I soon will return to my native land, to the bosom of my family; and in their embrace, I will enjoy peacefully **[fol. 1v.]** the reward of my labors.
   Today we stop in Amatitan, which is a small town situated amid ridges. Its streets are poorly laid out.[1] It has a few taverns, or rather places where *mescal* is made; a conduit in the plaza from which the inhabitants are provided with water; and a bad inn.

> AL ORO!—Varios de nuestros ciudada-
> nos estan preparandose para salir en bus-
> ca del oro, que se dice ò piensa haber ocul-
> to en las montañas que rodean esta ciu-
> dad.—Buen viaje

FIGURE 10. "¡Al Oro!" (To the gold!). The discovery of gold in California in 1848 quickly became known in the Spanish-speaking world, as word reached prospective miners in Mexico, Central America, South America, and Spain. The continuing draw of gold fever throughout the following decade is reflected in this notice from a Los Angeles Spanish-language newspaper, *El Clamor Público,* reporting local excitement over rumored gold strikes in southern California. (UCLA CESLAC.) Source: "¡Al oro!", Los Angeles *El Clamor Público,* May 10, 1856, 1.

FIGURE 11. A photographic view of Guadalajara in 1880. Justo Veytia left his home in the city on February 9, 1849, full of hope that he would strike it rich in California. Source: Vicente Riva Palacio, *México a través de los siglos. Historia general y completa del desenvolvimiento social, político, religioso, militar, artístico, científico y literario de México desde la antigüedad más remota hasta la época actual,* 5 vols. (Barcelona: Espasa y Cia., 1888–1889), 3:162.

Before one arrives, a little outside the travelers' lodge, one sees the corpses of three executed men hung by their necks from a horizontal beam placed atop two vertical ones. Their appearance is horrifying and causes fear: their limbs, half dried-out already by the heat of the sun and decayed in parts, present to view skeletons sheathed in tight, greasy skin that shines in the sunlight as if varnished. On a whitewashed board above them, one reads the following epigraph: "Thus does the law punish the thief and the murderer."

[February] 10.

We pass through Tequila, a pretty settlement: streets straight and paved, with sidewalks, reasonably good buildings, and a cheerful aspect.[2]

We arrive in Santo Tomás, a hacienda with a silver-processing concern and a mescal tavern. The entire machinery is driven by water, **[fol. 2r.]** and a little stream makes its mills and mortar go round at the same time. It is pretty and worth seeing.[3]

The road is rocky all the way to Mochitiltic, where we stop. There is a good inn there, with its arcade facing the countryside.[4]

[February] 11.

Today we pass through Yxtlan, a small and insignificant town.[5] Before one arrives, there is the beautiful canyon of Mochitiltic: long and deep, with its narrow passes sloping and rocky in parts. But a great deal of the road is open, along a steep cliff on the side of a lovely, imposing mountain, forming roadways.

The scenery of this ravine is lovely and romantic. The high tops of the ridges are eroded and full of narrow gorges, immense depths at whose bottom gently runs a little river, with its banks covered by different trees. It serves as asylum to a multitude of birds of beautiful plumage, such as magpies, parakeets, and various others. It all presents a majestic view, but especially as dawn breaks, when the first rays of the sun penetrate into those depths, sliding through the foliage of the trees and going on to be **[fol. 2v.]** reflected in the crystalline waters of the little rivulet that gently winds along that bed of perpetual greenness.

We arrive in Ahuacatlán, a small town with arcades on the plaza, an inn, and a church.[6]

At night there was a fandango at the end of one of the entrances to the plaza. The lighting was a single candle stuck in a wall, which gave light only to half the assembly, who were seated on the ground. The dancers stamped along to the discordant sound of a guitar, and it all presented an aspect more tedious than diverting.

[February] 12.

We pass through Santa Ysabel, which is an Indian village where we lunch and then take a road covered over to a great extent by immense trees. There are very thick, green woods on the ridges, making a very pretty scenery and countryside.

The volcano of Ceboruco is along this road, and it forms a mountain of melted crags, piled one on top of another, which look like iron.[7] It makes this part of the road very rocky, until one comes to San Leonel, which is a tiny, insignificant village of wretched aspect, with the odd house, a poor chapel, and an inn with three rooms and an arcade facing the countryside.[8]

[fol. 3r.] [February] 13.

We arrive in the morning at Tepic, a large and well-situated city on a vast plain watered by several springs.[9]

Its streets are broad and straight, and the greater portion of its buildings low: two churches, in which there is nothing notable; and another little church, or chapel, in the city's suburbs, which is called Santa Cruz because the vegetation within the narrow enclosure of four unroofed walls attached to the church has this shape, and the walled area communicates with it by means of a door with a grille through which a person can look.[10] The soil here is extremely moist, and the temperature very changeable. Extremes of cold and heat are experienced in a single day, which cause the thermometer to go up or down by 10 to 11 degrees.[11]

The greater part of the houses have sitting rooms facing the street, where the ladies sit and sew. In the rest of the rooms are hammocks, which serve so well to refresh people in the summer, and they even sleep in them at night.

Considerable luxury is apparent, especially in the furnishings of the houses; for nearly all of them, however poor they may be, have fine chairs, sofas, beds with curtains, dressing tables, and glass panes in the windows.

It seems that there is a good deal of immorality [fol. 3v.] in the local customs, and a lot of prostitution.

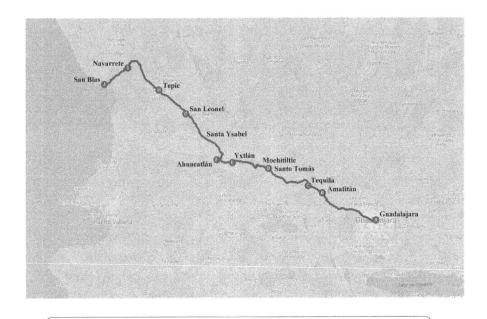

FIGURE 12. Guadalajara to San Blas. Veytia's journey through Mexico took him from Guadalajara through Tequila and Tepic to the coastal port of San Blas, where he embarked on a Peruvian ship, the *Volante,* for San Francisco. (UCLA CESLAC. Map by Paul Hsu.)

The plaza is surrounded by substantial ash trees, which create shade all around its circumference with their thick, interwoven boughs above the stone benches that they have to sit on there.

A fountain that stands in the middle of the plaza provides water to a portion of the population, but the rest carry it in from the nearby springs.

Three arcades and the front of a church form the square of this plaza, in which there is a market on Sundays. There is another fair-sized market in a small square, and some arcades in the middle of the city.

It has a tree-lined boulevard along the riverbank, next to the San Blas gate. It is bounded on one side by a wooden balustrade fixed on brick pillars sealed with mortar, upon parapets of the same material. The boulevard is planted with trees in rows, the greater portion of which are little orange trees. Between them is a multitude of rosebushes and northern flowers, planted in square beds. To conclude, the aspect of the city is cheerful, even though its sky is frequently cloudy, above all in the afternoons, due to the nearness of the seacoast.

[fol. 4r.] The 14th.

Today I left with a hired boy for San Blas, to see if our passages might be arranged there more easily.[12]

I walked as far as the Navarrete rancho.[13]

The 15th.

I arrived at the port around ten in the morning, having departed so early that I walked for a good part of the night along a path made through the woods.

I went immediately to see Don Carlos Tapia,[14] from whom I believed I might obtain two passages in the same ship in which Puga had arranged his[15]; but Tapia told me that Fernández Peral was in charge of arranging passages in that ship.[16] For that reason, I went to see him immediately. I got only one ticket. In order to please me, he told me that, purely for friendship's sake, he would get another ticket, for the *Republicano*, a ship that was leaving the same day as the *Volante*; and it would cost me two hundred pesos. In the end, practically at nightfall, he informed me that the second ticket had been secured, for [fol. 4v.] a hundred ninety pesos.

As a result of the many difficulties that presented themselves in obtaining transportation, and because the two ships were leaving on the same day, I decided to take them; albeit with great dismay, as it would be necessary to travel separately from Ygnacio, for it was not possible to change passage from one ship to the other.

So I was told that we had to be in San Blas by the 26th of this month, without fail, as the ships were to set sail the day after.

I delivered Puga's baggage to Pérez's house,[17] along with our own, so that they might load it on board; and I went to stay in a little hut that was on the shore. They gave me a hammock to sleep in there, and thus rescued me from the fleas—but I could not escape the mosquitoes.

The 16th of February.

I returned to Tepic.

I arrived at eleven in the morning at Navarrete's place, where I lunched and they told me that by taking the Palos Marias road I would come to Tepic around [fol. 5r.] seven at night.[18] I took their advice and went on.

But it was a road much worse than the other: more overhung by trees and even rockier.

As we were beginning to go up a hill, darkness covered us completely.

Neither one of us knew the road. The night was so dark, and the ravine we were beginning to go down so deep—as one could tell from the sound of the trees—that I believed we should not pass safely. But God willed it that, after we had traveled about two hours among mists and along several precipices without anything happening to us, we arrived at a little hut made of straw, around half past nine.

I woke the homeowners so that they might sell me something to eat, as my stomach found itself with considerable appetite, for I had eaten nothing since eleven in the morning. I got them to give me a plate of boiled beans, somewhat cold, and some tortillas, which I ate with a good appetite. They also sold me some [fol. 5v.] bundles of leaves and a little corn, which the hired boy gave to the pack animals we had with us.

With these operations concluded, I decided to go to sleep in the tiny porch of the hut—which was full of fleas, lice, and bedbugs[19]—for although the two homeowners had offered that I could sleep inside, I did not want to inconvenience them, since I did not wish to sleep long, in order to leave as early as I could.

The 17th.

I arrived in Tepic at eight in the morning.

Later, when I return to San Blas to embark, I will tell about the details of the journey, and the impression that the sight of the sea created in me. For now, I will occupy myself in amusing myself at Carnival, for there is quite an uproar going on.

[fol. 6r.] The 17th, 18th, and 19th—Sunday, Monday, and Tuesday of Carnival.

On these days, and especially the last one, Tepic is a city of crazy people and buffoons. From the time it gets dark, activity begins that does not stop all night. Hundreds of people of both sexes (from the lower classes) run around the streets with a lot of uproar and shouting, their faces whitened with flour, singing "Los papaquis" in discordant groups, to the sound of a tambourine or small drum.[20]

When people go out, they encounter so many people whose faces are covered in flour, no matter who they might be. Furthermore, ladies, joined by young men, do the same thing—although without as much racket—going into houses of people they know and people they don't, out into public, and along the arcades, to anoint the faces of everybody they meet.

After that, normally the dances begin, which last until dawn; and those who are animated by the most unrestrained glee and hidden by their whitened masks commit the greatest follies.

Until Tuesday, I had managed to avoid falling into the hands of the women face painters; but that very night Ygnacio and I were standing **[fol. 6v.]** in the doorway of a shop where we were wont to gather with other Guadalajarans[21] to listen to a young fellow who used to entertain us with his songs sing and play the guitar, when the storm broke over us.

We were alone, for the other people who usually gathered there were off walking around without having come into the shop. Nevertheless, I wanted to see what was going on in the streets. Well, a short time later, a big crowd passed through, with quite an uproar. We waited for it without fleeing, believing that we might stay there, hidden from their impudence, but we were mistaken. That multitude thirsty for pleasure flooded the street, looking for victims on whom to satisfy their crazy whims. They swooped down on the shop entrance. Four raving madwomen got inside, their faces whitened, their hair half disheveled, their expressions deranged. One of them came to where the shop clerk was and rubbed flour on his face, without the least resistance on his part. The other three addressed themselves to Ygnacio like Furies, taking up great fistfuls of flour, with which they sought to paint his face. He drove them roughly back and made for a door that led into a sitting room, where he tried to go to escape them; but in vain, for the door was closed. The women, seeing that they could not **[fol. 7r.]** paint his face so easily, threw great fistfuls of flour at him from a distance, which landed on his face and clothes. Afterward, taking advantage of a moment in which he was rubbing his eyes clear, they closed in and anointed him at will.

During the short interval between his initial resistance and the first fistful of flour that they threw at him, a feminine voice, more compassionate than the others, said, "Don't throw it on him! You're ruining his clothes." A hundred other voices at once were raised, disapproving of such compassion, and urging with loud shouts that they paint his face, leaving him at the mercy of those harpies, bathed in flour from head to toe.

Jumping over the shop counter—and landing on an oil lamp—I fled, but despite that did not escape. The men pursued me; and as I was running through unfamiliar territory and the night was dark, I was in danger of falling. For that reason, I decided it was better to take up a position on some firm ground, with my pocketknife in hand, to await the three good-for-nothings who, urged on by that crowd, were accosting me. Seeing that

I was armed, they hesitated; but before they retreated, they threw flour at me and left me thoroughly covered, then ran. [fol. 7v.] Since I had fled without knowing to where, I got lost when I tried to go home, and I had to wander around and around before I found it.

That was how Carnival in Tepic ended for us, whose baptism of flour, had we received it from other hands, we might have considered time well spent.

Our fellow Guadalajarans caused rather a scandal,[22] as a result of some fights that occurred between them and people of Tepic, especially against a stranger.

The 22nd.

Today our companion Puga left for San Blas, with whom we were to have gone to board the ships. But the matter was arranged differently, and we were left behind, waiting for another, more convenient passage.

Tonight, some Guadalajarans had a get-together at the house of Julián Romero, during which it was agreed that two individuals should be named from our number to arrange passage for all the members, or else to charter a ship for the whole group, whichever they should find more convenient. All of us were obligated not to separate from the group or get individual fares, so that if the passage should not be for all, it would not [fol. 8r.] be for any.[23]

Those thus commissioned were Don Andrés González and Julián Romero, in association with Canitrot.[24]

The 25th.

So far, nothing much has happened. Those who were commissioned have gone to San Blas to see about a ship that is in port.

The 26th.

Today, very early, we received a messenger from Fernández Peral, whom he sent to us with a letter in which he tells us we must depart at once to take up the passages I had arranged; for if we did not, we would have to pay for them anyway. We departed immediately and traveled until we reached Navarrete's big ranch.

A good deal of the road is covered by trees, and in the grass there is a multitude of ticks and other harmful insects. Despite the shade, we experienced excessive heat throughout its length.

The 27th.

We departed very early in the morning and walked through thickest darkness, along a road made through a wood of fat, thick trees, which stretched for quite some distance, forming a highway. We arrived at the port of San Blas at 8:00 in the morning.

[fol. 8v.] The sea can be seen from a little hill that overlooks the settlement.

At that moment, a spectacle new to me presented itself to my view: that immense sea, which is lost to view at the horizon, where it seems to join with the sky—its waters, at the time quiet and calm, upon which some vessels float—all of it, in short, is grand, magnificent, and tremendous. Upon beholding it, a soul naturally feels inclined to give thanks to the Maker of such grandeur.

We went down to the port, whose scant population lives in huts made of split poles set in the bare ground, covered with clay and thatched with palm fronds that the natives call *palapa*.

Only two or three buildings have tiled roofs, which are the Customs House and some private homes.

The heat was excessive and the mosquitoes abundant. We stayed there that day, and as night fell, we took a launch to go aboard the ship. In the meanwhile, we strolled around the beach a bit and bathed in the sea.

Fortunately for us, the brigantine *Republicano*, in which one of us was supposed to have embarked, [fol. 9r.] had already sailed.[25] But we were able to get passage for both of us in the *Volante*, a Peruvian brigantine, which was still there, and aboard which I previously had not been able to get more than one ticket—for which reason I had taken the other for the *Republicano*, which had already sailed.[26]

The two passages cost us $350, which turned out better for us, as traveling separately would have cost us $390.

As I have said earlier, we went aboard a launch and went out to where the ship was anchored.

We went up by means of the ladder when it was already night. I was aboard a ship, another new thing for me—and even more so for my stomach. As soon as it felt the rocking, even though it was slow, it could no longer keep down what it had in it, and made it come out of my mouth. My first bout of seasickness.

The brigantine is 400 tons in size; it is some 30 yards[27] in length or more, and about 6 yards in breadth.

She has about 1,500 half-bales in her hold,[28] 8 fat pigs, 8 live sheep, and a hundred-plus chickens confined in coops like cages lashed to the sides of the stern. [**fol. 9v.**] Her crew complement was made up of something like 15 men, and her number of passengers as many as 130.

The space between decks, or main compartment, in which Ygnacio and I were traveling, was a square room with a ceiling so low that it was necessary to go about bent over.

The cabins, or sleeping quarters, are distributed around the entire circumference of the ship, like boxes on the deck.

The scant light that these lodgings receive is through a trapdoor opened in the ceiling (or deck), barely more than a yard square, which they call a hatchway.

A long, broad table made of cedar, placed in the middle of the compartment, served at once as a way to climb up through the hatchway, a place to eat during the day, and for sleeping on at night.

A description of the rest of the ship would be very long and not very intelligible to anyone who is not familiar with vessels, and would not give an exact idea of her operation.

March 1, 1849.

Today, in the morning, we raised anchor and set sail in a light wind.

At the shout of the captain who was commanding the [**fol. 10r.**] maneuvers as he stood at the stern, the sailors carefully wound the long anchor-chain onto a windlass, or winch, at the same time intoning a sad sea chanty peculiar to themselves.[29] Others hoisted the broad sails to the wind, which unfolded themselves little by little as the crewmen hauled on the ropes, making the pulleys around which the ropes ran squeal. Finally, another man stood in front of the compass and had the wheel in his hands to steer the vessel. . . . [30]

The maneuvers were concluded; the wind filled the sails, and the ship, just noticeably, began to draw away from the shore. Then I said my farewell to that land I was leaving behind, to return to . . . when? perhaps never! . . . . This thought and many others tormented me, weighing terribly upon my heart. Nevertheless, my hopes for a swift and happy return home encouraged me again and made me brave, for a little while suppressing that heaviness—perhaps a secret presentiment of future misfortunes—and causing me to expect a promising, happy time to come.

March 15.

Fifteen days have passed! But such days—my God!—of suffering, of agony! [fol. 10v.] The great weakness and prostration in which I found myself, caused by terrible seasickness, kept me in a state of dazedness and indescribable illness. Most of my traveling companions were in the same state as I, or worse. Nothing was to be heard anywhere except the noise they made when vomiting their guts out: complaints, lamentations, and curses upon sailing.

The interior of the ship, below decks, presented painful scenes; but the constant dialogues to which all this had given rise caused laughter amid the distresses one suffered.

"So-and-so,[31] what do you say?" they would ask one another in faint voices. "If we had known about this, would we have come?"

"Like hell,"[32] the other would reply, taking strength from his own debility to lend his voice a certain vigor and air of firmness. "I would have gone by land, even if I knew that it would take me a year on the road and I would have to risk perishing at the hands of savages at any moment. At least I would have been able to drink fresh water and wouldn't be constantly throwing up whatever I eat."[33]

"Damn the *Volante*, and damn the hour in which I got the idea of coming aboard her," another would say. "If I had known about the miseries [fol. 11r.] I would have to endure here, damn me if I would have come, even if I knew I would come back loaded down with bags of gold!"

"They want gold? Well, let them have gold!" another would exclaim, giving his sepulchral voice a note of bitterest irony.

"Ah, gold! How much you cost!" another would murmur, with a dying note.

These and other, similar discussions, mixed with lamentations, imprecations, and vulgar expressions, took place in the main compartment, especially at night, when everyone was there.

In the morning, these remarks resumed, accompanied by terrible cries and curses caused by hunger.

"Bring the atole!!![34] When are they going to give us breakfast? Do they want to kill us with starvation?" said some. "At least give us a cracker!" said others.

When a sailor came below with the atole, a hundred bodies would stir in their bunks, some sticking their heads out, others slowly dragging themselves to the table, and everybody stretching out a hand for what they were giving them, causing a cry of "Me! Me! Me!" that deafened the poor fellow whose task it was to share out the food.

Those who were not seasick would go out on [**fol. 11v.**] deck early, and they would intercept the cauldron of atole before it went down to the main compartment, hastily taking one, two, or three cupfuls, or whatever they could. As a result of this, often there was not enough for those below, and some people were left without any breakfast. A similar scene would be repeated at dinnertime.

When the sun rose, they would begin to come out, one by one, from the mouth of the hatchway, wrapped up in their blankets: wan, disheveled, with sunken eyes, livid lips, and wasted faces, pale and corpselike. It looks like a grave had been opened and the dead had risen out of it.

They betook themselves, with unsteady gait, to the ship's rails to empty their stomachs or to sit down sadly somewhere.

Today, fortunately, the number of seasick now are few, and people's visages are recovering their natural color, along with a return of their appetites and the absence of illness.

During this period of time, we had some calms and also some spells of bad weather.

On the second day of sailing, we made out the Islas Marías,[35] which are tiny; and by the third or fourth day, we lost sight of the great white rock that could be seen ever since we left the shore,[36] which is a mass of stone made [**fol. 12r.**] white by the droppings of birds and marine fowl. Raised above the sea, it shines in the sun as though it were made of marble.

One calm night, we encountered a barque, and the next day a pinnace.[37]

We also saw, in the distance, some whales that, winding their way upon the waters, sent up great spouts of water shaped like fans, as frothy and transparent as if they had been made of silver and crystal.[38]

A multitude of dorados were seen around the ship, some among them very large. One day they fished one out, which was served at table in the main compartment, and it was exquisitely tasty.[39]

For a certain distance out from the land, a great number of gulls followed the ship: birds of ashy hue, the size of a sparrowhawk, which feed themselves on kitchen refuse.[40]

In the midst of the prostration in which I found myself, I could do no less than think about the anniversaries of certain days. The feast of Saint John of God—how many memories that brought to my mind, equally welcome and sorrowful, when I considered my present situation in light of that of a year before! That day on which, amid the tumult and joyfulness of the beautiful city of Gua– [**fol. 12v.**] dalajara, I had passed along the crowded street of San Juan de Dios,[41] in company with my friends, enjoying the happiness of the occasion. What comparisons were not made, what fancies and appetites were not aroused among my companions! What curses, moreover, at our bad luck in not being able to satisfy them!

An event that got the attention of all the passengers occurred on one of these days. Because a sort of rivalry existed between the passengers on the upper deck and those in steerage, as the former were treated better than the latter, a kind of rebellion broke out, for us to be given better food. One day, one of our company in steerage, instigated by another man—whether as a joke or in earnest—grabbed a platter of meat and potatoes that a servant was bringing to the first-class table. This attempt produced a predictable effect, which was, first, that one of the first-class passengers came from the upper deck to retrieve it, using language sufficiently insulting that some of the steerage passengers responded in kind.

Meanwhile, the dish in question, having gone down through the hatchway, went about from hand to hand, with each person quickly taking what he could from it. **[fol. 13r.]** But another first-class passenger soon arrived. Furious, he went below, insulting all the steerage passengers about it, and particularly the man who had committed the theft, challenging him to come up and fight him on deck.

The challenge was accepted, and the least imprudence on anybody's part could have produced the most deadly results. Fortunately, the most prudent and reasonable course was adopted that could have been in such a case, which was to keep quiet about it until both sides' angry emotions were soothed by the intervention[42] of respected persons, and even a certain satisfaction was given to the steerage passengers for the insult directed at them so generally and not deserved by all.

The 27th.

Twelve more days have passed: days of continual illness with intervals of relief—days of hunger, also, with intervals of bad food. How many days without breakfast or luncheon! Practically without food! And how many sacrifices, as well, to swallow it when they gave it to us!

In the morning, bad atole made from rice or maize flour, raw or else burned, and surely made with foul water: more suitable, truly, for inducing vomiting than for nourishment. For lunch, beans with rice or salt meat **[fol. 13v.]** or potatoes, and the same for dinner. That is, when there was any luncheon, and without anything more for dinner.

During the first days, they served coffee and tea at breakfast; but as they made it with salt water, very soon there was no one who wanted to drink it. Simply hearing it mentioned made your stomach turn.

Days worse than I would expect to spend in the worst prison in the world.

They say that, after tomorrow, we will sight land. God willing!

During these twelve days, there has been nothing special, apart from a promenade that two young whales made about the ship, and a strong north wind that blew upon us yesterday and the day before, during which the waves of the sea, raging, rose up like mountains, several times coming to break over the decks.

Today, the day dawned lovely and cloudless, preceded by a quiet, clear night in which the new moon shone amid the pure blue of a sky sown with stars.

The wind that has prevailed throughout these days, exceedingly cold and unbearable, has abated a little now; and the sky, previously cloudy and sad, begins to clear.

The 28th and 29th.

A cruel storm afflicted us during [fol. 14r.] these two days and put us in great danger. We came to the extreme of reefing the sails and heaving to; that is to say, dropping the anchor and leaving the ship to her own defenses.[43] The appearance that the sea presented was horrifying. The waves rose up like great mountains that spat briskly down on us, belching forth continuous deafening roars. The ship rolled strongly amid the waves, until she nearly lay over on her side, and the waves broke over her all the time, drenching the decks.

The 30th.

From this day on, it was more peaceful and quiet. In the morning it was announced to us that land would be sighted around two in the afternoon. Indeed, at that hour we made out a promontory in the distance, formed of several whitened peaks that projected from the waters.[44]

The feeling of pleasure we experienced was huge; and even more so as night was falling on the next day, the 31st, when, having passed through the mouth of the harbor, we finally dropped anchor. This event was celebrated with great demonstrations of joy. Gathered together below decks, many of our company sang together to the rhythm [fol. 14v.] of a guitar, frequently wetting our throats with wine, which was gotten out of the hold.

April 1.

As day broke, we raised anchor and began to enter the harbor. The picturesque and agreeable appearance it presented, with its small houses and wooden huts that seemed to be hanging on the lovely green hill, reanimated people's depressed spirits and induced a feeling of hopes and fears.

Around ten in the morning, we anchored in the bay, where something like 40 vessels, both large and small, swayed majestically up and down. Near us arrogantly streamed the flag of a Peruvian warship, a brigantine of 16 guns. Her captain at once came to visit ours, according to the custom of sailors.

Then the port captain came to visit our ship, and afterward other persons who had, or thought they had, a right to come aboard: friends or acquaintances, among them José María Ybarra, my cousin.[45] Great was the pleasure we experienced upon seeing each other, and much more so when he presented us with two beautiful loaves of fresh bread, a round cheese, and a bottle of wine. This repast seemed to us to have come down from the Heavens. **[fol. 15r.]** Our hunger was atrocious, and we were sick of ship's biscuit.

We eagerly devoured the bread and cheese in company with other friends after Ybarra had gone. Then we went on deck to view the harbor, the vessels, and the little boats that, rowing around to the ships, were offering to transport passengers to shore.

At last we had in our sight the much-desired Harbor of the Land of Gold, the object of so many hopes.[46] We had finished that sea voyage, so arduous and never to be forgotten. We were about to pursue a series of adventures already begun, and to undergo perhaps the greatest privations—and who knows but that it all might be in vain, with no reward. . . . We shall see.

We are waiting longingly for permission to go ashore.

The 4th.

Today, in the morning, I got into a little boat and went ashore, in company with Ygnacio and Games.[47]

The little settlement stretched the length of the beach, sometimes forming streets, with groups of buildings and individual houses scattered here and there, all made of wood with pitched roofs. Some had a porch, and all had glass in their windows, built with skill and grace and painted

FIGURE 13. Deserted ships in San Francisco Bay. Upon arriving in San Francisco, Veytia noted the large number of ships at anchor; many had been abandoned because their crews had run off to seek gold. (Wikimedia Commons.) Source: Photograph, Ships Abandoned in Yerba Buena Cove, San Francisco, During the California Gold Rush, ca. 1849, https://commons.wikimedia.org/wiki/File:Ships-abandoned-in-Yerba-Buena-Cove-San-Francisco-during-the-California-gold-rush.-1849.jpg.

> EX PHOENIX, VOLANTE, & FANNY.
> Liquors in 13 gallon barrels, sherry in do, claret in cases, sevilla wines in kegs, Havana cigars, vinegar, Mexican goods, assorted, etc. etc. For sale by
> PROBST, SMITH & CO.
> April 12, 1849   14 tf

FIGURE 14. The *Volante* arrives in San Francisco. This advertisement notes merchandise, including "Mexican goods," carried aboard the *Volante* on the voyage by which Justo Veytia came from San Blas to San Francisco, California. (UCLA CESLAC.) Source: "EX PHOENIX, VOLANTE, & FANNY," advertisement, San Francisco *Alta California,* April 12, 1849, 3.

various colors. **[fol. 15v.]** Furthermore, there was a multitude of makeshift shops for travelers who are going to the placers.[48]

The bustle is great and does not cease, all day. People on foot, men and wagons loaded down, go to and from the beach, where cargo is constantly being unloaded from the ships.

Nearly the entire population is Americans, a few foreigners, and very few Californios.[49]

There are fine warehouses and well-stocked commercial establishments, but most everything is expensive, especially foodstuffs. In the hotels, it costs $2 or $3 for dinner, as much for luncheon, and the food is not served very well.[50]

What is worth the most is human labor; but to get the greatest advantage from this, it is necessary to know English, as that is the tongue spoken almost exclusively here.

There are very few women here, and men do everything.

On this day, we bought a little tin of sardines and a loaf of bread, and we went to sit down among some shrubs to eat. As soon as we had finished, we went to the beach, where we got a little boat to go back aboard our ship.

The 6th.

Today we went ashore and spent the night in a sort of grotto made in the sand with **[fol. 16r.]** tree boughs, which Pepe relinquished to us.[51] I personally conveyed my baggage and saddle there, carrying them upon my own back, since nobody here is ashamed to do any type of work. Everyone is obliged to shift for himself, and it is, moreover, nothing unusual.[52]

The 20th.

Until today, nothing in particular has occurred. We spent 5 or 6 days in the grotto, suffering from cold and the uncomfortable consequences of its cramped interior,[53] and as many days in a sort of lean-to or shelter made from blankets; until yesterday, when we completed a makeshift tent and settled ourselves in it.

The greater part of this time Ygnacio has spent prostrate, with a couple of sores on one buttock that did not allow him to move.

The site where we are is picturesque and worthy of occupying the brush of some painter. At our backs a great wall rises from the sand, out of which is formed a hill entirely covered by bushes. In the shelter of this

> FOR SALE at the Tienda Española, the following assortment of newly arrived goods by the Hamburgh brig Conrad, from Buenos Ayres: superior Peiorato wine in pipes, jerked beef (tasajo) tongues, panocha (brown sugar,) superior leaf tobacco, claret wine in boxes, French clarified oil in boxes, vermicelli, frontignan wine, absynthe, American brandy, do gin, rice, segars, crockery, etc., etc. [nov22-47-2t]   DIAZ Y CIMA.

FIGURE 15. Goods offered by the Tienda Española on Washington Street, San Francisco, owned by José Díaz and Juan Cima. This English-language advertisement contains some of the earliest examples of code-switching between English and Spanish in California: "jerked beef (tasajo) . . . panocha (brown sugar)." The Tienda Española was one of many such establishments that Justo Veytia and his companions might have patronized when fitting out their expedition. (UCLA CESLAC.) Source: "FOR SALE at the Tienda Espanola," advertisement, San Francisco *Alta California,* November 29, 1849, 3.

cliff there were many makeshift houses, or huts, made with cargo sacking, sheets, poles, and pieces of wood, put together without any organization whatsoever. In them lived people **[fol. 16v.]** who were coming from or going to the placers. As a result, all of them were ephemeral, improvised structures at that site, at which often 5 or 6 of them, of different shapes and sizes, were put up inside a week.

The landscape is pure sand, in which one finds a multitude of little shells and snail shells, which indicates that, despite being high up, it was at one time covered by the waters of the sea.

To the right is the house of a rich merchant, to the north the town, and to the east the sea.[54]

We four companions, including Ybarra, shared among ourselves in turn all the necessary chores, such as cooking, fetching water, and getting firewood. Pepe Puga was the weakest, and it was necessary for another person to do his share for him.

The 21st.

Today a cart that we had bought for $50 arrived, and also 4 oxen, which cost $350. We loaded it with 5 or 6 half-bales of provisions; and before it had gone 12 steps, the axle broke—such was the poor condition the whole thing was in. It was necessary, for the time being, to look for

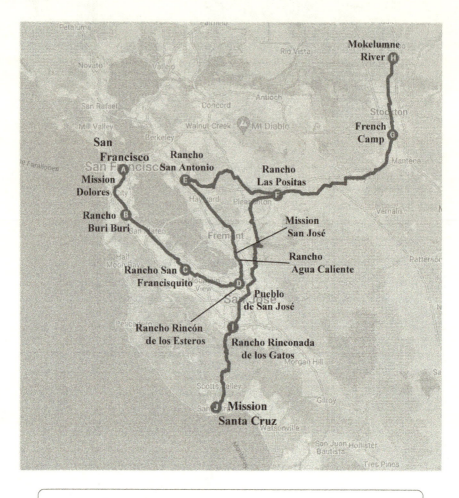

FIGURE 16. San Francisco to the Gold Country. Justo Veytia and his companions traveled south around San Francisco Bay, then east into the Gold Country. Unsuccessful there, Justo went to San José, then Santa Cruz, where he worked on the Arana ranch. Late in December 1849, he visited San Francisco again and witnessed one of its periodic destructive fires. His second trip to the Gold Country, in the spring and summer of 1850, was also unsuccessful, so he returned to San Francisco by stagecoach and boarded a steamship back to Mexico. (UCLA CESLAC. Map by Paul Hsu.)

an appropriate wooden pole with which to replace it, but none could be found, except one made of pine, and that for $8. Necessity compelled us to buy it, and then we set ourselves to work it into shape; [**fol. 17r.**] but that task could not be finished that day.

The 22nd.

Today, Sunday, we finished the axle, loaded up the cart, and set out for Mission Dolores, a town one league from the harbor.

We spent the whole day in getting there, for the road was so sandy that the wheels of the cart kept getting buried several inches deep,[55] and the oxen could not budge it, especially on some rising slopes, on which it was necessary to lighten their load, removing half-bales that we carried on our backs.

We traveled, of course, on foot, shod in huaraches[56]; I was wearing workpants and a cheap cloth duster.[57]

This first effort was supremely arduous for me, as much because of the badness of the road as because of the sun's burning rays that reflected off the sands.

As the sun was going down, we arrived at the Mission and unloaded in a sort of plaza that the buildings and fences formed. There the stock of Ygnacio's shotgun was broken, for a wheel of the cart ran over it.

We lit a fire and set ourselves to boiling beans. We roasted meat and ate with only one flour tortilla—[**fol. 17v.**] since we could get only one—as there was no bread.[58] Ygnacio and I slept there on some blankets, covered by other blankets to protect ourselves from the dew.

The 23rd.

Today, in the morning, I went with the hired boys and the cart to make another journey,[59] and Ygnacio stayed behind to take care of the supplies, to make some rails for the cart, and to prepare some food; for we had been reduced to boiled beans, as there was no bread, lard, or anything else.

We came back with the cart at 3 in the afternoon. We ate, and Ygnacio went to the harbor to arrange what was left for our final journey, which is to come tomorrow. Around 2 in the afternoon,[60] everyone arrived, with the cart. We ate boiled jerked meat and beans again and slept in a corridor of the mission.

Now it is time to give a description of the Mission in which we are staying.[61]

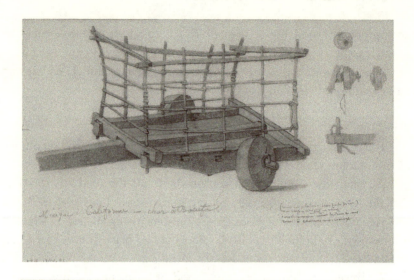

FIGURE 17. Oxcarts were commonly used for bulk transport in California. Justo Veytia and his companions bought one in San Francisco and used it for the next six months to haul their tools and supplies to the Gold Country. French-born artist Fritz Wikersheim drew this study of a typical California oxcart in 1851. (Bancroft Library, University of California, Berkeley.) Source: Fritz Wikersheim, "Mexique Californie—char à Boeufs," Bancroft Library, Robert B. Honeyman Jr., Collection of Early Californian and Western American Pictorial Material, University of California, Berkeley, BANC PIC 1963.002:1304:21–ALB.

It is a native village with pretensions to being a town. When someone enters it upon coming from the harbor, there are two or three semicircles of adobe buildings with tile roofs on the right-hand side, but mostly in ruins. On the left-hand side there are one or two more semicircles of buildings and some corrals. **[fol. 18r.]** An arcade with wooden pillars, roofed with tiles, stretches along the front, terminating at one end at a two-story building,[62] whose balcony has a wooden railing—if one can call three or four poles stuck together, now falling down, such a thing—and at the other end at the church, which also is made of adobe and roofed with tiles.

Its façade has columns attached to the wall, about the height of the door, crowned by capitals and cornices. On top of these pillars are more pillars, which go up almost to the roof-tiles; and between them are three bells that are rung from the outside by ropes and hang as if stuck to the wall.

The whole building is without whitewash, or even plastering.[63]

The interior offers quite a singular contrast. It is a sort of gallery,[64] long and dark, without paintings or ornaments on its bare walls, which are simply whitewashed. On the left-hand side is a small room that serves as the baptistry, painted and decent looking. On the right-hand side is a confessional; and down at its far end is the main altar, gilded in the old style, but decent looking and with a nice image of the Immaculate Conception. Near it, on the right- and left-hand sides, are two smaller altars, quite ugly ones. The floor in half the church [**fol. 18v.**] is made of loose boards, and the other half, nearest the door, has no floor at all.

Beside the far door there are attached living quarters, where the priest stays. The other quarters, which follow and form the rest of the Mission's buildings, are those where the Alcalde and two or three other private persons live.[65]

The climate is the same as that of the Harbor: windy and cold.

The inhabitants of the Mission are all natives of the country,[66] without any admixture of Americans, who dwell only around the harbor. There are among them some half-civilized Indians, and they have a singular appearance: a copper-colored face, more or less dark, in a few of them shading to black; a round countenance; a small, slightly snub nose; little, lively eyes; very prominent cheekbones; and lank black hair, which they wear very long, wound around their heads with a red or yellow cloth, kerchief, or head band with which they adorn themselves. They do not wear hats, and the remainder of their clothes are trousers and a jacket or duster. Some wear nothing but a shirt.[67]

Today we left the Mission with our cart at 4 in the afternoon; and we traveled a little more than a league, for the oxen could not go any further with the cart than a small rise, where it was necessary for us [**fol. 19r.**] to remain for the night.

With the canvas tent, we protected ourselves a bit, next to the cart, from the awful wind that was blowing. We lit a fire, made chocolate,[68] and after having drunk it, laid ourselves down to sleep on the green grass.

The 26th.

Today we went to a little ranch nearby, to obtain in any way possible another yoke of oxen so that we could continue our journey. With great pains, we managed to get the old rancher to rent us a pair, after he had gone to drop his wife off at a creek to do laundry, where he took her in a big cart.

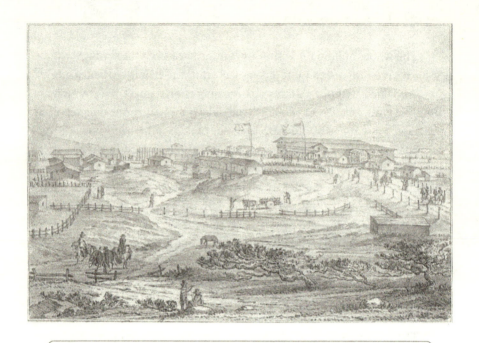

FIGURE 18. Mission Dolores, shown here in a lithograph by Quirot & Co. of San Francisco in the 1850s, was a little more than two miles from what is now downtown San Francisco. Note the oxcart, center. (Wikimedia Commons.) Source: "Mission Dolores," lithograph by Quirot & Co., http://www.fortwiki.com/File:Mission_Dolores_CA_LOC_32185v.jpg.

With their help, we managed all the difficult inclines that there were in this road, along which the old rancher accompanied us. We often had to give him swigs of mescal so that he would not take back his oxen too soon[69]; and so he helped us sufficiently and did not want any payment from us. Nonetheless, we presented him with a bottle of mescal and a pencil case, all of which left him very happy.

We traveled another short distance, as far as the oxen could go. I stayed with the cart, and Ygnacio and Puga continued to the Rancho Buri Buri to see if they might get some oxen.[70]

I lit a fire, made chocolate, drank it, and lay down [**fol. 19v.**] to sleep on my rain leathers, without protecting myself at all from the incredibly strong wind that was blowing. Moreover, there were lots of centipedes.

Today, we traveled through fields carpeted with yellow flowers interspersed with white ones and sunflowers, which presented very lovely views and gave one to understand that the land was very fertile.

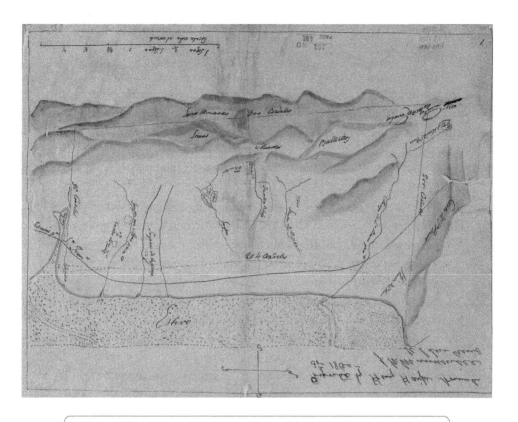

FIGURE 19. Diseño (plan) of Rancho Buri Buri in San Mateo County in 1860. Justo Veytia traveled south from San Francisco—from right to left on this map—along what is labeled here (bottom left) the *Camino p[ar]a S[a]n Fran[cis]co* (Road to San Francisco). (Bancroft Library, University of California, Berkeley.) Source: Diseño del Rancho Buri Buri: San Mateo Co., Calif. Bancroft Library, University of California, Berkeley, United States District Court Land Case Map D-231.

The 27th.

We left in the morning with a yoke of oxen that we bought for $120, and we arrived at the ranch where Ygnacio and Puga had stayed the night before. Then, in the afternoon, we continued our march.

After the sun already had set, we arrived at a wood, where we stayed to sleep, half covered by the tent canvas attached to the cart.

We made a fire to boil some toasted corn meal for atole and to roast meat, on which we dined, leaving for the following day a handsome goose that Ygnacio had shot.

The 28th.

After we had breakfasted on atole and chocolate, we stayed and waited for the hired boys, who had gone to look for the oxen. They arrived quite late, for they had had to go quite a distance. We yoked them up and continued traveling until the afternoon, when we stopped, very tired and sunburned, at a ranch called San Francisquito.[71]

The 29th.

We traveled today without any setback [**fol. 20r.**] whatsoever until 4 in the afternoon, at which point the axle of the cart broke while we were crossing a big irrigation ditch about a league distant from Cantúa's ranch.[72]

It was necessary for Ygnacio to go to the home of a little black fellow whom they called Portugués, near the ranch, to ask for the loan of a cart to move our supplies close to his house. They lent it to us, and in it we moved the supplies there, where we arrived when it was already nighttime, as we had been delayed by two bad spots in the road that the oxen got up only with great effort. We stopped at the edge of a creek overhung with trees along its banks, where we slept in the same fashion as we had on the previous night.

The 30th.

We put up the field tent, and Ygnacio and I went down to the river to wash the dirty clothes we had. We spent the whole day at this, and in hunting some partridge,[73] which we ate along with the handsome goose.

May 1st.

Today it fell to Ygnacio to cook. They gave us milk at Cantúa's ranch, and he made toasted-corn atole with it.

The family came from the ranch to visit us in our tent. We received them with chocolate, sweets, and other trifles, with which they were quite pleased; and afterward they gave us cheese, pudding, meat seasoned with chili pepper, rice, chicken, and flour tortillas. We got along quite well with all the ranch's people, and there we obtained an axle with a wheel, for 5 pesos, with which to replace the axle of our cart.

Of all the ranches we have passed, this one is the largest and the one on which one sees the greatest industriousness. All the others are smaller, some consisting of a single house or shack made of wood, with very few inhabitants and those very lazy ones. They did not work or cultivate the soil, except to sow a *fanega* of wheat, or only half of one.[74] They live off the proceeds of stock raising and of the milk they sell. On this ranch, there are some wooden buildings, a flour mill, and a herd of 16 milch cows.

The 2nd.

Today we worked on adjusting the axle and making our things ready to leave tomorrow.

Two Yankee sailors, deserters from a frigate, who had joined us along the road two days earlier, left today with some other comrades of theirs who passed through here. In the middle of the night, when we already were in bed, one of them came back, asking by means of signs for us to let him sleep inside the tent. As this arrival came at an unusual time, we thought he might [fol. 21r.] have other people with him and have evil intentions. But it was not so, for he simply went to sleep. The following day, his companion also showed up, doubtless having repented of having left us, given the hardships they would undergo without provisions and without any blankets to sleep in.

The 3rd.

Today Ygnacio shot 7 partridge and a dove,[75] as fat as chickens; he cooked them with a sauce he improvised, which we all enjoyed. We also ate a fine dish of rice and milk, and some refried beans that I made. In our situation, this meal was sumptuous, since only with difficulty will we come to enjoy these delicious dishes again, worthy of being served even at the tables of the wealthy.

Around 4 in the afternoon, we yoked up the oxen and traveled with our cart until the sun went down. We came to another ranch, called Agua Caliente, where we pitched the tent and slept.[76]

The 4th.

Today we came to the San Antonio ranch, where we slept after having dined on fresh meat.[77]

The 5th.

Today we traveled until 4 in the afternoon, and we stopped at the entrance to a canyon between hills covered with grass but without trees.

The ranch of Las Positas, which we passed through today, is the last one that may be encountered along this road.[78]

[fol. 21v.] Based on what I have observed until now, the manners and customs of the Californios are simple, but at the same time offensive to us.[79] They are boastful, coarse, lazy, and not at all industrious, thanks to the richness of the country, the abundance of livestock, and the limitations of their diet, as meat is the principal item in it. They like gambling and drunkenness; and although some of them are hospitable, most are self-interested and neither do nor give anything free of charge. This is diametrically opposed to what used to happen in the old days at the Missions, they say; for in those days the metallic riches of the country were unknown, and a stranger could journey throughout California and stay in one place or another however long he wished, without having to spend a peso.[80]

On all the ranches there are some Indians who were baptized at the old Missions, and they look the same as the ones I described earlier.

Mission San José, which we passed yesterday, and which I had forgotten to mention, is in ruins, more or less as badly as Mission Dolores. The church is a little better, and in the town there are some orchards of pears and apples; but one finds no foodstuffs or provisions of any sort there.

[fol. 22r.] The 6th.

Today we traveled about 4 leagues along a road made through a mountain range, with no more vegetation than short grass in some places and moss in others; and afterward, about another two leagues through an immense, dry plain. We stopped near a small lake, where a terrible wind blew upon us from afternoon on.[81]

The road was arduous, due to the heat of the sun and our thirst, for we were not carrying a drop of water; nor did we encounter any along the whole road, or any shade. I sat down in what shade a large rock gave, to write down yesterday's events.

How many thoughts and reflections come to mind at the sight of those plains, of that road to happiness or misfortune . . . ![82]

Now it is night, and I am in the field tent, writing these lines by the light of a single candle. The wind roars strongly, and its voice inspires my imagination to sad and melancholy notions. The moonbeams that shine amid the heavens, sliding softly across the waters of the lake, at times pass between the reeds where the duck, goose, and frog sleep tranquilly! Everything sleeps; only I am awake! My fevered fancy presents me, without ceasing, with images, [fol. 22v.] sometimes amusing, other times horrible.

My desire is to find myself at the mines, to try my luck. Already I

FIGURE 20. Mission San José. In May 1849, Justo Veytia and his companions passed by Mission San José on their way to the Gold Country. He described it as being in rather dilapidated condition. Bavarian-born artist Edward Vischer drew the mission in 1866. (Bancroft Library, University of California.) Source: Edward Vischer, "Sketch of the Church and Buildings of the Mission of San Jose, Upper California," Bancroft Library, The Mission Era: California Under Spain and Mexico and Reminiscences Collection, University of California, Berkeley, BANC PIC 19xx.039.28–ALB.

imagine myself back among my family and friends. Perhaps a time will come when this will happen, and may it be in favorable, fortunate circumstances!

The 7th.

A day of work. We traveled across the rest of the plain, until we arrived at one of the branches of the San Joaquín River.[83]

A little before arriving at it, it became necessary to bare our feet and legs, due to the muddiness of the footing.

On the riverbank, we unloaded the cart, which afterward crossed empty, and the supplies came across partly on a mule and partly on our backs.

I stripped myself naked here and was plunged into water up to my stomach, loaded down with a bale of supplies to carry it over to the other side. When Ygnacio went across with the first load, which was our bedclothes, he slipped as he was coming out and fell into the water and got wet. But in the end, after concluding these labors, we rested for a while in the shade of a tree, where we ate. In the afternoon, we loaded the cart again and traveled to the shore of another small lake, right next to which we stayed to sleep.

The 8th.

I am at the edge of the San Joaquín River. [**fol. 23r.**] After having shifted the most important part of the supplies onto four mules, which a Sonoran had leased to us,[84] we hung the baggage and the rest of the light items on the rails of the cart. We traveled about a league, through pools and mires, in some of which the water came up to our chests. Of course, we went along completely naked, so as not to soak our clothes.

Various other people, on foot and on horseback, were following the same road we were, and in the same Adamic attire. This scene was peculiar, grotesque, and ridiculous at the same time: seeing people of different colors, alone or at every step urging along the pack animals they had brought and pulling them out of the mud. This was so general that nobody took notice of the indecency of his appearance or paid any attention to "What would people say?"

Oh, gold, how much you cost! How many sufferings must be undergone to attain you! *Will* I attain you . . . ?[85]

The 9th.

On the shore of a tiny lake, whose still waters reflect the light of the moon that is rising majestically above the horizon, I am beneath the cart, covered by the tent canvas, resting from the fatigues of the day, which have been excessive.

At midday we crossed the river on a large raft that was pulled across on a cable: supplies, oxen, and cart. Afterward, we had to get into the freezing water [**fol. 23v.**] up to our necks, to work the raft free of a log on which it had stuck. Then it became necessary to move the supplies from that place to another, dry place, by getting through a bog half covered by bushes, into which everyone inevitably fell at every step, even when not loaded down. From there, we went a little further, on a track we laid using the side-rails of the cart; and it took three trips, because we could not carry everything across two more big ditches full of water that were along the way without its getting wet.

We finished when it was already nighttime. For that reason, we scarcely had time to make chocolate, and dined on that alone, so as to surrender ourselves to the rest so badly needed at this point.

Weary, covered in mud, pricked with thorns, and scraped up, nothing sustained me through all these ills but hope and the thought of a quick and happy outcome.

The 11th.

Beneath the shade of a leafy oak tree, amid a thick forest perhaps inhabited at some previous time by savages, I find myself writing these lines. What a lively scene to be described by a poet!

The sun is arriving at the halfway point of its journey, on a quiet, restful day! Everything is silent, and no more sound is heard than the light murmur that the trees' leaves make, softly **[fol. 24r.]** swayed by the wind, seeming like the faraway sound of running water.

The birds seem to be enjoying themselves amid the beauty of this wood formed by the Creator's hand. They sing continuously, hopping joyfully about in the boughs of the trees. The grackle screeches, the sparrows twitter, the dove and the partridge coo and sing,[86] a thousand other sorts of little birds trill in diverse manners, greeting with their songs the return of happy Springtime and forming a poetic and enchanting orchestra. But above all these tiny, innocent, unwary birds that sing so carefree moves another, which, swaying about on the winds and sometimes hovering upon them, sets a trap for its prey and awaits the opportune moment to hurl itself upon it: this is the predatory falcon.

In similar fashion do misfortunes and unhappy fates come to the careless man, falling upon him like the falcon upon its prey.

Yesterday, the 10th, after we had gone in a rowboat across the small lake on whose shores we had stopped, we swam the oxen across and then the cart, hauled by ropes. When everything was on the other side, we loaded up again and traveled beneath a burning sun, some three leagues, until four in the afternoon, the hour at which we arrived at this place, known by the name French Camp.[87] We have not been able to leave this place today because we have to wait for our companion who went to Stockton, a short distance **[fol. 24v.]** from here, to see if certain provisions belonging to us have had arrived there.[88]

I am surrounded by sleeping men, and the sight of them communicates

I know not what heaviness to my own eyelids, which keep falling shut. I feel strongly impelled to imitate them, and the efforts I make to hold Morpheus off are useless. . . .[89]

My thoughts are dazed, my senses grow sluggish. All that a brief time ago seemed to me poetic and enchanting now means little to me. All the sounds that previously made harmony in my hearing are nothing but a confused noise that the wind bears up on its wings . . . my head nods . . . my eyes shut at last . . . and my hands, no longer able to grasp the pen between their fingers . . . let it fall weakly. . . .[90]

The 13th [*sic*].[91]

The sun rises up, radiant on the horizon, gilding with its rays the crowns of the gigantic oaks in a beautiful forest blanketing the green and lovely fields; a light mist, produced by the evaporation of the abundant dew that fell during the night, moistly rises, creating a diaphanous cloud among the tree trunks. In the middle of this grove, a noiseless rivulet sends on its quiet, crystalline waters. **[fol. 25r.]** At its edge may be viewed the following scene:

Near a site where a cart stands in the water, one may see bales of supplies strewn upon the ground. Further on, next to a campfire, some men are making breakfast and others are eating it. Another man reclines upon the grass, with his gaze fixed on a shrub, on whose branches hang some articles of wet clothing. One sees another man sitting on a crate, whose torn pantaloon falls onto a broken shoe poorly mended with a piece of leather.[92] He has a paper in his hand and writes upon it, on another crate, where one may see some chocolate stains and a wax candle broken in pieces. . . .[93]

We slept in the open last night, since there was scarcely time to drink chocolate and rest from the afternoon's fatigues, which were many, after having traveled about 4 leagues to get here—and there is still another river we have to cross.

As soon as we had eaten, we set to the task, adopting the following method, or way, as the only one that could be managed under the circumstances. We laid a track made out of the cart rails. Onto this, we tossed three or four bales of supplies, and we conveyed the cart across on them, carried between two men, Ygnacio and Rico, **[fol. 25v.]** with the wheels held up between them on either side so that it would not tip over, and the other men pulling it to the opposite bank with a rope. It is easy to conceive the effort that this cost us: Climb up and get the bundles down from the cart, and walk (naked, of course) sunk in freezing water up to our necks, suffering from the restricted motion and from the multitude of mosquitoes and other insects that bit us all over our bodies when we emerged.[94] At the end of two hours of this coming and going, we finished, when it was already nighttime, worn out with fatigue and covered in bumps that itched unbearably. But in the end—they say that tomorrow we will reach the placers, that we have arrived at the desired goal of this wretched journey, where another period, one of brilliant prospects, should begin. We will see if my hopes will be in vain, and whether my labors will be rewarded or not.

The 13th.

We stayed here the entire day, because we found that one yoke of our oxen had strayed, and it was necessary to go looking for them.

This place, or arroyo, is known by the name Arroyo de las Calaveras.[95]

The 14th.

Today, at last, they left to look for the oxen, which had not reappeared, leaving me behind with a friend, the son of a Mexican who came here with the Colony of 1834.[96] This Mexican, his sons, [**fol. 26r.**] and some others have been traveling with us, or rather we with them, for 3 or 4 days; and as they also have carts, oxen, and loose cattle and horses they are driving, they seem to me like a wandering tribe that travels through immense deserts, looking for grazing for their herds.[97]

We traveled the entire day through a large wood where there was a multitude of mosquitoes that never stopped biting. We could not find our oxen, and we went to catch up with our companions, whom we found stopped near a river, where we also stopped. Profit is anticipated!

The 15th.

Today, before departing, it was necessary to treat me for a rash on my anus, caused by the ivy (a caustic plant),[98] for I had a lot of it, and there is a lot of it hereabouts. For a while now, I have not been able to sit a horse; and yesterday, when we were looking for the oxen, we ran about a lot. My rash became very red and inflamed.

The remedy I applied to myself was hot water. I went into a thicket; bare-arsed and with my pantaloons off, I received drenches of hot water at Ygnacio's hands, which he administered to me with a rag. And as I was there with my buttocks wholly exposed, the mosquitoes never stopped biting me, not for a moment. Once the operation was concluded, we departed and traveled about 5 leagues.

I find myself writing these lines by the light of a fire, in the middle of an uninhabited, shadowy, frightening forest, from which it seems to me [**fol. 26v.**] that at any moment I will see a numerous tribe of savages emerge, a forest watered by a river whose icy waters come down from snow-covered mountains.

On the opposite bank of the river a person may see two huts inhabited by Indians, who have fled. Throughout these woods are a multitude of antelope and deer of enormous size,[99] and a herd of wild horses, which the natives of the country call *mustangs*.[100]

The 16th.

We traveled little today because the road was so onerous, as it is all hills covered by very overgrown weeds, among which there are some aromatic plants that give off a sweet, agreeable scent when they are crushed beneath the wheels of the carts. We continued along the whole plain beside the river, which is called Vega de los Moquelamos,[101] where we made the first attempt,[102] or essay, to find gold in earth taken from the riverbank. It produced very small bits of gold, and only a tiny amount; so we decided to cross the river tomorrow, to go to some other of the other placers hereabouts.

The 17th.

We crossed the river on a raft made of tule reeds[103] that was there and brought the empty carts across by hauling them with a cable. We finished when it was already late, so we are staying here to pass the night. On the following day, the following scene was played out:

The 18th.

It was a cloudy, gloomy day. At the [**fol. 27r.**] river's edge, two carts were to be seen on the slope of a hill. Not far from them, two great fires were lit, and around them were many men holding various pieces of clothing in their hands, which they were drying at the fires.

"Friend," one said, "how did it go with you?"

"Absolutely miserable," replied the other. "Can't you see that not even my shirt stayed dry? And you—how long were you in the downpour?"

"Until water was running under me. Can't you see what a state my guns are in?"

"Well," said another man, drying his shoes out, "I tried, as soon as I woke up, to arrange myself so that I would not get too wet. But then I realized I was already soaking wet, so I stayed put, for I thought it would be even worse to move."

From these dialogues, a person will arrive at the understanding that during the night a heavy rain had drenched us, without leaving a dry stitch on our bodies.

We departed a bit late, due to this delay, and we traveled little, through mountains made of calcined stones and multicolored rubble. During our passage, we encountered some Indians, of both sexes, who were gathering certain plants and roots on which they feed themselves. Some of the women were adorned with necklaces of shells and glass beads, and they wore short skirts,[104] their bosoms covered by a sort of very coarse woolen shawl[105]; [**fol. 27v.**] and each had on her back a basket shaped like a drum ending in a point, made of sticks and a slender, strong kind of tule reed, into which they gather the seeds and roots.

Upon arriving at the bank of a creek where we stopped, we saw some young Indian men from a village nearby, dressed in different ways. Some had shirts of red wool, others military uniforms that they had bought from those who passed by, but most had ordinary clothing: pantaloons, shirts, and sashes, both old and new. But all were hatless, with a string, cloth, or red kerchief around their heads.

The 19th.

Today we were guided by an Indian wearing a captain's uniform to a creek where he told us there was a lot of gold. As a matter of fact, there were some Indians there, who were in the water, taking something out. But there was no grazing for the animals, and our companions thought it better to go somewhere else.

We traded rice and dried meat for gold with the Indians here. They all wore clothing, but it was easy to discern their old habits of nudity, in the manner in which they wore it and by their lack of concern about people they saw naked.[106]

Ygnacio and I went to sleep in company with two other men, [**fol. 28r.**] on the opposite bank of the river, our bodies serving as the gate to a corral where the oxen were penned up—as much because we had nothing with which to close it up as to take care of the oxen that night. On going to bed, I didn't give much for my head's chances, which I thought would be flattened by some ox's hooves before morning; but thanks be to God, nothing happened to me, and I am safe and sound, and ready to follow the thread of my adventures until St. John gives me the thumbs down.[107]

The 20th.

We spent[108] all day prospecting, but our attempts yielded no satisfactory result. Consequently, we decided to go back to another place nearby, which they say is better; and there is good grazing there for the animals.

The 21st.

We traveled about three leagues, as far as a little stream, where we set ourselves up to work.

The 22nd.

The results have not corresponded to our hopes. We worked all morning and part of the afternoon, and we got barely 3 drams of gold.[109] Our puny knowledge of the art of gold panning had too a great influence on the results, for some of our fellow prospectors got more than we did.[110] We decided to make a small sluice to wash the dirt,[111] for washing it in a pan takes more time, and gold is lost when a person doesn't know how to use that technique.

The 25th.

Three days have passed, which we employed in constructing a sort of sluice out of planks from crates that we took apart.[112] Today, in the afternoon, we [fol. 28v.] tried it out by washing some dirt. The result was good, as far as the device itself was concerned, but bad insofar as the dirt, for out of 6 arrobas of dirt,[113] we barely got two pesos' worth of gold.

Yesterday I found myself rather ill with some kind of fever, but thanks to a sudorific cordial that Ygnacio administered to me last night, I awoke today almost well.[114] This illness, without a doubt, was the consequence of having wet feet and of the fierceness of the sun, which already begins to embrace us.

The 28th.

Until today, all the prospecting and hard work we have done have produced the same result for us, so we have decided to look for another, better site. Therefore we broke camp in the morning today and began our journey into the Sierra, during which we underwent innumerable hardships in getting the carts through some places. Traveling through rocky, rugged mountains, we had at any given moment to help the oxen up inclines with ropes or keep the cart from overturning in places and move obstacles out of its path at every step, moving rocks or felling trees, and ceaselessly goading and encouraging the oxen with shouts.[115]

The day ended, and night found us still engaged in these labors. Fortunately, the moon poured forth a beautiful light, and with its aid we arrived, around 8:00, at the edge of a stream. Beneath **[fol. 29r.]** a leafy tree we lit a fire and made atole from toasted corn flour, which we had as our only nourishment that day since breakfast, which had been coffee with milk.

June 7.

Nothing special has happened in the time that has passed since my last entry.[116] For three or four days, I have been going with some other men to work a stream about a league away from our camp and coming back at night to eat. I have gotten very little or no benefit from this, and my efforts have been useless.

How many times, looking upon the fruitlessness of my labors, have I nearly lost hope and become discouraged, making my situation then utterly depressing to me! O adverse fortune! Will you not change someday? Must you always torment me?

Today! Corpus Christi Day![117] Oh! This day has been one of anguish and torments for me! The recollection of past celebrations of this day has fallen upon my memory, devastating and relentless! Comparisons of my past and my present situations also have descended upon my imagination, making my situation extremely agonizing and unhappy. Indeed, the difference is immense, and my heart is oppressed on contemplating it. How could it be the same for a person to live in his own country, among his family and friends, without so much worrying over how to survive, enjoying the domestic delights and comforts and the **[fol. 29v.]** advantages that society offers—and then for him to live in a strange, faraway land, in the midst of an uninhabited mountain range, subject to hard, painful labor and exposed to a thousand dangers? Is the life of the shopkeeper the same as that of the laborer? Is standing behind the counter of a shop the same as being in a field with a pick in his hand, digging the earth in the heat of the sun, or with his feet under water?[118] Is eating various delicious foods at a regular

FIGURE 21. *Los Tomadores de té* (The Tea Drinkers) in Mexico. On the Corpus Christi holiday in 1849, Justo Veytia waxed nostalgic for the comforts of urban Guadalajara, compared to his rough life in the gold fields of California. (*El Museo Mexicano,* 1845.) Source: *El Museo Mexicano,* 2nd ser., 1 (1845), unnumbered plate between pp. 476–77.

hour the same as eating only salt meat, rice, and beans with hardtack or a flour tortilla[119]—and all this prepared by himself? Is it the same to go to sleep beneath a roof, in a soft bed, as to sleep on the ground without any shelter but a field tent, and not even always that? And why this difference? Why has he left that agreeable, peaceful life and taken up this other one, turbulent, arduous, and filled with dangers? To look for gold—the very gold which we believed we would find so easily, but which we have scarcely seen. And will we ever see it? Who knows!

The 11th.

Today we broke camp and went deep into the north, to a site not far distant from the summits of the mountains designated on the map by the name of 'Snowy,'[120] where Arana's company had gone the day before yesterday to look at a placer that seemed richer to us, as far as we could see.[121]

We traveled the entire day, along a road rough [**fol. 30r.**] and difficult, and arrived when it was already evening, exhausted, broken down, and soaked by a rain that began to fall on us shortly before we arrived, and which became progressively heavier without giving us a chance to pitch our field tent. Expecting that it would stop, we stayed under some tree branches that hardly kept it off of us,[122] until, seeing that it was late and the rain was not stopping, Puga for once pitched the tent, where we soon found better refuge and went to sleep, <u>without supper</u>.[123]

The 12th.

Today I went with my companions to cut wood to make a corral in which we could keep the oxen and horses, and thus save them from the rapacity of a tribe of thieving Indians (like all Indians), who, led by their chief, Polo, made incursions into these placers at night to steal from the horse herds.[124]

The 14th.

"Up here, even a pig chitlin is worth a dollar."[125] The author of this maxim—who is a Mexican who came here 14 years ago as a settler[126]—today sold another man <u>eight feathers</u> from a hen, the only one left from the hens he brought, for <u>three pesos</u>,[127] which he was paid in gold. The fellow who bought them needed the feathers to treat a sick mule, so he said. . . .[128] That's what a mining camp is like! There are many people who pay excessive prices for some things, due to their scarcity; and others who exchange the gold they mine for silver coin, at around 5 pesos per ounce, when they need money with which to gamble—this being a [**fol. 30v.**] very common vice in the placers, at which even those people play who have never seen a deck of cards before.

Yesterday I went back to observe the efforts of some prospectors who were working here. They all are finding gold, and some have managed to get up to two pounds in one day. In view of this, we decided to stay here to work.

The 18th.

We have worked hard, but as bad luck follows us wherever we go, we have not gotten anything, and our hopes have dissipated entirely. We opened up a large digging, of the best dirt, and washed <u>two cartloads</u> of it, but we got no more than <u>four pesos</u> out of it.[129] Once again I will talk about what bad luck is: it's working without result in a place where nearly everybody else gets something, and digging precisely in a spot where there is nothing, even though all the rules say there should be. And what is the remedy for this? Nothing more than 'Patience, and shuffle the cards.'[130]

The 21st.

Today I went out to work with one of my companions, at a placer about a league away. I got up on his horse's crupper.[131] I took my pick in one hand and my gold-washing pan in the other—and when the horse was made to walk, he gave a violent buck, either because he was startled or because something stung him,[132] which threw me about three yards,[133] and I landed on my back. I got up immediately, without feeling anything wrong; but a little while later I could not even breathe because of the exceedingly strong pains that I felt in my back.

[fol. 31r.] The 25th.

It has been two days since I was able to work again, and in those days I have gotten about 14 pesos' worth of gold.

Today, when it was already very late, Arana arrived from Sacramento[134]; he had gone there with Ygnacio to buy some provisions we were lacking. He asked if Ygnacio had not arrived yet, for Ygnacio had departed much earlier than he had.[135] This question surprised me very much, and I immediately feared that Ygnacio must have lost his way and was at risk of perishing at the hands of the savages. I got ready to go look for him early the next day.

The 26th.

Arana and I had traveled about half a league, when we came upon Ygnacio, who was coming along with his two pack animals loaded down with provisions.

Because of certain superstitions of Arana's, which Ygnacio had made fun of, Arana had not wanted to leave Sacramento on the day Ygnacio did; so Ygnacio had loaded up his pack animals and gone on his way alone. He had not traveled far before he lost his way. He tried to correct his course, but that was not possible for him because he was traveling among rugged hills, full of trails, and he had to go now off to one side and now off to the other, to drive the pack animals along, which had become separated from each other. After four hours traveling through the mountains without seeing anyone, except a naked Indian as black as soot, he ended up in the same place he had left that morning!¹³⁶ He began to travel once more, uncertain and almost convinced he would lose his way again, and in fact that is what happened. He got lost again, and at **[fol. 31v.]** times he believed he had found his way, and thanked God; but his delusion disappeared when he saw that the path he was following was going to lose him on the slope of a mountain or in the depths of a canyon.

By the time it was growing dark, he decided to find a place where there was grazing and water for the animals and to stay there for the night. But without meaning to, he came upon an Indian village, which he could not then leave because the pack animals were very tired. He placed himself in the hands of Providence and unloaded them among the Indians.

To please them and win their good will, he gave them a small amount of hardtack and another of flour, with which they immediately made tortillas and gave some to him. After he had stayed with them for a while, he went away to sleep beneath the tree where he had put his load of supplies, in considerable fear that they would rob him of them by killing him. But thanks be to Heaven, nothing happened to him.

The following day, the pack animals, which an Indian had gone to fetch, did not turn up. Ygnacio could not go to look for them, so he begged the chief to get them. The chief left, but he brought back only one of them, saying that the other had not turned up. After repeated requests, he brought the other one. Ygnacio immediately saddled his horse and loaded up the pack animals, helped by the Indians. After making many **[fol. 32 r.]** promises and requests, he reached an agreement with the chief, giving him a pair of shoes, to guide him to the road to the placer. Fortunately the chief knew it, as he had gone there other times to buy provisions. The chief there had seen the carts that we had with us. During all this, Ygnacio had had to make himself understood by means of signs, as the chief knew very little Spanish.¹³⁷

So Ygnacio followed the chief, accompanied by other Indians armed with their bows and arrows. Going through hills, canyons, and streambeds, they arrived at the cart road, where the Indians stopped and did not wish to accompany him further. They asked him for hardtack, which he gave them. Then he continued on his way alone, until he found us only a short distance away.

July 3.

Today we broke camp to move further on. Luck has shown herself contrary till now, and we are going in pursuit of her. We traveled a short way, to the bank of a stream.

The 5th.

Yesterday we did not travel, as we had to wait for our companions, who were detained in making a new axle for their cart.

Today Ygnacio went with Marcos Arana to Arroyo Seco to collect ten pesos owed him,[138] and to see Don Ricardo Jones, to inquire if he might find employment for the two of them in the diving bell business.[139]

[fol. 32v.] I came with the cart. Here was where my labors were greatly increased—because only Rico and I were taking care of unloading the cart and harnessing the oxen, as Puga was no use to us—with this annoying result: as we were going up hills and passing through mires, we lost a pack with about two arrobas of flour,[140] a mining pick that a friend had given us, and some other trifles. We didn't know where we had lost them, so of course they stayed lost.

Ygnacio arrived when it was already late, without having found Jones. He went for wool but came back shorn,[141] for along the way he lost items worth just as much as the $10 he had gone to recover. Patience!

How many times, seeing the adversity of our fate, have I wished to go back to my own country, now not with the vast amounts of gold that, before I came here, I used to plan on getting—which in my mad enthusiasm, in the airy gardens my heated imagination showed to me, seemed so easy to get—but in my present state: poor, but with my health! But that is not possible for me. It is necessary for me to work to achieve this. I need to follow the iron thread of my destiny to see if any part of it is golden, even if it is at the end. In the end, it is necessary to overcome [fol. 33r.] adversity, to have courage and constancy, and to see if, by dint of our labor, we can defeat the bad luck of this whole year, or if death will cut our journey short, preventing us from returning to our native land in any state whatsoever.

The 6th.

Today Ygnacio and Puga have gone to Stockton to buy some provisions that we lack, in company with the Aranas, who are going to Santa Cruz, which is where they live.[142] The mutual sympathy that we had developed during the time that we stayed together has made us miss their company, as if it was natural to have it.

Señor Rico and I have stayed behind, under a tree near an Indian village, to take care of the oxen that remain to us and the cart, along with a few provisions. In the Indian village I obtained a bow and some arrows, with a quiver of tanned leather,[143] in exchange for a gold pan not worth a dime[144]—but which I had not been able to purchase previously for less than $10 cash. Even though I am not carrying any gold, at least I will bear these weapons.

The 9th.

Today Ygnacio and Puga came back.

The 10th.

We loaded up the cart and the horses and made our way to the right bank of the Mokelumne River,[145] whose waters are subsiding and leaving its banks dry, from which some gold is extracted. We arrived, and I believe that from here we will not take another step further with this damned [**fol. 33v.**] cart. I am sick of wandering about, and I want to settle myself somewhere. For even if what gold I find there should not be much, after two or three months I will have enough to get myself to my own country—to Guadalajara, among my family and friends. Oh! These are my constant desires, and my oppressed heart now yearns for nothing else.

The 18th.

Eight days have passed, of which I have used only the last five, because I have had to look after, and look for, oxen and horses. It seems that fortune, wearied of tormenting us, and perhaps defeated by our persistence, is at last yielding us some favor. It seems that it is beginning to smile on me, laying aside its old severity, for already I have gotten about fourteen pesos' worth of gold in a single day.

Today at midday, I went in company with Puga for San Francisco, for he arranged with Ygnacio that that the latter should stay behind with Rico, while I went with Puga, telling Puga that I would go with him back to Guadalajara. But that is not so, for I only will go with him to San Francisco, out of regard for his family; for Puga is losing his mind and is incapable of traveling alone, being such a coward. The only servant he had left now does not want to remain in his employ.[146]

We traveled about four leagues, with one pack animal laden and the other two saddled,[147] and we stayed on the bank of the Mokelumne River.

I also am going [fol. 34r.] to San Francisco to see a friend who has offered to provide us with a less strenuous way of earning money, by transporting fruit from the missions, which he will pay for with money he already has in this country.[148] I am carrying a letter for Ygnacio's mother, to give to Puga when he leaves.

The 19th.

Today, when it was already very late, we arrived in Stockton, with no more incident than having had to travel in the usual way, on foot, because the horse that I am riding scarcely can carry the saddle.

The 23rd.

Today we arrived in San José. Thanks to our acquaintance with a man from Tepic, whom we joined after we left Stockton, we stayed in the porch of a house that Forbes's nephew Wester [*sic*] had rented to sell his Mexican goods.[149]

August 4.

Twelve days have already passed, during which we have stayed in San José. I spent them fixing some saddles, for which Forbes paid me two pesos apiece.[150] Thanks to this aid, yesterday I bought an unbroken mare for three ounces of gold, since I could not find a horse broken to saddle, even for a hundred pesos. Tomorrow I will go to San Francisco to see Arana.

The 6th.

I have returned from San Francisco without finding the friend I was looking for. A useless journey! But it served for me to give that damned mare a fair long workout. Twice she tried to buck me off, but fortunately did not throw me.

[fol. 34v.] Tomorrow—what a difference! Puga is leaving for San Francisco, where he is to take ship for San Blas to return to Guadalajara.

Fortunate man, who will have the satisfaction of clasping his beloved family in his arms! It is not given to me to enjoy this pleasure. How could it be possible, as I have no money and am in a situation where I have no likelihood of getting any?[151] Should I abandon my undertaking without even being compensated for what I have laid out upon this journey, at least? No, for me it is not possible. Yet if I should stay three months longer where I left Ygnacio, I would be left disillusioned, with my body so worn out that it would not be able to endure physical work for a long time; for the work of a prospector[152] is hard and made doubly arduous by the strength of the sun during this season. To have to spend the entire day digging up dirt, or plunged into the water to wash it, to obtain a few grains of the desired gold—for someone who has come so far, for someone who has suffered so much and will suffer more. . . .[153] So tomorrow I, too, am striking out on a different course, for the placers. I will have to spend five days on the road, alone, riding an unbroken horse, to reach them. Along that road, I will not come across more than one town—Stockton—and along the way there are bears and other wild animals. I am, in short, without more provisions than some little containers of hardtack, sugar, tea, and a little tin pot in which to make the tea. I can carry nothing more, as it would add extra baggage, and I already risk **[fol. 35r]** the mare throwing me along the road. But Divine Providence accompanies me, and I trust that nothing bad will happen.

The 11th.

Today in the afternoon, I arrived where Ygnacio had been, without anything having happened to me. Two days ago, though, the mare tried to buck me off, but I stayed on well, as God didn't want me to be thrown. But that same night, I dreamed that I had been thrown and dragged. What a strange thing for me! I rarely dream, but such was the fear the beast instilled in me.

The 12th.

For about 15 days Ygnacio and Rico were feeding an American whose companion, who had a canoe, had left him here alone, ill and abandoned. Even though he says he has a ranch in Napa,[154] that means nothing here, both because it is far away and because he had nobody here from his company. For the 3 days previous, he had taken no nourishment. Even though he had some hardtack with him, he could not eat it. When Ygnacio and Rico saw this for the first time, they brought him something to eat. He could scarcely move, due to the swelling he had in his legs as a consequence of gout. The only shelter he had from the intemperate weather was a lean-to made of branches, into which he barely fit and which really did him no good.

Now that I had arrived and we had a beast of burden, the horse he owned was brought from a nearby ranch, for previously he had not found anyone to bring it to him. We [fol. 35v.] saddled it, made ready, and helped him to mount—which he did, although with great effort—to go to a ranch from which he could be brought to his own home. He seemed very grateful to us; and all the more so should he have been, for the benefits he received were not at the hands of his own countrymen, but rather from Mexicans: from the enemy, it could be said.[155] But with the state this poor man was in, no one could pay attention to his origins, but only to humanity. We had to help him, even had he been a personal enemy—to do good, in short, without considering who he was, according to the Lord's commandment.[156]

The 13th.

Today, in the morning, a Black man informed us that the American had spent the night out in the open, as he had not been able to travel further. As he surely needed aid, Ygnacio decided to go help him get back on his horse (that is, if he was able) and go with him to the ranch. He went with him until he left him at the ranch, some three leagues away—after having helped him get back on the horse, the two or three times the man fell along the way. Ygnacio came back very late, without any misfortune besides two blisters on his feet.[157]

The 14th.

Last night, I was attacked by a strong pain in my side[158]; but fortunately Ygnacio remembered having heard that horse straw, burned and mixed with water, was good for this if drunk. He gave it to me, and I woke up quite relieved.

[fol. 36r.] The 24th.

Ten days have passed without anything notable having occurred. I recovered within two days,[159] but Señor Rico has been very ill, with a high fever.

Today was like a holiday for us, for we had fresh meat and lard from a cow, things that we had been lacking for a long time now, as there was no one who was selling them. We had a good, well-cooked stew, which fortified our feeble stomachs, fed for a number of days only on rice and beans—both items barely cooked—and flour tortillas.

The 25th.

Although I am fed up by everything around me, and the nature of my present situation seems to offer little or no delight to my feelings, wearied and dulled by the force of so many impressions, nevertheless there are moments in which my soul feels naturally inclined to—or, better said, made to face—contemplation, and to view things through this fantastic, divine veil that is called Poetry. Such a thing has befallen me on this occasion. The following scene had made a certain impression upon my mind, but I have not occupied myself with it until now, as I was busy with other things.[160]

It was night! But what a night! Quiet and serene! The sweet zephyrs, passing softly through, refreshed the atmosphere, making the temperature delightful. [fol. 36v.] The new Moon shed its gentle radiance as it descended through the pure blue of a Heaven embroidered with Stars. Amid the silence, there came only the murmur of the waters of the river that snaked in foaming waves through the rocks. They created a sort of mysterious cadence, together with the continuous creaking of the cicadas and the measured, monotonous singing of the frogs. . . .[161] This silence was interrupted from time to time by the noise bottles made, crashing together, the shouts of joy, and the choruses of a band of Sonorans who had been working the opposite bank, whose harmonies, as the wind carried them upon its wings, came in the end to mingle with this concert of Nature. . . . Meanwhile we, under our tent, lay in bed with our heads tied up, as we all had headaches, contemplating in silence this majestic scene: in truth, an interesting one, but a sad one for us, as we had come so far from our homeland.

The slow flight of the bat and other nocturnal birds that flittered around us began to increase the horror of our situation and to cast down our spirits, always inclined under such circumstances to superstition and to seeing fatal portents and ill omens in the simplest of things. . . .[162] [fol. 37r.] At last the singing and the noisy bacchanal ceased in sleep; everything once again was left in peace, and the grave, solemn silence of this night now was disturbed by the voice of no human being. . . .

The 27th.

Today we left the placer, with the intention of staying two months in San José, where we are going. We sold the provisions and tools that we had, for what they gave us, to rid ourselves of encumbrances. Our departure was already late, for the mare we had to carry our baggage started bucking under the load as soon as we put it on her. She threw it off and broke the pack saddle into pieces. So it was necessary to look for somebody who might agree to take her in trade for a trained pack animal that would not do the same thing. We found someone in the end, after a great deal of effort, and we had to give an additional ounce of gold as well, for a very feeble horse, practically dead. But it was necessary, and we set out with him.

The 29th.

Stockton. Today we arrived at this place, where we had the good fortune to buy, for an ounce of gold, a strong, healthy mare to carry the load, for our sorry Rocinante barely got here under it.[163] Tomorrow we will continue our journey to San José, where we are going to look for another way of making a living, another kind of life, less exposed to sickness and other kinds of misadventures. **[fol. 37v.]** Goodbye, placers! Goodbye! maybe forever, for I hope never to see you again—you who have so poorly recompensed my labors and have given me such cruel disappointments; you who have shrunk your gifts to a mere atom of my hopes, and who perhaps would have taken from me the only true treasure I possess, which is my health. Goodbye. . . . Goodbye. . . .

September 3.

Today we arrived in San José, with only the mare, as Rocinante got the colic on us along the road. We could not get him up, so we decided it was best to leave him cast aside there. There goes another profit of four ounces of gold!

It is incredible how much this settlement has grown in such a short time, since I last saw it, even though the buildings are scattered about here and there, some made of adobe, others of wood, and many only tents. It should grow quickly, as a result of the great migration that is happening. Every day people come in, and every day they put up new buildings.

As we had no place to lodge ourselves, we slept up against the wall of a house, where they gave us permission to do so.

FIGURE 22. Diseño (plan) of Rancho Potrero y Rincón de San Pedro Regalado, José Arana's ranch in Santa Cruz. The inset shows a closeup of the Casa de Arana (Arana's house). (Bancroft Library, University of California, Berkeley. Inset by Víctor Zúñiga.) Source: Diseño del Rancho Potrero y Rincon de San Padro Regalado, Calif., Bancroft Library, United States District Court Land Case Map B-1432, University of California, Berkeley, https://oac.cdlib.org/ark:/13030/hb4779n8mr/?layout=metadata&brand=oac4.

Tomorrow I am going to Santa Cruz, which is eleven leagues from here, across the mountains (so they have told me), to see Arana, upon whom I have fixed my old hopes, and whom I went in search of in San Francisco, in vain. [fol. 38r.] When I return, we will see to what we are devoting ourselves or what we may undertake to make some money for ourselves.

The 8th.

Today I came back from Santa Cruz. What an arduous journey! I left San José in the afternoon and spent the night at the foot of the mountains, at a little ranch there.[164] Early the next day, after I had broken my fast, I saddled up. I informed myself thoroughly about the road and mounted up to follow it. All day I journeyed along a hellish path. I had to go on foot on all the uphill stretches, so that my beast would not become exhausted under me. Finally, after many travails, by nightfall I arrived at the Mission,[165] where I found the Aranas, who showed me great affection and made me a guest in their home.

I stayed there for a day, arranging with Don Felipe Arana how I should work in the mountains to make wooden shingles.[166] He assured me that it is very easy. Shingles are quite scarce, so one can earn an ounce of gold a day. He has promised to form a company with us. They also have told me that we can take advantage of an opportunity to lease a sawmill. Therefore I decided to go get Ygnacio and come back to try it. We'll see if this also is piling up gold by the shovelful.[167]

I departed very early yesterday, so that I could reach the ranch where I stayed on the day I left San José,[168] as there is no other shelter along the entire road. But it did not turn out that way, for my mare started to get tired before we had covered half the distance. So I went on foot and led her along behind. I walked something like two leagues, **[fol. 38v.]** and still I could not go a step on the unfortunate mare. Surely it was because the other animals that were at Arana's had not let her eat. The sun had already set, and still I was some two and a half leagues out from the ranch. No matter what I did, I could not make the mare go faster. I coaxed her, I cursed her, I whipped her. Finally I unsaddled her for a bit, so that she could rest. Then I saddled her again, but still she could not go. I decided to load my rain leathers and bedding on my own back and go to the ranch, leaving the mare tethered where there was grazing, with my saddle hidden nearby. But then, considering that it already was night and I was so far away, I could lose my way, stumble over a precipice, or encounter a bear that might tear me to shreds (they are very numerous in those mountains, and I had seen many signs of them). So, after I tethered the mare securely and hid the saddle, I got a kettleful of water from a nearby creek and made a fire. And once the food Arana had given me was warm, I had supper and placed myself in the hands of Providence, lying down to sleep beneath a tree, with no more defense than a pocketknife.

I stopped lying down as soon as the wolves and coyotes began to howl in the depths of the ravines,[169] the sound resonating so loudly in my ears that it made me tremble. But in the end sleep came, to put my spirit at ease until dawn, when I awoke safe and well, which no one would have believed without seeing it. **[fol. 39r.]** With the rest she had gotten that night, the mare now was able to carry the saddle all the way to San José, where I arrived today after noon.

The 11th.

The pilgrimage continues. It seems we are descended from the Hebrew nation and that our destiny is to wander about far from our homeland. Today we are resuming our journey, on foot and leading our humble Rocinante, who does us the favor of bearing upon her skinny back a trunk and a bundle containing our bedding. Thus do we follow the invisible hand of our mischievous destiny, which guides us from adventure to adventure until we stop . . . where? I don't know. Let us go on, and we will find out.

The 14th.

Today, in the morning, after having traveled for two days, we arrived at Mission Santa Cruz. We stopped at Arana's house, which is about a quarter of a league from the Mission. The family is very genial and seems to be the most civilized among all the Californios, who in general are hard to deal with.[170] We arrived hungry because the coyotes had eaten our bread the night before, in the spot where we slept—and at that, they did it twice, because the previous night they also had eaten our meat, right next to our pillows!

The 22nd.

It is a foggy, gloomy morning. The sun's rays—slipping through the **[fol. 39v.]** clouds at times and penetrating the thick foliage of the gigantic pitch pines, or redwoods,[171] whose tops seem to vanish into the clouds—usually reach down to the bottom of a deep ravine covered along its entire length by these and many other trees. Down the middle of the ravine runs a little stream of cold, delicious water. Near this is pitched a field tent, which serves as shelter for four men who are making shingles. We are these men. We arrived yesterday afternoon, and we set ourselves up here to work, after having with much difficulty acquired some tools, borrowed to begin the work. This place is about two leagues from the Mission, where we go to supply ourselves with the necessary provisions.

The 29th.

Until today, we have accomplished nothing, for we wasted our time chopping up a fallen tree that was useless, as it did not split well into shingles. We were working under the direction of Don Felipe Arana, who is the boss—but who, I believe, knows no more about it than I do.[172] Nonetheless, we have been making some benches for stripping the bark off the shingles and getting all the tools ready.

The 30th.
A day of religious ceremony. Yesterday we went to the Mission to watch the ceremony that is celebrated in honor of St. Michael, its patron saint. I attended the Mass, which the priest celebrated with all the solemnity possible in the ruined church of the town. [fol. 40r.] The orchestra was composed of some Indians who sang, accompanied by violins, triangles, a drum, and a base drum, creating a din that almost equalled that of the little cannon they shot off outside from time to time.[173] All the aristocracy of the settlement and its surrounding area attended the Mass; and as soon as they left, they took themselves off to the plaza, where there were two bulls penned up for a bullfight. The bull ring was made of cut poles, so weak and poorly put together that the bull could get out through any place he liked; and the stands for the spectators were no more than the half-collapsed balcony of a nearby house and the roof of another house, atop which there were some women who were hanging onto the roof to keep from sliding off.

They brought in the first bull. They knocked him down and cut off half of each horn; and as soon as they let him up, he ran away, knocking down the poles of the ring on one side. They brought in the other bull, which had been fought before and was experienced; he did not take one step forward unless it was to deal a sure blow. However many horses as they put in front of him, and however many times as they tested him with the light touch of their lance shafts, and however many drunken Indians came into the ring, he shredded them all as easily as if they were so many rabbits, leaving one Indian half dead. In the end, they drove him out of the ring, saving the three other bulls for the second spectacle, in the afternoon—which did not take place because the bulls got out of the plaza.

[fol. 40v.] At night was the dance. It began during the afternoon, in a narrow little room. Let's hear it for the famous dances, in which the manner of asking the ladies to dance is among the most courtly, refined, and polite that could be performed. The man claps his hands before the young lady whom he wishes for his partner, or else shakes a silk neckerchief or handkerchief in front of her. No lady refuses, and she goes immediately to dance. This they do to the rhythm of violins that make the most annoying noises I have ever heard in my life. This is the way most dances in California are held, with the exception of one or two that they hold in San José, Monterey, and other more populated places, where the presence of foreigners makes the people a little more civilized.[174]

Thus closed the day of the most important festival Santa Cruz has, at which—no doubt to increase its solemnity—there was plenty of drunkenness, shouting, and the other things that usually result.

October 1.

Today, in the afternoon, when the sun was nearly down, we returned to the ravine where we were working. As it was evening and the fog that was coming up was very thick, it got dark very quickly, and we got lost in the labyrinth of trails that wander through the many hills. We walked for a long time, going astray by chance, until, weary from so much useless going up and down, [**fol. 41r.**] we resolved to stay under a tree until dawn should come, to look for the road then. So we did, and we spent the night there, wrapped in our blankets, which fortunately we had brought (our only bed), but nearly dead from hunger because we had not breakfasted well or eaten dinner or indeed had supper.

It was a wretched night, but—patience! For we are in California, where we have come to dig up gold by the shovelful.

On the morning of the following day, the 2nd, we continued our journey.[175] We soon found the way and arrived at our house,[176] without finding anything amiss, other than fewer pieces of meat on the pole where they had been. To judge by the signs we saw, the ever-courteous coyotes were the ones who had done us the favor of helping us eat our provisions.

The 6th.

It is night! Murky[177] and frightening! The thick mist that covers the earth contributes to increasing the darkness and horror of the shadowy night. The faint light of the Heavens may be seen only in places through the dense foliage of the thick forest, and to an extent along the narrow path through the ravine. Perhaps it may be made out amid the shadows of the nearest trunks of the massive, gigantic trees, which cover it like the immense columns of a temple. [**fol. 41v.**] Everything around me is terrifying, and the noises that strike my ears are frightening as well. The sinister call of the owl and other strange birds, the constant creaking of a multitude of insects that live in the grasses, the deafening roar of the turbulent waves of the sea—everything, in short, combines to give this night a most horrid and ominous aspect. Next to our field tent burns a small fire, and beside it, by the light of a candle, I write about this scene that I contemplate.

The 10th.

The day before yesterday, I came back from San José with a handsaw I had gone to buy. This journey was very different, for instead of taking the poor, weak mare, I rode one of Arana's horses, a very good one, and in just over half a day I arrived in San José.

Yesterday we busied ourselves with sharpening the saw and fitting it together. But as that did not turn out well, it was necessary to take it to a blacksmith at the Mission so that he might make it ready to use. Ygnacio was given this commission and charge to the smith. They struck a bargain, and he came back. A heavy rain fell during his return trip, but he considered this wetting well worthwhile, both because the saw had been fixed and because he was the bearer of good news. I say "good" because it brought back to us the peace and tranquility that we had enjoyed earlier, without the two little boys Don Felipe's wife had. (She had come to live with her husband here). They gave us **[fol. 42r.]** headaches day and night. Today we were rid of this conflict because the Aranas' brother Marcos sent by Ygnacio to say that he was going to Monterey and would be leaving the house empty if they did not go to take care of it. So she had to leave, and her damned boys with her.[178]

November 10.

It has been raining for a little over a week,[179] and it already seems as if a flood has been announced. The rain is constant, with very few pauses, so that in all this time there scarcely has been a clear, cloudless day, and only one on which we were able to work. Today dawned with rain falling, and we were in the tent when we received a message from the lady owner of the nearest ranch.[180] She said that we should go to her house to stay during the worst of the downpour and that we should bring with us whatever we wished so that it would not get soaked. Due to a mistake by the messenger, we believed that it was an express command, either a party or some matter of business. We got on the road for the aforesaid ranch, about a quarter of a league distant. When we arrived, our feet were thoroughly muddy and our clothes quite soaked.

FIGURE 23. The trees commonly called redwoods (*Sequoia sempervirens*) grow on the California coast, and the closely related species sequoia (*Sequoiadendron giganteum*) grow inland. Working on the Arana ranch in Santa Cruz, Veytia felled redwoods to make boards and shingles. A decade later, a Spanish artist illustrated these "giant trees" near Yosemite, showing scale by placing two human figures at their base. (*El Museo Universal,* April 3, 1864, 108.) Source: Illustration, "Espedicion al Pacífico—Arboles gigantes, la Madre y el Hijo," *El Museo Universal* 8, no. 14 (April 3, 1864), 108; http://www.cervantesvirtual.com/obra/el-museo-universal--315/.

At the lady's first words, we realized that they had gotten the message wrong, and we had come for no particular purpose; but now we were there, and there was no help for it. They had us sit down on some extremely low benches, and then she commanded that a big brazier filled with coals be brought, which she set at our feet—so that we might get warm, she said. Now who would think of drying out soaking wet shoes by the heat of a fire when they're still on someone's feet? Only these people! Discretion made us keep quiet and suffer, even though we knew that it would cause us some harm. But it is the custom of the country. She is a person to whom we owe kindness and favors, and there was nothing for it but to please her; for had we done the opposite, she would have believed that she was being scorned.

It rained the whole day, and we were there the whole day, with the brazier at our feet. When we took our leave in the evening to go back, my legs were paining me and I was numb from having spent so much time sitting, which we did, playing cards with members of the family after eating luncheon. **[fol. 43r.]** So we got our feet soaked again, after having had them heated (a very beneficial thing). But finally we were got free from the torture we had undergone from the low seats and being right next to the fire.

The 29th.

Today we are going to leave the mountains. A week ago,[181] we finished the tree we were working on, which produced 18 thousand shingles—which we have not sold yet because we have not found any merchant.

Now it is time to write an essay on the kind of life we have had during our stay here. I already have said earlier that this place is two leagues from the Mission, where we have to go every 6 or 8 days to supply ourselves with necessary provisions. It is easy to imagine the difficulty of these journeys, and much more so in the present weather. As we have no pack animal here, it is necessary to carry on our own backs the flour, sugar, candles, and other provisions that we have to bring and, under these conditions, traverse steep hills, creeks, and marshes. At the exit from the ravine is the ranch of the lady owner from whom we received, as I have related, much kindness and favor; for, in addition to having allowed us **[fol. 43v.]** to work on her land without any payment whatever for the wood, every time we pass by her house she gives us lunch or supper and loads us down with vegetables that she gives us from her garden. Ygnacio made a bed for her, which she had ordered from him—without taking anything from her, of course—as a way to recompense her in some way for even a part of her many kindnesses.

All this while, we have lived under a field tent that a friend lent us, which does not preserve us entirely from the wet when it rains, because it is fairly worn out. We have made a kitchen next to a tree trunk, in which we three companions take turns cooking—for Arana left off working with us more than a month ago, on the excuse of illness. Many times we have returned from our supply trips to the Mission when it was already nighttime, and some of those times I came back by myself. On those occasions, I imagined myself one of those mysterious characters whom novels portray, dwellers in the wild forests, who sometimes are glimpsed by the last rays of the setting sun, walking with solemn, measured tread along a winding path, with a pensive attitude, and then are lost amid the denseness of the woods.

December 6.

On the 30th of last month, we [**fol. 44r.**] left Santa Cruz for San Francisco, where we have come with the goal of recovering some items that we left when we were here last—for which we were paying $4 a month storage fees—and to see if we could succeed in selling the shingles we had in Santa Cruz.

We stopped at Mission Dolores, at the home of a fellow countryman,[182] whence we went on foot to San Francisco.

In the course of this journey, I had some difficulties that tended to distract me from the pleasant prospect of the road, which runs entirely along the coast without leaving the seashore, which presents varied and majestic scenes. The constant roar of the turbulent waves that, crashing into the cliffs, eat away at them and destroy them, forming in some places archways or pyramids that stand alone amid the waters and are assaulted ceaselessly by the waves that dash against them, groaning, and fall back, foamy and as white as if they were made of silver.[183] Never had I seen so beautiful a horizon as the one that presented itself to my view on the first day.[184] The sun seemed to sink into the waters, and its dying rays, reflected in the [**fol. 44v.**] atmosphere, gave it a brilliant purple hue. And this immense horizon, this vault, in the reaches of which I believed I saw its great Creator appear surrounded by glory, became lost in the immensity of space, in which my vision wandered, lost, from one side to another without being able to tear itself away from that grandiose and magnificent scene.[185]

On this day I traveled on foot for a while, with Arana carrying my saddle on his horse's crupper, for we had encountered a friend of his, who hired a horse from us for $5 to go to a ranch where he kept his own animals—which was fifteen leagues away—from which he was to loan me one of his beasts. Ygnacio went on foot a day before to the same ranch where we were keeping the mare and, riding her bareback, went to San Francisco.

Two days were the most trying of this expedition.[186] The second day on the road, one has to pass along the beach very near the water, and this can be done only when the tide is low. The day we passed through, the surf was fairly choppy. Both Arana and I were unfamiliar with the route. Thus it was that, when we got onto the beach, it seemed to us that it would be all right, for even when [fol. 45r.] a very large wave came, it hardly reached the horses' hooves.[187] In this fashion, we had traveled some 300 yards, with two sections made very difficult by rocks, when the sea, now very turbulent, began to wash over us as high as our saddle-pommels. We did not know which way to turn. As for going back, the danger was obvious, for the rocks already were covered by the tide, and we could no longer see the fissures in them. Accordingly, we decided to press on, to look for some place where we could climb up off the beach, as the waves had us pinned up against a fairly high cliff. So we went on, and we traveled some 200 yards, until we found a path on which we climbed up.[188] As soon as we were safe, we stripped ourselves completely naked to dry our clothes; for the waves had rolled us over three times, horses and all, so it was necessary to dismount and take everything out to dry. We had left at ten o'clock in the morning, and by the time we had finished laying out our clothes and saddles to dry, we sat down naked on the grass to have lunch. Also, the food we were carrying was thoroughly soaked.

That day, we arrived at the ranch, where we waited for Ygnacio, and we changed our clothes, to be able to leave together the next day. But that was not to be, because Ygnacio had gone ahead with three other companions. So I left afterward with Arana. The animal that [fol. 45v.] they loaned me was a stallion, quite stout and hard to handle. About three leagues further along the road, my companion took it into his head to make some strange noises at the stallion with his rain leathers.[189] This spooked the horse, and he started running with a will. I tried to get him under control, but seeing that this was impossible, and that the reins were very weak, I threw myself off and let him go. Arana, who was not very far away, immediately went in pursuit of him, telling me that I should wait for him at this same place, so we might not lose each other. My patience was all used up, and hunger afflicted me. But it was necessary for me to stay there, as I was not very sure of finding the ranch from which we had started, and that would have been even worse.

As soon as it grew dark, I lost all hope that he would return that day, so I strove to make myself comfortable as best I could, putting my rain leathers (which the stallion had thrown off) under me.[190] The umbrella that Arana had left with me so that it might not hinder him, I placed on the side from which the wind was blowing so strongly, anchoring it with my sash to some plants that grew there. I used my hat as a pillow and wrapped myself in two serapes that my companion had left me, to protect myself from the light rain that began to fall as soon as it grew dark, but which soon stopped. I must have been there for an hour after I lay down, when I heard shouts from my [fol. 46r.] companion, who was searching for me, to which I responded immediately.

It seemed to me as though I had heard the voice of an angel speaking to me, such was the delight I felt, because now I would not have to spend the night alone, exposed to the risk that some bear might tear me to shreds. At last he arrived, with two different horses because he had left behind the ones we had been riding, which were worn out from having run most of the day. We decided not to keep going, so as not to run the risk of getting lost, for the night was dark.

The next day when we arose, the serape that we had over us had turned white from the heavy snow that fell in the early morning. On this day we caught up with our other companions.

The 9th.

Today we lost the gold that we had left in a little bag that I carried in the pocket of my jacket.[191] The previous night when I went to bed, I had put this next to my head, which was near the door; and now, when I got up, it was not where I had put it. As there were various people in the house, it could not be determined which of the ones who left that morning had taken it. Another misfortune!—Patience, for our fate is to suffer.

The 27th.

Tomorrow we are going to leave for Santa Cruz, on foot and with our baggage on our backs. I will make a [fol. 46v.] summary of the difficulties and sufferings that we have had during our stay here.

I went to fetch the animals we had sent to Sánchez's ranch to be taken care of,[192] for now that we have lost the gold, no resource is left to us but to

> For SANTA CRUZ, MONTEREY and
> Santa Barbara.—The fast sailing clipper brig 'MA-
> LEK ADHEL, Wright master, will have immediate dispatch
> for the above ports. For freight or passage, apply to
> m23-4   WOODWORTH & MORRIS, Clay st. Wharf.

FIGURE 24. Advertisement for the voyage of the brig *Malek Adel* on which Justo Veytia attempted to ship his saddle and clothes to Santa Cruz. Due to strong winds, however, the ship was unable to complete offloading in Santa Cruz and left for southern California, carrying Justo's belongings with it. (UCLA CESLAC.) Source: "For SANTA CRUZ, MONTEREY and Santa Barbara," advertisement, San Francisco *Alta California,* March 25, 1850, 3.

leave here as soon as possible. I looked for them in the company of the person who had taken them there, but I could not find them. For this reason, we suspected that he must have left them somewhere else or even must have sold them, as he was not a man of very good character. Moreover, he was drunk when he took them. It was necessary to demand that he hand them over, and he went in search of them, leaving us dismounted, without half a dollar to spend. And I was without my hat because, on the day I went out to look for the animals, a wind caught me on the road that was so strong it carried off my hat a great distance away, so that it was not easy to find it. To this was added hail so big and heavy that I was not able to see. At the ranch they lent me a hat so that I could return to the Mission, where I stayed for two days while Ygnacio got some money in San Francisco and bought me a hat.

Under such circumstances, with little hope of recovering our animals and without money on which to live, we thought of going to Santa Cruz by sea, for we had seen a ship that was going there. They wanted us to pay our [fol. 47r.] passage aboard this ship in advance, but the cargo master happened to be an acquaintance of Arana's, and we had come to an agreement that we would pay in Santa Cruz instead. We already had handed over our saddles and some clothing to have them put aboard, and we expected that on the following day we would go aboard the *Malek Adel,* which was leaving that day, according to what we had been told.[193]

Every day we went into San Francisco in the morning and returned at night to the Mission, to the house where we slept. On that day, Ygnacio and Arana remained in San Francisco, confident that they would go on the following day, and I returned to the Mission; for we had agreed that I would stay behind to get news of our animals and to look for some position, so that I could survive while I remained here. Three or four days passed, my companions staying to sleep in San Francisco, where I went to see them every day, and I would return in the afternoon to the Mission—until, on the last day, the following events occurred.

It was very early in the morning on the day of Jesus Christ's nativity. All was silent. Everyone was asleep, with the exception of a few people gathered together in the Parker House Hotel, attending a public dinner party held in honor of this holiday. Their drunkenness lasted long, and so did the shouting that [fol. 47v.] echoed throughout the house. Suddenly a voice is raised that strikes fear into all the guests: "Fire!" they shout. And the word leaps from mouth to mouth. The banquet comes to a halt. Terrified, everyone throws themselves down the stairs toward the street. All at once, the whole world is moving. Meanwhile, the fire spreads from building to building—all made of wood—and draws near to where Ygnacio and Arana were sleeping, in a little room where a Sonoran had permitted them to spend the night. The shouts and running feet woke them; and, hearing that the fire was coming near, Ygnacio got up quickly, believing it was much closer than it was. He put on only his jacket, took up his serape, and crossed streets full of mud, running toward the hills. When he tried turn back to save his clothes, the crowd of people that flooded the plaza would not let him, and they carried him along from one side to another. Meanwhile, the blaze is spreading voraciously and already is drawing near the room where they had been sleeping. So he returned to his first idea, running toward the hills to escape, believing that people would come to put the fire out.[194]

When I came to San Francisco from the Mission, the sun was beginning to appear, but its rays were clouded by torrents of thick black smoke that were rising from the midst of the flames. [fol. 48r.] This was horrifying: boards, rags, and other objects were flying about, impelled by gunpowder that was blowing up and barrels of liquor that had caught fire—they burst with a horrible crash, as if they were artillery.[195] Nobody could contain the voracity of that fire, which spread with great rapidity, consuming one after another of the buildings it invaded, despite the fact that there was no wind. The buildings' owners, and many other persons who helped them, were engaged in saving at least the most valuable and moveable objects, tossing them out of doors and windows and off balconies into the street, into the mud. Other people took them from there and piled them up in the middle of the plaza; but many other persons, taking advantage of the disorder and confusion, stole as much as they could.

You saw long lines of men stretching down to the sea, passing buckets full of water from hand to hand, which they threw upon the fire to extinguish it. Some men dealt terrible axe blows to the foundations of buildings, while others were trying to pull the buildings down with ropes.[196] Yet others were laying out a multitude of water-soaked blankets so that the fire might not spread further; until, in the end, after more than two hours of effort, they managed—aided by a fire engine, as well—to put out the blaze, [**fol. 48v.**] which had consumed almost the entire block, which had been quite large.

When the fire finally was put out, little by little I drew near to the plaza. I saw nothing but heaps of ashes where before there had been huge commercial warehouses and magnificent hotels—and not a sign of the little room where my friends had been sleeping. Some have since calculated the loss at two million dollars, but others have made that figure much higher. After staying in the plaza for a while, I found Arana, who told me that Ygnacio had run off, he did not know to where, but that he himself had come back after he first had left the room and saved the clothing they had left behind. I was very upset because I could not find Ygnacio, until at last, I saw him appear at one edge of the plaza; for he was coming down from the hills, from which, as he told me later, he had watched the scene.[197]

Having no place now to sleep that night or the following nights, they had to go back with me to the Mission, to the building where we had stayed previously, for the ship still had not sailed. The persons in charge of accepting passengers had been putting them off constantly, and now they had no clear idea what the day of departure would be. Meanwhile, we were suffering from a thousand wants and shortages. [**fol. 49r.**] Our resources were completely exhausted. We had no means of subsistence whatever, for the friends and fellow countrymen on whom we had been depending already had made us several loans. We had no one to employ us, nor anything with which to employ ourselves to earn something. We went several days without eating, due to our lack of money, contenting ourselves with drinking a cup of coffee. Finally, tired of the ship's tardiness and despairing of our situation, we decided to go back to Santa Cruz on foot, bearing on our backs only the most necessary items for sleeping, having previously left our saddles and clothing behind so that those might travel there aboard the ship, for we could not carry them.

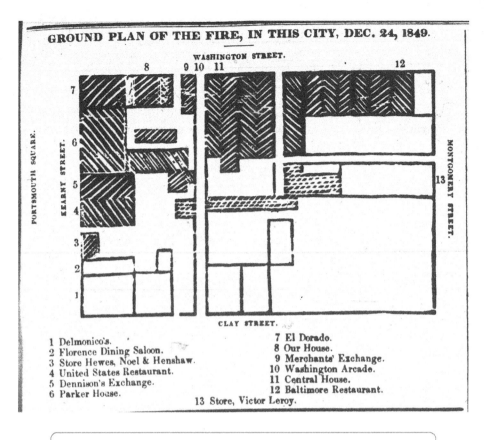

FIGURE 25. Contemporary diagram of destruction caused by the fire of December 24, 1849, in San Francisco, which was described by Veytia in his diary. (UCLA CESLAC.) Source: "Ground Plan of the Fire, in This City, Dec. 24, 1849," San Francisco *Alta California,* December 29, 1849, 3.

I will say something, if only in passing, about San Francisco, about this new Rome, populated by men, among whom one sees only one or two women. Its growth is rapid. Every day they are putting up buildings and erecting new hotels and warehouses. The population is rather large already, and the countryside, which provides the city with a view from some commanding position, is pleasant and varied. Although the ground is very uneven, as it is all hills, the streets are straight, and the [**fol. 49v.**] settlement extends from the plaza, where there are a great number of buildings, all the way down to the water and a long pier for the loading and unloading of goods from ships, as well as two or three smaller piers. The harbor is covered with shipping, whose masts, gathered together, resemble a pine forest in winter,[198] presenting to view a mass of bare poles amid the waters. Commerce is very active, and traffic never ceases. A multitude of carts go along the streets all day long, transporting goods from the piers to the warehouses, and from the latter to other places. People never stop traveling, by foot or on horse, despite the deep mud in the streets and the frequency of the rains in this season. In short, all is motion, and the principal occupations of the inhabitants (almost all Americans) are business and gambling.

January 1, 1850.

Today I woke up in Santa Cruz. I arrived last night quite broken down and worn out by weariness and fatigue.

We left Mission Dolores on foot, as I have said, with our baggage on our backs, with no more resources than 4 dollars that a countryman from Tepic had lent us, with whom I left [fol. 50r.] my saber [as collateral]. On that day, we arrived at Sánchez's ranch, 7 leagues away, where we had the good fortune to encounter, on the following day, one of the mares we had lost. This was a great relief indeed, for we carried our baggage on her, and took turns riding for short distances to rest.

On the next day, we arrived at another ranch, where we found another mare, which we had left in their care there, so that they could send her to the ranch where we previously had been. On the third day, we found the rest of our animals, which had come back by instinct, and on the fourth, we rode them bareback until arriving here, which was at midnight.

We underwent great travails due to the badness of the road, the great quantity of water that was in it along its length, and the need we had to travel along the edge of the sea, which was angry at times, and to cross estuaries—in one of which Ygnacio found himself in danger, in water up to his neck and pulled at strongly by the waves. Fortunately, however, he got out without incident, and then we were able to get across in greater safety.

Finally the year '49 expired: a year of sorrows, of travails and useless labors; a year of [fol. 50v.] misfortunes and bad luck, which even in its last days made its last and most terrible attempts to cast me down, and which, even while breathing its last, aimed its most desperate blows at me, so as to leave me with an eternal memory of its name and an indelible remembrance of all my sufferings, particularly the last ones. The new year that has followed it, the year '50—will it be as faithless as its predecessor? Has it succeeded the other only to lengthen the list of my sorrows? Or, perhaps made compassionate by them, will it show itself more benevolent, granting me some kindness? We will see. Hope and dreams are what nourish a man, especially young men. They still sustain me, leading me to expect something favorable and to look for the reverse of the medal, whose obverse until now has been one of misfortunes.

January 31.
A month has passed, a month of inaction and dreadful lethargy. Oh, how slowly has this time passed, and how bitter have been its hours! How many demoralizing sufferings have I borne! How I have seen my passions, my pride, and my self-esteem brought low! I find myself with no money, and I have to live at the expense of a friend, from whom we have [**fol. 51r.**] received a double favor, since he finds himself in a situation very similar to our own! O poverty, how cruel you are! To how many humiliations, insults, and slights do you expose your victims! No one can know you until he has tried you and until he has drained your bitter cup to the dregs! How many times, oh! how many times have I fervently begged God to give me enough resignation to be able to rise above my sorrows and bear my misfortune with patience! O holy religion! In those moments, I used to feel it lightening my heart of the great weight that oppressed it, and I thought of myself as having sufficient courage to overcome adversity and calmly await the high designs of Providence, trusting that it would not forsake me! For it is certain that man forgets his God when he is living amid abundance, in prosperity and delight. He has recourse to Him only in moments of desperate bitterness, when he can hope for nothing from his fellow men! Then we remember that we profess a holy and consoling religion, and we take refuge in it, as the only guide to salvation! No one is made mock of when he prays from the heart; and nor have I [**fol. 51v.**] been on this occasion, for Providence at last has furnished me with means of subsistence through work.

An unfortunate event has led indirectly to our benefit. A house on the beach caught fire a few days ago, and for this reason its owners have bought shingles from us to repair it. Even though at a very low price, it is still income. To this is added the price of 1,500 boards for the same purpose, each 4 feet long, for which we contracted at 35 dollars the thousand, and which we will make in the same ravine where we made the shingles—as soon as the weather allows us to, for it does not stop raining.

February 3.

Today we went to the ravine, to begin work on the morrow.

The 18th.

Today we left the woods, as we have now finished the boards. We felled a tree and tossed off 1,500 boards more than they told us to make. All this while, our food was limited to beans, as we were unable to come by meat or anything else; but, in short, we ate them when we were hungry, and as much as we wanted, without becoming indebted to anyone for them—so, above all, in freedom. Fortunately, it did not rain all this while, so we did not lose any time. Now we will return to Arana's house [**fol. 52r.**] and to our old sorrows.

March 7.

Tomorrow I am going to begin a new job. Don José Arana, Marcos, and I have made a contract with some Americans in a sawmill,[199] to haul 200 logs for $300. The Americans provide the oxen and equipment and will receive half the money; Marcos and I will provide the actual labor, for which a fourth part of the money will belong to us, once the $1.50 per day wages have been deducted,[200] which we are paying a boy who is helping us. They say that a man can haul out 15 to 20 logs a day. We shall see. It's worse to be idle.

April 30.

Finally! At last God has willed it! 54 days now have passed, during which I was kept occupied with the following things:

Some days, when the hired boy was ill, I used to get up early and go out straight away on foot to find the oxen and bring them back to the house to yoke them up, getting soaked up to the knee from the dew that was falling and the grass, which was tall. Then we would go to the mill, which was about a league away. We would bring the oxen across a creek that cut across the road, and we would go across on a log that had fallen onto the bank of the river, which served us as a bridge. We had to bring the logs down hillsides that were very steep and heavily obstructed by trees, and afterward, we dragged them, two at a time, for half a mile,[201] which is how far it is to the mill. A person will understand already how difficult it was to bring them down, from[202] [**fol. 52v.**] what has already been explained; now add to this the fact that three yoke of oxen were young and balky, and we had only one yoke of tame oxen.

We could not leave because we had not completed the contract for the logs. Now that we are winding up our accounts, I have come out very badly; for, after having lost several days due to the rain, and many more because of our employers, the latter have not paid more than half of what they owe us, and they have gone to San Francisco, saying that they will come back <u>in a short while</u> to pay the rest.[203] All I received from this, according to the agreement that we had and after what we paid the boy has been deducted, has been $30. A vast amount! With this and the proceeds from 3,500 shingles with which we were left, and which we sold at <u>4 dollars the thousand</u>, plus ten dollars that they paid us for a large table we made for Arana, we are going to leave tomorrow for the gold fields, first paying a few odd sums we owe. Our provisions for the road are extremely limited because we are traveling very uncomfortably. Ygnacio is <u>bareback</u> on a mare,[204] seated only on a sort of saddle that he will make out of blankets.[205] He will have great difficulty carrying his baggage and saddlebags with the cooking utensils. I am on another mare, which I traded for with Arana in exchange for 4 thousand shingles, and whose tack is reduced to an [**fol. 53r.**] old saddletree that has no more leather on it than that with which it is trimmed, with the stirrups and stirrup-leathers made out of some bits of straps. This has to carry my baggage of clothing, two gold-washing pans, and a pick. But a man has to have patience, for my saddle has been lost.

It and the clothing that we had left in keeping in San Francisco, which should have come aboard the *Malek Adel*, have not reappeared. For although the ship finally came and was more than a day unloading on the beach, our things did not come off, nor did many other items which still remained to be offloaded, because on the third day there was a bad storm. Hauling anchor, the ship left for other places she was going, and she has not been seen since, nor have we had news of her whereabouts.[206]

All this time, Ygnacio has been occupied in making a bed and a table and in mending two clock cases in Arana's house, and in other works of carpentry that he did for the lady who owns the ravine.[207] She gave him, as her entire payment, a pair of gold-washing pans worth $8, a little sack of wheat flour, and three cheeses, which we are bringing to eat while on the road. It is easy to understand the desire I have to leave, to try my luck anew in the gold fields.

In the large scene of adventures that I have had in Santa Cruz, my luck has always been [**fol. 53v.**] adverse, for all my adventures have been misadventures.[208] All can be reduced into three principal periods. The first was being a shingle maker: having worked so long, hoping to see the fruit of my labors in the form of a price that would compensate me for so many fatigues and privations . . . hopes of which I was cheated. The second, the journey to San Francisco: the loss of the gold and our animals, shortages, and calamities, one after another. The third: some periods of inactivity and others with some work, for which I was paid, as they say, like a dog, with food or with payments that amounted to the same thing. Everything here has been labors, hardships, and miseries during the time of my residence in Santa Cruz. Can I have any agreeable memory of this ill-fated Mission, where I have experienced nothing but physical and mental suffering? No. I will have always before me the unpleasant memories that this series of unfortunate events has created in me, and they will form a part of my life.

May 9.

Today we arrived at a placer called Las Mariposas,[209] without any mishap along the road, which we traveled without a hitch. After having traversed the immense San Joaquin Valley,[210] we crossed the San Joaquin River, then the [**fol. 54r.**] Merced River,[211] and went deep into the mountains, until arriving at this point, which is to the south of the other placers with which we were familiar until now, all of them situated in the snowy mountains. There are a great many people here, a fair amount of commerce, pool halls, and a plaza where some Mexican acrobats used to put on shows, all in canvas tents or structures made of rubblework, that is, stones stuck together with mud.[212] The greater part of the prospectors get very little gold, for which reason we are going to another ravine nearby, called Agua Fría.[213]

The 12th.

Tomorrow, as there is almost nothing here, we will leave this place in company with Don Juan Smith and his siblings,[214] with whom we joined forces on the road at a point a little ways back, not far from the Merced River. The people who are here get little or no gold. Our own efforts have yielded no result; and moreover, there is no place to stake a claim because everything is being worked already. In recent days, a law has been passed that all foreigners who work in the mines must pay 20 dollars a month henceforward. We're all right, though; we already see how we will avoid paying this tax.[215]

The 15th.

Yesterday we arrived at this stream, where a large village of Indians live at its edge, in shelters made out of branches. They are preparing to receive a chief [**fol. 54v.**] from another village, whom they have invited to come

Chap. 97.

AN ACT *for the better regulation of the Mines, and the government of Foreign Miners.*

Passed April 13, 1850.

The People of the State of California, represented in Senate and Assembly, do enact as follows:

§ 1. No person who is not a native or natural born citizen of the United States, or who may not have become a citizen under the treaty of Guadalupe Hidalgo (all native California Indians excepted), shall be permitted to mine in any part of this State, without having first obtained a license so to do according to the provisions of this Act. [Certain persons not to mine without a license.]

FIGURE 26. Opening text of the Foreign Miners' Tax, 1850. (*The Statutes of California, Passed at the First Session of the Legislature,* 221) Source: "An Act for the better regulation of the Mines, and the government of Foreign Miners," *The Statutes of California, Passed at the First Session of the Legislature, Begun the 15th Day of Dec. 1849, and Ended the 22d Day of April, 1850, at the City of Pueblo de San José. With an Appendix and Index* (San José, CA: J. Winchester, 1850), 221–23.

eat a deer with them; for it is, I believe, the most opportune time to hunt this animal. We will begin today to work at mining, and we will see how it turns out for us. Need afflicts us, and hunger has bothered us quite a lot these last two days, during which we have not had anything to nourish us except a little toasted corn flour that we had left. Our purse is completely empty, and we have nothing with which to supply ourselves with the necessary provisions. Patience! What else is to be done?

The 19th.

I am on the left bank of the Merced River, beneath the much-desired shade of a leafy holm oak, which gives me shelter from the rays of the midday sun. Oh, what a turbulent life, so full of misadventures! When will it end? I find myself, one might say, like a fugitive here, together with my companions, not knowing yet which way to turn.

Last night, we went away from where we were, traveling for part of the night by the light of the moon, fleeing from two enemies that threatened us at the same time. One was a fire that spread with great speed toward where we were, eating up the **[fol. 55r.]** dry grass across a vast width of the landscape, whose burning the wind encouraged. The other was the Indians,[216] who, gathered in great numbers and excited by drunkenness, gave terrible shrieks and threatened a Californio who was selling provisions and liquor with throwing him out of the place. He was the cause of it all because he had given them credit, and above all because he had sold them liquor. Therefore we left, based on the decision of our companions, who assured us that they had seen many Indians as they were passing through the village, whose intentions toward those of us who were there were very wicked. They also pointed out the few means of defense we could count on in case of attack.

We followed a road on which the Indians would not see us, which went according to plan,[217] and we arrived at a place about a league and a half away, where we slept. We would like to go back today to see if anything happened; but as we already are near the river, where the Smith family is,[218] we will go on to that place.

During the days we worked there, we got enough gold to support ourselves, plus about an ounce more than that.

The 21st.

Today I am going to Stanislaus,[219] [fol. 55v.] in company with Don Antonio Smith,[220] with the goal of seeing my cousin Ybarra there, who has a commercial establishment,[221] and to inform myself about the state of things: as much about the clash between the Americans and foreigners over the law about taxes on foreign miners as to see if I might find a position in some other line of work, in which I could earn enough for us to go home. Here almost no gold has been found. I worked only a short time yesterday, and I got about 6 reales' worth of gold.[222] At first the Americans prohibited us from working here, but not now, because of the identity we have assumed here: we have said we are Californios.[223]

The 24th.

The day before yesterday, I arrived at the city of Stanislaus, which is fairly well populated, with a few houses made of wood and adobe, but most are canvas tents. I stopped at the house of my cousin Ybarra, who in partnership with another man has a cantina and eight gambling tables that they rent out at night. He has made great efforts to get me to stay, to the point that he has offered that his firm will put up the money and I will be a card dealer, in return for which a third share of the business will be mine. We shall see if I earn anything by gambling.

Today, Smith returns to the Merced River.[224] I am sending the two mares with him, for Ygnacio, and also a letter telling Ygnacio that within [fol. 56r.] twelve days I expect him in this town.

June 18.

I have spent twenty-five days in my position as a cardsharp, during which I won only fifty-some dollars, of which my share was about eighteen—which leaves me free to seek some other destiny. I say "free" because yesterday the partners had to pay a debt of $500, and they had to use the funds of their partnership, which I think they will not get together again now. A man who has been a cardsharp will know the bad times that caused me to conduct my play between the alternatives of <u>winning</u> or <u>losing</u>.[225]

Ygnacio still has not come. I will wait for him for a week, and meanwhile I will go to the nearby canyons to look for gold, so as not to be idle, and to see if anything may be gotten. And if he should not come during that time, I will go to look for him at the Merced River, in company with Silvano Valencia, who has offered to accompany me, to decide what we should do.[226]

The 29th.

Tomorrow I am going, in company with two other men, to a placer that they call Los Melones,[227] with my bedclothes and a little sack of provisions [**fol. 56v.**] on my back. It is six leagues away. They tell me it is a good place, and a person can get an ounce of gold a day. Here I have gotten almost nothing.

July 12.

Today I returned from my expedition, without anything in particular having befallen me. All the gold I have left to me after expenses is worth $20, which I lent to a friend today.

The 25th.

Finally! At last I am going to leave for my own country! My own country, to which I always have longed to return! I will return, although not with the pleasure that I had imagined a little more than a year ago, due to the interference of these circumstances:

1st, because my health is completely broken, on account of a serious inflammation that began eleven days ago and as a result of which I found my life in great danger. I was in bed for a week, suffering from excessive fever in addition to my aches, since my house was a canvas tent and the sun we suffer under in these months is burning hot. Doctor Rodgers—an American, who next after God has saved my life, with his medicines and able attendance—has told me that I should leave [**fol. 57r.**] this place as quickly as I can, for if I have a relapse, then there will be no remedy, since my constitution is very debilitated. He himself is leaving tomorrow for Guadalajara, and he offers to accompany me in whatever adventures may befall me along the way.[228]

LINEA DIARIA DE COCHES

PARA

STOCKTON, SACRAMENTO, SONORA, MOKELUMNE HILL I MARIPOSA.

Los pasajeros que deseen ir para cualquiera de los puntos mencionados, deberá partir a bordo del vapor que sale del muelle de la calle Jackson para Ouckland todas las mañanas a las 8 en punto, en donde estará un coche dispuesto para conducirlos a Stockton.

Saliendo de Stockton a las 6 i 1|2 de la mañana, los pasajeros llagaran a San Francisco a las 4 de la tarde.

Este camino atraviesa la seccion mas pintoresca del Estado i es digna de verla.

Esta linea se corresponde con la de Martinez i San José conduciendo pasajeros de San José a Stockton en 10 horas.

La oficina en San Francisco esta en Wilson Exchange, calle Sansome, i en Stockton en la oficina jeneral de dilijencias, en donde se pueden asegurar asientos a cualpuiera hora del dia

A. McCLOUD,
Propietario.

44 20a 1m

FIGURE 27. Stagecoach advertisement in Spanish, 1854. Ships, stagecoaches, railroads, buses, and now airlines routinely have advertised in Spanish to the Latino market, from 1849 to 2023. (UCLA CESLAC.) Source: "LINEA DIARIA DE COCHES," advertisement, San Francisco *La Crónica,* December 15, 1854, 3.

2nd, in leaving my true friend Ygnacio without knowing where or how he is.

And, 3rd, in returning to my country not only without[229] the riches that my imagination had created, but also without even my health, which I had recovered but which, along with everything else, I lost again.

Tomorrow, therefore, I will leave in company with the Doctor, on the stagecoach that goes to Stockton, a seat on which has cost me $25.

The 30th.

Yesterday, as soon as I arrived in San Francisco, I went to see if I could get passage in the steamship that is leaving for San Blas on the 1st, but I found that all the spaces already were sold. Fortunately, I met with Ygnacio Tapia, who had bought two of them for his brother and himself and two for their servants. He sold me one of the servants' tickets, for $100, and bought another passage in a sailing ship for his servant, for $35.[230]

The Doctor did not obtain the two spaces on the steamship that he needed. As a result, he arranged one on a sailing ship and will depart later. I am very sorry [**fol. 57v.**] that we may not go together, but perhaps I will go accompanied by some friends and fellow countrymen.

The day I left Stanislaus, I arrived in Stockton at night, and I stayed at a hotel where they treated me very well. I was there for two days, waiting for the steamship that makes the run to San Francisco. I have still not gotten well, and the burning sensations in my stomach have not yet stopped. Thanks to Don Roque Delgado,[231] who is going to Mazatlan, I now am lodging in a little room belonging to a friend of his, which is not very far from the docks, and which is costing me nothing.

August 2.

Yesterday afternoon I left San Francisco, bringing my baggage on board before noon to get a good space for myself before the other passengers came, as it is my lot to sleep on deck—for cabin passage costs $200.

At last I have left California. We have passed the mouth of the harbor and lost sight of San Francisco. At the time, mixed feelings excited my heart and various thoughts occupied my imagination, as they had at another, similar time, when I lost sight [**fol. 58r.**] of San Blas when coming to California. What a difference! Then, illusions and hopes drew me on; now, terrible disenchantments and costly experience bear me along: in short, the force of bitter, horrible reality.

PACIFIC MAIL STEAMSHIP COMPANY, connecting with the United States Mail Steamers Cherokee and Philadelphia at Chagres.—The Pacific Mail Steamship Company's Steamer PANAMA, D. G. Bailey, Commander, will leave for PANAMA, touching at the usual ports, on THURSDAY August 1, 1850, at 5 o'clock P. M. Treasure for shipment received at the Company's office, foot of Howison's Pier, Sacramento street, on Tuesday 30th and Wednesday 31st until 12 A. M. Passengers are requested to be on board at noon of the day of departure. The Panama connects with the U. S. Mail steamer Cherokee to leave Chagres on arrival of the passengers and treasure. The undersigned are prepared to give drafts on Messrs. Howland & Aspinwall, New York, on the most favorable terms and have open policies of insurance by each steamer to the extent of $500,000 to cover shipments of gold dust to the United States or the Bank of England.

jy17.   ROBINSON, BISSELL & Co.

FIGURE 28. Advertisement for the steamship *Panama*, leaving San Francisco on August 1, 1850, for Panama, "touching at the usual ports." This most likely was the ship that brought Justo Veytia from San Francisco back to Mexico. (UCLA CESLAC.) Source: "PACIFIC MAIL STEAMSHIP COMPANY," advertisement, San Francisco *Alta California,* July 30, 1850, 1.

The 6th.

Today is my saint's day. In order to congratulate me, they have stolen my silver watch, which Pepe gave me, from beneath my pillow. As I have said, I am sleeping on deck. Doubtless some nosy person saw where I put it last night, and that sleep enveloped me. When I awoke, I had to get up quickly, gathering up my clothes so they would not get wet, for already buckets of water were being poured out to wash the ship. I missed my watch immediately and began to question various persons about it. Some told me that they did not know who would have taken it, but the majority—who were Americans—did not respond, either because they did not want to answer me or because they did not understand me. I tried to speak to the Captain, so that he might order a search; but they told me that an interpreter was necessary, and I don't know what other things, and that, with more than 400 passengers—and tomorrow we will arrive at Mazatlan, where many of them will disembark—[**fol. 58v.**] it is very difficult to investigate.[232] Thus it is that, to my sorrow, I am resigning myself to its loss and to not arriving home with either of the two watches that I was carrying. The other one, a gold watch, which Pepe also gave me, I gave as security to Doctor Rodgers on the 9th,[233] for the $100 to pay for my passage. He remained behind in San Francisco, and perhaps I will never see him again.

The 9th.

Today, in the morning, we arrived at San Blas, and in a short time I leaped onto dry land: that land so longed for, at the sight of which my heart throbbed powerfully within my breast. But was it from joy? I do not know. Was it from sorrow? Perhaps. Am I not going to see my family, my friends? Then why is there such a mixture of joy and sadness? What is the reason that the latter predominates? I don't know that either, but perhaps it is because my return is not what I had hoped it would be and because, instead of the riches of fortune that I had thought to bring, nothing comes with me save the story of my sufferings and misfortunes and the torment of a costly disillusionment. This is very sad, in truth: to return to the bosom of my family without being able to help them or give them what I wished. Oh! This is a double suffering.

About 5 in the afternoon, I departed for Tepic [**fol. 59r.**] in company with the Tapias, on some mules that we have hired.

The 13th.

Three days ago, we arrived in Tepic and stayed at the San José Inn. We have not been able to leave because it was hard for us to find cheap mounts. Today, finally, we have gotten some, and I believe that tomorrow we will continue our journey.

I bought a saddle for four pesos, out of the little that remained to me, and with ten pesos that Tapia loaned me I have bought a rather skinny horse. But I think he will get me there.

The 18th.

Today, at half past ten in the morning, I arrived in Guadalajara. The closer I came to the city and perceived its towers and buildings more clearly and distinctly, the more my heart was stifled by sorrow—when, in other times, even after a brief absence, the sight of this city upon my return used to cause me an inexplicable joy!

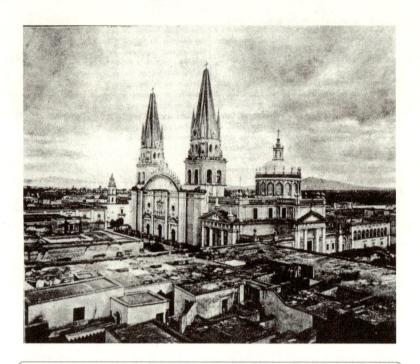

FIGURE 29. A photographic view of the cathedral in Guadalajara, *ca.* 1880. Returning from his miserable, unsuccessful voyage to California, Justo Veytia found that the sight of these towers saddened him. As he passed by, he met his family leaving ten o'clock mass. Source: Vicente Riva Palacio, *México a través de los siglos,* 3:164.

The people were coming out from ten o'clock mass in the sanctuary when I arrived, and I found my entire family well. But Tula had strong palpitations, so that at first, she could not speak to me. Surely my sudden arrival caused this, [fol. 59v.] after an absence of more than eighteen months.

The End
Guadalajara, the year 1850
J.V.

Ygnacio arrived at this city on the 19th of May 1851.

Epilogue

After Justo Veytia Returned to Mexico, 1850–2022

Luis Jaime Veytia Orozco, Justo Veytia's Great-Grandson

My great-grandfather, Justo Veytia y Valencia, was born here in Guadalajara in 1820.[1] At the beginning of 1849, when he was twenty-eight and still single, he went to California as a prospector in search of riches. From what he had heard at the time, fortunes were being found there. It's like migrant farmworkers in recent times following the Mexican dream of getting money abroad. So Justo Veytia went, following his dream.

Justo died in 1870, more than fifty years before I was born, so I never knew him personally, but I had always heard about him in my father's stories. Some anecdotes about my great-grandfather always came up. I heard so much about Justo that he sometimes seemed present. My father often held up Justo as an example of how things should be done, saying, "Do as my grandfather did." He was always a model to follow.

We used to hear that Justo's journey to California was counterproductive for him materially, but that it was very good for him in other ways, for he learned there that money isn't easily earned. His example made us understand that it isn't easy to achieve one's dreams. We learned that to achieve prosperity for oneself and one's family, a person has to work hard.

I was already grown the first time I read Justo's diary. The narration of his journey fascinated me. He states that, after leaving Guadalajara, he passed through various villages on his way to the port of San Blas. These villages continue to exist as small towns like Tepic and Nayarit. He went through Tequila, which is known as the cradle of tequila liquor, near Guadalajara. And San Blas continues to be a very interesting town because of its shrimp farms, and there is even a farm for raising crocodiles. It also has beautiful canals.

Throughout his entire journey, Justo Veytia was not alone. He was accompanied by other people, although sometimes they separated and each one traveled a different way for a time. But he was always accompanied by his cousin "Nacho"—that is to say, Ygnacio Arana.[2] Rather surprisingly, though, once Justo returned to Mexico, he didn't write anything more about Ygnacio. We have no written account of his later activities.

Owing to the difficult life of a Mexican in California, he found the most support among other Mexicans. It wasn't easy, and supplies were limited, making it hard to feed the group. Nevertheless, there were local people who were really kind, who opened their doors to them without knowing them and without asking for anything in return. In his diary, Justo talks a great deal about the Californios. On leaving San Francisco the first time, he made friends with the Arana family of Santa Cruz. They loaned horses to him during his stay in California. When he had no luck finding gold, they gave him work, and they even loaned him money to buy passage aboard a ship for his return home. On the other hand, some people were quite unfriendly.[3] There were all kinds.

My great-grandfather was not the only person from Guadalajara who traveled to California in search of riches. I can say that many groups went there from Guadalajara and its environs. For example, members of the Lancaster-Jones family also traveled to Alta California, although they went as a group, an expeditionary force. They brought a diving bell to lower into rivers to search for gold.[4] They were more productive than my great-grandfather and made a good profit. But when they were about to return to Guadalajara, they were afraid to go back all together with the money. They took a vote and they left one person behind to safeguard the gold, but that person never came back to Guadalajara—he was somehow lost, together with all the gold.[5] So it was a frustrating experience for them to come back without the fortune they had dreamed about and once actually possessed.

Members of the Orendáin family from the town of Tequila also went to California.[6] They went from Jalisco to California as merchants, to sell tequila. Two brothers went. One dedicated himself to sales and the other to the protection of their profits. It is logical to assume they came with a group because going around alone in San Francisco at that time could result in being assaulted and robbed. There was so much banditry, it was necessary to have the protection of good people around. The Orendáins had better economic support than Justo Veytia, and their journey was better organized. Moreover, they did not go with the intention of looking for gold, but of selling merchandise. They did very well, too.

The sad thing is that, after Justo made this journey—after so much effort and suffering—things unfortunately did not go well for him. He came back to Guadalajara with empty hands, although he had learned to improvise. After he lost the little amount of gold he had scraped together while staying in San Francisco, he worked for the Aranas in Santa Cruz, making wooden shingles, and managed to earn some money with which to go back to Mexico.[7]

Upon returning without the wealth he had hoped to get, he had to somehow make a living. Once back in Mexico, he leased a company store at a hacienda that belonged to a relative near Lake Chapala and went to live near there. Later, he leased another store as well, and after that, he leased the entire hacienda and dedicated himself to managing haciendas.

Subsequently he went to live in a little village called Santa Ana Tepetitlán. Now it's called Santa Ana Acatlán, or Santa Ana de Juárez, because Benito Juárez was there when his enemies came to arrest him in 1858, but local people hid him and he escaped.[8] Justo lived in that village for a time. He was a hardworking man and was able to amass some capital. There are still connections between my family and some of the families who lived there.

He married Mercedes Reyes y Delgado in 1863. Their daughter, Matilde de Jesús Veytia y Reyes, was born two years later.[9] Mercedes died the same year as Matilde's birth, of unknown causes.

His wife's death did not dishearten Justo. Probably, in different ways, the journey to California was an apprenticeship that enabled him to triumph later in life. He had a good education, albeit only primary school,[10] but it seems to me the voyage to California was his university. It was there he got the ideas and values that served him well later, when he was working in agriculture.

I believe he ended up having several farms around Guadalajara, and some money. In 1867, he bought a house in Guadalajara, which was no common house, but an old, very beautiful building facing the Degollado Theater.

Things apparently were going well, but then another blow fell: Justo died suddenly in 1870, only fifty years old. His daughter, Matilde, was left an orphan at the tender age of five. Scarcely having begun her life, she was alone in the world.

Matilde de Jesús Veytia Reyes

Being alone and very small, Matilde was delivered into the care of the Hospicio Cabañas (Cabañas Hospice), an orphanage and school in Guadalajara. This orphanage gave my grandmother an education and formed her character.

My sister, who also is called Matilde, says that we are a matriarchal family, thanks to my grandmother Matilde's force of personality. Whatever Doña Matilde said should be done, was done. Finding herself completely alone in the world had helped build her character. Even before women were liberated, my grandmother Matilde knew how to liberate herself.

The Cabañas Hospice is a very large building, full of courtyards. There are a lot of great halls, and between each hall and the next there is a courtyard for light and ventilation. They are very soundly built, with huge walls and lovely columns. When she was a grown woman, Matilde used to take my father there—for she continued to visit the hospice—and she used to tell him about the constant fights she had had in the hospice and the games the children used to play when she lived there. Later, with my father, I also used to come to visit the hospice. I would let my imagination wander, thinking about when my grandmother was there: which room she slept in, where she ate, where she played, where she chatted, and where she quarreled with her companions or with the nuns. I don't think it was easy for my grandmother, but that was essentially where she grew up. Without family members around, she formed a very strong personality.

Given that she went to the orphanage when only five years old, she didn't keep many of her father's possessions. The good thing is, she did keep his diary. I imagine that, at the time, it was just loose pages. I don't know what it was like then, and I can't give a description of it; but there must have been booklets or loose pages that she gathered with care. It seems to me that she transferred her tender feelings for her father to the diary, to sort it, put it together, and transcribe it completely. She was very little when she went to the orphanage, and I have to think that she saved the diary because she liked to read the accounts her father had written—so much so that she later wrote on it "Property of Matilde."[11] It was her inheritance, a treasure for her, and she in turn bequeathed it to us.

She left the Cabañas to marry her first cousin, Luis Veytia, going to live at the property she had inherited from my great-grandfather, the house facing the Degollado Theater, in the very center of the city. It was a colonial-era house in the Spanish style, with courtyards and arcades of hewn stone and very large bedrooms. Curiously, the bathrooms were way in the back of the house; one had to cross the entire building to get to them. My father was born in that house, along with his siblings, as were my siblings and I. So, in a sense, it was not just my grandmother's inheritance but something more since it made us always remember Justo and Matilde.

Salvador Veytia y Veytia

My father, Salvador Veytia y Veytia, was the youngest of six children: four boys and two girls. My father, who had the same personality as his mother, Matilde, was the person on whom my grandmother most relied. She turned to my father for everything. My father had the character of both Don Justo and my grandmother. If my grandmother wanted something, he would automatically give it to her.

My father, as it turned out, was the center of the family. Even though he was the youngest, all his brothers came to him for help in one way or another: in finances, love affairs, or other matters.

For us, my grandmother's house was fabulous, a place where we held all the family's parties and celebrations. My sister Laura even got married there. My cousins used it for *quinceañeras*, first communions, and wedding parties. Basically, the house was the family heritage of all of us. There we continued to come together, always celebrating the birthday of my grandmother. Although my father was only eight years old when his father died, my grandmother used her deceased husband's birthday as an occasion to bring the family together every year. For us, living in that house was the essence of family unity.

The house in Guadalajara where Matilde lived no longer exists. Governor González Gallo built very broad streets around the cathedral, which formed a plaza in the shape of a cross.[12] In order to do this, he had to tear down a lot of old houses in that neighborhood; and in consequence, all those houses have disappeared, which at the time were the best ones in Guadalajara.

My father rebuilt that house stone by stone, exactly the same, on another property. Later, unfortunately, it fell down in an earthquake. There was no defense against that. Nevertheless, the building's stones and arcades still exist at a hotel in Zihuatanejo, in the state of Guerrero, with the inscription "Building stones from the Veytia family home." Those stones continue to have value, and thus we preserved them and a few other, small things from the house with great care.

From that experience, my father and I were impressed with the value of objects used in the past. My father began to rescue old things that are no longer used, and that was how he learned history, by discovering and acquiring tools and utensils, learning about them, their history, and the people who originally acquired them.

For my grandmother Matilde, Justo's diary represented part of a family tree. Let's say it was a kind of legacy transmitted to my father. Although he had several brothers, she left it directly to my father, who she noticed had the most feelings for Justo and the greatest appreciation for what he had done.

In 1975 my father, together with Ricardo Lancaster-Jones, had two hundred copies made of Justo's diary. They were interested in having my great-grandfather's odyssey become better known. So many years before, at the age of twenty-eight, he had gotten the urge to go in quest of gold. The two wanted recognition of the sophisticated nature my great-grandfather had in carrying a diary so well produced, so artfully written, that presented the story of his travels.

These two hundred copies were distributed among friends and relatives. Out of the people who received them from my father's hands, though, maybe two out of ten ever read the diary. The other eight merely said, "Oh, what nice handwriting. How interesting," but had no interest in reading it. It did not really speak to them, for not everyone enjoys such things.

Luis Jaime Veytia Orozco

Thirty-some years later, David Hayes-Bautista visited the Madero Bookstore in Mexico City, between the Zócalo and the Casa de Azulejos, and by chance came across one of these two hundred copies. How had a copy ended up in a used bookstore? Some of the friends and relatives had moved to the Federal District, including the director of a bank that my father had opened there in Mexico City. Upon his death, some of his household furnishings were sold, and his copy of the diary was given to that bookstore.

I think it wasn't a coincidence. Things come to those who wait for them, to those who look for them. That copy passed through various hands, and it didn't interest them. How many bookstore customers might have turned its pages, without it arousing their curiosity? But the fact that Hayes-Bautista came to that bookstore is incredible to me, as is the interest he showed in it when it caught his attention, and that he should have tracked us down.

The first contact he made was with Vanesa, a great-great-granddaughter of Justo. She happens to be a coworker of my daughter, Bárbara. Chatting with her, Vanesa said, "They're looking for a person related to this book," and Bárbara said, "I think my dad is the right one." My daughter came to me, and that was when I got in touch with Hayes-Bautista. If he had talked to any other people, I fear they would not have responded, would not have been interested. But now we are colleagues, coauthors, and friends in bringing my great-grandfather's diary to light.

About ten years ago, in collaboration with some friends and partners here in Guadalajara, we put together an exhibit of sacred art. Our goal was to show off the treasures we have in the region's churches. Sacred art is richly cultural, artistic, and religious. What the exhibit was trying to do was to show the artistic value those pieces have.

I thought about the exhibit for many years. We began with silversmiths—putting on an exhibit of religious items made of silver, which the jewelers of past times made—and stumbled into the idea of putting on a larger exhibit of religious art. I was occupied with planning this for two years, forming a group who were interested, and finally we were able to make it happen. We worked on it for two years, gathering the objects and restoring them.

We decided to hold the exhibit in the Cabañas Hospice (now the Cabañas Cultural Institute), where my grandmother had lived as a girl 150 years ago. The Hospice itself needed restoring, and we gathered private funds for the initiative, convincing the government and the Cardinal that we would do the restoration, and they allowed us to use the site for the exhibit.

The exhibit lasted thirty days. It was the most-visited exhibit of recent years. There were long lines every day to get in. It was really a success, because all the treasures, mainly religious ones, were brought together in one place. People wanted it to run longer, but unfortunately that was not possible. The various communities of the region wanted to keep praying to their saints, but we had them in the exhibit, so we had to return them![13]

We restored the Cabañas Hospice and improved its floors, its lighting, and the security of the building. It was an interesting project. When I visited the exhibit, I would always remember my grandmother. It's strange how places where Justo, Matilde, or my own father lived put my memories in touch with my present activities. And all this—because it was a passion of mine, or, better said, a dream—ultimately resulted in the exhibit. I spent more than five years dreaming and planning to do it someday, without

FIGURE 30. Justo's great-grandson, Luis Jaime Veytia Orozco, and his wife Pilar in Guadalajara, 2019. (Courtesy of Luis Jaime Veytia Orozco.)

knowing where, how, when, or anything. This dream lasted longer than Justo's whole journey to Alta California.

I think Justo's diary shows the roots of the conquest of 1848. It says to everyone, "We Mexicans were here." Many of California's Latinos today share these roots. Sometimes they may be indistinct, or even lost, but indeed they have them, even if not everyone has discovered them. My wish is for them to feel pride in their ancestors and fellow countrymen, and in what they have accomplished.

Justo Veytia y Valencia was a Mexican who came to California in 1849, along with other Mexicans, who shared a mix of indigenous and Spanish heritage, a heritage which many of the more than 15 million Latinos in California share today. These are the roots of California.

Luis Jaime Veytia Orozco
Guadalajara, Jalisco, Mexico

Appendix 1

Relative Population Composition Factors for San Francisco, Los Angeles, San Luis Obispo, and Tuolumne Counties and Combined Counties for 1850, 1860, and 1870 Censuses

Year/County	Males	Females	Children	Relative Composition Ratio
1850				
San Francisco*	—	—	—	—
Los Angeles	768	592	1,680	2.50
San Luis Obispo	64	47	182	4.56
Tuolumne**	—	—	—	—
Total	**832**	**639**	**1862**	**4.00**
1860				
San Francisco	349	449	611	4.04
Los Angeles	2,448	1,608	3,677	3.16
San Luis Obispo	374	204	611	3.18
Tuolumne	517	226	297	2.00
Total	**3,688**	**2,487**	**5,196**	**3.07**
1870				
San Francisco	543	763	1,097	4.43
Los Angeles	1,661	1,353	3,445	3.88
San Luis Obispo	461	266	918	3.58
Tuolumne	182	99	214	2.21
Total	**2,847**	**2481**	**5674**	**3.86**

* The detailed census returns for 1850 San Francisco were lost in a fire, hence no data are shown.

** The geography of Tuolumne County in 1854 changed radically when Stanislaus County was formed out of the western portion of it. As result, we only include data for the reduced Tuolumne County for 1860 and 1870.

Appendix 2

Data to Estimate Latinos as Percent of California Population, 1860 and 1870

Year	California Total Population	Undercount Fraction	Latino Population Estimate	Latinos as % of California Total
1850	92,597	—	—	—
1860	379,994	1/2	Low: 79,366	20.8%
		1/3	Mid: 119,048	31.3%
		1/4	Mid: 158,731	41.8%
		1/5	High: 198,967	52.4%
1870	560,247	1/2	Low: 99,789	17.8%
		1/3	Mid: 149,683	26.7%
		1/4	Mid: 199,577	35.6%
		1/5	High: 249,472	44.5%

Notes

Preface

1. United States Census 2020, Official Questionnaire OMB No. 0607-1006, accessed October 10, 2021, https://www2.census.gov/programs-surveys/decennial/2020/technical-documentation/questionnaires-and-instructions/questionnaires/2020-informational-questionnaire-english_DI-Q1.pdf.
2. Aida Hurtado, David E. Hayes-Bautista, R. Burciaga Valdez, and Anthony C. R. Hernández, *Redefining California: Latino Social Engagement in a Multicultural Society* (Los Angeles: UCLA Chicano Studies Research Center, 1992), table 6.1, p. 59.
3. With apologies to the singer Celia Cruz, whose original term was "Latinos en Estados Unidos, ya casi somos una nación," on Fania Records, accessed August 26, 2022, https://www.youtube.com/watch?v=7r0YTmP5_RU.
4. "El Domingo pasado, dos Californios, llamado el uno Luis Rubio y Joaquin Blanco, el otro, tuvieron una disputa . . ." "Horribles Asesinatos," *Los Angeles Star*, November 8, 1851.
5. "Se dice que se ha tirado una linea de partido formando una parte los Americanos y otra los nativos Californios." "Eleccion de Santa Barbara," letter to the editor, dated December 20, 1852, *Los Angeles Star*, January 15, 1853.
6. "Seria muy vergonzozo y aun degradante para los hijos del pais, vivir en una sociedad silvestre, mientras que los hombres que vengan de otras partes ocupan los mejores lugares en la sociedad y se lleven toda la atención y consideraciones que no pueda conseguir el rustico aldeano." "Un Colegio en la Ciudad de los Angeles," *Los Angeles Star*, July 12, 1851.
7. "Los mexicanos residentes en California han celebrado por todas partes el glorioso aniversario de la independencia de su patria." Untitled editorial, (Los Angeles) *El Clamor Público*, October 2, 1855.
8. "Hemos visto en manos de un Sonorense que llegó recientemente una hermosa chispa de oro que pesaba cerca de tres onzas." "Los Placeres—Mucho Oro!," *Los Angeles Star*, February 8, 1855.

9. Un infeliz Mexicano . . . se ofreció a torear a pié . . . los innumerables espectadores . . . se divertian en celebrar las gracias de la fiera, con las palabras de '*que bonito levanta el toro al cholo!*'" "Comunicado," (Los Angeles) *El Clamor Público*, August 22, 1857.

10. "Sirvanse vdes. SS. EE., insertar en las columnas de su apreciable periódico esta produccion sencilla de una mujer que carece de talento por desgracia para dar mas espansion a sus ideas, pero que como hispana-americana solo aspira al bien estar de su raza." Untitled news item, *Los Angeles Star*, September 21, 1854.

11. In one untitled Spanish-language editorial, both "Hijos del pais" and "Españoles" were used when referring to Latinos eligible to vote: "Yá ha llegado el tiempo, en que los Hijos del pais aprovechandose de su derecho como buenos Ciudadanos, deban comparecer cada uno á depositar su Voto . . . Esperamos ahora que nuestros conciudadanos Españoles, mirarán con otro aspecto dichas elecciones para ellos tan importantes, y que todos que tienen derechos no faltarán el martes de aprovechar la ocasion de votar conforme su consciencia y su juicio." *Los Angeles Star*, October 30, 1852.

12. "Una de las primeras obligaciones de un periodico traducido en Español el seguir los acontecimientos de la política de las Republicas Hispano-americanas, para tener al corriente de las noticias de sus respetivos paises a los innumerables hijos de ellos que se encuentran en este Estado." "Reflecciones sobre Mejico," *Los Angeles Star*, May 7, 1853.

13. "Y aún no deja de conducir nuestros intereses americanos a cierto genero de descendimiento moral, algo mas que desdeñal, desfavorable à nosotros los de la raza latina." "EQUIVOCACION AL APLICAR LA PALABRA 'AMERICANO,' Solo al que es Originario de Norte America," (Los Angeles) *El Clamor Público*, April 25, 1857.

14. "On Friday last, a Mexican found a lump of gold lying near the surface, weighing four pounds seven ounces." "San Joaquin and Placer Intelligence," (San Francisco) *Alta California*, May 14, 1850.

15. "We learn from a private source that in consequence of the probable enforcement of the mining tax the Sonoranians are leaving for their own 'stamping grounds,' in large bodies." "THE SONORANIANS," (San Francisco) *Alta California*, May 24, 1850.

16. "In place of the high bred Spanish cavaliers, a few greasers with their hateful looking *sombreros* and greasy serapes appear." "The Bull Fighter's Champion," (San Francisco) *Alta California*, May 24, 1850.

17. "A greaserita, by the name of Carolina, and an American by the name of

Hyde . . . presented the appearance of a very interesting pair" "A Nice Little Scrape," (San Francisco) *Alta California*, May 3, 1852.

18. "She is a mongrel Mexican, loves rum to distraction, and drinks to intoxication. There is no use in fining or imprisoning her; just as sure as she is turned out, she will be picked up in less than five hours, in some fence corner, beastly drunk." "A Deplorable Fact," (San Francisco) *Alta California*, May 8, 1852.

19. "Digging for gold was a new and untried vocation to the Anglo Saxon who sought these shores in the early times of their prosperity." "The Sonora Troubles," (San Francisco) *Alta California*, August 9, 1850.

20. "We feel the importance of bringing into requisition the true spirit of Yankee energy and enterprise, in order to fairly present our country abroad." "The Immigration—Yankee Enterprise," (San Francisco) *Alta California*, April 9, 1850.

21. "Resolved. That the following regulations, concerning the election ordered to be held on the fifteenth day of January next, be ordained. 1st. None but white male persons, and of twenty-one years of age and upwards, shall be entitled to vote." "*TOWN COUNCIL.* ELECTION NOTICE," (San Francisco) *Alta California*, January 11, 1849.

22. "The American hearts beat strongly and proudly, as they felt that they had planted the flag under which they were born and reared upon this wild western shore of the new continent." "Signing the Constitution," (San Francisco) *Alta California*, November 22, 1849.

23. "[San Francisco] is perhaps, the most perfectly cosmopolitan city on earth. All tints of complexion, from the deep cerberean hue of that bell-ringing Cuffee, the city-crier, to the white Caucasian skin that shows the complexion of Power's Greek Slave . . . are found here." "San Francisco Now and to Be," (San Francisco) *Alta California*, December 14, 1850.

24. "A representation of the landing of the Pilgrims on Plymouth [R]ock, was very well executed. Over the picture was the inscription, '*Religion, Liberty and Law*,' and on the reverse '*Sons of the Pilgrims on the shores of the Pacific*.'" "THE CELEBRATION," (San Francisco) *Alta California*, October 31, 1850.

25. "It has long been known that the tendency of Civilization is to progress towards the realms of the sitting sun. . . . In the thickly settled States of the Atlantic, the rage for removing towards the setting sun is this year the theme of much remark." "West Moving West," (San Francisco) *Alta California*, July 10, 1851.

26. "The staid matron and quiet maid of our own Atlantic States—the gay and sparkling daughters of Erin, and the beautious [*sic*] gazelle-eyed maidens of

Alta California shone conspicuously in the dance." "BALL AT THE PARKER HOUSE," (San Francisco) *Alta California*, May 24, 1849.
27. "The omnibusses commenced running over the plank road to the Mission yesterday. How many pleasant and unpleasant remembrances these vehicles recall to the mind . . . all come in with the memories of omnibus riding in the cities of the Atlantic." "CITY INTELLIGENCE," (San Francisco) *Alta California*, June 2, 1851.
28. "The following company left this place on the 6th inst., for their homes in the Atlantic States." "SACRAMENTO NEWS," (San Francisco) *Alta California*, June 15, 1852.

Introduction

1. United States Census Bureau, United States Census 2020, official questionnaire, question 8, https://www2.census.gov/programs-surveys/decennial/2020/technical-documentation/questionnaires-and-instructions/questionnaires/2020-informational-questionnaire-english_DI-Q1.pdf.
2. Aida Hurtado, David E. Hayes-Bautista, R. Burciaga Valdez, and Anthony C. R. Hernández, *Redefining California: Latino Social Engagement in a Multicultural Society* (Los Angeles: UCLA Chicano Studies Research Center, 1992), 59, table 6.1.
3. J. S. Holliday, *The World Rushed In: The California Gold Rush Experience* (New York: Simon & Schuster, 1981).
4. David E. Hayes-Bautista, *El Cinco de Mayo: An American Tradition* (Berkeley, Los Angeles, & London: University of California Press, 2012).
5. David E. Hayes-Bautista, *La Nueva California: Latinos from Pioneers to Post Millennials*, 2nd ed. (Berkeley, Los Angeles, & London: University of California Press, 2017).
6. "Libreria Madero. Quienes Somos," www.libreriafimadero.com/madero.html.
7. David E. Hayes-Bautista, Werner Schink, and Jorge Chapa, *The Burden of Support: Young Latinos in an Aging Society* (Stanford, CA: Stanford University Press, 1987).
8. David E. Hayes-Bautista, *La Nueva California: Latinos in the Golden State*, 1st ed. (Berkeley & Los Angeles: University of California Press, 2004).
9. Doris Marion Wright, "The Making of Cosmopolitan California. An Analysis of Immigration, 1848–1870," *California Historical Society Quarterly* 19, no. 4 (December 1940): 323–43.

10. Richard L. Nostrand, "Mexican Americans circa 1850," *Annals of the Association of American Geographers* 65, no. 3 (September 1975): 378–90.
11. Leonard Pitt, *The Decline of the Californios* (Berkeley: University of California Press, 1966).
12. Julian Samora and Patricia Vandel Simon, *A History of the Mexican-American People* (Notre Dame, IN: University of Notre Dame Press, 1993), 113.
13. Leo Grebler, Joan W. Moore, and Ralph C. Guzman, *The Mexican-American People: The Nation's Second Largest Minority* (New York: Free Press, 1970), 44.
14. Arthur F. Corwin, "Mexican-American History: An Assessment," in *The Chicano*, ed. Norris Hundley Jr. (Santa Barbara, CA: Clio Books, 1973), 8.
15. A modern edition is Richard Henry Dana, *Two Years Before the Mast. A Personal Narrative of Life at Sea*, ed. Thomas Philbrick (New York & London: Penguin, 1981).
16. Paul G. Sweetser, "History of Fiesta," *Old Spanish Days Santa Barbara—Fiesta* (2022), https://www.sbfiesta.org/history-santa-barbara-fiesta.
17. Jo Mora, *Californios: The Saga of the Hard-Riding Vaqueros, America's First Cowboys* (Garden City, NY: Doubleday, 1949).
18. United States Census Bureau, *Quick Facts*, Lompoc city, California, https://www.census.gov/quickfacts/lompoccitycalifornia;.
19. "On the Wing," *Lompoc Record*, October 9, 1875, 2.
20. "Married," *Lompoc Record*, April 1, 1876, 3.
21. "Died," and "Pedro Barrara," *Lompoc Record*, February 14, 1880, 2.
22. "Brief Items," *Lompoc Record*, March 6, 1880, 3.
23. "Brief Items," *Lompoc Record*, August 20, 1887, 3.
24. "Notice of Intention," *Lompoc Record*, June 8, 1889, 2.
25. Many of these newspapers only survive today in incomplete runs or are missing occasional issues. Microfims of all these newspapers are archived at the UCLA CESLAC offices and are available for on-site public use. As of this writing, with the exception of the San Francisco *Alta California* and the Los Angeles *La Crónica* and *El Clamor Público*, they have not yet been digitized in the California Digital Newspaper Collection maintained by the Center for Bibliographical Studies and Research at the University of California, Riverside, https://cbsr.ucr.edu/CDNC.
26. Maria del Carmen Ferreyra and David S. Reher, eds. and trans., *The Gold Rush Diary of Ramon Gil Navarro* (Lincoln: University of Nebraska, 2000); Edwin A. Beilharz and Carlos U. Lopez, eds. and trans., *We Were 49ers: Chilean Accounts of the California Gold Rush* (Pasadena, CA: Ward Ritchie, 1976).
27. Gregorio Mora-Torres, *Californio Voices: The Oral Memoirs of José María Amador and Lorenzo Asisara* (Denton: University of North Texas Press,

2005); Robert Ryal Miller, *Juan Alvarado, Governor of California, 1836–1842* (Norman: University of Oklahoma Press, 1998).
28. Doyce B. Nunis Jr., ed., *Tales of Mexican California. Cosas de California* (Santa Barbara, CA: Bellerophon Books, 1994), 53–65.
29. Anselm Strauss and Barney Glaser, *The Discovery of Grounded Theory: Methods for Qualitative Research* (Chicago: Aldine, 1967).
30. Kathy Charmaz, *Constructing Grounded Theory* (Thousand Oaks, CA: Sage, 2006).
31. Richard Henry Morefield, "Mexicans in the California Mines, 1848–1853," *California Historical Society Quarterly* 35, no. 1 (March 1956): 37–46.
32. *Chino* can mean, variously, "kid," "curly-haired," "halfbreed," or even "Chinese." Without knowing more about this individual, it is hard to say which connotation his nickname bore.
33. Nunis, ed., *Tales*, pp. 55–56.
34. Beilharz and Lopez, *We Were 49ers*, 103–4.
35. "Aviso sobre minas," (San Francisco) *La Voz de Méjico*, August 13, 1863, 3.
36. "La mina de Zaragoza," (San Francisco) *La Voz de Méjico*, March 19, 1863, 2.
37. "Las Minas de Long Pine, Owens Valley," (San Francisco) *El Nuevo Mundo*, June 29, 1867, 2.
38. "Correspondencia de La Cronica," (Los Angeles) *La Crónica*, August 15, 1874, 2; "Santa Barbara," (Los Angeles) *La Crónica*, September 9, 1874, 3; "James William BRECK . . . Boston to California 1829–30," https://www.ancestry.com/boards/thread.aspx?mv=flat&m=17&p=surnames.breck.
39. "Latest from the Mines. Mockelumne Diggings, May 29, 1849," (San Francisco) *Alta California*, June 21, 1849, 2.
40. "San Joaquin Intelligence. A Lump Weighing 13 Pounds," (San Francisco) *Alta California*, October 14, 1850, 2.
41. Persons from the Mexican state of Sonora were known as *sonorenses*—or, in contemporary English, "Sonoranians"—but during the Gold Rush this also became a generic term for any recent Mexican immigrants, regardless of their state of origin. The origins of the *sonorenses* in Coronel's group, therefore, are not entirely clear.
42. Nunis, ed., *Tales*, 53–55.
43. "Del rio de las Salinas," (San Francisco) *La Voz de Méjico*, September 26, 1863, 3. *Hijos del pais* (native sons) was a term commonly used in the period for Californios.
44. "From the Southern Mines," (San Francisco) *Alta California*, August 1, 1851, 2.

45. "A Hard Case," (San Francisco) *Alta California*, October 20, 1851, 2.
46. "San Joaquin Intelligence—Died," (San Francisco) *Alta California*, October 4, 1851, 2.
47. "Correspondencia particular de La Crónica—Lone Pine," (Los Angeles) *La Crónica*, November 5, 1873, 2. Victor was the brother of Prudent Beaudry, who became mayor of Los Angeles in 1874. See also *Frenchtown Confidential*, http://frenchtownconfidential.blogspot.com/2017/01/the-forgotten-beaudry-brother.html.
48. Philip Wayne Powell, *Mexico's Miguel Caldera: The Taming of America's First Frontier (1548–1597)* (Tucson: University of Arizona Press, 1977), 4–9.
49. "Stanislaus 'Diggings' Jamestown," (San Francisco) *Alta California*, June 21, 1849, 2.
50. "San Joaquin Intelligence," (San Francisco) *Alta California*, October 6, 1851, 2.
51. "Sonora Correspondence," (San Francisco) *Alta California*, March 25, 1853, 1.
52. "Mining on Kern and White Rivers," (San Francisco) *Alta California*, March 15, 1860, 1.
53. "Sale Postponed," (San Francisco) *Alta California*, September 17, 1851, 3.
54. "Minas de Zaragoza y Todos Santos," (San Francisco) *La Voz de Méjico*, December 13, 1862, 2.
55. "Aviso a los Hispano-Americanos" [advertisement], (San Francisco) *Alta California*, August 30, 1849, 2.
56. "Fatal Accident," (San Francisco) *Alta California*, December 6, 1856, 1.
57. "Accident at the San Gabriel Mines," (Los Angeles) *El Clamor Público*, October 22, 1859, 3.
58. "Los Mejicanos en Nueva Almaden," (San Francisco) *El Nuevo Mundo*, February 10, 1865, 2.
59. David E. Hayes-Bautista and Jorge Chapa, "Latino Terminology: Conceptual Bases for Standardized Terminology," *American Journal of Public Health* 77, no. 1 (1987): 61–68.
60. The Census holds the names of individuals confidential for seventy-two years. See United States Census Bureau, "The 72-Year Rule," *Census History*, rev. January 26, 2022, https://www.census.gov/history/www/genealogy/decennial_census_records/the_72_year_rule_1.html.
61. Most returns for the 1890 census were destroyed by a fire in 1921. United States Census Bureau, "Availability of 1890 Census," *Census History*, rev. December 8, 2021, https://www.census.gov/history/www/genealogy/

decennial_census_records/availability_of_1890_census.html; Kellee Blake, "'First in the Path of the Firemen.' The Fate of the 1890 Population Census," pts. 1–2, *Prologue* 28, no. 1 (Spring 1996), US National Archives website, https://www.archives.gov/publications/prologue/1996/spring/1890-census-1.html; and https://www.archives.gov/publications/prologue/1996/spring/1890-census-2.html.

62. David L. Word and R. Colby Perkins Jr., "Building a Spanish Surname List for the 1990's—A New Approach to an Old Problem," U.S. Bureau of the Census, Population Division, Technical Working Paper No. 13 (Washington, DC: U.S. Bureau of the Census, 1996), 13.

63. Lyman D. Platt, *Hispanic Surnames and Family History* (Baltimore: Genealogical Publishing, 1996); Gutierre Tibón, *Diccionario etimológico comparado de los apellidos españoles, hispano-americanos y filipinos*, 3rd ed. (Mexico City: Fondo de Cultura Económica, 2001).

64. Ted Gosten, *Southern California Vital Records*, vol. 1, *Los Angeles County, 1850–1859* (Sherman Oaks CA: Generations, 2001).

65. The odd pronunciation of this name by English speakers persists in a local place name; see "Palm Trees, Sandy Beach Belies [sic] a Checkered Past," *Lompoc Record*, February 28, 2006, A2.

66. Juan Francisco Dana, *The Blond Ranchero: Memories of Juan Francisco Dana* (Arroyo Grande, CA: South County Historical Society, 1999), 65–67.

67. Jeffrey S. Passel, Mark Hugo Lopez, and D'Vera Cohn, "U.S. Hispanic Population Continued Its Geographic Spread in the 2010s," Pew Research Center, February 3, 2022, https://www.pewresearch.org/fact-tank/2022/02/03/u-s-hispanic-population-continued-its-geographic-spread-in-the-2010s/.

68. US Census Bureau." Census Bureau Releases Estimates of Undercount and Overcount in the 2020 Census," March 10, 2022, https://www.census.gov/newsroom/press-releases/2022/2020-census-estimates-of-undercount-and-overcount.html.

69. "Interview of the Select Committees of the Senate of the United States and of the House of Representatives to Make Provision for Taking the Tenth Census, with Prof. Francis A. Walker, Superintendent of the Census," *Miscellaneous Documents of the Senate of the United States for the Third Session of the Forty-Fifth Congress, 1878–'79*, 4 vols. (Washington, DC: Government Printing Office, 1879), vol. 1, Miscellaneous Document 26, p. 15. On issues of using Census data for historical research generally, see Richard H. Steckel, "The Quality of Census Data for Historical Inquiry: A Research Agenda," *Social*

Science History 15, no. 4 (Winter 1991): 579–99, https://doi.org/10.1017/S0145553200021313.
70. Louisiana Clayton Dart, ed., *La Fiesta de San Luis Obispo, Inc. La Fiesta '69: Portola's Trek 1769* (San Luis Obispo, CA: San Luis Obispo County Historical Museum, 1969), 21.
71. Hayes-Bautista, *El Cinco de Mayo*, chaps. 2–3.
72. David E. Hayes-Bautista, Cynthia L. Chamberlin, Branden Jones, Juan Carlos Cornejo, Cecilia Cañadas, Carlos Martinez, and Gloria Meza, "Empowerment, Expansion and Engagement: Las Juntas Patrióticas in California, 1848–1869," *California History*, 85, no. 1 (2007), 4–23.
73. The role of Latina women in California during the Gold Rush and US Civil War deserves much further study, including statistical study. The rancheros list and the junta patriótica lists used here contain both men and women, often intermingled; for any future works focusing on Latina women, they would have to be disaggregated by sex. Given more time for the lengthy process of identification of individuals and disaggregation of our data sets by sex, we will be able to treat males and females separately in future publications.
74. "1850 Census Records," United States National Archives website, revised August 23, 2022, https://www.archives.gov/research/census/1850.
75. Hayes-Bautista, et al., "Empowerment, Expansion, and Engagement."
76. "The Californian Race," (San Francisco) *Alta California*, June 5, 1852, 6.
77. Richard Griswold del Castillo, *The Los Angeles Barrio 1850–1890: A Social History* (Berkeley: University of California Press, 1979), 74–77.
78. Rodolfo Acuña, *Occupied America: A History of Chicanos*, 4th ed. (New York: Addison Wesley Longman, 2000), 143.
79. These parish records, extending through 1850, still exist and have been extracted and digitized by the Early California Population Project at the Huntington Library, San Marino, California, https://www.huntington.org/ecpp.
80. Although the Spanish-language term for a female Californio was *Californiana*, the term Californio here is used to refer to both sexes, for readability.
81. A paper submitted and currently undergoing peer review provides and analyzes marriage data from the Los Angeles County Recorder's Office for the years 1851–1910. While the birthplaces of bride and groom were routinely included in these records from 1873 through 1910, generally the spouses' birthplaces were not recorded before 1873, with an anomalous exception of the twenty-two months from June 1858 through March 1860. The overall

pattern of endogamous and exogamous marriages observed in 1873–1910—two-thirds to three-quarters endogamous—also holds true in the marriages recorded during that brief period in 1858–1860 during which the spouses' birthplaces were recorded. Therefore, the 106 couples who married in those twenty-two months represent patterns of endogamous marriage during the Gold Rush and Civil War very similar to those in 1873–1910, indicating a regular practice. David E. Hayes-Bautista, Cynthia L. Chamberlin, and Paul Hsu, "Latino Marriage Patterns Recorded in Los Angeles County, 1851–1910."

82. "Bando aboliendo las castas y la esclavitud entre los mexicanos. El bachiller don José María Morelos, cura y juez eclesiástico de Carácuaro, teniente del excelentísimo señor don Miguel Hidalgo, Capitán General de la América (17 de noviembre de 1810)," in Ernesto de la Torre Villar, ed., *La Constitución de Apatzingán y los creadores del Estado Mexicano*, 2nd ed. Instituto de Investigaciones Históricas, Serie Documental, 5 (Mexico City: UNAM-Instituto de Investigaciones Históricas, 2010), 331. See also Alice L. Baumgartner, *South to Freedom: Runaway Slaves to Mexico and the Road to the Civil War* (New York: Basic Books, 2020), 51–97, 111–20.

83. English-born William E. P. Hartnell (1798–1854) originally came to California as a merchant in 1822 and subsequently converted to Roman Catholicism, became a Mexican citizen, and married María Teresa de la Guerra y Noriega. This made Hartnell a brother-in-law of delegate Pablo de la Guerra y Noriega.

84. English text in J. Ross Browne, ed., *Report of the Debates in the Convention of California, On the Formation of the State Constitution, in September and October, 1849* (Washington, DC: John T. Towers, 1850), 63; contemporary Spanish translation: "El S[eño]r Botts dijo, que no ponia objecion al color, escepto en cuanto indicase las razas inferiores de la especie humana," in J. Ross Browne, ed., *Relacion de los debates de la Convencion de California sobre la formacion de la Constitucion del Estado, en Setiembre y Octubre de 1849* (New York: S. W. Benedict, 1851), 67.

85. "The American public . . . the most energetic and adventurous of modern races," in Browne, ed., *Report of the Debates*, 405; "El pueblo angloamericano . . . la raza moderna mas activa y emprendedora," in Browne, ed., *Relacion de los debates*, 376.

86. In 1849 there were as yet very few Asians in California, although that would change by the following year. This explains the relative absence of mention of Asians in the debates of the constitutional convention. When Asians did begin to arrive in the state, however, they also were instantly relegated to the status of "inferior races" by the white majority of Atlantic Americans.

87. Browne, ed., *Report of the Debates*, 137; Spanish translation in Browne, ed., *Relacion de los debates*, 143: "Son perezosos por costumbre, dificil de gobernarse por leyes, inútiles y mal educados."

88. "In God's name, I say, let us make California a place where free white men can live," in Browne, ed., *Report of the Debates*, 148; Spanish translation in Browne, ed., *Relacion de los debates*, 154: "Por Dios, Señores, hagamos á California un lugar donde pueden vivir los hombres blancos." For a general survey of historical policies of exclusion of nonwhites in the United States, see Juan F. Perea, "On the Management of Non-Whites: Deportation and Exclusion as Techniques of White Supremacy," SSRN, February 25, 2020, https://ssrn.com/abstract=3544349 or http://dx.doi.org/10.2139/ssrn.3544349; also Reginald Horsman, *Race and Manifest Destiny: The Origins of American Racial Anglo-Saxonism* (Cambridge, MA: Harvard University Press, 1986). For precedents and parallel developments in Great Britain, see Reginald Horsman, "Origins of Racial Anglo-Saxonism in Great Britain Before 1850," *Journal of the History of Ideas* 37, no. 3 (July–September 1976): 387–410, https://www.jstor.org/stable/2708805.

89. William Marvin Mason, *Los Angeles Under the Spanish Flag: Spain's New World* (Burbank: Southern California Genealogical Society, 2004), 66, https://www.scgsgenealogy.com/free/media/los-angeles-under-the-spanish-flag-wmason.pdf.

90. Dana, *Two Years Before the Mast*, 127.

91. "Speech of Mr. Buchanan, of Pennsylvania," in *Appendix to the Congressional Globe, for the First Session, Twenty-Eighth Congress: Containing Speeches and Important State Papers*, eds. Francis Preston Blair and John C. Rives (Washington, DC: Blair & Rives, 1844), 722.

92. New York–born delegate Edward Gilbert implicitly recognized this possibility when he argued against restricting voting rights to white men: "We wish to give every Mexican citizen residing in California, who becomes a citizen of the United States, the free right to vote," in Browne, ed., *Report of the Debates*, 62; Spanish translation in Browne, ed., *Relacion de los debates*, 66: "Deseamos conceder el libre sufrajio a todo mejicano ciudadano residente en California que se haga ciudadano de los Estados Unidos."

93. "But there was one doctrine urged here, that really astonished him—that the treaty of peace between the United States and Mexico . . . could prescribe to this Convention what persons it should make voters in the State of California! The Congress of the United States could not do it. . . . The States of this Union are free and sovereign," in Browne, ed., *Report of the Debates*,

64; Spanish translation in Browne, ed., *Relacion de los debates*, 68–69: "Pero que aquí se arguia una doctrina que realmente le sorprendia—de que el tratado de paz entre los Estados Unidos y Méjico . . . pudiese dictar á esta Convencion la clase de personas á quienes debe conceder el derecho de votar en el Estado de California. Que el Congreso de los Estados Unidos no podia hacerlo . . . [q]ue los Estados Unidos eran libres y soberanos, y determinaban por sí el derecho del sufragio." In the Spanish version of this passage, "los Estados Unidos eran libres y soberanos" is a bad translation of what delegate Botts actually said, which was "the *States of this Union*," not the United States, "are free and sovereign." For a legal scholars' survey of the use of the states' rights doctrine to exclude specified groups from voting, see Guy-Uriel E. Charles and Luis Fuentes-Rohwer, "State's Rights, Last Rites, and Voting Rights," *Connecticut Law Review* 47, no. 2 (December 2014): 481–527, https://www.repository.law.indiana.edu/cgi/viewcontent.cgi?article=3046&=&context=facpub&=&sei-redir=1&referer=https%253A%252F%252Fscholar.google.com%252Fscholar%253Fhl%253Den%2526as_sdt%253D0%25252C5%2526q%253DStates%252527%252Brights%252Band%252Bvoting%252B19th%252Bcentury%2526btnG%253D#search=%22States%20rights%20voting%2019th%20century%22.

94. "What are the rights of citizens of the United States? . . . Does it necessarily follow that the right of suffrage is one of these rights? . . . It is not necessarily the right of a citizen. He believed that the States in their sovereign capacity have a right to make their own regulations in respect to this matter. . . . The right of suffrage is not possessed by all citizens; it is not a general right." Browne, ed., *Report of the Debates*, 67; Spanish translation in Browne, ed., *Relacion de los debates*, 71: "¿Cuáles son los derechos de los ciudadanos de los Estados Unidos? . . . ¿Pretende alguno asegurar que estamos obligados á esto? No; pues ese no es necesariamente el derecho de un ciudadano. El . . . pensaba que los Estados, en sus atribuciones soberanas, tenian derecho de formar sus propias reglas respecto á estae asunto. . . . El derecho de sufragio no lo posee todo ciudadano; no es un derecho general."

95. "Un hombre podia ser ciudadano de los Estados Unidos, sin que por esto tuviese el derecho de votar. No es el Congreso el que decida esta cuestion; decídela el Estado. La constitucion concede a los Estados el derecho de determinar quienes hayan de ser los votantes." Browne, ed., *Relación de los debates*, 73.

96. "All he asked was that citizens of Mexico who had become citizens of the United States should be placed upon the same footing with ourselves; that white citizens alone should be admitted to the right of suffrage." Browne, ed., *Report of the Debates*, 63. The speaker was Virginia-born Charles T. Botts, a delegate

from Monterey. Spanish translation in Browne, ed., *Relacion de los debates*, 67:"Que todo lo que pedia era que los ciudadanos de Méjico que se hiciesen ciudadanos de los Estados Unidos estén con nosotros bajo el mismo pié, admitiéndose al goce de derecho de sufrajio a los ciudadanos blancos únicamente."

97. "The meaning of the word 'white,' in the report of the Committee, was not generally understood in this country [California], though well understood in the United States." Browne, ed., *Report of the Debates*, 62; Spanish translation in Browne, ed., *Relacion de los debates*, 66–67: "Dijo que el sentido de la palabra 'blanco' que contiene el informe de la comision, no se comprendia jeneralmente en este pais, aun que se comprendia muy bien en los Estados Unidos."

98. "[De la Guerra y Noriega] desired that it should be perfectly understood in the first place what is the true signification of the word 'white.' Many citizens of California have received from nature a very dark skin; nevertheless, there are among them men who have heretofore been allowed to vote, and not only that, but to fill the highest public offices. It would be very unjust to deprive them of the privilege of citizens merely because nature had not made them white." Browne, ed., *Report of the Debates*, 63; Spanish translation in Browne, ed., *Relacion de los debates*, 67: Relacion de los debates, "Deseaba se entendiese perfectamente, en primer lugar, cuál era la verdadera significacion de la palabra 'blancos.' Que muchos ciudadanos de California habian recibido de la naturaleza una tez morena; y sin embargo hay entre ellos hombres que hasta ahora han sido admitidos a votar, y no solo eso, sino á llenar los puestos públicos mas altos; y sería muy injusto privarles del privilejio de ciudadanos, meramente porque la naturaleza no los hubiese hecho blancos."

99. "Mr. Gwin asked the gentleman from Santa Barbara . . . whether Indians and Africans were entitled to vote according to Mexican law." Browne, ed., *Report of the Debates*, ; Spanish translation in Browne, ed., *Relacion de los debates*, 68: "El S[eñ]or Gwin preguntó al representante por Santa Bárbara . . . si los indios y los africanos tenian derecho á votar, segun las leyes mejicanas." For Gwin as a slave owner, see Rachel St. John, "The Unpredictable America of William Gwin. Expansion, Secession, and the Unstable Borders of Nineteenth-Century North America," *Journal of the Civil War Era* 6, no. 1 (March 2016), 60.

100. "Mr. Noriego said that, according to Mexican law, no race of any kind is excluded from voting. Mr. Gwin wished to know if Indians were considered Mexican citizens? Mr. Noriego said that so far were they considered citizens, that some of the first men in the [Mexican] Republic were of the Indian race." Browne, ed., *Report of the Debates*, 63; Spanish translation in Browne, ed.,

Relacion de los debates, 68: "El S[eñ]or Noriego dijo que, según las leyes mejicanas, ninguna raza, de cualquier clase que fuese, estaba escluida de votar. El S[eñ]or Gwin dijo que deseaba saber si los indios estaban considerados como ciudadanos mejicanos. El S[eñ]or Noriego dijo que, estaban tan considerados como tales, que algunos de los primeros hombres de la Republica eran de raza india."

101. "If such is the fact, all of the African race living in California . . . would be included as citizens, and would of course be entitled to aspire to the position of Governor." Browne, ed., *Report of the Debates*, 158; Spanish translation in Browne, ed., *Relacion de los debates*, 164: "Si tal es el caso, todos los individuos de raza africana que vivían en California . . . se considerarían como ciudadanos, y por consiguiente con derecho a aspirar al empleo de Gobernador."

102. "There was a[s] great mixture of population in Louisiana as there is here. The Constitution of that State says: 'In all elections held by the people, every free white male . . . shall have the right of voting." Browne, ed., *Report of the Debates*, 67–68; Spanish translation in Browne, ed., *Relacion de los debates*, 72: "Tengase presente que en la Luisiana habia una poblacion tan mista como la de aquí. La Constitucion de aquel Estado dice: que 'Tendrá derecho a votar en todas las elecciones que tenga el pueblo, todo hombre blanco libre.'"

103. "Every free male who [is] . . . a citizen of the Republic of Texas . . . *Indians not taxed, Africans, and descendants of Africans, excepted* . . . shall be deemed a qualified elector, &c." Browne, ed., *Report of the Debates*, 64; Spanish translation in Browne, ed., *Relacion de los debates*, 69: "Toda persona libre, varon . . . [que] sea ciudadano de la República de Tejas . . . *excepto los indios que no pagan contribuciones, los africanos y los descendientes de africanos*, será considerado como elector idóneo, &c."

104. "We do not debar the Spanish, or the French, or the Italians from voting by the use of this word ['white']. They are darker than the Anglo-Saxon race, but they are white men." Browne, ed., *Report of the Debates*, 72; Spanish translation in Browne, ed., *Relacion de los debates*, 77: "Usando esta palabra ['blanco'] no escluimos de votar á los españoles, ni á los franceses, ni á lo italianos, que aunque son mas trigueños que la raza anglo-sajona, son hombres blancos."

105. "Mr. Semple . . . saw no better way of settling the difficulty than by adopting the word 'white' before male citizen, which is sufficiently explained in the courts of the United States. . . . Mr. Gilbert . . . objected to the words 'white male citizen' on the ground that they were not sufficiently explicit. They might be very well understood in our courts, but it was necessary that every citizen

should understand the provisions of this Constitution, without going into court to have them explained." Browne, ed., *Report of the Debates*, 72; Spanish translation in Browne, ed., *Relacion de los debates*, 77: "El S[eñ]or Semple . . . no veia mejor modo de arreglar la dificultad, que insertando la palabra 'blanco' entre las palabras 'hombre' y 'ciudadano,' lo cual está suficientemente esplicado en todos los tribunales de los Estados Unidos. . . . El S[eñ]or Gilbert . . . [t]enia objecion á las palabras 'hombre blanco ciudadano,' en el concepto de que no eran suficientemente esplicitas. Que podian entenderse muy bien en nuestros tribunales, pero que era necesario que todos los ciudadanos entendiesen las disposiciones de esta Constitucion, sin tener que ir á los tribunales á enterarse de su espíritu."

106. "This constitution, in its unavoidable conformity to American principles, restricts from the right of suffrage numbers of Indians, descendants of Africans, &c., whom it is asserted possessed that right under the Mexican supremacy." Browne, ed., *Report of the Debates*, 406; Spanish translation in Browne, ed., *Relacion de los debates*, 377: "Esta Constitucion bajo la forma reconocida por el pueblo de los Estados Unidos que niega el derecho de sufragio á los indios, descendientes de la raza africana, etc., que segun se ha dicho gozaban de aquel derecho bajo el régimen mejicano."

107. In northern California, where because of the Gold Rush the population quickly became dominated by an Atlantic American majority, leaving such decisions to the courts proved detrimental to Latinos. In southern California, however, where Latinos still comprised most of the population until after ca. 1880, Latino men frequently served on juries—whose members were drawn from the voter rolls—and a few, such as Ygnacio Sepúlveda, were even judges. A statistical survey of Los Angeles jury trials during that period also indicates no regular pattern of prejudice against Latino defendants. Paul R. Spitzzeri, "On a Case by Case Basis: Ethnicity and Los Angeles Courts, 1850–1875," *California History* 83, no. 2 (Fall 2005): 26–39.

108. Baumgartner, *South to Freedom*, passim.

109. Eric Foner, "Racial Attitudes of the New York Free Soilers," *New York History* 46, no. 4 (October 1965): 311–29.

110. "It has likewise been asserted that the people of the southern part of the country are in favor of slavery; this is entirely false. They have equally as much desire as any portion of the people of California to avoid the curse of slavery." Browne, ed., *Report of the Debates*, 446; Spanish translation in Browne, ed., *Relacion de los debates*, 410–11: "Se ha dicho tambien que el pueblo de la parte meridional del pais está en favor de la esclavitud; esto es absolutamente

falso. El pueblo de aquella parte del pais es tan opuesto á la esclavitud, como lo puede ser cualquier otro."

111. "We have introduced into our bill of rights a clause permitting foreigners to exercise the same rights in reference to holding lands and enjoying the political privileges of this country which we enjoy ourselves. What will be said of our Constitution if we assert one thing in our bill of rights—extend the privileges of our free institutions to all classes, both from foreign countries and our own, and then in another exclude a class speaking our own language, born and brought up in the United States, acquainted with our customs, and calculated to make useful citizens[?]" Browne, ed., *Report of the Debates*, 140; Spanish translation in Browne, ed., *Relacion de los debates*, 146: "Hemos puesto en nuestro bill de facultades una cláusula que permite á los estrangeros el ejercicio de los mismos derechos en cuanto á poseer tierras, y gozar en este pais de los mismos privilegios políticos que nosotros gozamos.... ¿Que se dirá de nuestra Constitucion si acordamos una cosa en nuestro bill da facultades, haciendo estensivo todas clases nuestra libres instituciones, y despues acordar en otra parte la esclusion de una clase que habla nuestro idioma, nacida y educada en los Estados Unidos; que tiene nuestras mismas costumbres, y aptan como cualquiera otra clase para ser ciudadanos útiles[?]"

112. "There is now a respectable and intelligent class of population in the mines; men of talent and education; men digging there in the pit with the spade and pick, who would be amply competent to sit in these halls. Do you think they would dig with the African? No, sir, they would leave this country first." Browne, ed., *Report of the Debates*, 333; Spanish translation in Browne, ed., *Relacion de los debates*, 308: "Hay ahora en las minas una clase de poblacion respetable é inteligente; hombres que trabajan en los placeres con la pala y el azadon y que serian muy competente para ocupar un asiento en esta Asamblea. ¿Creeis que trabajarian mezclados con los africanos? No, señor; antes saldrian de este pais." John M. Rozett, "Racism and Republican Emergence in Illinois: A Re-evaluation of Republican Negrophobia," *Civil War History* 22, no. 2 (June 1976): 101–15.

113. "We should protect them against the monopolies of capitalists who would bring their [N]egroes here. We should protect them against a class of society that would degrade labor, and thereby arrest the progress of enterp[r]ise and greatly impair the prosperity of the State." Browne, ed., *Report of the Debates*, 140; Spanish translation in Browne, ed., *Relacion de los debates*, 146: "Debemos protegerlos contra el monopolio de los capitalistas que quisiesen traer sus negros aquí. Debemos protegerlos contra una clase de hombres que

degradarían el trabajo, y por consiguiente detrendrian el progreso de las empresas, y serian perjuiciales, en gran manera, á la prosperidad del Estado."
114. "An immense and overwhelming population of [N]egroes, who have never been freemen; who have never been accustomed to provide for themselves.... . The whole country would be filled with emancipated slaves—the worst species of population—prepared to do nothing but steal, or live upon our means as paupers." Browne, ed., *Report of the Debates*, 138; Spanish translation in Browne, ed., *Relacion de los debates*, 144: "Tendriamos una inmensa poblacion de negros, que nunca han sido libres, ni han estado jamas acostumbrados á buscarse la vida.... Se llenaria todo el país de negros emancipados, que es la peor clase de poblacion—dispuesta á no hacer nada mas que robar, ó vivir a nuestras espensas como mendigos." For a history of white slaveowners' and other whites' negrophobia, see Lacy K. Ford, *Deliver Us from Evil: The Slavery Question in the Old South* (Oxford & New York: Oxford University Press, 2009).
115. "When [N]egroes are free, they are the freest of all human beings; they are free in morals, free in all the vices of brutish and depraved race. They are a most troublesome and unprofitable population.... Of all classes of population, the free [N]egroes are the most ignorant, wretched, and depraved." Browne, ed., *Report of the Debates*, 144; Spanish translation in Browne, ed., *Relacion de los debates*, 150: "Cuando los negros adquieren su libertad, son los seres humanos mas libres. Son desmoralizados y se abandonan libremente á los vicios de una raza bruta y depravada, viniendo á ser la poblacion mas molesta y desventajosa. ... De todas las clases de la poblacion, la de negros libres es la mas ignorante, miserable, y depravada."
116. "Why, sir, of all the States that I have any knowledge of, free or slave States, it is admitted by all, whether philanthropists for blacks or for all mankind, that the free [N]egro is one of the greatest evils that society can be afflicted with." Browne, ed., *Report of the Debates*, 140; Spanish translation in Browne, ed., *Relacion de los debates*, 146: "¿Por qué se admite por todos los Estados que conozco, tengan ó no esclavos, que el negro libre es uno de los mas grandes males que pueden afligir á una sociedad?" Hartnell's Spanish translation of Wozencraft's racist declaration is somewhat imprecisa, but it maintains the gist of his meaning.
117. "No population ... could be more repugnant to the feelings of the people, or injurious to the prosperity of the community, than free [N]egroes. They are idle in their habits, difficult to be governed by the laws, thriftless, and uneducated." Browne, ed., *Report of the Debates*, 137; Spanish translation in

Browne, ed., *Relacion de los debates*, 143:"Ninguna poblacion . . . puede ser mas repugnante á los sentimientos del pueblo, ni mas perjudicial a la prosperidad del Estado, que los negros libres. Son perezosos por costumbre, difícil de gobernarse por leyes, inútiles, y mal educados."

118. "I am opposed to the introduction into this country of [N]egroes, pœons [*sic*] of Mexico, or any class of that kind; I care not whether they be free or bond. It is a well established fact, and the history of every State in the Union clearly proves it, that [N]egro labor, whether slave or free, when opposed to white labor, degrades it." Browne, ed., *Report of the Debates*, 143; Spanish translation in Browne, ed., *Relacion de los debates*, 149: "Estoy opuesto á que se introduzcan en este pais negros, peones de Méjico, ú otra clase semejante; no me cuido de que sean libres ó esclavos. Es un hecho bien patente, y la historia de todos los Estados de la Union lo comprueba claramente, que al trabajador blanco lo degrada." The Spanish translation of the last phrase has omitted "when opposed to white labor."

119. "In Alabama some years ago . . . a law was passed . . . requiring that all the free [N]egroes who were not residents in the State for a certain number of years antecedent to the law, should have a certain time to leave the State, and in the event of their not leaving by that time, they were liable to be seized upon by any person and sold as slaves." Browne ed., *Report of the Debates*, 332; Spanish translation in Browne, ed., *Relacion de los debates*, 307: "En Alabama hace algunos años . . . adoptó una ley previniendo que á todos los negros libres no residentes en el Estado por cierto número de años antes, se les concediese algun tiempo para salir del Estado, y sino [*sic*, si no] lo verificaban durante este tiempo quedaban sujetos a ser arrestados por cualquier persona, y vendidos como esclavos."

120. "Article II. *Right of Suffrage*. Sec. 1. Every white male citizen of the United States, and every white male citizen of Mexico who shall have elected to become a citizen of the United States . . . shall be entitled to vote at all elections . . . provided, that nothing herein contained, shall be construed to prevent the Legislature . . . from admitting to the right of suffrage, Indians or the descendants of Indians, in such special cases as . . . the legislative body may deem just and proper." Browne, ed., Report of the Debates, iv; Spanish translation in Browne, ed., *Relacion de los debates*, iv: "Articulo II. *Derecho de Sufragio*. Sec. 1. Todo ciudadano varon blanco de los Estados Unidos y todo ciudadano varon blanco de Méjico que prefiera ser ciudadano de los Estados Unidos . . . tendrá derecho á votar en todas las elecciones . . . advirtiendo que nada de lo aquí contenido podrá interpretarse como impedimento para que la Legislatura

deje de admitir al derecho de sufragio . . . á los indios, ó á los descendientes de los indios, en los casos especiales en que . . . la Legislatura lo creyere justo y oportuno."

121. "I speak knowingly when I say a large portion of that district do not desire such a provision. . . . The native inhabitants of the country do not desire it." Browne, ed., *Report of the Debates*, 151; Spanish translation in Browne, ed., *Relacion de los debates*, 157: "Hablo con conocimiento del asunto cuando aseguro que la majoría de aquel Distrito no desea tal disposición. . . . Los naturales del pais no lo desean."

122. Browne, ed., *Report of the Debates*, 337–40; Browne, ed., *Relacion de los debates*, 311–14.

123. Heath Dillard, *Daughters of the Reconquest: Women in Castilian Town Society, 1100–1300* (Cambridge: Cambridge University Press, 1984); Peter Thomas Conmy, *The Historical Spanish Origin of California's Community Property Law and Its Development and Adaptation to Meet the Needs of an American State* (San Francisco: Native Sons of the Golden West, 1957).

124. For the debate on marital community property, see Browne, ed., *Report of the Debates*, 257–69, with Francis Lippitt's fears for the foundations of civilization at pages 257–58; the final text of Article XI, Sec. 14, is at page xi. Spanish translation in Browne, ed., *Relacion de los debates*, 252–64, esp. 252 and xi.

125. Conmy, *The Historical Spanish Origin*, 24; Robert I. Burns, Introduction, *Las Siete Partidas*, ed. Robert I. Burns, vol. 1, *The Medieval Church: The World of Clerics and Laymen* (Philadelphia: University of Pennsylvania Press, 2001), xxiv–xxvi.

126. Browne, ed., *Report of the Debates*, xi; Spanish translation in Browne, ed., *Relacion de los debates*, xi: "Todas las leyes, decretos, reglamentos y ordenanzas, que por su naturaleza hubiera de ver la luz pública, seran publicados en ingles y en español."

127. See, for example, fols. 20r., 21v., 39r., 40rv., 42r. of his diary.

128. Robert N. Bellah, *Habits of the Heart: Individualism and Commitment in American Life* (New York: Harper & Row, 1985).

129. C. Alan Hutchinson, *Frontier Settlement in Mexican California. The Hijar-Padrés Colony and Its Origins, 1769–1835* (New Haven, CT: Yale University Press, 1969).

130. C. Alan Hutchinson, "An Official List of the Members of the Hijar-Padres Colony for Mexican California," *Pacific Historical Review* 42, no. 3 (August 1973): 407–18.

131. An image of the register of the church of San José y Nuestra Señora del

Sagrado Corazón in Mexico City, showing Felipe Arana's baptism on February 7, 1819, can be found at México, Distrito Federal, registros parroquiales y diocesanos, 1514–1970, database with images, *FamilySearch* website, https://familysearch.org/ark:/61903/1:1:NYQ7-4P1; Felipe de Jesus Jose Maria Arana Alderete, 1819, accessed August 26, 2022. The list of the Híjar-Padrés colonists transcribed in Hutchinson, "An Official List," mistakenly subtracts three years from Felipe's age and misgenders him as female (410).

132. Fol. 15r.

133. Browne, ed., *Report of the Debates*, 405–6; Spanish translation in Browne, ed., *Relacion de los debates*, 376–77: "Señor, ¿de qué manera obtuvo este territorio el pueblo angloamericano? . . . Fué por medio de una posesion armada. . . . Bajo la forma reconocida por el pueblo de los Estados Unidos que niega el derecho de sufragio á los indios, descendientes de la raza africana, etc., que segun se ha dicho gozaban de aquel derecho bajo el régimen mejicano." Although there were occasional unofficial efforts to interfere with their voting rights, in practice adult male Latinos usually retained the franchise, whatever their physical appearance, especially in Latino-majority areas like southern California; see, for example, Hayes-Bautista, *El Cinco de Mayo*, 31, 34–35, and nn. 73 and 82 on 202–3.

134. "Foreign Miners," (San Francisco) *Alta California*, April 5, 1850, p. 3.

135. Fol. 54r.

136. "Your paper of the 30th contains an article from the Sacramento Transcript, which states . . . that the Sheriff of Tuolumne County, in attempting to compel the foreigners to comply with the enactment taxing them, was killed. . . . This statement is entirely incorrect. . . . Only one person was killed, and that was a Mexican, who made an attempt on the life of the Sheriff . . . The most critical moment was at the time of the death of the Mexican. Several of his countrymen, who stood by, drew and cocked their fire-arms; upon which the Americans drew their revolvers. There was a pause, but fortunately neither party fired." "San Joaquin and Placer Intelligence," (San Francisco) *Alta California*, June 3, 1850, p. 2; Ramón Gil Navarro, *The Gold Rush Diary of Ramón Gil Navarro*, ed. and trans. María del Carmen Ferreyra and David S. Reher (Lincoln & London: University of Nebraska Press, 2000), 126–27; "San Joaquin Intelligence," (San Francisco) *Alta California*, September 2, 1850, p. 2; "San Joaquin Intelligence," (San Francisco) *Alta California*, July 24, 1850, p. 2.

137. Fols. 41v–42r.

138. The Huntington Library, Early California Population Project Database

(2006), Santa Cruz Mission marriage record 00885 and baptism records 02770 and 02795.
139. Untitled article, (San Francisco) *Alta California*, October 1, 1854, p. 2.
140. "Hai un Individuo Centroamericano" [advertisement], (San Francisco) *La Crónica*, December 15, 1854, p. 4.
141. "Public Schools in Sonora," *Sonora Union Democrat*, September 18, 1858, p. 2.
142. "Anglicismos," (San Francisco) *La Voz de Méjico*, May 26, 1863, p. 2.
143. "Pankekes, Tortillas y Pan En Santa Barbara," (Los Angeles) *El Clamor Público*, July 12, 1856, p. 4; "Estrella de Chile. Groserias de Familias, Jose Alcayaga" [advertisement], (San Francisco) *La Crónica*, December 15, 1854, p. 3.
144. "Cronica local, dia de muertos," (Los Angeles) *El Clamor Público*, November 7, 1857, p. 3; "Proclama de Acción de Gracias" [advertisement], (Los Angeles) *El Clamor Público*, November 24, 1855, p. 3.
145. "Celebration of the Anniversary at Santa Cruz" [letter to the editor], (San Francisco) *Alta California*, July 8, 1852, p. 4.
146. "Police Court," (San Francisco) *Alta California*, July 14, 1853, p. 2.
147. "Declaracion de Independencia. Julio 4 de 1776," (Los Angeles) *El Clamor Público*, July 3, 1855, p. 3.
148. "La Sociedad de Señoras de Mount Vernon, Al Pueblo de California," (Los Angeles) *El Clamor Público*, March 5, 1859, p. 1.
149. "Distinguished South American Dancers," (San Francisco) *Alta California*, June 29, 1853, p. 2.
150. "Musical—Theatrical," (San Francisco) *Alta California*, July 22, 1853, p. 2.
151. "Libreria Española" [advertisement], (San Francisco) *La Crónica*, December 15, 1854, p. 3. A *galop* was a contemporary dance similar to a polka.
152. "The [steamship] *Santa Cruz* brought up a number of Mexican political refugees, belonging to the Church party, who have been banished from the country by Pesquiera [*sic*, Pesqueira]. These gentlemen, it is stated, have been accused of no other than political offences, and are not to be regarded in a criminal light." "Later from Mexico," (San Francisco) *Alta California*, May 13, 1859, 2; "History," Central American Resource Center (CARECEN) website, 2022, https://www.carecen-la.org/history?locale=en.
153. "El tratado de Guadalupe Hidalgo nos ha concedido amplios privilegios. . . . Somos verdaderos ciudadanos, y como tales es nuestro deber tomar parte activa en los negocios públicos." "La Independencia de Mexico, el 16 de Setiembre," (Los Angeles) *El Clamor Público*, September 27, 1856, 2.
154. "Somos Californio por nacimiento y Americano por adopcion. El escudo

de la libertad y de la ley, nos defenderá contra las amenazas y los insultos." Untitled article, (Los Angeles) *El Clamor Público*, December 25, 1858, 2.

155. Hayes-Bautista, *El Cinco de Mayo*, especially chap. 4, for descriptions of patriotic celebrations in California, and chap. 5, for details on Latinos in the military.

156. With apologies to the great salsa singer Celia Cruz. One of her greatest hits was titled "Latinos en Estados Unidos, Ya casí somos una nación," music and lyrics by Titti Soto. Sony Records, 1994. Lyrics, https://globallessons.files.wordpress.com/2009/04/celiacruz-latinos-en-estados-unidos1.pdf.

157. "The Tug-of-War," *Los Angeles Times*, December 12, 1891, 8; "Santa Monica," *Los Angeles Times*, August 5, 1889, 7; "The Foresters. The Union Picnic at Santa Monica Canyon Yesterday," *Los Angeles Times*, August 16, 1893, 2.

158. A *niña bien educada* is a well brought-up, well-mannered girl or woman, regardless of social class. The colloquial term *niña bien*, however, deliberately denotes elevated social class. It does not translate readily into a word or phrase in US English, but carries connotations of gentility, elevated taste, and upper-class identity. In British English, it would translate as "posh girl." See Guadalupe Loaeza, *Las niñas bien: 25 años después*, 3rd. ed. (Mexico City: Editorial Océano de Mexico, S.A. de C. V., 2010).

159. The title page Matilde Veytia made for her fair copy of her father's diary proclaims it to be *Propiedad de Matilde V. de Veytia* (Property of Matilde V. de Veytia). It was a frequent custom for a married woman in Mexico to retain her maiden name and simply add her husband's surname at the end, preceded by the particle *de*; and a widow often reverted to the use of her maiden name, followed by the descriptive phrase *viuda de* (widow of) plus her late husband's surname. The *V* in Matilde's assertion of ownership, therefore, is an abbreviation either for *Veytia* or for *viuda*. Either way, it is clear that the title page and the facsimile it introduces must have been made after Matilde married her cousin Luis Veytia Villaseñor in 1890, thereby becoming Matilde Veytia de Veytia—and possibly not until after she was widowed in 1915, when she became Matilde Veytia, viuda de Veytia.

160. Justo Veytia, *Viaje a la Alta California, 1849–1850*, ed. Cuauhtémoc Velasco Ávila. Papeles de Familia (Mexico City: Instituto Nacional de Antropología e Historia, Universidad Nacional Autónoma de México, 2000).

161. As the planned premiere date will suggest, this exhibit unfortunately was sidelined by the COVID-19 pandemic.

162. David E. Hayes-Bautista, Marco Antonio Firebaugh, Cynthia L. Chamberlin,

and Christina Gamboa, "Reginaldo Francisco del Valle: UCLA's Forgotten Forefather," *Southern California Quarterly* 88, no. 1 (Spring 2006): 1–35; David E. Hayes-Bautista and Cynthia L. Chamberlin, "Cinco de Mayo's First Seventy-Five Years in Alta California: From Spontaneous Behavior to Sedimented Memory, 1862 to 1937," *Southern California Quarterly* 89, no. 1 (Spring 2007): 23–64; David E. Hayes-Bautista, Cynthia L. Chamberlin, Branden Jones, Juan Carlos Cornejo, Cecilia Cañadas, Carlos Martines, and Gloria Meza, "Empowerment, Expansion, and Engagement: *Las Juntas Patrióticas* in California, 1848–1869," *California History* 85, no. 1 (2007): 4–23, 66–70; David E. Hayes-Bautista and Cynthia L. Chamberlin, "Cinco de Mayo in Tuolumne County, 1862–1865: A New Light Shines on Tuolumne County's Latinos," *Chispa, the Quarterly of the Tuolumne County Historical Society* 48 (2008): 1715–22; David E. Hayes-Bautista, Cynthia L. Chamberlin, and Nancy Zuniga, "A Gold Rush Salvadoran in California's Latino World, 1857," *Southern California Quarterly* 91, no. 3 (Fall, 2009): 257–94; Paul Bryan Gray, David E. Hayes-Bautista, and Cynthia L. Chamberlin, "'The Men Were Left Astonished': Mexican Women in *las Juntas Patrióticas de Señoras*, 1863–1866," *Southern California Quarterly* 94, no. 2 (Summer 2012): 161–92; David E. Hayes-Bautista, Cynthia L. Chamberlin, and Seira Santizo-Greenwood, *El Cinco de Mayo en la Alta California / The Cinco de Mayo in Alta California* (Puebla: Gobierno del Estado de Puebla, 2023).

163. Paul Bryan Gray, *Forster vs. Pico. The Struggle for Rancho Santa Margarita* (Spokane, WA: Arthur H. Clark, 1998).

164. Paul Bryan Gray, *A Clamor for Equality: Emergence and Exile of California Activist Francisco P. Ramirez* (Lubbock: Texas Tech University Press, 2012).

Spanish Text of Justo Veytia's Diary

1. El nombre del pueblo, Amatitán, en el municipio de Amatitán, se deriva de la palabra indígena *amathe*, que significa "pequeño bosque de árboles de amate". Sus primeros habitantes fueron indios nahuatlacas, quienes se establecieron en un cerro llamado Chiquihuitillo. *Enciclopedia temática de Jalisco*, vol. 8, *Municipios*, 1, ed. Fernando Martínez-Réding (Guadalajara: Gobierno del Estado de Jalisco, 1992), 35–36.

2. El nombre Tequila se deriva de la palabra indígena *tequillan*, que significa "lugar donde uno corta". Sus primeros habitantes fueron indios nahualtecas, toltecas y otomíes. En 1600, Don Pedro Sánchez de Tagle, marqués

de Altamira, construyó aquí la primera fábrica de tequila. En los tiempos de Veytia, Tequila era meramente un pueblo, aunque hoy es la cabecera del municipio de Tequila. *Enciclopedia temática de Jalisco*, vol. 10, *Municipios*, 3, ed. Fernando Martínez-Réding (Guadalajara: Gobierno del Estado de Jalisco, 1992), 82–83.

3. Santo Tomás se encuentra en el municipio de Hostotipaquillo, cuyo nombre deriva de la palabra indígena *oztotipa*, que significa "encima de una caverna". Unas minas de hierro fueron descubiertas en la región en 1605. *Enciclopedia temática de Jalisco*, vol. 9, *Municipios*, 2, ed. Fernando Martinez-Réding (Guadalajara: Gobierno del Estado de Jalisco, 1992), 28–29.

4. Venta de Mochitiltic se encuentra a unos cinco kilómetros al oeste de Santo Tomás. Según una guía de 1965, "La Venta de Mochitiltic . . . es una antigua hacienda con una típica casa antigua y una pequeña capilla. Todavía se puede ver el antiguo camino empedrado al pasar. El nombre La Venta se refiere a un tipo de posada que se ubicaba a lo largo de los caminos para brindar alimento y hospedaje a los viajeros y alimento para sus animales". El grupo de Veytia podría haberse alojado en una posada así de camino a la costa. Las barrancas de Mochitiltic son una serie de cañones que desembocan en el Río Grande de Santiago. *Enciclopedia temática de Jalisco*, vol. 9, *Municipios*, 2, 28; Howard E. Gulick, *Nayarit, Mexico. A Traveler's Guidebook to This Historic and Scenic State of Mexico's West Coast and its Capital, the City of Tepic*. Clark Guidebooks, 3 (Glendale, CA: Arthur H. Clark Co., 1965), 138–39.

5. El pueblo de Ixtlán del Río es la cabecera del municipio de Ixtlán, en el estado mexicano de Nayarit. El nombre deriva de un término náhuatl que significa "lugar de obsidiana". Gulick, *Nayarit*, 135.

6. "Ahuacatlán . . . fue un importante cacicazgo indígena independiente antes de la conquista española. . . . Pronto se convirtió en un centro importante después de que se abrieran minas en el área". El pueblo es cabecera del municipio del mismo nombre, que se extiende hasta el río Ameca. Su nombre indígena significa "lugar de aguacates". Indicando la fama de cultivo de alimentos de la región, cerca hay otro pueblo llamado Camotlán, del náhuatl que significa "lugar de camotes". Gulick, *Nayarit*, 130–31.

7. El camino de Guadalajara a Tepic atraviesa la Faja Volcánica Transmexicana, una cadena montañosa que incluye el Ceboruco de 2.200 metros de altura. Este volcán entró en erupción más recientemente en 1870, enviando lava de movimiento lento por los lados del volcán durante casi dos años. Los flujos de lava endurecida se pueden ver a ambos lados de la carretera Guadalajara-Tepic. La lava que vió Veytia, sin embargo, era de erupciones anteriores, dos

de las cuales ocurrieron en el siglo XVI. *Enciclopedia temática de Jalisco*, vol. 1, *Geografía*, ed. Fernando Martínez-Réding (Guadalajara: Gobierno del Estado de Jalisco, 1992), 142–43.

8. En 1965 San Leonel fue descrito como una antigua hacienda. Gulick, *Nayarit*, 126.

9. El nombre de Tepic puede derivar de la palabra náhuatl *tepicle*, una variedad de maíz que madura en cincuenta días. Un censo español de 1525 señaló que Tepic estaba habitada en gran parte por indios de habla náhuatl. Tepic se convirtió en un floreciente centro comercial después de que se estableciera el puerto de San Blas en 1768, ya que la ruta principal desde ese puerto a Guadalajara pasaba por Tepic. Poco después de la independencia de México de España, en 1823 o 1824, Eustace Barron, un súbdito británico de ascendencia irlandesa y española nacido en Cádiz, España, llegó a Tepic, donde se desempeñó como cónsul británico y formó la famosa casa comercial de Barron Forbes con dos socios nacidos en Escocia, Alexander Forbes y James Alexander Forbes (no relacionados entre sí). Barron Forbes tenía intereses comerciales que iban desde Ecuador hasta la mina de Nueva Almaden justo al sur de San José en Alta California. Tepic tenía una gran cantidad de comerciantes de América Central, Bélgica, Italia, Francia, Alemania, España y EE. UU., y en el momento del viaje de Veytia era un importante centro comercial, dominado económicamente por Barron Forbes. John Fox, *Macnamara's Irish Colony and the United States Taking of California in 1846* (Jefferson, NC, y Londres: McFarland, 2000), 21, 80, 118–19, 131; Gulick, *Nayarit*, 96; Marina Anguiano, *Nayarit. Costa y altiplanicie en el momento de Contacto* (Mexico City: Universidad Nacional Autónoma de México, 1992), 54, 57; Jean Meyer, *Breve historia de Nayarit* (Mexico City: Fondo de Cultura Económica, 1997), 73, 94–95.

10. La palabra "nada" está interlineada.

11. El diario tiene "comunicadas [*sic*] con esta", pero el antecedente debe ser en realidad el recinto de cuatro paredes, no las paredes mismas.

12. En aquel tiempo, México aún no usaba la escala de temperatura Celsius, que se introdujo en 1857 como un aspecto de las reformas nacionales de ese año, pero no fue obligatoria hasta el Tratado del Metro de 1890 (Tratado del Sistema Métrico). Antes de eso, los pesos y medidas de México se basaban en los españoles introducidos durante el período colonial, que podían variar de una región a otra. Como resultado, no está exactamente claro qué escala de temperatura estaba usando Veytia aquí, excepto que no era Celsius. Lucero Morelos Rodríguez, "A peso el kilo. Historia del sistema métrico decimal en México", repaso de H. Vera, *Libros de escarabejo* (Mexico City, 2007), en

Investigaciones Geográficas 69 (2009):132–35, https://www.researchgate.net/publication/43530987_Resena_de_A_peso_el_kilo_Historia_del_sistema_metrico_decimal_en_Mexico_de_H_Vera.

13. El puerto de San Blas fue fundado por el Virrey de la Nueva España el marqués de Croix en 1768, específicamente para servir de base a los barcos y expediciones a la Alta California. Fue diseñado por el ingeniero Miguel Costansó, quien en 1769 acompañó al padre Junípero Serra en la expedición que fundó la primera misión en Alta California, San Diego. Más tarde caminó a lo largo del estado con el Capitán Gaspar de Portolá hasta la Bahía de Monterey. El diario del viaje de Costansó proporciona detalles fascinantes sobre la Alta California en aquel momento. María Luisa Rodríguez-Sala, Karina Neria Mosco, Verónica Ramírez Ortega, and Alejandra Tolentino Ochoa, *Los cirujanos del mar en la Nueva España (1572–1820), ¿miembros de un estamento profesional o una comunidad científica?* Serie Los cirujanos del mar en la Nueva España, 1 (Mexico City: Universidad Nacional Autónoma de México, 2004), 58–59; *The Portolá Expedition of 1769–1770: Diary of Miguel Costansó*, ed. Frederick J. Taggart. Publications of the Academy of Pacific Coast History, 2:4 (Berkeley, CA: University Press, 1911). San Blas seguía siendo el principal puerto de la Costa del Pacífico para viajar a Alta California durante el viaje de Justo Veytia, pero para 1855, el desvío del comercio hacia los puertos más profundos de Mazatlán y Acapulco había provocado una caída de dos tercios en el tonelaje que llegaba a San Blas; y en la década de 1860, San Blas estaba siendo evitado por todos menos los barcos locales. Meyer, *Breve historia*, 99–100.

14. El pueblo agrícola de Navarrete está a unas diecisiete millas al noroeste de Tepic, ubicado en el antiguo camino de Tepic a San Blas. Gulick, *Nayarit*, 85.

15. Carlos Tapia no está identificado. A su regreso a México, Justo compró su boleto de pasaje, en una transacción privada, de un tal Ygnacio Tapia (fol. 57r.), pero no se ha establecido si él y Carlos Tapia tenían alguna relación.

16. No hasta el fol. 16v. menciona Justo el primer nombre de Puga, Pepe. Este individuo viajó por un tiempo con Justo y sus compañeros en California, hasta regresar a Guadalajara en agosto de 1849. El barco en cuestión, como aclara Justo más adelante, era el *Volante*.

17. Fernández Peral no ha sido identificado.

18. Pérez no ha sido identificado.

19. En la zona de Tepic, *palomaría* se refiere a un árbol de la familia *Clusiaceae*. Presuntamente tales árboles estuvieron cerca de la carretera de Palos Marías en algún momento. Francisco J. Santamaría, *Diccionario de mejicanismos*, 7th ed. (Mexico City: Porrúa, 2005).

20. *Papaqui* proviene de una palabra náhuatl, *papaquiliztli*, que significa "felicidad" o "alegría". Este era un estilo tradicional de música y celebración de Carnaval. "Papaqui", en Santamaría, *Diccionario de mejicanismos*, 7ª ed.

21. Justo usa la palabra "tapatíos", que significa gente de la ciudad de Guadalajara o, por extensión, del estado de Jalisco. Proviene de la palabra náhuatl *tlapatiotl*. "Tapatío", en Santamaría, *Diccionario de mejicanismos*, 7ª ed.

22. Esto ilustra el fuerte apego contemporáneo que la mayoría de la gente sentía por su ciudad o región natal, hasta el punto de verla, en cierto sentido, como una cultura o estado diferente de las de otras regiones de México.

23. Los gambusinos latinos que participaban en la Fiebre del Oro de California a menudo formaban compañías, algunas bastante grandes. Por ejemplo, José María Amador, un californio por quien fue nombrado el Condado de Amador, organizó una compañía de unos treinta hombres, con una recua de animales de carga y dieciséis cabezas de ganado, para ir del Condado de Santa Clara al pueblo de Coloma en 1848. Un argentino, Ramón Gil Navarro, se incorporó a una compañía formada en Concepción, Chile, que tenía capital suficiente para comprar su propio barco, el *Carmen*, y equiparlo para el viaje a California. Los américo-atlánticos también formaron compañías, aunque muchas de ellas se disolvieron en el camino o después de llegar a los campos de oro. Ramón Gil Navarro, *The Gold Rush Diary of Ramón Gil Navarro*, ed. y trad. María del Carmen Ferreyra and David S. Reher (Lincoln y Londres: University of Nebraska Press, 2000), 1–2; *Californio Voices: The Oral Memoirs of José María Amador and Lorenzo Asisara*, ed. y trad. Gregorio Mora-Torres (Denton: University of North Texas Press, 2005), 197; Cecil K. Byrd, *Searching for Riches: The California Gold Rush* (Bloomington: Lilly Library, Indiana University, 1991), 8.

24. Estos individuos no han sido identificados.

25. Un bergantín es un barco de dos mástiles; el trinquete tiene aparejo cuadrado y el palo mayor tiene aparejo proa-popa. *The Oxford Companion to Ships and the Sea*, ed. Peter Kemp (Oxford: Oxford University Press, 1988), 109. El *Republicano* llegó a San Francisco el 12 de abril, 32 días después de hacer escala en Mazatlán. (San Francisco) *Alta California*, April 5, 1849, 2.

26. Una vez que México logró su independencia, se levantaron las restricciones comerciales coloniales y California pronto se unió al creciente mundo del comercio del Pacífico. William Heath Davis, nacido en Hawaii y radicado en San Francisco, agregó a sus memorias un "Registro de barcos que llegaron desde 1774 hasta 1847". Muestra que desde la década de 1820 aumentó considerablemente el número de barcos que hacían escala en San Francisco,

al igual que el número de países de los que procedían. William Heath Davis, *Seventy-five Years in California*, ed. John Howell (San Francisco: John Howell, 1929), 397–409.

27. Justo usa el término *varas*; una vara equivalía a aproximadamente 0.84 de un metro. La vara como unidad de medida se usó en Alta California durante los períodos de la colonia española y la república mexicana, y durante años después de la anexión de los Estados Unidos. Incluso diez años después del viaje de Justo Veytia, un anuncio en un periódico en inglés de San Francisco ofrecía a la venta "A 100 vara lot" ("Un lote de 100 varas"). "For Sale Cheap", anuncio, (San Francisco) *Alta California*, October 27, 1859, 4.

28. Justo usa el término "tercios" para referirse a fardos o bultos de mercancías. Originalmente se cargaba una mula con un tercio por cada lado, totalizando dos tercios. Según el tamaño y la fuerza de la mula, un tercio podía pesar entre 18.15 y 36.29 kg. El *Diccionario de mejicanismos* da "tercio" como sinónimo para "paca". "Tercio", en Santamaría, *Diccionario de mejicanismos*, 7ª ed.; "Tercio", en *Diccionario de autoridades*, vol. 3.

29. La aparente elipsis parece ser del propio Justo, para un efecto dramático, en lugar de una indicación de alguna omisión.

30. La palabra "Marzo" está interlineada.

31. Matilde, quizás como una supresión deliberada, ha escrito ¡*Que capaz!*, lo cual tiene poco sentido. Su padre pudo haber escrito originalmente ¡*Qué caray!*

32. La principal ruta terrestre desde el norte de México hasta California atravesaba el desierto de Sonora y era tan difícil que recibió el apodo de *El Camino del Diablo*. Los primeros europeos exploraron esta ruta en el siglo XVII, pero la evidencia arqueológica sugiere que los pueblos indígenas la habían utilizado durante más de 7.000 años. En 1774 la expedición de Juan Bautista de Anza la estableció como la ruta terrestre aceptada de México a California. Richard F. Pourade, *Anza Conquers the Desert: The Anza Expeditions from Mexico to California and the Founding of San Francisco: 1774 to 1776* (San Diego: Copley, 1971), 7–49. Esta era la ruta que el pasajero mareado deseaba haber tomado.

33. Las Islas Marías son tres islas que forman un archipiélago a unos setenta kilómetros mar adentro desde San Blas. María Madre es la más grande. María Magdalena es la mediana y María Cleofas la más pequeña. Meyer, *Breve historia*, 17.

34. A mediados del siglo XIX, una barca era cualquier barco con tres o más mástiles y un plan de vela que usaba aparejo proa-popa en el mástil de popa y velas cuadradas en los otros mástiles. Eran los barcos oceánicos más utilizados

en ese momento porque su aparejo permitía que el barco se navegara con una tripulación más pequeña que un barco con aparejo completo o con aparejo de bergantín, pero lo hacía casi igual de rápido y fácil de manejar. El tipo de pinaza que Justo vio mientras estaba a bordo del *Volante* era una pinaza con aparejo completo, un barco algo más pequeño que una barca, con velas aparejadas en sus dos o tres mástiles. Las pinazas con aparejo completo a menudo se usaban como barcos mercantes. El término "pinaza" también se puede usar para un bote pequeño, pero tal barco no habría estado tan lejos en el mar como lo estaba el *Volante* en esta ocasión. *Oxford Companion to Ships and the Sea*, 61–62, 649.

35. Estas probablemente fueron las primeras ballenas grises (*Eschrichtius robustus*) que regresaron a las aguas del Pacífico norte desde las zonas de cría frente a Baja California. Los que salen durante febrero y marzo son los machos y las hembras que no tienen crías nuevas. Las nuevas madres siguen la migración hacia el norte unas semanas más tarde, a fines de marzo y abril.

36. *Coryphæna hippurus*.

37. Muy probablemente la gaviota occidental muy difundida, *Larus occidentalis*.

38. San Juan de Dios es uno de los barrios más antiguos de Guadalajara, fundado en 1551. La Orden de San Juan de Dios, comúnmente conocida como los Hospitalarios, tenía allí una iglesia y un hospicio para 1557. Los molinos harineros se construyeron en el río San Juan a mediados del siglo XVIII y la naciente industria propició un marcado crecimiento de la población. Antonio de Jesús Mendoza Mejía, "El barrio de San Juan de Dios", *El Occidental*, 12 junio 2017, https://www.eloccidental,com.mx/analisis/el-barrio-de-san-juan-de-dios-1282189.html.

39. La palabra "caso" interlineada.

40. El diario tiene "interpretación", pero por el contexto evidentemente se entiende el sentido de "intervención" o "mediación". Esto puede ser un error de copia de Matilde.

41. Aunque la frase que usa Justo es "poner el buque á la capa", su descripción del procedimiento es algo imprecisa. Véase "Estar à la capa" bajo "Capa", *Diccionario de autoridades*, vol. 1.

42. Este "promontorio" muy probablemente fue los Marin Headlands, en la costa norte de la entrada a la Bahía de San Francisco, aunque normalmente los promontorios no parecen pálidos o "blanqueados", como los describe Justo.

43. Justo menciona varias veces en su diario a su primo José María Ybarra, particularmente en el fol. 55v., que presenta su breve empleo de Justo como repartidor de cartas en el bar y casa de juego de Ybarra en Stanislaus, California.

44. San Francisco recibió su nombre de San Francisco de Asís. La Misión San Francisco de Asís se estableció en 1776 a orillas de un arroyo que Juan Bautista de Anza había llamado Arroyo de los Dolores porque llegaba allí el Viernes de Dolores, el viernes anterior a la Semana Santa. De ahí que la misión a veces también se llama Misión Dolores. A unas tres millas de distancia, en la misma bahía, había una ensenada donde descargaban los barcos, llamada Yerba Buena. El capitán William A. Richardson, ciudadano mexicano naturalizado originario de Inglaterra, fue nombrado primer capitán de puerto por el gobernador José Figueroa. En 1835 erigió el primer edificio permanente en Yerba Buena. En 1847, después de la ocupación estadounidense, el asentamiento de Yerba Buena pasó a llamarse formalmente San Francisco y pasó a incluir toda el área entre la bahía y el océano. Mildred Brooke Hoover, Hero Eugene Rensch, y Ethel Grace Rensch, *Historic Spots in California*, ed. nueva (Stanford, CA: Stanford University Press, 1948), 290–93; Erwin G. Gudde, *California Place Names: The Origin and Etymology of Current Geographical Names*, ed. William Bright, 4th ed. (Berkeley y Los Angeles: University of California Press, 1998), 335.

45. Games no se identifican de otra manera.

46. Los pláceres son depósitos superficiales de oro que se pueden separar de la tierra, lavándolos en una batea con agua, generalmente en un arroyo o río. La mayor parte de la actividad en los primeros años de la Fiebre del Oro tuvo lugar en los pláceres. En California, la palabra "plácer" se ha prestado comúnmente al inglés para referirse a este tipo de depósito de oro y las actividades en torno a su funcionamiento. El Condado de Placer en California lleva el nombre de los muchos pláceres que hay allí. Cuando los pláceres se agotaron, la extracción del oro de rocas de cuarzo, que requería más mano de obra y capital, se hizo más común.

47. Extrañamente, Justo aquí no se percataba de las bien documentadas comunidades de inmigrantes mexicanos y sudamericanos de San Francisco. Muchos angloparlantes de la época también imaginaban, erróneamente, que la población de habla hispana de California estaba "desapareciendo" por completo. A fines de 1853, la población de San Francisco se estimó en 50,000 habitantes, de los cuales supuestamente 33,000 eran angloparlantes, incluidos ciudadanos estadounidenses e inmigrantes británicos, y 3000 "españoles", es decir, hispanohablantes de cualquier nacionalidad. El uso que hace Justo de "americano" para referirse específicamente a un ciudadano de los Estados Unidos, en lugar de cualquier habitante de América del Norte o del Sur, era común en el español de México a mediados del siglo XIX, y estándar en los periódicos en español publicados en California en las décadas de 1850 y 1860.

"Foreign Immigration", (San Francisco) *Alta California*, 20 febrero 1850, 2; "The Californian Race", (San Francisco) *Alta California*, 30 mayo 1852, 2; "San Francisco at the End of 1853", (San Francisco) *Alta California*, 9 januario 1854, 2.

48. Según un convertidor de moneda histórico en línea, $2 (USD) en 1849 valían aproximadamente $75 en la moneda de 2022 (https://futureboy.us/fsp/dollar.fsp).

49. Pepe es el compañero de viaje de Justo Pepe Puga.

50. El hecho de que Justo esté comentando con tanto énfasis sobre lo común que es en el San Francisco de la Fiebre de Oro cuidar de uno mismo en lugar de tener sirvientes revela cuán inusual fue eso en su propia experiencia, viniendo de un entorno de buen tono en la zona urbana de Guadalajara.

51. La famosa ocurrencia "El invierno más frío que pasé fue un verano en San Francisco", aunque comúnmente atribuida al autor Mark Twain, en realidad no fue pronunciada por él. Se desconoce su verdadero origen. Sin embargo, describe bastante bien muchos días de verano con niebla, viento y humedad en San Francisco, especialmente cuando los turistas que no están vestidos adecuadamente para las condiciones.

52. El mar, por supuesto, está al oeste de San Francisco. Podría ser que por "mar" Justo se estuviera refiriendo a la Bahía de San Francisco. O Matilde, quien probablemente no estaba familiarizada con la geografía de Alta California, pudo haber copiado mal "Oriente" cuando su padre originalmente escribió "oeste".

53. La unidad de medida que cita Justo es la "cuarta", un palmo, es decir, el ancho de una mano adulta, aproximadamente 10 centímetros.

54. Guaraches—Justo, o Matilde, usa una variante ortográfica de "guarachis", también deletreado "huaraches"—era considerado un calzado primitivo, usado a menudo por los indígenas en México. Hubiera sido impensable que Justo alguna vez hubiera usado guaraches en la Guadalajara urbana, pero mencionar que lo hizo en Alta California indica cuán primitiva encontró su situación allí. "Guarache", Santamaría, *Diccionaro de mejicanismos*, 7[a] ed. Una "pantalonera" era un pantalón vaquero ceñido al cuerpo, que por lo general tenía botones ornamentales a los lados; un "paltó" era una chaqueta o abrigo destinado a protegerse del polvo, especialmente para usar en un viaje. Esta sobrecubierta en particular, señala Justo, estaba hecha de "pañete", es decir, material de calidad inferior. Evidentemente se sentía vestido como un vagabundo. "Paltó" y "pantalonera", Santamaría, *Diccionaro de mejicanismos*, 7[a] ed.; "Pañete", *Nuevo pequeño Larousse ilustrado: Diccionario enciclopédico*,ed.

Claude Augé y Paul Augé, 43.ª ed., versión en español por Miguel de Toro y Gisbert (Buenos Aires: Editorial Larousse, 1964).
55. Las tortillas han sido un alimento básico de la cocina mexicana desde la época precolombina. Castelló Yturbide, *Presencia de la comida prehispánica*, 24.
56. Presumiblemente, esto fue para obtener más suministros.
57. Parece haber cierta inconsistencia en el momento de los eventos que Justo describe aquí. Como esta entrada está fechada el 23 de abril y la próxima entrada es para el 26 de abril, Justo puede estar describiendo eventos que ocurrieron en días diferentes.
58. Conocida popularmente como Misión Dolores por un manantial y arroyo cercano, la Misión San Francisco de Asís fue la sexta misión franciscana que se estableció en California, el 9 de octubre de 1776. Maynard Geiger, "New Data on the Buildings of Mission San Francisco", *California Historical Society Quarterly* 46, no. 3 (septiembre 1967), 195, https://www.jstor.org/stable/25154111; "Dolores, Mission", en Gudde, *California Place Names*, 111.
59. Matilde ha escrito "enfarrar", que no tiene sentido. Dado el contexto, Justo probablemente tuvo "enyesar", es decir, "tapar con yeso".
60. Matilde ha escrito "galera", pero presumiblemente Justo escribió, o al menos quiso decir, "galería".
61. El Alcalde, en este caso, habría sido el cacique del pueblo indígena ubicado en la misión.
62. Justo usa el término "del pais" en el sentido de "nativo", aquí y en otras partes del diario para referirse a cosas—personas, productos, costumbres, gustos, et cétera—particulares de la Alta California de habla hispana. "Nativos del pais" se refiere a los californios, habitantes de habla hispana nacidos en Alta California, no a los inmigrantes recientes de otras partes de México, a quienes llama "mexicanos", o a los indígenas que nacieron en California pero que no compartían completamente la sociedad de habla hispana. Y aquí otra vez usa la palabra "americanos" para referirse solo a ciudadanos de EE.UU.
63. Más adelante en el diario (fol. 27v.), Justo también comenta sobre la costumbre indígena de usar solo prendas individuales del atuendo "civilizado" en lugar de trajes completos.
64. Para la historia del chocolate, véase Simon Varey, "Three Necessary Drugs", *1650–1850: Ideas, Aesthetics, and Inquiries in the Early Modern Era*, 4 (1998); Sophie Coe y Michael Coe, *The True History of Chocolate* (Londres y Nueva York: Thames & Hudson, 1996).
65. En 1835, Rancho Buri Buri, también conocido como el Rancho Sánchez, está cerca del pueblo moderno de San Bruno. Originalmente un pueblo de

indios sobre el cual la Misión Dolores reclamaba jurisdicción, un rancho grande con este nombre fue otorgado provisionalmente a José Antonio Sánchez en 1827 y le fue confirmado en 1835, al jubilarse del Presidio de San Francisco. A la muerte de Sánchez en 1843, el rancho contaba con una casa de adobe de cinco cuartos, rebaños de ganado y caballos, campos de cultivo, un molino tirado por mulas y un embarcadero en un estero cercano. Frank M. Stanger, "A California Rancho under Three Flags: A History of Rancho Buri Buri in San Mateo County", *California Historical Society Quarterly* 17, no. 3 (septiembre 1938), 252, https://www.jstor.org/stable/25160788. Un relato de un viaje en diligencia desde San Francisco a San José en 1850 se refiere al "rancho de Sánchez" como un lugar de parada habitual para conseguir caballos frescos para la diligencia. Los diez hijos de José Antonio Sánchez se vieron obligados a defender su derecho al rancho a partir de 1852; finalmente ganaron su caso en 1872 y pronto tuvieron que vender la propiedad para pagar los costos legales y los impuestos atrasados. El Aeropuerto Internacional de San Francisco ahora ocupa parte del antiguo rancho. Bancroft Library, University of California, Berkeley, Collection BANC MSS Land Case Files, 1852–1892, case no. ND 101; Gudde, *California Place Names*, 52; Hoover et al., *Historic Spots in California*, 315–16; "A Stage Ride to San Jose", (San Francisco) *Alta California*, 3 agosto 1850, 2.

66. El Arroyo de San Francisquito actualmente corre desde el Acelerador Lineal de Stanford moderno hasta la Bahía de San Francisco, desembocando justo al norte de Moffett Field. El Rancho San Francisquito, otorgado originalmente a Antonio Buelna en 1839, se encontraba al sureste del arroyo. Buelna murió en 1842; su viuda, Concepción Valencia, se casó con el viudo Francisco Rodríguez, originario de Monterey, California, en 1844. El hijo mayor de Rodríguez, Jesús, construyó una casa cerca, y esta familia combinada vivía en la propiedad cuando Veytia pasó por allí en 1849. Más tarde, Leland Stanford compró gran parte de la propiedad. DeLorme Mapping Company, *Northern California Atlas & Gazeteer*, 6ª ed. (Yarmouth, ME: DeLorme, 2003), 115; Hoover et al., *Historic Spots in California*, 340.

67. No se registró ningún rancho en la zona que haya sido otorgado a ningún miembro de la familia Cantúa. El "Rancho de Cantúa" probablemente fue una parte del Rancho Rincón de los Esteros en el Condado de Santa Clara, ocupado en 1849 por Manuela Cantúa de Alviso (1820–1914), viuda de José María Alviso (1807–1846), y sus cuatro hijos. Debido a que era común que las mujeres casadas y las viudas en la sociedad californiana usaran solo sus apellidos de soltera, ella habría sido conocida como Manuela Cantúa, y Justo Veytia pudo

haber asumido que Cantúa era el apellido de toda la familia. El Rancho Rincón de los Esteros estaba ubicado en el extremo sur de la Bahía de San Francisco, entre el Río Guadalupe y el Arroyo Penitencia, y de hecho se encontraba a lo largo de la ruta de Justo Veytia entre el Rancho San Francisquito mencionado anteriormente (fol. 19v.) y el Rancho Agua Caliente mencionado a continuación (fol. 21r.). John Arvizu, *Building California: 200 Years of Arvizu History* (Gilroy, CA: autopublicación, 2007), 21; Charles A. Tuttle, *Reports of Cases Determined in the Supreme Court of the State of California*, vol. 44 (San Francisco: Bancroft-Whitney, 1906), case no. 2,879: Maria Ygnacio Alviso Bernal, Pedro Bernal, Juan Ygnacio Alviso, and Louisa Alviso Vincent, et al., *v*. Charles Wade, Estefano Alviso Wade, Rafael Alviso, Augustia Alviso Dias, and Lautario Dias, et al., pp. 663–67. Gudde, *California Place Names*, 11; Plat del Rancho Rincón de los Esteros, finalmente confirmado a Rafael Alvisa et al. (Condado de Santa Clara, California). Inspeccionado bajo instrucciones del Agrimensor General de EE.UU., por John Wallace, Depy. Survr., http://content.cdlib.org/ark:/13030/hb029001z3/?order=2&brand=calisphere.

68. Veytia los llama "perdices", pero sin duda se trataba de codornices de California (*Callipepia californica*).

69. La medida de grano tradicional española llamada "fanega" puede variar de aproximadamente 23 a 56 litros, dependiendo de la localidad. "Fanega", *Gran diccionario español-inglés. English-Spanish Dictionary*, ed. íntegra, ed. Ramón García-Pelayo y Gross (Paris: Larousse, 1993). Los ranchos de California se dedicaban principalmente a la cría de ganado y, por lo tanto, cultivaban solo los cereales y las verduras que necesitaban para su propio uso.

70. El término "huilota", que aquí Justo o Matilde deletrea "guilota", deriva del náhuatl *vilotl*, que significa paloma de luto (*Zenaida macroura*). "Huilota", en Santamaría, *Diccionario de mejicanismos*, 7ª ed.

71. El lugar en el sur del Condado de Alameda ahora conocido como Warm Springs fue una vez parte del Rancho Agua Caliente, otorgado originalmente a Fulgencio Higuera en 1839. Está a unas dos millas al sur de la Misión San José. Hoover et al., *Historic Spots in California*, 220. La estación Warm Springs/South Fremont del sistema de tránsito Bay Area Rapid Transit (BART) se abrió en 2017.

72. Extendiéndose desde lo que ahora es la ciudad de San Leandro hasta la de Albany, Rancho San Antonio fue otorgado a Luis María Peralta en 1820. En 1842, dividió el rancho entre sus cuatro hijos. Antonio Peralta recibió la parte que contenía la casa familiar original, en lo que actualmente es el este de Oakland, y vivía allí cuando pasó Justo Veytia. Hoover et al., *Historic Spots in California*, 217–18.

73. Robert Livermore, un marinero inglés, abandonó el barco en 1822; más tarde se convirtió en ciudadano mexicano y, junto con William Gulnac, se le concedió Rancho Las Positas en 1839. Livermore construyó una casa de adobe que luego se convirtió en un punto de parada común para quienes viajaban a Stockton. Cuando pasó Justo Veytia, Livermore aún vivía en el rancho. Livermore Valley lleva su nombre. Hoover et al., *Historic Spots in California*, 220–21.
74. Este pasaje muestra que los cuentos de la hospitalidad ilimitada de los californios eran mitos incluso en 1849. En todos los relatos, la práctica de una hospitalidad tan espléndida e incondicional siempre se ubicó en alguna imaginaria antigua Edad de Oro de California. A fines de la década de 1840, como aquí, se ubicaba "en los viejos tiempos, en las misiones", mientras que en generaciones posteriores se ubicaba en las décadas de 1830–1850. A pesar de su falsedad, el mito resultó persistente; cuando los románticos de la primera mitad del siglo XX le preguntaban al respecto, Reginaldo F. del Valle (n. 1854), quien creció en un rancho en el sur de California, respondía sin rodeos: "That's a lot of bunk" (Eso es un montón de tonterías). "Along El Camino Real with Ed Ainsworth," *Los Angeles Times*, 22 septiembre 1938, A15.
75. Por su descripción del paso a través de las montañas y los fuertes vientos predominantes, Justo probablemente estaba en o cerca del paso de Altamont, al este de Livermore, a través del cual serpenteaba el camino a Stockton. El paso es ahora el sitio de un parque eólico.
76. Otra de las elipses de Justo para un efecto dramático, más que una omisión.
77. El Río San Joaquín es uno de los dos ríos principales que transportan agua desde la Sierra Nevada hasta la Bahía de San Francisco. El Río Sacramento fluye de norte a sur y el San Joaquín de sur a norte. Fray Juan Crespí vió por primera vez el río en 1772 y lo llamó San Francisco. Casi treinta años después, hacia 1805, Gabriel Moraga lo nombró San Joaquín. DeLorme Mapping Company, *Northern California Atlas & Gazetteer*, 117–18; Gudde, *California Place Names*, 337.
78. Por supuesto, literalmente un "sonorense" era alguien del estado mexicano de Sonora. Pero en ese momento, la palabra también se usaba genéricamente en Alta California, tanto por hablantes de español como de inglés, para referirse a cualquier inmigrante mexicano reciente, porque muchos de ellos de hecho venían de Sonora durante la Fiebre del Oro. Véase al Preface.
79. Otra elipsis para el efecto dramático.
80. Justo Veytia no era naturalista y, por lo tanto, solía llamar a la flora y fauna de Alta California con los nombres de aves y plantas que le eran familiares, ya sea de su Guadalajara natal o de la literatura. Llamó al pájaro chillón "zanate",

que específicamente significa el zanate mexicano (*Quiscalus mexicanus*). Los zanates, sin embargo, no son nativos de California, por lo que el "zanate" de Justo probablemente era un cuervo local de aspecto y sonido similar (*Corvus brachyrhynchos hesperis*). Mientras que Justo escribió "tórtola" y "perdiz", esas aves en realidad habrían sido palomas de luto (*Zenaida macroura*) y codornices de California (*Callipepia californica*). Estos últimos, de hecho, no cantan, aunque ocasionalmente emiten pío-píos.

81. Ahora conocido como French Camp, Campo de los Franceses fue otorgado en 1844 a William Gulnac, un ciudadano mexicano naturalizado nacido en Estados Unidos, y a Charles M. Weber, nacido en Alemania, quien más tarde fundó Stockton. Los tramperos francocanadienses de la Hudson's Bay Company habían utilizado previamente el sitio como un campamento de verano anual, ya en 1832. En 1845, Gulnac vendió su participación a Weber por $60. Para atraer a los pobladores, Weber prácticamente regaló la mayor parte de la propiedad, aunque más tarde se le confirmó el título. Hoover et al., *Historic Spots in California*, 150–51.

82. Charles M. Weber fundó la ciudad actual de Stockton en 1847 como Tuleburg, llamada así por los densos pantanos de juncos de tule de la zona. Dos años más tarde, Tuleburg fue encuestada nuevamente y renombrada en honor al comodoro estadounidense Robert F. Stockton. Se convirtió en uno de los principales puntos de partida para los mineros que se dirigían a las colinas. Hoover et al., *Historic Spots in California*, 151.

83. Otra elipsis para un efecto dramático, más que para indicar una omisión. Morfeo era una deidad grecorromana menor, hijo del dios del sueño, y se le consideraba responsable de enviar sueños a las personas mientras dormían.

84. Más elipses dramáticas.

85. Esto parece ser un error para "12".

86. Otra de las elipses dramáticas de Justo.

87. Asumiendo que "de la cintura" no es un error de copia de Matilde, Justo parece usar la palabra "cintura" en el sentido de "meter en cintura". "Cintura", *Diccionario de autoridades*, vol. A–C. A los insectos los llama "mosquitos" y "zancudos"; por lo general, las dos palabras son sinónimas, por lo que presumiblemente aquí se refiere a mosquitos y otros insectos que pican, como las moscas negras (*Simúlidos*).

88. Según Hoover et al., *Historic Spots in California*, 77, el Río Calaveras fue nombrado por Gabriel Moraga en 1808, posiblemente porque vio allí gran cantidad de esqueletos humanos, producto de la guerra o la hambruna. Pero Gudde, *California Place Names*, 58, 59, dice que fue el grupo de John Marsh en 1836–1837 quien

vio los restos y le dió nombre al río. Este río se une al Río San Joaquín justo al oeste de Stockton. El Arroyo de las Calaveras habría sido parte de la cuenca. DeLorme Mapping Company, *Northern California Atlas & Gazetteer*, 106–7.

89. El "mejicano que vino aquí en la Colonia el año de 1834" y sus hijos luego son identificados como la familia Arana de Santa Cruz; véase abajo, nota 109. La República de México fomentó y facilitó el movimiento de población a la Alta California, como lo había hecho el Virreinato de la Nueva España antes de la independencia de México. La "Colonia" a la que se refiere Justo fue la expedición colonizadora Hijar-Padrés, llamada así por los apellidos de sus líderes. José María Hijar era de una destacada familia tapatía; fue miembro del Congreso mexicano a partir de 1832 y partidario del presidente Valentín Gómez Farias, quien también era de Guadalajara. Cuando la colonia fue autorizada por el Congreso, Hijar fue nombrado gobernador de la Alta California, en reemplazo de José Figueroa. José María Padrés, originario de la Ciudad de México, había ido a Alta California anteriormente, en 1825, en el equipo del gobernador José María Echeandia. La colonia a veces se llama colonia Gómez Farias, en honor al presidente de México que en 1834 autorizó la concesión de antiguas tierras de las misiones a los pobladores y sufragó los gastos de unos 230 pobladores. Los pobladores fueron reclutados principalmente de la Ciudad de México y de Guadalajara, e incluyeron médicos, farmacéuticos, maestros y artesanos. Su grupo recorrió el mismo camino que hizo Justo Veytia de Guadalajara a Tepic, luego a San Blas. Cuando los barcos coloniales *Morelos* y *Natalia* llegaron a Alta California, Antonio López de Santa Anna había reemplazado a Gómez Farias como presidente de México; envió un mensaje especial al gobernador Figueroa revocando la carta de la colonia, especialmente su reclamo sobre las antiguas tierras de las misiones. C. Alan Hutchinson, *Frontier Settlement in Mexican California: The Hijar-Padrés Colony and Its Origins, 1769–1835* (New Haven, CT: Yale University Press, 1969), 127, 182–86, 215, 265.

90. Matilde ha escrito erróneamente "buseando" en lugar de "buscando".

91. Aunque Justo llama a la planta "yedra", no crece ningun tipo de hiedra en California que pudiera haberle causado sarpullido a alguien. Por lo tanto, debe haber sido el ubicuo roble venenoso del Pacífico (*Toxicodendron diversilobum*), que a veces se enrolla alrededor de los troncos de los árboles de una manera similar a la hiedra. Dada la ubicación muy específica de la erupción de Justo, debe haber usado hojas de roble venenoso sin saberlo como papel higiénico.

92. El texto de Justo tiene "berrendos" y "buras". Los "berrendos" son antílopes berrendos (*Antilocapra americana* o *mexicana*), que se encuentran comúnmente en el norte de México, pero no en las Sierras de Alta California. "Bura"

es una palabra de origen indígena tarahumara, posiblemente una corrupción indígena de la palabra española "burro", pero significa "venado" en lugar de "burro", especialmente el venado de cola negra (*Odocoileus hemionus columbianus*), que se encuentra en el norte de México y es muy común en Alta California. "Berrendo" y "Bura", en Santamaría, *Diccionario de mejicanismos*, 7ª ed. Pero debido a que Veytia dice que los "buras" y "berrendos" eran "de enorme tamaño", algunos de ellos probablemente eran wapitis de Roosevelt (*Cervus canadensis roosevelti*). La Mesta fue una institución castellano fundada en la Edad Media, como una corporación de ganaderos trashumantes y pastores con facultades de autorregulación para decidir la propiedad de los animales y los derechos de pastoreo. La institución fue importada a las Américas luego de la conquista y colonización española. El ganado que pertenecía a la Mesta, más que a propietarios privados individuales, se llamaba "mesteños", que es en última instancia el origen de la palabra inglesa *mustang*. Julius Klein, *The Mesta: A Study in Spanish Economic History, 1273–1836* (Port Washington, NY: Kennikat, 1964), esp. 49–135; Charles Julian Bishko, "The Peninsular Background of Latin American Cattle Ranching", *Hispanic American Historical Review* 32 (1952), 491–515; "Mostrenco", en Joan Corominas, *Diccionario crítico etimológico castellano e hispánico*, vol. ME–RE. Biblioteca Románica Hispánica 5, Diccionarios, 7 (Madrid, Gredos, 1997); "Mustang", *Oxford English Dictionary*, http://www.oed.com/viewdictionaryentry/Entry/124238.

93. "Vega de los Moquelamos" hace referencia a las orillas del Río Mokelumne, que atraviesa el pueblo de Lodi, a medio camino entre Stockton y Sacramento. El nombre muy probablemente es de origen miwok, posiblemente significando "gente de la red", y fue utilizado por primera vez por Fray Narciso Durán, miembro de la expedición de Luis Argüello al Valle Central, en 1817. Gudde, *California Place Names*, 243; Hoover et al., *Historic Spots in California*, 143. Cada letra de la palabra "tentadura" está subrayada por separado. Justo significa su primer intento de encontrar oro.

94. Matilde, evidentemente poco familiarizada con el término y copiando el diario en una fecha muy posterior, ha escrito "hule", que significa "caucho", en lugar de "tule", "junco" (*Schoenoplectus acutus*). Las balsas de goma aún no existían durante la Fiebre del Oro de California, por lo que la balsa de Justo se habría fabricado con estas cañas.

95. Justo o Matilde escribió "schal" por "chal".

96. Algunas omisiones parecen haber ocurrido aquí, posiblemente errores de copia de Matilde pero posiblemente originados por el propio Justo. El texto dice "por el ningun cuidado que les da los vean desnudos"; quizás debería leerse "por el ningun cuidado que les dan a los que ven desnudos".

97. Justo mezcla unas alusiones clásicas aquí, con una referencia a seguir un hilo a través del Laberinto de Creta y una imaginación humorística de su santo cristiano favorito como un emperador romano que decide si alguien en la arena debe vivir o morir.
98. Probablemente por un lapsus cálami, Matilde ha escrito "Estivimos" para "Estuvimos".
99. Un "adarme" era una unidad de peso tradicional igual a 0.4 g., por lo que el trabajo de su día había producido un mero 1.2 g. de oro.
100. Casi trescientos años antes del descubrimiento de oro en California en 1848, se encontraron extensos depósitos de plata en Zacatecas, México, en 1548. Posteriormente se descubrieron otras minas de plata en puntos más al norte de los desiertos mexicanos. Tan importante se volvió la explotación de estas minas para la economía mexicana que la Escuela de Minería se estableció en la Ciudad de México en 1797. Como resultado, muchos mexicanos, especialmente en el norte del país, tenían una amplia experiencia en minería, la cual trajeron consigo a la Fiebre del Oro de California. Philip Wayne Powell, *Mexico's Miguel Caldera: The Taming of America's First Frontier (1548–1597)* (Tucson: University of Arizona Press, 1977), 8–14.
101. El término que Justo usa por primera vez para "esclusa" es "maquinita", pero queda claro por el contexto que la "máquina" en cuestión era una esclusa.
102. Una "arroba" era una unidad tradicional española y mexicana de peso o volumen líquido. Justo probablemente tenía en mente el peso de la tierra que procesaban, así que seis arrobas serían unos 68 kg. "Arroba", in *Gran diccionario español-inglés*.
103. Un "cordial sudorífico" habría sido una suspensión alcohólica de ciertas sustancias, probablemente hierbas, que inducían la sudoración. En la creencia médica de la época, esto habría acelerado la "crisis" de la fiebre—en términos modernos, el cese de la fiebre—que se caracterizaba por la sudoración, como señal de que la infección estaba saliendo del cuerpo y la enfermedad había desaparecido.
104. Matilde ha escrito "animando sin cesas [*sic*, por 'sin cesar'] con gritos á los bueyes".
105. Originalmente establecido como una fiesta litúrgica de la iglesia católica romana en 1264, esta celebración de la eucaristía llegó a ser utilizada por las autoridades civiles y religiosas en el México colonial para reforzar públicamente las imágenes de la conquista española de los pueblos indígenas. Sin embargo, después de la independencia de México, la festividad fue remodelada en un intento de crear una identidad compartida para el nuevo país. Patricia Lopes Don, "Carnivals, Triumphs, and Rain Gods in the New World: A Civic Festival

in the City of México-Tenochtitlán in 1539", *Colonial Latin American Review* 6 (1997): 17–40; Flor de María Salazar Mendoza, "Vestigios novohispanos en la formación de un estado nacional: Celebraciones cívicas en San Luis Potosí, México, en la década de 1820", *Fronteras de la Historia* 20 (2015), 174–99.

106. Después de su regreso a México, Justo Veytia finalmente se convirtió en comerciante y gerente de haciendas. Véase el epílogo.

107. "Galleta dura" era un tipo de galleta densa hecha con harina y agua, a veces salada, a veces no, y horneada varias veces para eliminar prácticamente toda la humedad. Tenía que empaparse en un líquido, como caldo o simplemente agua, para que se hiciera comestible. Galleta dura era fácilmente transportable y duraba meses o incluso años sin estropearse, lo que en una era anterior a la refrigeración lo convirtió en un alimento básico para ejércitos, armadas, exploradores y personas en situaciones como la de Justo Veytia, sus compañeros y los otros '49ers.

108. Es decir, la Sierra Nevada de California.

109. El mencionado "mexicano que vino aquí con la Colonia en 1834" era el cabeza de familia Arana de Santa Cruz, José Arana, padre, hijo natural de Francisco Arana y María de los Ángeles Arteaga de la Ciudad de México. Con su familia llegó a la Alta California en 1834 como parte de la Colonia Hijar-Padrés. Tenía entonces 41 años (incorrectamente enumerados en los registros de la colonia como 37), su profesión figuraba como fabricante de pólvora. Su esposa, Feliciana Alderete de Arana, tenía 36 años (incorrectamente listada como 30). Ya tenían cuatro hijos: José, hijo, 18 años (incorrectamente listado como 14); Felipe, 15 años (incorrectamente catalogada como hija de 12 años, "Felipa"); Marcos, de 11 o 9 años (pero incorrectamente listado como 6); y Florencia (incorrectamente catalogada como hijo, "Florencio"), de 3 años. Pronto se establecieron en Santa Cruz, donde José, padre, y Feliciana tuvieron al menos dos hijos más: José de Jesús Homobono, nacido ca. 1836; y María de Jesús Senona, nacida en 1844. Entre los hijos que Justo menciona por nombre en su diario estaban Felipe y Marcos; no está claro si José, hijo, también estaba en la compañía minera de su familia en 1849. C. Alan Hutchinson, "An Official List of the Members of the Hijar-Padrés Colony for Mexican California, 1834," *Pacific Historical Review* 42 (1973), 410; la Huntington Library, Early California Population Project Database (2006), los registros de bautismo de la Misión Santa Cruz núms. 02263 y 02710. Las imágenes de los registros de bautismo originales que indican los años de nacimiento correctos de varios miembros de la familia Arana están disponibles en el sitio web de FamilySearch, bautismo de José

María Francisco Xavier Pánfilo Arana, 2 junio 1793, https://www.familysearch.org/ark:/61903/3:1:939D-8Y9H-PV?i=674&cc=1615259; bautismo de María Dolores Feliciana Alderete, 1 abril 1798, https://www.familysearch.org/ark:/61903/3:1:939D-ZBYY-L?i=137&cc=1615259; bautismo de José María Antonio Arana, 26 noviembre 1816, https://www.familysearch.org/ark:/61903/3:1:S3HY-XKT9-KNP?i=217&cc=1615259; bautismo de Felipe de Jesús José María Arana, 7 febrero 1819, https://www.familysearch.org/ark:/61903/3:1:S3HY-XKT9-2W4?i=320&cc=1615259; bautismo de María de Jesús Florencia Arana, 25 febrero 1831, https://www.familysearch.org/ark:/61903/3:1:939D-8YS9-DM?i=612&cc=1615259. Marcos Arana puede ser José Macario Antonio Arana, bautizado el 10 marzo 1823, o José María Mateo Arana, bautizado el 22 septiembre 1825: https://www.familysearch.org/ark:/61903/3:1:S3HY-XKT9-2QQ?i=478&cc=1615259, https://www.familysearch.org/ark:/61903/3:1:S3HT-6PV9-BP7?i=932&cc=1615259.
110. Matilde ha escrito "ramajos" en lugar de "ramajes".
111. Subrayado en el texto original.
112. En septiembre de 1849, se informó que el cacique Polo había sido asesinado por otro indio por la recompensa de 5.000 pesos ofrecida en respuesta a los robos de caballos. Navarro, *Gold Rush Diary*, 51.
113. Esto puede ser una referencia al amigo de Justo, José Arana, padre. Véase nota 109, arriba.
114. Subrayado en el original.
115. Una de las elipses de Justo para un efecto dramático, no una omisión.
116. Subrayado en el original.
117. Proverbio citado por Sancho Panza en el *Quijote* de Cervantes, aunque Justo no lo indica como tal entre comillas u otros medios. La esencia es que una persona puede esperar que la próxima mano que de la vida sea mejor.
118. Es decir, Justo se levantó detrás de su compañero en el caballo, de modo que no quedó sentado en la silla sino casi en la grupa del caballo.
119. Véase nota 27, arriba, para la definición de "vara".
120. Nombrada por Gabriel Moraga en 1808, Sacramento, a partir de 1849, aún no era la capital de California. La ciudad no alcanzó ese estatus hasta 1854. Hoover et al., *Historic Spots in California*, 143, 147.
121. Subrayado en el original.
122. Para 1849, después de unos ochenta años de presencia de habla hispana en California, el idioma europeo más familiar para los pueblos indígenas era el español, e incluso en la remota Región del Oro, algunos indígenas podían hablar un poco. Ese mismo año, el sucesor de Polo en la jefatura habló en

español al defender a su pueblo de las acusaciones de que habían matado a dos estadounidenses; afirmó que otro grupo de indios, encabezados por un tal José Santos, en realidad eran los responsables. Navarro, *Gold Rush Diary*, 56.

123. No hay ningún sitio llamado oficialmente Arroyo Seco en esta parte de California. Sin embargo, los hispanohablantes pueden haber usado el nombre de manera informal para Drytown en el Condado de Amador, llamado así porque el arroyo que lo atraviesa no proporcionaba suficiente agua para la extracción de oro, especialmente en verano. O posiblemente, aunque menos probable, se usó para Campo Seco en el Condado de Calaveras. Gudde, *California Place Names*, 63, 144.

124. Según Ricardo Lancaster-Jones, editor de la edición de 1975 del diario de Veytia, el "Don Ricardo Jones" mencionado aquí fue su antepasado, quien, junto con tres de sus hijos, visitó Alta California durante la Fiebre del Oro. Era Richard Maddox Jones, quien se casó con Elizabeth Lancaster, hija del educador cuáquero inglés Joseph Lancaster (1778–1838), creador del sistema lancasteriano de enseñanza. Richard y Elizabeth Jones emigraron a México en 1825, por invitación del presidente Guadalupe Victoria, para establecer escuelas en el sistema lancasteriano. Se establecieron en Guadalajara, donde criaron ocho hijos; a pesar de los orígenes ingleses de la familia y sus antecedentes cuáqueros, todos sus descendientes nacidos en México eran católicos de habla hispana. Jones inicialmente tuvo bastante éxito en la extracción de oro en California, solo para perder todo lo que había ganado cuando un socio se fugó con todo el dinero que le habían confiado. La "empresa de la campana de busear" que Veytia menciona fue un proyecto de Jones, para extraer oro del lecho del Río San Joaquín, enviando hombres en un dispositivo de este tipo. Sin embargo, debido a la malversación de fondos por parte de su socio, la empresa quedó en nada y parece no haber dejado rastro en el registro histórico, fuera del diario de Veytia. Otro plan para emplear una campana de buceo para buscar oro en el mismo río fue emprendido posteriormente por John L. Moffatt en Stockton en 1852, también sin éxito. El equipo de Moffatt se destruyó cuando el río creció abruptamente como resultado de las lluvias invernales. Ricardo Lancaster-Jones, Introducción, en Veytia, *Viaje* (1975), 9; "Guadalajara's Lancaster-Joneses and the British Connection", 8 septiembre 2006, http://guadalajarareporter.com/features-mainmenu-95/908-features/19223-guadalajaras-lancaster-joneses-and-the-british-connection.html; accedido 14 junio 2012 (link muerto); Newell D. Chamberlain, *The Call of Gold: True Tales of the Gold Road to Yosemite* (Mariposa, CA: Gazette, 1936), 93–95; Mary Hill, *Gold: The California Story* (Berkeley y Los Angeles: University of California Press, 1999),

246; "RFG-382. Moffat & Co. Prospectus for the San Joaquin Diving Bell Mining Company, San Francisco, CA 1852", http://www.holabirdamericana.com/HKA-Spring2008-Cat1/Cal07.html (link muerto); accedido 2 abril 2012. Una campana de buceo se había usado en la minería de oro por lo menos una vez previamente, en el estado de Georgia de EE.UU. Otis E. Young, "The Southern Gold Rush: Contributions to California and the West", *Southern California Quarterly* 62, no. 2 (verano 1980), 132, https://www.jstor.org/stable/41170867.

125. Esta frase originalmente decía "Con esta fatiga: de subiendo lomas y pasando atascaderos", pero luego se tachó la palabra "de".
126. Justo usa el término "arroba", que era como 11.34 kg., así que un total de 23kg. aquí. Ver nota 102, arriba, para la definición de "arroba".
127. Esta frase originalmente se escribió "pobre aunque con salud", pero la ubicación correcta de "aunque" se ha indicado por medio de una flecha.
128. El nombre de Santa Cruz se le dió por primera vez a un arroyo en la costa del Pacífico al norte de Monterey por la expedición Portolá en 1769. Aunque el primer asentamiento español allí en 1797 se llamó oficialmente Villa Branciforte, el pueblo moderno, fundado en 1849, tomó el nombre de Santa Cruz en cambio. La legislatura del estado de California también le dió este nombre al condado en 1850. En 1842, a José Arana, padre, se le había otorgado el Rancho Potrero y Rincón de San Pedro Regalado en el área de Santa Cruz; un diseño de 1855 de la concesión muestra la "Casa de Arana" en el extremo occidental del Arroyo de San Pedro Regalado. Véase a la figura 27. La selva y la empresa de fabricación de tajamaniles que Justo describe más adelante en su diario (fols. 38r.–39v.) estaban en las tierras de este rancho. Gudde, *California Place Names*, 346; Diseño del Rancho Potrero y Rincon de San Pedro Regalado, Calif., http://imgzoom.cdlib.org/Fullscreen.ics?ark=ark:/13030/hb4779n8mr/z1&&brand=calisphere.
129. Matilde escribió "surron de sorra" en lugar de "zurrón de zurra".
130. El término "tlaco" es de origen náhuatl, que significa literalmente "la mitad de algo", y se usaba para referirse a la moneda de menor denominación en el México colonial, que valía solo un sesenta y cuatro cuarto de un peso de plata. "Tlaco", en Francisco J. Santamaría, *Diccionario de mejicanismos*, 4ª ed. (Mexico City: Porrúa, 1983).
131. El Río Mokelumne.
132. Justo escribió "no quiso seguirlo", en el sentido, un tanto anticuado aún en la época, de referirse a un criado como "seguidor". El significado es que el sirviente ya no quería trabajar para Puga.

133. Justo usa el término "bestia", que normalmente se usa para referirse a mulas, pero las referencias posteriores sugieren que los tres animales eran caballos, o al menos que lo eran los dos que iban montados.
134. El amigo en cuestión parece haber sido José Arana, padre. Véase la entrada del diario a continuación para el 4 de agosto.
135. "Wester" debió ser porque Justo escuchó mal o Matilde leyó mal el apellido *Welch*. El individuo mencionado aquí es casi con certeza Guillermo Angelo Welch (nacido el 4 de julio de 1829), hijo mayor del inmigrante irlandés en California William Welch y su esposa nacida en California, María Antonia Galindo; Huntington Library Early California Population Project Database (2006), registro de bautismo núm. 08297 de la Misión de Santa Clara, 6 julio 1829. James Alexander Forbes (véase nota siguiente) era el esposo de la hermana menor de Antonia Galindo de Welch, Ana María Galindo, lo que lo convertía en tío de Guillermo Welch.
136. James Alexander Forbes (1804–1881), hijo bilingüe y bicultural de padre escocés y madre española, fue criado en gran parte por su tío William Forbes, un comerciante activo en el comercio con España y con la América del Sur de habla hispana. James llegó por primera vez a California en 1831, trabajando como agente mercantil para la Hudson's Bay Company, y se convirtió en ciudadano mexicano naturalizado en 1833. Al año siguiente, se casó con Ana María "Anita" Galindo (1815–1884) y se estableció en San José, donde se convirtió en un destacado terrateniente e inició varios negocios. En 1842 fue nombrado vicecónsul de Gran Bretaña en California. Bernard Glienke, *James Alexander Forbes, 1804 to 1881: His Descendants for Four Generations*, 2da ed. (n.p.: CreateSpace, 2015), 4–74.
137. Matilde parece haber omitido un negativo aquí, escribiendo "sin recursos y en situación en que tengo probabilidad de adquirirlos", cuando, por el contexto, Justo debe haber significado "sin recursos y en situación en que [no] tengo probabilidad de adquirirlos".
138. El diario aquí tiene "gambuceo" en lugar de "gambusino", que significa "minero" o "prospector".
139. Otra de las elipses de Justo para el efecto dramático.
140. En ese momento, varios américo-atlánticos poseían ranchos en Napa, pero no hay suficientes detalles en la descripción de Justo para permitir la identificación de este estadounidense. Existe desacuerdo sobre el origen y significado de la palabra "Napa", aunque en 1914 el Dr. Platón Vallejo, quien había aprendido a hablar el idioma suisun patwin desde niño, dijo que significaba "patria" en esa lengua. Hoover et al., *Historic Spots in California*, 280, 283; Gudde, *California Place* Names, 255–56.

141. Justo alude a la Guerra México-Estadounidense recientemente concluida, en la que México había perdido territorios que ahora forman los estados de California, Nevada, Arizona y Nuevo México de Estados Unidos, en el Tratado de Guadalupe Hidalgo.
142. Como en la mayor parte de la sociedad occidental durante el siglo XIX, había muy pocos programas de asistencia pública en California en ese momento para los enfermos y débiles. La filantropía era tradicionalmente un asunto privado y voluntario. Por ejemplo, una familia mexicana que atravesaba tiempos difíciles en San Francisco en la década de 1860 apeló a sus compatriotas a través de un artículo escrito por el editor de un periódico en español en San Francisco. El editor instó a sus lectores: "Si hay compasion en los pechos de los mejicanos y mejicanas ésta es la mejor oportunidad de manifestarla". Una organización filantrópica latina se estableció formalmente en San Francisco en 1860, la Sociedad Hispano-Americana de Beneficencia Mútua, que finalmente tuvo agentes en doce comunidades desde Sacramento hasta Virginia City, Nevada. Sin embargo, como se puede ver en este incidente del diario de Justo, la compasión a veces cruzaba las fronteras étnicas. "Socorro à la desgracia", (San Francisco) *La Voz de Méjico*, 7 junio 1862, 2; "Sociedad Hispano-Americana de Beneficencia Mùtua", (San Francisco) *El Éco del Pacífico*, 7 junio 1860, 1.
143. Esto sugiere que Ygnacio caminó toda la distancia hasta el rancho y de regreso.
144. Eso es, presumiblemente, por el dolor de costado.
145. Otra elipsis para el efecto dramático, como es la más adelante en el mismo párrafo.
146. Otra elipsis dramática, como son la que sigue en este párrafo.
147. Justo aquí se refiere sarcásticamente a su caballo de carga con el nombre de Rocinante, el caballo de don Quijote. Matilde, sin embargo, parece no haber estado familiarizada con el *Quijote*, ya que no lo escribió con mayúscula como nombre propio. Ella parece haberlo tomado simplemente como una forma de "rocín", que es de hecho la raíz etimológica del nombre grandilocuentemente caballeresco que don Quijote otorga a su viejo caballo averiado cuando se incorpora a la caballería andante.
148. Este "ranchito" debió ser el Rancho Rinconada de los Gatos, otorgado en 1840 a José María Hernández y Sebastián Fabián Peralta. Se cree que el rancho recibió su nombre de los gatos salvajes, ya sea gatos monteses (*Lynx rufus*) o pumas (*Puma concolor*), o ambos, nativos de la cercana Sierra de Santa Cruz. Esta concesión de tierras abarcó lo que ahora son los pueblos de Los Gatos y Monte Sereno, así como partes de San José, Campbell y Saratoga. Gudde,

California Place Names, 141–42; Hoover et al., *Historic Spots in California*, 326; George G. Bruntz, *History of Los Gatos, Gem of the Foothills* (Fresno, CA: Valley, 1971), 8; "About Los Gatos", *Town of Los Gatos, California* website, https://www.losgatosca.gov/515/About-Los-Gatos.

149. La Misión Santa Cruz fue fundada por misioneros franciscanos en 1791. En 1857, casi ocho años después de la estancia de Justo Veytia en Santa Cruz, el terremoto de Fort Tejón dañó gravemente la estructura de adobe de la misión, que luego se derrumbó tras un mes de fuertes réplicas. Zephyrin Engelhardt, *Missions and Missionaries of California*, vol. 2, *Upper California*, pt. 1, *General History* (San Francisco: James H. Barry, 1912), 454, https://archive.org/details/missionsmissiona02enge/page/454; Francis J. Weber, *Encyclopedia of California's Catholic Heritage* (Mission Hills, CA: Arthur H. Clark, 2000), 60–61; Hoover et al., *Historic Spots in California*, 555–57; "Fort Tejon Earthquake", Southern California Earthquake Data Center, California Institute of Technology, http://scedc.caltech.edu/significant/forttejon1857.html; Duncan Carr Agnew, "Reports of the Great California Earthquake of 1857" (La Jolla, CA: Institute of Geophysics and Planetary Physics, Scripps Institution of Oceanography, 2006), esp. p. 54, https://escholarship.org/uc/item/6zn4b4jv.

150. Originalmente se escribió la palabra "molino", luego se tachó y se sustituyó por "aserredero".

151. Justo pretende aquí una metáfora escéptica, preguntándose si estas promesas de ganancias fáciles resultarán tan esquivas como las riquezas que esperaba obtener mediante la prospección de oro.

152. Justo dice "el día que salí de este pueblo"; evidentemente escribió esta entrada de diario después de regresar a San José, que es el pueblo al que se refiere. El rancho al que se hace referencia es, nuevamente, Rinconada de los Gatos.

153. Aunque los lobos grises (*Canis lupus*) fueron reportados en California en el siglo XVIII, ya eran raros en 1827 y se encontraban casi exclusivamente en la parte más al norte del estado y en la cordillera de Sierra Nevada. Por lo tanto, es muy poco probable que los aullidos que escuchó Justo Veytia en las montañas de Santa Cruz provengan de otra cosa que coyotes (*Canis latrans*). Roger Schlickeisen, Mark Shaffer, Robert M. Ferris, y William J. Snape, "Northern California/Southwestern Oregon Gray Wolf Designated Population Segment", peticionado al US Fish and Wildlife Service, United States Department of the Interior, 30 abril 2001. Washington, DC: Defenders of Wildlife, http://www.defenders.org/resources/publications/programs_and_policy/wildlife_conservation/imperiled_species/wolf/pacific_west_wolves/northern_california-southwestern_oregon_gray_wolf_dps.pdf (link muerto); accedido 14 abril 2012.

154. El término "intratables" puede significar "poco sociables", tal vez incluso con matices de "poco socializados". Sin embargo, esta estaba muy lejos de ser la impresión que obtuvieron la mayoría de los visitantes américo-atlánticos y europeos de la antigua California, quienes escribieron extensamente sobre la hospitalidad y la afición de los californios por los bailes y las fiestas.
155. Al no estar familiarizado con la flora y la fauna locales, Justo al principio llama a estos inmensos árboles "pinavetes" (*Pinus rigida*), pero luego da como alternativa su nombre correcto, "palos colorados" (*Sequoia sempervirens*).
156. Los misioneros franciscanos trajeron estilos musicales europeos a California a partir de 1769, y los indígenas que se unieron a las misiones aprendieron al canto coral y a tocar música secular y sagrada, en órganos, instrumentos de cuerda, instrumentos de viento de madera, metales y percusión. Sus orquestas y coros actuaban en las misas y también en las fiestas de los pueblos cercanos a las misiones. La mayoría de los visitantes de California que presenciaron sus actuaciones los tenían en mayor estima que a Justo Veytia. William John Summers, "California Mission Music", http://californiamissionsfoundation.org/articles/californiamissionmusic/.
157. Monterey fue fundada en 1770 como misión y presidio. Fue la capital efectiva de la Alta California durante el período colonial español y durante gran parte del período de la República Mexicana. Una parte de la primera convención constitucional del estado se llevó a cabo en Monterey, del 1 de septiembre al 13 de octubre de 1849. Hoover et al., *Historic Spots in California*, 264–66, 277.
158. Una palabra femenina que indica viaje, tal vez "jornada", ha sido accidentalmente omitida por Matilde después de "nuestra".
159. El subrayado de "casa" está en el original, para énfasis sarcástico.
160. Matilde escribió sobre la letra inicial de la palabra "lobrega", haciendo que la palabra fuera difícil de descifrar. Una transcripción del diario de Justo Veytia elaborado por Salvador Villanueva Veytia en 2000 con el auspicio del Instituto Nacional de Antropología e Historia da la palabra como "lóbrega". Justo Veytia, *Viaje a la Alta California, 1849–1850*, ed. Cuauhtémoc Ávila (Mexico City: Insituto Nacional de Antropología e Historia, 2000), 59.
161. Marcos Arana se casó en Santa Cruz en enero de 1849 con Dolores Leyva. Él y su hermano Felipe, con sus esposas y los hijos de Felipe, figuran en el Censo de los Estados Unidos de 1850 para el Condado de Santa Cruz como viviendo en un hogar conjunto no muy lejos del de su padre, José, padre. Según las actas de bautismo de sus hijos Epifanio Genovevo (nacido en 1847) y José Ygnacio (nacido en 1848), la esposa de Felipe era Esperanza Guadalupe Amaya; estos hijos deben haber sido los "maldecidos muchachos" que tanto molestaron a Justo. El

censo tergiversa los nombres de la esposa y el hijo mayor de Felipe como "María" y "Juan", respectivamente, en lugar de Esperanza y Genovevo, aunque nombra correctamente al segundo hijo como Ygnacio. La Huntington Library, Early California Population Project Database (2006), registro de matrimonio núm. 00885 y registros de bautismo núms. 02770 y 02795 de la Mission Santa Cruz.

162. El sentido de "Hace poco más de ocho días" es más como "un poco más de una semana". Esta expresión tradicional "ocho días" para significar una semana se usa varias veces en el diario.

163. Literalmente, el rancho más cercano habría sido Rancho Arroyo del Rodeo, pero no era propiedad de una mujer; desde 1845, había sido propiedad de John Daubenbiss y John Hames. Sin embargo, el próximo rancho al sur, Rancho Soquel, era propiedad de Martina Castro de Cota de Lodge de Depeaux (1807–1890), quien según la historia oral de su nieta era una mujer de carácter decidido; entonces ella puede ser la vecina bien intencionada mencionada aquí. Carrie Lodge, "The Martina Castro Lodge Family", entrevista de historia oral por Elizabeth Spedding Calciano (Santa Cruz: Regional History Project, University of California, Santa Cruz, Library, 1965), 4–17, 21–34; Hoover et al., *Historic Spots in California*, 566–67.

164. Mientras que la frase "del pais" se refería a alguien o algo nativo de California, "paisano" se usaba para indicar a alguien de su mismo país de origen que vivía en California.

165. El diario tiene "se estrellan en ellas", con "en ellas" posteriormente tachado.

166. La sintaxis de Justo en este punto se torturó un poco, al menos como la presenta su hija, quien obviamente tuvo problemas con ella en este punto.

167. Justo relata aquí hechos ocurridos una semana antes, alrededor del 1 de diciembre de 1849.

168. Matilde ha escrito "estaviada", pero esto debe ser un error por "extraviada". Además, el diario originalmente tenía "sin poder apartarse de un lado *á* otro cuadro", con "de un lado *á* otro" posteriormente tachado.

169. Originalmente el diario tenía "y en donde se fue"; luego se tachó "en donde" y arriba se escribió "la que".

170. Alrededor del 2 al 3 de diciembre de 1849.

171. Justo usa aquí la palabra "pesuña", aunque normalmente significa una pezuña hendida, como la de una vaca o una cabra; "casco" es la palabra adecuada para la pezuña no hendida de un caballo.

172. Gary Griggs identifica el sitio de esta desventura casi fatal como la playa debajo de Waddell Bluffs, al sur de Año Nuevo Point en el Condado de San Mateo. Según Griggs, normalmente "los primeros viajeros, ya sea a caballo, en

diligencia o en un automóvil 'Stanley Steamer,' esperaban la marea baja y luego corrían por la playa lo más rápido que podían" en esta sección de la ruta costera de Alta California. No fue hasta la década de 1940 que se construyó con éxito una carretera, State Highway 1, a lo largo de la ruta de la costa, incluido Waddell Bluffs; pero incluso hoy, Waddell Bluffs es una de las secciones de esa carretera notoriamente propensa a deslizamientos de rocas y lodo durante los inviernos lluviosos. "Coastal Cliffs and Rolling Rocks", *Santa Cruz Sentinel*, 18 diciembre, 2010, https://www.santacruzsentinel.com/2010/12/18/gary-griggs-our-ocean-backyard-coastal-cliffs-and-rolling-rocks/.

173. El diario usa el término "armas de montar", que eran solapas de cuero adheridas a la silla de montar, que el jinete colocaba sobre sus piernas para protegerlas contra las inclemencias del tiempo, la maleza, et cétera. En la década de 1870, este equipo de protección se modificó en las icónicas "chaps" de vaqueros de EE.UU. (del español "chaparreras") que se llevan en las piernas del jinete en lugar de en la silla de montar. Pero durante las décadas de 1840 y 1850, las armas de montar originales todavía formaban parte de la silla de montar. Fay E. Ward, *The Cowboy at Work* (Nueva York: Hastings House, 1958; repub. Mineola, NY: Dover, 2003), chap. 25, esp. pp. 225–27. Sin embargo, posteriormente en este pasaje Justo usa la palabra "chaparreras" aparentemente para referirse al mismo equipo. Porque precisa que el caballo desbocado "había tirado" estas chaparreras, estas no podían ser prendas que llevaba el jinete. El último término, por lo tanto, ya estaba en uso en 1849–1850, aunque para referirse a armas de montar en lugar de las chaparreras más modernas.

174. Matilde sin darse cuenta omitió un sustantivo, escribiendo "que yo tenía en de la chaqueta". Presumiblemente se pretendía alguna palabra como "bolsillo"; aunque "bolsillo" es masculino, y el artículo femenino precede a la palabra que falta.

175. Es decir, en Rancho Buri Buri Véase nota 65, arriba.

176. Originalmente construido en Nueva York en 1840 para México como buque mercante, más tarde en ese mismo año el *Malek Adel* fue incautado por el USS *Enterprise* en Bahía, Brasil, y traída a Baltimore, luego de informes de que su tripulación se había involucrado en actos de piratería contra otros barcos mercantes a lo largo de la costa atlántica de Estados Unidos, en el curso de un viaje de Nueva York a Guaymas. El tribunal determinó que el Capitán José Núñez había practicado piratería sin el conocimiento de los armadores, por lo que el bergantín fue incautado pero la carga fue devuelta a sus propietarios. Durante la Guerra México-Estadounidense, *Malek Adel* fue equipado como un bergantín de diez cañones para las fuerzas navales mexicanas. El 7 de

septiembre de 1846 fue capturada en Mazatlán por el USS *Warren* y llevado a la Marina de los Estados Unidos. Después de que terminó la guerra, fue vendido en 1848 y, a partir de entonces, fue un barco mercante civil. En la edición del 6 de diciembre de 1849 de *Alta California* apareció un anuncio del "bergantín clíper de navegación rápida" *Malek Adel*, programado para salir de San Francisco "Hacia Monterey, Santa Bárbara, San Pedro, San Diego y las Islas Sandwich" en el 15 de diciembre. (El nombre del barco parece haber sido escrito a veces como *Malek Adel* y a veces como *Malek Adhel*.) Este es el viaje al que Justo y sus compañeros esperaban unirse como pasajeros. No hay ninguna mención en el itinerario anunciado de Santa Cruz, un puerto muy pequeño, pero les aseguraron verbalmente que harían una parada allí, o planeaban desembarcar en Monterey y viajar por tierra a Santa Cruz. El barco en realidad llegó a San Francisco desde Monterey, sin embargo, hasta el 10 de diciembre. Justo y sus compañeros habrían puesto sus pertenencias a bordo el día 14. Sin embargo, como deja en claro el diario de Justo, ella no se fue a tiempo, o por algún tiempo después. United States *v.* the Brig Malek Adhel, 43 US 210 (1844), http://supreme.justia.com/cases/federal/us/43/210/case.html; *Dictionary of American Naval Fighting Ships*, 8 vols., vol. 4, L–M, ed. James L. Mooney (Washington, DC: Navy Department, Office of the Chief of Naval Operations, Naval History Division, 1959–81), 206; "Marine Journal", (San Francisco) *Alta California*, 15 diciembre 1849, 3.

177. Matilde comenzó a escribir "pasar por alli", pero se dió cuenta del error después de las dos primeras letras de "por", que luego tachó.

178. En este pasaje sobre el fuego, los tiempos verbales de Justo cambian repetidamente entre el pasado y el presente histórico, reflejando la urgencia y la inmediatez de la experiencia.

179. Justo usó una forma singular, "cual si fuera pieza de artillería", cuando en realidad tenía un antecedente plural, "las pipas de aguardiente". Este es el error gramatical común de tomar el objeto de la frase adjetiva, "aguardiente", como el antecedente, ya que está más cerca de la cláusula dependiente "cual si fuera pieza de artillería" que el sujeto real, "las pipas".

180. Según la descripción, estos hombres estaban aplicando una de las pocas técnicas efectivas de extinción de incendios urbanos de la época, creando un cortafuegos al demoler una franja de edificios no quemados en el camino del fuego, para que el fuego no pudiera llegar al resto de la ciudad al otro lado del cortafuegos.

181. Un relato detallado del incendio apareció en el periódico de San Francisco *Alta California*, 26 diciembre 1849, 2, bajo el título "Appalling and Destructive

Conflagration!!" Este artículo confirma el informe de Justo sobre los métodos utilizados para combatir el incendio, incluido el camión de bomberos, y estima los daños sufridos como resultado entre $1,000,000 y $1,500,000. En el siguiente número del periódico, el 28 de diciembre, apareció un diagrama de las áreas quemadas (3) y un editorial sobre la necesidad urgente de un departamento de bomberos en San Francisco (2).

182. Los pinos, por supuesto, son árboles de hoja perenne y no perderían su follaje en invierno. Pero Justo podría haber tenido en cuenta el hecho de que muchos mástiles de barcos estaban hechos de pinos.
183. Matilde ha escrito por error "recomendada" por "encomendada".
184. El diario originalmente tenía "ultimos" ante "mas terribles esfuerzos"; esto fue luego tachado. Probablemente Justo se dió cuenta de que "postreros" y "ultimos" eran prácticamente sinónimos y los sustituyó por "mas terribles".
185. Los estadounidenses mencionados aquí pueden haber sido John Daubenbiss (1816–1896), en realidad un inmigrante bávaro, y John Hames (1811–1894), quien construyó un aserradero en el Arroyo Soquel en la década de 1840, que era el límite entre su Rancho Arroyo del Rodeo y el Rancho Soquel de Martina Castro de Cota de Lodge de Depeaux (véase nota 163, arriba). Comprado por Daubenbiss y Hames en 1845 al concesionario original Francisco Rodríguez, el Rancho Arroyo del Rodeo colindaba con el Rancho Potrero y Rincón de San Pedro Regalado de José Arana en el sur. Hoover et al., *Historic Spots in California*, 572–73; *Decisions of the Department of the Interior and General Land Office in Cases Relating to the Public Lands, from July, 1881, to June, 1883*, ed. S. V. Proudfit, rev. ed., vol. 1 (Washington, DC: Government Printing Office, 1887), 260; "Soquel Pioneer John Hames", *Santa Cruz Sentinel*, 28 diciembre 1947, 9; Edward Martin, *History of Santa Cruz County, California* (Los Angeles: Historic Record Co., 1911), 48, https://archive.org/details/historyofsantac00mart/page/n5; E. S. Harrison, *History of Santa Cruz County* (San Francisco: Pacific Press, 1892), 301, https://books.google.com/books?id=unAUAAAAYAAJ&pg=PA289&lpg=PA289&dq=John+Daubenbis&source=bl&ots=7NnPstetf9&sig=43GzQSetlMQVf6wZow9q8N_dy6I&hl=en&sa=X&ved=2ahUKEwiu6aamobbeAhWqJTQIHfSXAD0Q6AEwDHoECAQQAQ#v=onepage&q=John%20Daubenbis&f=false.
186. Justo utiliza una abreviatura monetaria, "rs", transcrita en la edición de 2000 del diario como "12 reales". Veytia, *Viaje*, ed. Cuauhtémoc Ávila, 71.
187. Ya sea Justo o Matilde ha escrito "y", pero por el contexto debería ser "de".
188. Subrayado en el original.

189. Subrayado en el original. Justo usa el término "albardón", que ordinariamente significa una silla de estilo inglés, que carece de un cuerno prominente. Sin embargo, el contexto deja en claro que no había una silla de montar real involucrada aquí, solo una almohadilla improvisada que Ygnacio fabricó con mantas dobladas. "Albardón", en Santamaría, *Diccionario de mejicanismos*, 7ª ed.

190. Un anuncio en el *Alta California*, 6 diciembre 1849, 3, anunciaba que, el 15 de diciembre de 1849, el *Malek Adel* zarparía de San Francisco hacia Monterey, Santa Bárbara, San Pedro, San Diego y luego las Islas Sandwich (es decir, Hawai), para regresar "a principios de la primavera" (véase nota 176, arriba). Luego, se registra que el *Malek Adel* llegó debidamente a San Francisco el 22 de marzo de 1850. Del 25 al 28 de marzo y el 2 de abril, los anuncios en el *Alta California* anunciaron que el *Malek Adel* pronto partiría hacia Santa Cruz, Monterey y Santa Bárbara. El anuncio del 4 de abril declaraba que "navegará positivamente hacia los puertos mencionados el jueves 4 de abril". Sin embargo, según la columna de "Shipping Intelligence" ("Inteligencia de barcos") del 6 de abril, no salió de la Bahía de San Francisco hasta el 5 de abril. O la ropa y la silla de Justo nunca se subieron a bordo en San Francisco en primer lugar, o no llegaron a tierra durante la descarga abortada en Santa Cruz. "Shipping Intelligence," *Alta California*, 23 marzo 1850, 2, y anuncios de 25 marzo 1850, 3; 26 marzo 1850, 1; 27 marzo 1850, 1; 28 marzo 1850, 1; 2 abril 1850, 3; 4 abril 1850, 1; "Shipping Intelligence", 6 abril 1850, 3.

191. La "Señora dueña de la cañada" probablemente fue Martina Castro de Cota de Lodge de Depeaux de Rancho Soquel; véase notas 163 y 185, arriba.

192. Gabriel Moraga usó la forma plural, Las Mariposas, para referirse a un lugar en lo que ahora es el Condado de Merced. Juan Bautista Alvarado nombró a su rancho en esa área Las Mariposas en 1844. La forma singular, Mariposa, se usó para nombrar un arroyo, un pueblo y una mina en las colinas, en lo que ahora es el Condado de Mariposa. Justo Veytia llama a la mina Las Mariposas, que no parece corresponder a ninguno de estos lugares; probablemente se refería a la Mina Mariposa, a lo largo de la actual Ruta 49. Hoover et al., *Historic Spots in California*, 108; Gudde, *California Place Names*, 228; Metsker's Map of Mariposa County.

193. El diario habla de atravesar el inmenso "Valle de San José". No existe tal lugar en la parte de California que Justo atravesaba camino a la mina que él llama Mariposas. Como deja en claro su mención de los ríos San Joaquín y Merced, en realidad estaba cruzando el Valle de San Joaquín; entonces o él o Matilde escribió el nombre geográfico equivocado. En 1806 Gabriel Moraga

nombró al Río de Nuestra Señora de la Merced. Empezando en el Valle de Yosemite, el Río Merced se junta con el San Joaquín casi cincuenta millas al sur de Stockton. Hoover et al., *Historic Spots in California*, 112; DeLorme Mapping Co., *Northern California Atlas*, 108–11, 117–18.

194. Un canadiense, William Perkins, describió el pueblo minero de Sonora durante el verano de 1849: "Las habitaciones estaban construidas de lona, tela de algodón o de palos verticales sin tallar con ramas y hojas verdes y enredaderas entretejidas, y decoradas con llamativos tapices de sedas, algodones de fantasía, banderas, artículos brillantes de todo tipo; el zarape mexicano de muchos colores, la rica manga, con sus bordados de oro, las bufandas chinas y los chales de la más costosa calidad; sillas de montar, bridas y espuelas bañadas en oro y plata estaban esparcidas en todas direcciones. . . . ¡Pero qué artículo era demasiado costoso para los hombres que podían pagarlo con puñados de polvo de oro, el producto de unas pocas horas de trabajo!" Los circos y artistas itinerantes mexicanos visitaban con frecuencia a la Alta California durante la Fiebre del Oro y las décadas posteriores, y se conoce al menos una compañía de artistas nativos de California. William Perkins, *Three Years in California: William Perkins' Journal of Life at Sonora, 1849–1852*, eds. Dale L. Morgan y James R. Scobie (Berkeley y Los Angeles: University of California Press, 1964), 101; "Letter from Los Angeles", (San Francisco) *Alta California*, 28 febrero 1858, 1; "Noticias Sueltas del Pacífico", (Los Angeles) *La Crónica*, 9 abril 1873, 3.

195. Agua Fria era la sede del condado original de Mariposa. Está a orillas del Arroyo Agua Fría, afluente del Río Merced, cerca de la intersección de las Rutas 140 y 49; Metsker's Map of Mariposa County.

196. Los "Don Juan Smith y sus hermanos" aquí mencionados eran la mayoría de los hijos e hijas de Thomas Smith y su esposa María Meza, de Baja California. En español, "hermanos" puede significar específicamente hermanos varones o más generalmente hermanos de ambos sexos; y la documentación indica que los hermanos Juan, Manuel, José María, Juan Bautista (también conocido como Washington), Salvadora, Nieves y Antonio Felix Smith estaban en California por esta época. Juan (n. 1810) era el mayor de los hermanos. Donna Przecha, "Smith Family of Baja California," http://docplayer.net/32077214-Smith-family-of-baja-california-donna-przecha.html.

197. El 13 de abril de 1850, la Legislatura del Estado de California aprobó una "Ley para una mejor regulación de las minas y el gobierno de los mineros extranjeros". Esta estipulaba que las personas que no eran ciudadanos de Estados Unidos y no eran elegibles para "tener convertirse en ciudadanos bajo el tratado de Guadalupe Hidalgo"—es decir, indígenas y negros—no tenían

permitido hacer minería en California, a menos que primero hubieran obtenido una licencia, que costaba $20 al mes. La licencia tenía que ser renovada cada mes. Aunque el lenguaje de la ley simplemente se refería vagamente a "mineros extranjeros", sin especificar ningún país o países de origen, en la práctica tenía como objetivo desalentar a los mineros de México y otros países de habla hispana, así como a los mineros chinos. Esto se hizo explícito en una versión posterior de la ley, que fue revisada para eximir del impuesto a cualquier "persona blanca libre", independientemente de su origen nacional. *The Statutes of California passed at the First Session of the Legislature, Begun the 15th Day of Dec, 1849 and ended the 22nd day of April, 1850, at the city of Pueblo de San Jose* (San José: J. Winchester, 1850), 221–23; Jean Pfaelzer, *Driven Out: The Forgotten War Against Chinese Americans* (Nueva York: Random House, 2007), 50.

198. El diario tiene incorrectamente la forma plural del verbo "eran", pero el sujeto es singular, "El otro".

199. Por el contexto, está claro que los indígenas no los vieron. Posiblemente Matilde insertó accidentalmente el "no" negativo, o bien escribió "no" en lugar de "nos". O puede ser que aquí se enredó un poco la sintaxis de Justo, como ocasionalmente en el diario, y quiso decir que lo que no pasó fue que los indígenas lo vieron a él y a sus compañeros. En cualquier caso, el sentido parece ser que tomar ese camino en particular les permitió escapar de la atención de los indígenas, como esperaban.

200. Esta palabra originalmente se escribía "há", pero luego se tachó la H.

201. Estanislao, un indígena neófito, huyó de la Misión de San José al Valle Central en la década de 1820 y fomentó una rebelión contra el gobierno mexicano que no fue sofocada hasta 1829. El río a lo largo de cuya orilla sus fuerzas finalmente fueron derrotadas llegó a ser conocido en la década de 1830 como el Río Estanislao. John C. Frémont se refería al area por la traducción en inglés del nombre de Estanislao, "Stanislaus". Stanislaus City fue fundada en 1849 pero renombrada Ripon en 1879. Gudde, *California Place Names*, 318, 373.

202. Antonio Félix Smith (n. 1831) era el menor de los hermanos Smith de Baja California; véase nota 196, arriba.

203. De hecho, como se hará evidente, su primo Ybarra dirigía una cantina y una casa de juego.

204. Según los términos del Tratado de Guadalupe Hidalgo, todos los californios que permanecían en California se habían convertido en ciudadanos de Estados Unidos en 1848 y, como tales, teóricamente estaban exentos del impuesto a los mineros extranjeros. Véase nota 197, arriba.

205. Este es Antonio Smith; véase notas 196 y 202, arriba.
206. Es decir, "tahúr".
207. Subrayado en el original.
208. Silvano Valencia no ha sido identificado.
209. Los Melones se encuentra a orillas del Río Stanislaus en el Condado de Calaveras. El nombre puede provenir de la descripción de los mineros latinos del oro de placer que se encuentra allí, como parecido a las semillas de melón; aunque esta etimología ha sido cuestionada. Olaf P. Jenkins, ed. dir., *The Mother Lode County*, ed. Centennial. Geologic Guidebook along Highway 49—Sierran Gold Belt, Bulletin 141 (San Francisco: California Department of Natural Resources, Division of Mines, 1948), 55; Hoover et al., *Historic Spots in California*, 78; Gudde, *California Place Names*, 233
210. "Dr. Rodgers" puede ser Samuel Josiah Smith Rogers (1824–1904), nacido en Massachusetts, que acababa de llegar a San Francisco en 1850. Finalmente se estableció en Marysville, California. J. M. Guinn, *History of the State of California and Biographical Record of the Sacramento Valley, California: An Historical Story of the State's Marvelous Growth from Its Earliest Settlement to the Present Time* (Chicago: Chapman, 1906), 1618; https://www.findagrave.com/memorial/132029864.
211. El texto tiene "con" en lugar de "sin", muy probablemente un error de copia de Matilde.
212. Aunque Justo no nombra el barco en el que regresó a México, el *Panama*, de la Pacific Mail Steamship Company, salió de San Francisco a las 5:00 p.m. el 1 de agosto de 1850, con destino a Panamá, con paradas intermedias no especificadas, probablemente muy parecidas a las de un barco de vapor anterior del Pacific Mail que hizo escala en Mazatlán, San Blas, Acapulco y Panamá. Como el *Panama* era el único barco de vapor programado para salir de San Francisco ese día, lo más probable es que Justo Veytia estuviera a bordo. (San Francisco) *Alta California*, 29 julio 1850, 1, y 5 abril 1849, 1.
213. Originalmente se omitió la palabra "los", luego se comprimió entre "que" y "ajustó".
214. Roque Delgado no ha sido identificado.
215. La ligera incoherencia de la prosa de Justo aquí refleja la confusión y la frustración que obviamente sintió en ese momento.
216. Es decir, el 9 julio 1850.
217. Las palabras "un doble" originalmente se escribieron dos veces, luego se tachó la segunda aparición.

English Translation of Justo Veytia's Diary

1. The name of the town, Amatitán, in the county of Amatitán, is derived from the indigenous word *amathe*, which means "small forest of amate trees." Its earliest inhabitants were Nahuatlaca Indians, who established themselves on a ridge called Chiquihuitillo. *Enciclopedia temática de Jalisco*, vol. 8, *Municipios*, 1, ed. Fernando Martínez-Réding (Guadalajara: Gobierno del Estado de Jalisco, 1992), 35–36.

2. The name Tequila is derived from the indigenous word *tequillan*, which means "place where one cuts." Its first inhabitants were Nahualtec, Toltec, and Otomi Indians. In 1600, Don Pedro Sánchez de Tagle, marquess of Altamira, built the first tequila factory here. In Veytia's day, Tequila was merely a town, although today it is the seat of the county of Tequila. *Enciclopedia temática de Jalisco*, vol. 10, *Municipios*, 3, ed. Fernando Martínez-Réding (Guadalajara: Gobierno del Estado de Jalisco, 1992), 82–83.

3. Santo Tomás is in the county of Hostotipaquillo, whose name derives from the indigenous word *oztotipa*, which means "on top of a cavern." Iron mines were discovered in the region in 1605. *Enciclopedia temática de Jalisco*, vol. 9, *Municipios*, 2, ed. Fernando Martinez-Réding (Guadalajara: Gobierno del Estado de Jalisco, 1992), 28–29.

4. Venta de Mochitiltic is located about five kilometers west of Santo Tomás. According to a guidebook in 1965, "La Venta de Mochitiltic . . . is a former *hacienda* with a typical old house and a small chapel. The cobblestone-paved old road is still to be seen passing through. The name La Venta refers to a type of inn which was located along the roads to furnish food and lodging to travelers and feed for their animals." Veytia's party might have stayed in such an inn on their way to the coast. The *barrancas*, or ravines, of Mochitiltic are a number of canyons that drain into the Santiago River. *Enciclopedia temática de Jalisco*, vol. 9, *Municipios*, 2, 28; Howard E. Gulick, *Nayarit, Mexico: A Traveler's Guidebook to This Historic and Scenic State of Mexico's West Coast and its Capital, the City of Tepic*. Clark Guidebooks, 3 (Glendale, CA: Arthur H. Clark, 1965), 138–39.

5. The town of Ixtlan del Río is the seat of the county of Ixtlan, in the Mexican state of Nayarit. The name derives from a Nahuatl term meaning "place of obsidian." Gulick, *Nayarit*, 135.

6. "Ahuacatlan . . . was an important independent Indian chiefdom before the Spanish conquest. . . . It early became an important center after mines were opened up in the area." The town is the seat of the county of the same

name, which extends to the Ameca River. Its indigenous name means "place of avocados." Indicating the food-growing fame of the region, nearby is another town called Camotlan, from the Nahuatl for "place of sweet potatoes." Gulick, *Nayarit*, 130–31.

7. The road from Guadalajara to Tepic crosses the Transmexican Volcanic Belt, a mountain chain that includes the 2,200-meter-high Ceboruco. This volcano erupted most recently in 1870, sending slow-moving lava down the sides of the volcano for nearly two years. The hardened lava flows can be seen on either side of the Guadalajara-Tepic road. The lava Veytia saw, however, was from earlier eruptions, two of which had occurred in the sixteenth century. *Enciclopedia temática de Jalisco*, vol. 1, *Geografía*, ed. Fernando Martínez-Réding (Guadalajara: Gobierno del Estado de Jalisco, 1992), 142–43.

8. In 1965 San Leonel was described as a former hacienda. Gulick, *Nayarit*, 126.

9. The name of Tepic may derive from the Nahuatl word *tepicle*, a variety of corn that matures in fifty days. A Spanish census of 1525 noted that Tepic was largely inhabited by Nahuatl-speaking Indians. Tepic became a flourishing trade center after the port of San Blas was established in 1768, as the major route from that port to Guadalajara went through Tepic. Shortly after Mexico's independence from Spain, in 1823 or 1824, Eustace Barron, a British subject of Irish and Spanish ancestry born in Cádiz, Spain, arrived in Tepic, where he served as British consul and formed the famed trading house of Barron Forbes with two Scottish-born partners, Alexander Forbes and James Alexander Forbes (not related to each other). Barron Forbes had comercial interests ranging from Ecuador to the New Almaden mine just south of San José in Alta California. Tepic had a large number of merchants from Central America, Belgium, Italy, France, Germany, Spain, and the United States, and at the time of Veytia's journey was a major trading center, dominated economically by Barron Forbes. John Fox, *Macnamara's Irish Colony and the United States Taking of California in 1846* (Jefferson, NC, & London: McFarland, 2000), 21, 80, 118–19, 131; Gulick, *Nayarit*, 96; Marina Anguiano, *Nayarit. Costa y altiplanicie en el momento de Contacto* (Mexico City: Universidad Nacional Autónoma de México, 1992), 54, 57; Jean Meyer, *Breve historia de Nayarit* (Mexico City: Fondo de Cultura Económica, 1997), 73, 94–95.

10. The diary has *comunicadas* [sic] *con esta*, "[the walls] communicate with it," but the antecedent must actually be the four-walled enclosure, not the walls themselves.

11. At this time, Mexico did not yet use the Celsius temperature scale, which

was introduced in 1857 as one aspect of that year's national reforms but not mandated until the 1890 Tratado del Metro (Metric System Treaty). Before then, Mexico's weights and measures were based on Spanish ones introduced during the colonial period, which could vary from region to region. As a result, it is not clear exactly which temperature scale Veytia was using here, except that it was not Celsius. Lucero Morelos Rodríguez, "A peso el kilo. Historia del sistema métrico decimal en México," review of H. Vera, *Libros de escarabejo* (Mexico City, 2007), in *Investigaciones Geográficas* 69 (2009): 132–35, https://www.researchgate.net/publication/43530987_Resena_de_A_peso_el_kilo_Historia_del_sistema_metrico_decimal_en_Mexico_de_H_Vera.

12. The port of San Blas was founded by the viceroy of New Spain, the marquess de Croix, in 1768, specifically to serve as a base for ships and expeditions to Alta California. It was designed by the engineer Miguel Costansó, who in 1769 joined Father Junípero Serra on the expedition that founded the first mission in Alta California, San Diego. He later walked the length of the state with Captain Gaspar de Portolá to Monterey Bay. Costansó's journal of his journey provides fascinating details about Alta California at the time. María Luisa Rodríguez-Sala, Karina Neria Mosco, Verónica Ramírez Ortega, and Alejandra Tolentino Ochoa, *Los cirujanos del mar en la Nueva España (1572–1820), ¿miembros de un estamento profesional o una comunidad científica?* Serie Los cirujanos del mar en la Nueva España, 1 (Mexico City: Universidad Nacional Autónoma de México, 2004), 58–59; *The Portolá Expedition of 1769–1770: Diary of Miguel Costansó*, ed. Frederick J. Taggart. Publications of the Academy of Pacific Coast History, 2:4 (Berkeley, CA: University Press, 1911). San Blas was still the major port on the Pacific Coast for travel to Alta California at the time of Justo Veytia's journey, but by 1855, diversion of trade to the deeper harbors of Mazatlán and Acapulco had caused a two-thirds drop in tonnage arriving in San Blas; and by the 1860s, San Blas was being bypassed by all but local ships. Meyer, *Breve historia*, 99–100.

13. The farming village of Navarrete is about seventeen miles northwest of Tepic, located on the old road from Tepic to San Blas. Gulick, *Nayarit*, 85.

14. Carlos Tapia is otherwise unidentified. On his return to Mexico, Justo bought his passage ticket, in a private transaction, from one Ygnacio Tapia (fol. 57r.), but it has not been established if he and Carlos Tapia were any relation.

15. Not until fol. 16v. does Justo mention Puga's first name, Pepe (a nickname for José). This individual traveled for a time with Justo and his companions in California, until returning to Guadalajara in August 1849. The ship in question, as Justo makes clear later, was the *Volante*.

16. Fernández Peral has not been identified.
17. Pérez has not been identified.
18. In the Tepic area, *palomaría* refers to a tree of the *Clusiaceae* family. Presumably such trees stood near the Palos Marías road at some point. Francisco J. Santamaría, *Diccionario de mejicanismos*, 7th ed. (Mexico City: Porrúa, 2005).
19. Justo's original wording was *pulgas, gorupos y chinchis*. The *Diccionario de mejicanismos* defines *gorupo* as a mammalian louse. *Chinchi* is a variant spelling of *chinche*, "bedbug." "Chinche," in *Diccionario de autoridades*, facs. ed. Biblioteca Románica Hispánica, ser. 5, Diccionarios, 3 (Madrid: Gredos, 1990), vol. 1, A–C; "Gorupo," in Santamaría, *Diccionario de mejicanismos*, 7th ed.
20. *Papaqui* comes from a Nahuatl word, *papaquiliztli*, which means happiness or joy. This was a traditional style of Carnival music and celebration. "Papaqui," in Santamaría, *Diccionario de mejicanismos*, 7th ed.
21. Justo uses the word *tapatíos*, meaning people from the city of Guadalajara or, by extension, from the state of Jalisco. It comes from the Nahuatl word *tlapatiotl*. "Tapatío," in Santamaría, *Diccionario de mejicanismos*, 7th ed.
22. The phrase in Spanish translated here as "our fellow Guadalajarans," *nuestros paisanos*, literally means "our fellow countrymen." It is clear that Justo meant by this his fellow Guadalajarans, as contrasted with the people of Tepic (*tepiqueños*) with whom they got into the fights during Carnival. This again illustrates the contemporary strong attachment most people felt to their hometown or region, to the extent of viewing it as, in a sense, a different culture or polity from those of other regions of Mexico.
23. Latino prospectors participating in the California Gold Rush often formed companies, some quite large. For example, José María Amador, a Californio after whom Amador County was named, organized a company of about thirty men, with a train of pack animals and sixteen head of cattle, to go from Santa Clara County to the town of Coloma in 1848. An Argentine, Ramón Gil Navarro, joined a company formed in Concepción, Chile, which had sufficient capital to buy its own ship, the *Carmen*, and fit her out for the journey to California. Atlantic Americans, too, formed companies, although many of them dissolved en route or after arriving in the gold fields. Ramón Gil Navarro, *The Gold Rush Diary of Ramón Gil Navarro*, ed. and trans. María del Carmen Ferreyra and David S. Reher (Lincoln & London: University of Nebraska Press, 2000), 1–2; *Californio Voices: The Oral Memoirs of José María Amador and Lorenzo Asisara*, ed. and trans. Gregorio Mora-Torres (Denton: University

of North Texas Press, 2005), 197; Cecil K. Byrd, *Searching for Riches: The California Gold Rush* (Bloomington: Lilly Library, Indiana University, 1991), 8.

24. These individuals have not been identified.

25. A brigantine is a ship with two masts; the foremast is square-rigged and the mainmast fore-and-aft-rigged. *The Oxford Companion to Ships and the Sea*, ed. Peter Kemp (Oxford: Oxford University Press, 1988), 109. The *Republicano* arrived in San Francisco on April 12, thirty-two days after making a stop at Mazatlán. (*Alta California*, April 5, 1849, 2).

26. Once Mexico achieved independence, colonial trade restrictions were lifted and California soon joined the growing world of Pacific trade. Hawaiian-born and San Francisco-based William Heath Davis appended to his memoirs a "Record of Ships Arriving from 1774 to 1847." It shows that from the 1820s the number of ships calling in San Francisco greatly increased, as did the number of countries from which they came. William Heath Davis, *Seventy-five Years in California*, ed. John Howell (San Francisco: John Howell, 1929), 397–409.

27. Justo uses the term *varas*; a *vara* was equivalent to 33 inches, close enough to the yard used in English-speaking countries that we have used the English measure in the translation. The vara as a unit of measurement was used in Alta California during the Spanish colonial and Mexican republic periods, and for years after US annexation. Even ten years after Justo Veytia's journey, an advertisement in an English-language newspaper in San Francisco offered for sale "A 100 vara lot" ("For Sale Cheap," advertisement, (San Francisco) *Alta California*, October 27, 1859, 4).

28. Justo uses the term *tercios* to mean bales or bundles of goods. Originally a mule was loaded with one tercio on each side, totaling two tercios. Depending upon the size and strength of the mule, a tercio could weight from forty to eighty pounds. The *Diccionario de mejicanismos* gives *tercio* as a synonym for *paca*, "bale." "Tercio," in Santamaría, *Diccionario de mejicanismos*, 7th ed.; "Tercio," in *Diccionario de autoridades*, vol. 3.

29. Sea shanties have been well studied in the English-speaking marine tradition, but very little literature seems to exist on the equivalent tradition among Spanish speakers.

30. The apparent ellipsis seems to be Justo's own, for dramatic effect, rather than an indication of any omission.

31. Here Justo uses the word *fulano*, similar to the English "What's-his-name," ordinarily used of a third person. Either he discreetly chose not to name any

one person, or else the sort of conversation he describes was so common that any one of his fellow passengers could have said this at any given point during the voyage.

32. Matilde, perhaps as a deliberate suppression, has written ¡*Que capaz!*, which makes little sense. Her father may have originally written ¡*Qué caray!*, an interjection commonly used in the Americas, which is a somewhat milder form of a common Romance-language vulgarity based on male anatomy. "Carajo," in Joan Corominas, *Diccionario crítico etimológico castellano e hispánico*, vol. A–CA. Biblioteca Románica Hispánica V, Diccionarios, 7 (Madrid, Gredos, 1997). Here we translate with the contextualized sense, not the literal words, of how Justo used the expression.

33. The main land route from northern Mexico to California ran through the Sonora desert and was so difficult that it was nicknamed *El Camino del Diablo*, "the devil's highway." The first Europeans explored this route in the seventeenth century, but archaeological evidence suggests that indigenous peoples had used it for more than 7,000 years. In 1774 the expedition of Juan Bautista de Anza established it as the accepted land route from Mexico to California. Richard F. Pourade, *Anza Conquers the Desert: The Anza Expeditions from Mexico to California and the Founding of San Francisco, 1774 to 1776* (San Diego: Copley, 1971), 7–49. This was the route the seasick passenger wished he had taken.

34. *Atole* is a traditional Mexican beverage in use since pre-Columbian times, made usually of cornmeal boiled in water to the consistency of thin porridge, with sugar and other flavorings added, although it can also be made of rice flour or other flours. It is commonly consumed at breakfast. Many regional varieties exist in Mexico. Teresa Castelló Yturbide, *Presencia de la comida prehispánica* (Mexico City: Banamex, 1986), 20.

35. The Islas Marías are three islands forming an archipelago about seventy kilometers out to sea from San Blas. María Madre is the largest. María Magdalena is the medium-sized one, and María Cleofas is the smallest. Meyer, *Breve historia*, 17.

36. Justo wrote *desde tierra*, literally "since land," meaning "since leaving shore."

37. By the mid-nineteenth century, a *barque* (in US English, sometimes spelled *bark*) was any ship with three or more masts and a sail plan using fore-and-aft sails on the aftermost mast and square sails on the other masts. They were the most commonly used ocean-going ships at the time because their rigging enabled the ship to be worked with a smaller crew than a full-rigged or

brig-rigged ship, yet made it nearly as fast and easy to handle. The sort of *pinnace* Justo saw while aboard the *Volante* was a full-rigged pinnace, a somewhat smaller vessel than a barque, with ship-rigged sails on its two or three masts. Full-rigged pinnaces often were used as merchant ships. The term *pinnace* also can be used for a small boat, but such a vessel would not have been as far out to sea as the *Volante* was on this occasion. *Oxford Companion to Ships and the Sea*, 61–62, 649.

38. These probably were the first gray whales (*Eschrichtius robustus*) returning to northern Pacific waters from the calving grounds off Baja California. Those leaving during February and March are males and those females who do not have new calves. New mothers follow the northward migration a few weeks later, in late March and April.

39. *Coryphæna hippurus*, also known as the common dolphinfish or mahi-mahi.

40. Most likely the widespread Western gull, *Larus occidentalis*.

41. San Juan de Dios is one of Guadalajara's oldest neighborhoods, founded in 1551. The Order of St. John of God, commonly known as the Hospitallers, had a church and hospice there by 1557. Flour mills were built on the San Juan River in the mid-eighteenth century, and the nascent industry led to marked growth in population. Antonio de Jesús Mendoza Mejía, "El barrio de San Juan de Dios," *El Occidental*, June 12, 2017, accessed August 29, 2022, https://www.eloccidental.com.mx/analisis/el-barrio-de-san-juan-de-dios-1282189.html.

42. The diary has *interpretación*, that is, "interpretation," but from context evidently the sense of "intervention" or "mediation" is meant. This may be a copying error by Matilde.

43. The phrase Justo uses for heaving-to is *poner el buque á la capa*. His description of the procedure, however, is somewhat imprecise. See "Estar à la capa" under "Capa," *Diccionario de autoridades*, vol. 1.

44. This "promontory" most likely was the Marin Headlands, on the northern shore of the entrance to San Francisco Bay, although ordinarily the headlands do not appear pale or "whitened," as Justo describes them.

45. Justo mentions his cousin José María Ybarra several times in his diary, particularly in fol. 55v., which features his brief employment of Justo as a card dealer in Ybarra's bar and gambling house in Stanislaus, California.

46. San Francisco was named for St. Francis of Assisi. Mission San Francisco de Asís was established in 1776 along the banks of a creek that Juan Bautista de Anza had named the Arroyo de los Dolores because he arrived there on the *Viernes de Dolores*, the Friday before Holy Week. Hence the mission sometimes

also is called Mission Dolores. About three miles away, on the bay itself, was a cove where ships unloaded, called Yerba Buena. Captain William A. Richardson, a naturalized Mexican citizen originally from England, was made the first harbormaster by Governor José Figueroa. In 1835 he erected the first permanent building at Yerba Buena. In 1847, after the US occupation, the settlement of Yerba Buena was formally renamed San Francisco and came to include all the area between the bay and the ocean. Mildred Brooke Hoover, Hero Eugene Rensch, and Ethel Grace Rensch, *Historic Spots in California*, new ed. (Stanford, CA: Stanford University Press, 1948), 290–93; Erwin G. Gudde, *California Place Names: The Origin and Etymology of Current Geographical Names*, ed. William Bright, 4th ed. (Berkeley & Los Angeles: University of California Press, 1998), 335.

47. Games is not otherwise identified.

48. Placers (*placeres* in Spanish) are surface deposits of gold that can be separated from dirt by washing in a gold pan in water, usually in a stream or river. Most activity in the early years of the Gold Rush took place in the placers. In California, the word "placer" has been commonly borrowed into English to refer to this type of gold deposit and the activities around their working. Placer County in California is named after the many placers there. When the placers played out, the more labor- and capital-intensive quartz mining became more common.

49. Justo here seems oddly unaware of San Francisco's well-documented communities of Mexican and South American immigrants. Many English speakers of the period also fondly imagined, wrongly, that the Spanish-speaking population of California was "disappearing" altogether. Late in 1853, San Francisco's population was estimated at 50,000, of which allegedly 33,000 were English speakers—including both US citizens and British immigrants—and 3,000 "Spaniards," that is, Spanish speakers of any nationality. Justo's use of *americano* (American) to mean specifically a citizen of the United States, rather than any inhabitant of North or South America, was common in Mexican Spanish in the mid-nineteenth century, and standard in Spanish-language newspapers published in California in the 1850s and 1860s. "Foreign Immigration," (San Francisco) *Alta California*, February 20, 1850, 2; "The Californian Race," (San Francisco) *Alta California*, May 30, 1852, 2; "San Francisco at the End of 1853," (San Francisco) *Alta California*, January 9, 1854, 2.

50. According to an online historical currency converter, $2 (USD) in 1849 was worth approximately $75 in 2022 currency, https://futureboy.us/fsp/dollar.fsp.

51. Pepe is Justo's traveling companion Pepe Puga.
52. The fact that Justo is commenting with such emphasis on how ordinary it is in Gold Rush San Francisco to look after oneself rather than having servants betrays how unusual that was in his own experience, coming from a genteel background in urban Guadalajara.
53. The famous quip "The coldest winter I ever spent was a summer in San Francisco," although commonly attributed to author Mark Twain, was not actually uttered by him. Its true origin is unknown. It does, however, fairly describe many a foggy, windy, damp summer day in San Francisco, especially when experienced by tourists inadequately dressed for the conditions.
54. The sea, of course, is to the west of San Francisco. It could be that by "sea," Justo was referring to San Francisco Bay. Or Matilde, who probably was not familiar with the geography of Alta California, might have miscopied *Oriente* ("east") when her father originally wrote *Oeste* ("west").
55. The unit of measurement Justo cites is *cuarta*, a span or handspan, that is, the width of an adult hand, approximately four inches.
56. *Guaraches*—Justo, or Matilde, uses a variant spelling of *guarachis*, also spelled *huaraches*—are considered primitive footware, often used by Indians in Mexico. They are sandals, consisting of a leather sole held to the foot by a series of interwoven leather straps. It would have been unthinkable for Justo ever to have worn guaraches in urban Guadalajara, but mentioning that he did so in Alta California indicates how primitive he found his situation there. "Guarache," Santamaría, *Diccionaro de mejicanismos*, 7th ed.
57. Justo uses the terms *pantalonera*—referring to a vaquero's close-fitting workaday pants, which usually had ornamental buttons down the sides—and *paltó*, defined as a jacket or coat meant to keep off dust, especially for use on a journey. This particular dust jacket, he says, was made of *pañete*, or inferior quality material. Evidently he felt he was dressed like a vagabond. "Paltó" amd "pantalonera," Santamaría, *Diccionaro de mejicanismos*, 7th ed.; "Pañete," *Nuevo pequeño Larousse ilustrado: Diccionario enciclopédico*, ed. Claude Augé and Paul Augé, 43rd ed., Spanish version by Miguel de Toro y Gisbert (Buenos Aires: Editorial Larousse, 1964).
58. In Mexican culture, a *tortilla* is a sort of flatbread made from either corn or wheat flour, round in shape, and varying in size and thickness from region to region. Usually it is filled with other foods, such as meat or beans, and folded or rolled up, although pieces of tortilla also can be used to scoop up other foods, or it can even be eaten by itself. Tortillas have been a staple of Mexican cuisine since pre-Columbian times. Castelló Yturbide, *Presencia de la comida prehispánica*, 24.

59. Presumably this was to fetch more supplies.
60. There seems to be some inconsistency in the timing of events that Justo describes here. As this entry is dated April 23 and the next entry is for April 26, Justo may be describing events that took place on different days.
61. Popularly known as Mission Dolores from a nearby spring and stream, Mission San Francisco de Asís was the sixth Franciscan mission to be established in California, on October 9, 1776. Maynard Geiger, "New Data on the Buildings of Mission San Francisco," *California Historical Society Quarterly* 46, no. 3 (September 1967), 195, https://www.jstor.org/stable/25154111; "Dolores, Mission," in Gudde, *California Place Names*, 111.
62. The term here translated as "two-story building" is *alto*, which literally means a floor of a building with two or more floors. Since few adobe buildings in Alta California at this time had even two stories, and virtually none had more than two, it is safe to assume this structure at Mission Dolores had only two. "Alto," *Nuevo pequeño Larousse*, 43rd ed.; "Altos," *Diccionario de autoridades*, vol. 1.
63. Matilde has written *enfarrar*, which makes no sense. Given the context, Justo probably had *enyesar*, "to plaster."
64. Matilde has written *galera*, "galley," but Justo presumably wrote, or at least meant, *galería*, "gallery."
65. The Alcalde, in this case, would have been the headman of the indigenous village located at the mission.
66. Justo uses the term *del país*, literally "of the country" in the sense of "native," here and elsewhere in the diary to refer to things—people, products, customs, tastes, and so on—particular to Spanish-speaking California. *Nativos del país* refers to the Californios, Spanish-speaking inhabitants born in California, not to recent immigrants from other parts of Mexico, whom he calls *mexicanos*, or to Indians who were born in California but did not completely share in Spanish-speaking society.
67. Later in the diary (fol. 27v.), Justo also comments on the Indian custom of wearing only individual articles of "civilized" attire instead of complete suits of clothing.
68. For the history of chocolate, see Simon Varey, "Three Necessary Drugs," *1650–1850: Ideas, Aesthetics, and Inquiries in the Early Modern Era*, 4 (1998); Sophie Coe and Michael Coe, *The True History of Chocolate* (London & New York: Thames & Hudson, 1996).
69. Mescal is an alcoholic beverage distilled from the leaves and heart of the maguey cactus (*Agave mexicana*). "Mexcal," in Santamaría, *Diccionario de mejicanismos*, 7th ed.

70. Rancho Buri Buri, also known as the Sánchez rancho, is near the modern town of San Bruno. Originally an Indian village over which Mission Dolores claimed jurisdiction, a large ranch with this name was granted provisionally to José Antonio Sánchez in 1827 and confirmed to him in 1835, on his retirement from the San Francisco Presidio. By Sánchez's death in 1843, the ranch had a five-room adobe house, herds of cattle and horses, cultivated fields, a mule-powered grist mill, and a landing place (*embarcadero*) on a nearby estuary. Frank M. Stanger, "A California Rancho under Three Flags: A History of Rancho Buri Buri in San Mateo County," *California Historical Society Quarterly* 17, no. 3 (September 1938), 252, https://www.jstor.org/stable/25160788. An account of a journey by stagecoach from San Francisco to San José in 1850 refers to "Sánchez's rancho" as a regular stopping place to get fresh horses for the coach. José Antonio Sánchez's ten children were obliged to defend their claim to the rancho beginning in 1852; they finally won their case in 1872, and promptly had to sell the property to pay legal costs and back taxes. San Francisco International Airport now occupies part of the former rancho. Bancroft Library, University of California, Berkeley, Collection BANC MSS Land Case Files, 1852–1892, case no. ND 101; Gudde, *California Place Names*, 52; Hoover et al., *Historic Spots in California*, 315–16; "A Stage Ride to San Jose," (San Francisco) *Alta California*, August 3, 1850, 2.

71. San Francisquito Creek currently runs from the modern Stanford Linear Accelerator to San Francisco Bay, debouching just north of Moffett Field. Rancho San Francisquito, originally granted to Antonio Buelna in 1839, lay southeast of the creek. Buelna died in 1842; his widow, Concepción Valencia, married widower Francisco Rodríguez, originally from Monterey, California, in 1844. Rodríguez's eldest son, Jesús, built a house close by; and this combined family were living on the property when Veytia passed by in 1849. Leland Stanford later purchased much of the property. DeLorme Mapping Company, *Northern California Atlas & Gazeteer*, 6th ed. (Yarmouth, ME: DeLorme, 2003), 115; Hoover et al., *Historic Spots in California*, 340.

72. No ranch in the area was recorded as having been granted to any member of the Cantúa family. "Cantúa's ranch" most likely was a portion of the Rancho Rincón de los Esteros in Santa Clara County, occupied in 1849 by Manuela Cantúa de Alviso (1820–1914), widow of José María Alviso (1807–1846), and her four children. Because it was common for married women and widows in Californio society to use their maiden names, she would have been known as Manuela Cantúa, and Justo Veytia may have assumed Cantúa was the whole family's surname. Rancho Rincón de los Esteros was located at the southern

end of San Francisco Bay, between the Guadalupe River and Penitencia Creek, and indeed lay along Justo Veytia's route between the previously mentioned Rancho San Francisquito (fol. 19v.) and next-mentioned Rancho Agua Caliente (fol. 21r.). John Arvizu, *Building California: 200 Years of Arvizu History* (Gilroy, CA: self-published, 2007), 21; Charles A. Tuttle, *Reports of Cases Determined in the Supreme Court of the State of California*, vol. 44 (San Francisco: Bancroft-Whitney, 1906), case no. 2,879: Maria Ygnacio Alviso Bernal, Pedro Bernal, Juan Ygnacio Alviso, and Louisa Alviso Vincent, et al., *v*. Charles Wade, Estefano Alviso Wade, Rafael Alviso, Augustia Alviso Dias, and Lautario Dias, et al., 663–67. Gudde, *California Place Names*, 11; Plat of the Rancho Rincon de los Esteros, finally confirmed to Rafael Alvisa et al. (Santa Clara Co., Calif.). Surveyed under instructions from the US Surveyor General, by John Wallace, Depy. Survr., accessed August 26, 2022, http://content.cdlib.org/ark:/13030/hb029001z3/?order=2&brand=calisphere.

73. Veytia calls them *perdices*, "partridges," but undoubtedly these were California quail (*Callipepia californica*).

74. The traditional Spanish grain measurement called a *fanega* can vary from approximately 23 to 56 liters, depending on locality. "Fanega," *Gran diccionario español-inglés. English-Spanish Dictionary*, ed. Ramón García-Pelayo y Gross, unabr. ed. (Paris: Larousse, 1993). California ranchos were mainly devoted to raising cattle and therefore grew only what grain and vegetables they needed for their own use.

75. The term *huilota*, which either Justo or Matilde here spells as *guilota*, derives from the Nahuatl *vilotl*, meaning the mourning dove (*Zenaida macroura*). "Huilota," in Santamaría, *Diccionario de mejicanismos*, 7th ed.

76. The place in southern Alameda County now known as Warm Springs was once part of Rancho Agua Caliente ("Warm Water"), originally granted to Fulgencio Higuera in 1839. It is about two miles south of Mission San José. Hoover et al., *Historic Spots in California*, 220. The Warm Springs/South Fremont station of the Bay Area Rapid Transit (BART) system opened in 2017.

77. Extending from what is now the city of San Leandro to Albany, Rancho San Antonio was granted to Luis María Peralta in 1820. In 1842, he divided the ranch among his four sons. Antonio Peralta received the portion containing the original family home, in what is currently east Oakland, and was living there when Justo Veytia passed through. Hoover et al., *Historic Spots in California*, 217–18.

78. Robert Livermore, an English sailor, jumped ship in 1822; he later became

a Mexican citizen and, along with William Gulnac, was granted Rancho Las Positas in 1839. Livermore built an adobe house that later became a common stopping point for those traveling to Stockton. When Justo Veytia passed by, Livermore was still living on the ranch. Livermore Valley is named after him. Hoover et al., *Historic Spots in California*, 220–21.

79. Justo uses the term *chocante*, which derives most likely from the cognate English *shock* or *shocking* (Dutch, *schokken*), in the sense of "offputting," or possibly from the Nahuatl term *chocani*, literally "crybaby." "Chocar," in Corominas, *Diccionario crítico etimológico castellano e hispánico*, vol. A–CA.; "Chocante," in Santamaría, *Diccionario de mejicanismos*, 7th ed.

80. This passage shows that tales of unbounded Californio hospitality were myths even in 1849. In all tellings, the practice of such lavish and unquestioning hospitality was always located in some imagined past Californio golden age. At the end of the 1840s, as here, it was located "in the old days, at the Missions," whereas in later generations, it was located in the 1830s–1850s. Despite its falsity, the myth proved persistent; when asked about it by romantics in the first half of the twentieth century, Reginaldo F. del Valle (b. 1854), who grew up on a rancho in southern California, would reply bluntly, "That's a lot of bunk." "Along El Camino Real with Ed Ainsworth," *Los Angeles Times*, September 22, 1938, A15.

81. From his description of the pass through the mountains and the strong, prevailing winds, Justo probably was in or near the Altamont Pass, east of Livermore, through which the Stockton road wound. The pass is now the site of a wind farm.

82. Another of Justo's ellipses for dramatic effect, rather than an omission.

83. The San Joaquin River is one of the two major rivers carrying water from the Sierra Nevada to San Francisco Bay. The Sacramento River flows north to south, and the San Joaquin south to north. Friar Juan Crespí first saw the river in 1772 and named it the San Francisco. Nearly thirty years later, around 1805, Gabriel Moraga named it the San Joaquin. DeLorme Mapping Company, *Northern California Atlas & Gazetteer*, 117–18; Gudde, *California Place Names*, 337.

84. Literally a *Sonorense* was someone from the Mexican state of Sonora. But at this time, the word also was used generically in California, by speakers of both Spanish and English ("Sonoranian [*sic*]," in English), to mean any recent Mexican immigrant, as many of them during the Gold Rush did in fact come from Sonora. See preface.

85. Another ellipsis for dramatic effect.

86. Justo Veytia was not a naturalist and therefore tended to call California's

flora and fauna by the names of birds and plants familiar to him, either from his native Guadalajara or from literature. He called the screeching bird a *zanate*, which specifically means the great-tailed grackle (*Quiscalus mexicanus*). Grackles, however, are not native to California, so Justo's *zanate* probably was a similar-looking and -sounding local crow (*Corvus brachyrhynchos hesperis*). While Justo wrote *tortola* and *perdiz*, those birds actually would have been mourning doves (*Zenaida macroura*) and California quail (*Callipepia californica*). The latter, in fact, do not sing, although occasionally they make peeping noises.

87. Now known as French Camp, Campo de los Franceses was granted in 1844 to William Gulnac, a US-born naturalized Mexican citizen, and German-born Charles M. Weber, who later founded Stockton. French Canadian trappers from the Hudson's Bay Company previously had used the site as an annual summer camp, as early as 1832. In 1845, Gulnac sold his interest to Weber for $60. To entice settlers, Weber virtually gave away most of the property, although title was later confirmed to him. Hoover et al., *Historic Spots in California*, 150–51.

88. Charles M. Weber founded the current city of Stockton in 1847 as Tuleburg, called after the dense tule reed swamps in the area. Two years later, Tuleburg was resurveyed and renamed in honor of US Commodore Robert F. Stockton. It became one of the major jumping-off points for miners going into the foothills. Hoover et al., *Historic Spots in California*, 151.

89. Another ellipsis for dramatic effect, rather than to indicate an omission. Morpheus was a minor Greco-Roman deity, a son of the god of sleep, and was considered responsible for sending dreams to people in their sleep.

90. More dramatic ellipses.

91. This seems to be a mistake for "12th."

92. The term used for the piece of leather is *guarache*, which has the secondary meaning of an ordinary shoe mended by an amateur. "Guarache," in Santamaría, *Diccionario de mejicanismos*, 7th ed.

93. Another of Justo's dramatic ellipses.

94. Assuming that *de la cintura* is not a copying error by Matilde, Justo seems to use the word *cintura* in the sense of *meter en cintura*, to restrict someone's freedom or oblige them to do something. "Cintura," *Diccionario de autoridades*, vol. A–C. He calls the insects *mosquitos y zancudos*; ordinarily, the two words are synonymous, so presumably here he means mosquitoes and other biting insects, such as black flies (various members of the *Simuliidæ* family), whose bites do indeed cause intensely itchy swellings.

95. According to Hoover et al., *Historic Spots in California*, 77, the Calaveras River was named by Gabriel Moraga in 1808, possibly because he saw great numbers of human skeletons there, the result of either war or famine. *Calavera* means "skull" in Spanish. But Gudde, *California Place Names*, 58–59, says it was the John Marsh party in 1836–1837 who saw the remains and named the river. This river joins the San Joaquin River just west of Stockton. The Arroyo de las Calaveras would have been part of the watershed. DeLorme Mapping Company, *Northern California Atlas & Gazetteer*, 106–7.

96. The "Mexican who came here with the Colony of 1834" and his sons are later identified as the Arana family of Santa Cruz; see below, note 121. The Republic of Mexico encouraged and facilitated population movement to Alta California, as the Viceroyalty of New Spain had before Mexican independence. The "Colony" Justo refers to was the Hijar-Padrés colonizing expedition, called after the surnames of its leaders. José María Hijar was from a prominent Guadalajaran family; he was a member of the Mexican Congress beginning in 1832 and a supporter of President Valentín Gómez Farias, who also was from Guadalajara. When the colony was authorized by the Congress, Hijar was appointed governor of Alta California to replace José Figueroa. Mexico City native José María Padrés had gone to Alta California previously, in 1825, on Governor José María Echeandia's staff. The colony sometimes is called the Gómez Farias colony, after the president of Mexico who in 1834 authorized the granting of former mission lands to the colonists and underwrote the expenses of some 230 colonists. The colonists were recruited primarily from Mexico City and Guadalajara and included physicians, pharmacists, teachers, and artisans. Their party traveled the same road that Justo Veytia did from Guadalajara to Tepic, then on to San Blas. By the time the colony ships *Morelos* and *Natalia* reached Alta California, Antonio López de Santa Anna had replaced Gómez Farias as president of Mexico; he sent a special message to Governor Figueroa revoking the colony's charter, especially its claim on former mission lands. C. Alan Hutchinson, *Frontier Settlement in Mexican California: The Hijar-Padrés Colony and Its Origins, 1769–1835* (New Haven, CT: Yale University Press, 1969), 127, 182–86, 215, 265.

97. Matilde has erroneously written *buseando* for *buscando*.

98. Although Justo calls the plant *yedra*, "ivy," no ivy grows in California that could have given anyone a rash. It must, therefore, have been the ubiquitous native poison oak (*Toxicodendron diversilobum*), which sometimes winds about tree trunks in a fashion similar to ivy. Given the very specifically named location of Justo's rash, he must have unwittingly used poison oak leaves as toilet paper.

99. Justo's text has *berrendos y buras*. *Berrendos* are pronghorn antelope (*Antilocapra americana* or *mexicana*), commonly found in northern Mexico but not usually in the California Sierras. *Bura* is a word of Tarahumara Indian origin, possibly an indigenous corruption of the Spanish word *burro*, but means a deer rather than a donkey, especially the black-tailed deer (*Odocoileus hemionus columbianus*), found in northern Mexico and very common in California. "Berrendo" and "Bura," in Santamaría, *Diccionario de mejicanismos*, 7th ed. But because Veytia says the *buras y berrendos* were "of enormous size," some of them probably were Roosevelt elk (*Cervus canadensis roosevelti*).

100. The Mesta was a Castilian Spanish institution founded in the Middle Ages as a corporation of transhumant livestock owners and herders with self-regulatory powers to decide ownership of animals and grazing rights. The institution was imported to the Americas following Spanish conquest and colonization. Livestock that belonged to the Mesta, rather than to individual private owners, were called *mesteños*, which is ultimately the origin of the English word *mustang*. Julius Klein, *The Mesta: A Study in Spanish Economic History, 1273–1836* (Port Washington, NY: Kennikat, 1964), esp. 49–135; Charles Julian Bishko, "The Peninsular Background of Latin American Cattle Ranching," *Hispanic American Historical Review* 32 (1952), 491–515; "Mostrenco," in Joan Corominas, *Diccionario crítico etimológico castellano e hispánico*, vol. ME–RE. Biblioteca Románica Hispánica 5, Diccionarios, 7 (Madrid, Gredos, 1997); "Mustang," *Oxford English Dictionary*, http://www.oed.com/viewdictionaryentry/Entry/124238.

101. *Vega de los Moquelamos* refers to the banks of the Mokelumne River, which runs through the town of Lodi, halfway between Stockton and Sacramento. The name most likely is of Miwok origin, possibly meaning "people of the fish net," and was first used by Friar Narciso Durán, a member of Luis Argüello's expedition to the Central Valley, in 1817. Gudde, *California Place Names*, 243; Hoover et al., *Historic Spots in California*, 143.

102. Each letter of the word *tentadura*, "attempt," is underlined separately. Justo means their first attempt to find gold.

103. Matilde, evidently unfamiliar with the term and copying the diary at a much later date, has written *hule*, which means "rubber," instead of *tule*, "bulrush" or "cattail reed" (*Schoenoplectus acutus*). Rubber rafts did not yet exist during the California Gold Rush, so Justo's raft would have been fashioned instead out of these reeds.

104. Justo uses the word *enaguas*, usually meaning a petticoat or underskirt. "Enagua," in Santamaría, *Diccionario de mejicanismos*, 7th ed.

105. Either Justo or Matilde wrote *schal* for *chal*, "shawl."
106. Some omissions seem to have occurred here, possibly copyist's errors by Matilde but possibly originating with Justo himself. The text reads *por el ningun cuidado que les da los vean desnudos*; it should perhaps read *por el ningun cuidado que les dan a los que vean desnudos.*
107. Justo mixes Classical allusions here, with a reference to following a thread through the Cretan Labyrinth and a humorous imagining of his favorite Christian saint as a Roman emperor deciding if someone in the arena should live or die.
108. Probably due to a slip of the pen, Matilde has written *Estivimos* for *Estuvimos*.
109. The text has *3 adarmes*. A dram was a traditional unit of weight equal to one-sixteenth of an ounce, so their day's work had yielded a mere three-sixteenths of an ounce of gold.
110. Almost three hundred years before the discovery of gold in California in 1848, extensive deposits of silver were found in Zacatecas, Mexico, in 1548. Subsequently other silver mines were discovered at points further north in the Mexican deserts. So important did the exploitation of these mines become to the Mexican economy that the School of Mining was established in Mexico City in 1797. As a result, many Mexicans, especially in the north of the country, had extensive mining experience, which they brought with them to the California Gold Rush. Philip Wayne Powell, *Mexico's Miguel Caldera: The Taming of America's First Frontier (1548–1597)* (Tucson: University of Arizona Press, 1977), 8–14.
111. The term Justo first uses for "sluice" is *maquinita*, literally "little machine," but it becomes clear from context that the "machine" in question was a sluice.
112. Now Justo uses the more precise term *lavadero* for the sluice.
113. An *arroba* was a traditional Spanish and Mexican unit of weight or liquid volume. Justo probably had in mind the weight of the dirt they processed, so six arrobas would be about 150 pounds. "Arroba," in *Gran diccionario español-inglés*.
114. A *cordial sudorífico* would have been an alcoholic suspension of certain substances, probably herbs, that induced sweating. In the medical belief of the time, this would have hastened the "crisis" of the fever—in modern terms, the breaking of the fever—which was marked by sweating, as a sign that the infection was leaving the body and the illness was over.
115. Matilde has written *animando sin cesas* [*sic*, for *sin cesar*] *con gritos á los bueyes*.
116. Justo has merely *Nada de particular ha acaecido en los dias que han pasado*,

literally "Nothing in particular has happened in the days that have passed"; but from context he evidently means in the days since his last diary entry.

117. Originally established as a liturgical feast day of the Roman Catholic Church in 1264, this celebration of the Eucharist came to be used by civil and religious authorities in colonial Mexico to publicly reinforce imagery of the Spanish conquest of the indigenous peoples. Following Mexican independence, however, the holiday was refashioned in an attempt to create a shared identity for the new country. Patricia Lopes Don, "Carnivals, Triumphs, and Rain Gods in the New World: A Civic Festival in the City of México-Tenochtitlán in 1539," *Colonial Latin American Review* 6 (1997), 17–40; Flor de María Salazar Mendoza, "Vestigios novohispanos en la formación de un estado nacional: Celebraciones cívicas en San Luis Potosí, México, en la década de 1820," *Fronteras de la Historia* 20 (2015), 174–99.

118. After his return to Mexico, Justo Veytia eventually did become a shopkeeper and manager of haciendas. See epilogue.

119. Hardtack (Spanish, *galleta dura*) was a dense kind of cracker made with flour and water—sometimes salted, sometimes not—and baked multiple times to remove virtually all moisture from it. It had to be soaked in a liquid, such as broth or plain water, to be made edible. Hardtack was easily transportable and lasted for months or even years without going bad, which in an age before refrigeration made it a staple food for armies, navies, explorers, and people in situations like that of Justo Veytia, his companions, and their fellow '49ers.

120. That is, the Sierra Nevada range, *nevada* meaning "snowy" in Spanish.

121. The previously mentioned "Mexican who came here with the Colony in 1834" was the head of the Arana family of Santa Cruz, José Arana Sr., natural son of Francisco Arana and María de los Ángeles Arteaga of Mexico City. With his family, he arrived in Alta California in 1834 as part of the Híjar-Padrés Colony. He was then forty-one (incorrectly listed in colony records as thirty-seven), his profession listed as gunpowder maker. His wife, Feliciana Alderete de Arana, was thirty-six (incorrectly listed as thirty). They already had four children: José Jr., age eighteen (incorrectly listed as fourteen); Felipe, age fifteen (incorrectly listed as a twelve-year-old daughter, "Felipa"); Marcos, aged either eleven or nine (but incorrectly listed as six); and Florencia (incorrectly listed as a son, "Florencio"), age three. They soon settled in Santa Cruz, where José Sr. and Feliciana had at least two more children: José de Jesús Homobono, born ca. 1836; and María de Jesús Senona, born in 1844. The sons whom Justo mentions by name in his diary included Felipe and Marcos; it is not clear if José Jr. also was with his family's mining company in 1849.

C. Alan Hutchinson, "An Official List of the Members of the Hijar-Padrés Colony for Mexican California, 1834," *Pacific Historical Review* 42 (1973), 410; The Huntington Library, Early California Population Project Database (2006), Santa Cruz Mission baptismal records 02263 and 02710; images of the original baptismal records indicating various Arana family members' correct birth years are available on the FamilySearch website: baptism of José María Francisco Xavier Pánfilo Arana, June 2, 1793, https://www.familysearch.org/ark:/61903/3:1:939D-8Y9H-PV?i=674&cc=1615259; baptism of María Dolores Feliciana Alderete, April 1, 1798, https://www.familysearch.org/ark:/61903/3:1:939D-ZBYY-L?i=137&cc=1615259; baptism of José María Antonio Arana, November 26, 1816, https://www.familysearch.org/ark:/61903/3:1:S3HY-XKT9-KNP?i=217&cc=1615259; baptism of Felipe de Jesús José María Arana, February 7, 1819, https://www.familysearch.org/ark:/61903/3:1:S3HY-XKT9-2W4?i=320&cc=1615259; baptism of María de Jesús Florencia Arana, February 25, 1831, https://www.familysearch.org/ark:/61903/3:1:939D-8YS9-DM?i=612&cc=1615259. Marcos Arana may be either José Macario Antonio Arana, baptized March 10, 1823, or José María Mateo Arana, baptized September 22, 1825: https://www.familysearch.org/ark:/61903/3:1:S3HY-XKT9-2QQ?i=478&cc=1615259, https://www.familysearch.org/ark:/61903/3:1:S3HT-6PV9-BP7?i=932&cc=1615259.

122. Matilde has written *ramajos* for *ramajes*.
123. Underlined in the original text.
124. In September 1849, it was reported that Chief Polo had been killed by another Indian for the 5,000-peso reward offered in response to the horse thefts. Navarro, *Gold Rush Diary*, 51.
125. In Spanish, this rhymes: *En tal altura vale un peso un asadura*. In translation, it has been rendered in prose for the sake of clear meaning, with no attempt to imitate the playfulness of the original rhyme.
126. This may be a reference to Justo's friend José Arana Sr. See note 121, above.
127. Underlining in original.
128. One of Justo's ellipses for dramatic effect, not omission.
129. Underlining in original.
130. A proverb quoted by Sancho Panza in Cervantes's *Don Quixote*, although Justo does not indicate it as such by quotation marks or other means. The gist is that a person can hope the next hand life deals will be better.
131. That is, Justo got up behind his companion on the horse so that he was sitting not in the saddle but almost on the horse's rump.
132. *Reparar* is the act of a horse hopping and arching its back to throw off the

rider. Santamaría, in *Diccionario de mejicanismos*, defines *reparar* as a synonym for *corcovear*, "to buck, to curvet." The word *reparo* was commonly used in California to describe the bucking of a horse; see Arnold Rojas, *The Vaquero* (Charlotte, NC, & Santa Barbara, CA: McNally & Loftin, 1964), 17–18: "Y si un caballo repara, te tumba?" ("And if a horse bucks, does it fling you off?")

133. Justo has *como tres varas*; see note 27, above, for the definition of this unit of measurement.

134. Named by Gabriel Moraga in 1808, Sacramento, as of 1849, was not yet the capital of California. The town did not attain that status until 1854. Hoover et al., *Historic Spots in California*, 143, 147.

135. Justo's original text here contains only pronouns, making it a bit difficult to follow, so proper antecedents have been supplied here in the translation.

136. Underlining in original.

137. By 1849, after some eighty years of Spanish-speaking presence in California, the European language most familiar to indigenous peoples was Spanish, and even in the remote Gold Country some Indians could speak a little. That same year, Polo's successor as chief spoke in Spanish when defending his people against accusations that they had killed two Americans; he claimed that another group of Indians, led by one José Santos, actually were responsible. Navarro, *Gold Rush* Diary, 56.

138. There is no site officially called Arroyo Seco in this part of California. The name may have been used informally, however, by Spanish-speakers for Drytown in Amador County, so called because the creek (in Spanish, *arroyo*) running through it did not provide sufficient water for gold panning, especially in summer. Or possibly, though less likely, it was used for Campo Seco in Calaveras County. Gudde, *California Place Names*, 63, 144.

139. According to Ricardo Lancaster-Jones, editor of the 1975 edition of Veytia's diary, the "Don Ricardo Jones" mentioned here was his ancestor, who, together with three of his sons, visited California during the Gold Rush. This was Richard Maddox Jones, who married Elizabeth Lancaster, daughter of the English Quaker educator Joseph Lancaster (1778–1838), originator of the Lancasterian system of teaching. Richard and Elizabeth Jones migrated to Mexico in 1825, by invitation of President Guadalupe Victoria, to set up schools on the Lancasterian system. They settled in Guadalajara, where they raised eight sons; despite the family's English origins and Quaker background, all their Mexican-born descendants were Spanish-speaking Catholics. Jones initially was rather successful at mining gold in California, only to lose everything he had gained when a partner absconded with all the money entrusted

to him. The "diving bell business" Veytia mentions was a project of Jones's, to mine gold from the bed of the San Joaquin River by sending men down in such a device. Due to his partner's embezzlement of the funds, however, the venture came to nothing, and it seems to have left no trace in the historical record outside of Veytia's diary. Another scheme to employ a diving bell to look for gold in the same river was undertaken subsequently by John L. Moffatt in Stockton in 1852, also without success. Moffatt's equipment was destroyed when the river rose abruptly as a result of winter rains. Ricardo Lancaster-Jones, "Introduction," in Veytia, *Viaje* (1975), 9; "Guadalajara's Lancaster-Joneses and the British Connection," September 8, 2006, http://guadalajarareporter.com/features-mainmenu-95/908-features/19223-guadalajaras-lancaster-joneses-and-the-british-connection.html, accessed June 14, 2012 (dead link); Newell D. Chamberlain, *The Call of Gold: True Tales of the Gold Road to Yosemite* (Mariposa, CA: Gazette Press, 1936), 93–95; Mary Hill, *Gold: The California Story* (Berkeley & Los Angeles: University of California Press, 1999), 246; "RFG-382. Moffat & Co. Prospectus for the San Joaquin Diving Bell Mining Company, San Francisco, CA 1852," http://www.holabirdamericana.com/HKA-Spring2008-Cat1/Cal07.html, accessed April 2, 2012 (dead link). A diving bell had been used in gold mining at least once previously, in the US state of Georgia. Otis E. Young, "The Southern Gold Rush: Contributions to California and the West," *Southern California Quarterly* 62, no. 2 (Summer 1980), 132, https://www.jstor.org/stable/41170867.

140. Justo uses the term *arroba*, which was about twenty-five pounds, so a total of fifty pounds here. See note 113, above, for the definition of *arroba*.

141. Justo's original *Fue por lana y volvió tresquilado* contains a nice pun on *lana*, "wool," which is also a Mexican slang term for money. "Lana," in Santamaría, *Diccionario de mejicanismos*, 7th ed.

142. The name Santa Cruz was first given to a creek on the Pacific Coast north of Monterey by the Portolá expedition in 1769. Although the first Spanish settlement there in 1797 was officially called Villa Branciforte, the modern town, founded in 1849, took the name Santa Cruz instead. This name was also given to the county by the California State Legislature in 1850. In 1842, José Arana Sr. had been granted the Rancho Potrero y Rincón de San Pedro Reglado in the Santa Cruz area. An 1855 *diseño* (sketch) of the grant shows the "Casa de Arana" at the western end of the Arroyo de San Pedro Regalado; see figure 27. The forest and the shingle-making enterprise Justo describes later in his diary (fols. 38r.–39v.) were on the lands of this rancho. Gudde, *California Place Names*, 346. Diseño del Rancho Potrero y Rincon de San Padro

Regalado, Calif., http://imgzoom.cdlib.org/Fullscreen.ics?ark=ark:/13030/hb4779n8mr/z1&&brand=calisphere.
143. Matilde wrote *surron de sorra* for *zurrón de zurra*.
144. The expression used is *que no valia un tlaco*. The term *tlaco* is of Nahuatl origin, meaning literally "half of something," and was used to refer to the coin of smallest denomination in colonial Mexico, worth only one sixty-fourth of a silver peso. The colloquialism means about the same as the English "not worth a dime." "Tlaco," in Francisco J. Santamaría, *Diccionario de mejicanismos*.
145. Here spelled *Moquélamos*.
146. Justo wrote *no quiso seguirlo*, literally "does not want to follow him," in the sense, rather old-fashioned even at the time, of referring to a servant as a *follower*. The meaning is that the servant no longer wanted to work for Puga.
147. Justo uses the term *bestia*, "pack animal," which ordinarily is used to mean a mule, but subsequent references suggest that all three animals were horses, or at least that the two under saddle were.
148. The friend in question appears to have been José Arana Sr. See the diary entry below for August 4.
149. "Wester" must be either Justo's mishearing or Matilde's misreading of the last name *Welch*. The individual mentioned here is almost certainly Guillermo Angelo Welch (born July 4, 1829), eldest son of Irish immigrant to California William Welch and his Calfornia-born wife, María Antonia Galindo; Huntington Library Early California Population Project Database (2006), Santa Clara mission baptismal record 08297, July 6, 1829. James Alexander Forbes (see following note) was the husband of Antonia Galindo de Welch's younger sister Ana María Galindo, making him Guillermo Welch's uncle.
150. James Alexander Forbes (1804–1881), the bilingual, bicultural son of a Scottish father and a Spanish mother, was largely raised by his uncle William Forbes, a merchant active in trade with Spain and Spanish-speaking South America. James first came to California in 1831, working as a mercantile agent for the Hudson's Bay Company, and became a naturalized Mexican citizen in 1833. The following year, he married Ana María 'Anita' Galindo (1815–1884) and settled in the San José area, where he became a prominent landowner and started several businesses. In 1842 he was named Great Britain's vice consul in California. Bernard Glienke, *James Alexander Forbes, 1804 to 1881: His Descendants for Four Generations*, 2nd ed. (n.p.: CreateSpace, 2015), 4–74.
151. Matilde seems to have omitted a negative here, writing *sin recursos y en situacion en que tengo probabilidad de adquirirlos*, when, from context, Justo must have meant *sin recursos y en situacion en que [no] tengo probabilidad de adquirirlos*.

152. The diary here has *gambuceo* instead of *gambusino*, meaning a miner or prospector.
153. Another of Justo's ellipses for dramatic effect.
154. A number of Atlantic Americans owned ranches in Napa by this time, but there is not enough detail in Justo's description to allow identification of this American. There is disagreement about the origin and meaning of the word *Napa*, although in 1914 Dr. Platón Vallejo, who had learned to speak the Suisun Patwin language as a child, said that it meant "motherland" in that tongue. Hoover et al., *Historic Spots in California* 280, 283; Gudde, *California Place* Names, 255–56.
155. Justo alludes to the recently concluded Mexican-American War, in which Mexico had lost territories that now form the US states of California, Nevada, Arizona, and New Mexico to the United States, in the Treaty of Guadalupe Hidalgo.
156. As in most of Western society during the nineteenth century, there were very few public assistance programs in California at this time for the ill and infirm. Philanthropy traditionally was a private, voluntary affair. For example, a Mexican family fallen upon hard times in San Francisco in the 1860s appealed to their countrymen via a piece written by the editor of a Spanish-language newspaper in San Francisco. The editor urged his readers, "If there is compassion in the breasts of Mexican men and women, this is the best chance to demontrate it" (Si hay compasion en los pechos de los mejicanos y mejicanas ésta es la mejor oportunidad de manifestarla). A Latino philanthropic organization was formally established in San Francisco in 1860, the Sociedad Hispano-Americana de Beneficencia Mútua (Hispanic-American Mutual Benefits Society), which eventually had agents in twelve communities from Sacramento to Virginia City, Nevada. As can be seen from this incident in Justo's diary, however, compassion sometimes crossed ethnic lines. "Socorro à la desgracia," (San Francisco) *La Voz de Méjico*, June 7, 1862, 2; "Sociedad Hispano-Americana de Beneficencia Mùtua," (San Francisco) *El Éco del Pacífico*, June 7, 1860, 1.
157. This suggests that Ygnacio walked the entire distance to the ranch and back.
158. The term used is *dolor de costado*.
159. That is, presumably, from the pain in his side.
160. Justo's actual expression was *por reunirse otras circunstancias*, "because of meeting other circumstances," but the sense seems to be that he had been busy with other matters.
161. Another ellipsis for dramatic effect, as is the one later in the same paragraph.

162. Yet another dramatic ellipsis, as is the one that follows.
163. Justo here sardonically refers to their packhorse by the name of Don Quixote's horse, Rocinante. Matilde, however, seems not to have been familiar with *Don Quixote*, for she did not capitalize this as a proper noun. She seems to have taken it merely as a form of *rocín*, "nag," which is indeed the etymological root of the grandiosely chivalric name Don Quixote bestows upon his broken-down old horse when he takes up knight-errantry.
164. This "little ranch" must have been the Rancho Rinconada de los Gatos, granted in 1840 to José María Hernández and Sebastián Fabián Peralta. The rancho is thought to have been named for the wild cats—either bobcats (*Lynx rufus*) or cougars (*Puma concolor*), or both—native to the nearby Santa Cruz Mountains. This land grant encompassed what is now the towns of Los Gatos and Monte Sereno, as well as parts of San José, Campbell, and Saratoga. Gudde, *California Place Names*, 141–42; Hoover et al., *Historic Spots in California*, 329; George G. Bruntz, *History of Los Gatos, Gem of the Foothills* (Fresno, CA: Valley, 1971), 8; "About Los Gatos," *Town of Los Gatos California* website, https://www.losgatosca.gov/515/About-Los-Gatos.
165. Mission Santa Cruz was founded by Franciscan missionaries in 1791. In 1857, almost eight years after Justo Veytia's sojourn in Santa Cruz, the Fort Tejón earthquake heavily damaged the mission's adobe structure, which then crumbled following a month of strong aftershocks. Zephyrin Engelhardt, *Missions and Missionaries of California*, vol. 2, *Upper California*, pt. 1, *General History* (San Francisco: James H. Barry, 1912), 454, https://archive.org/details/missionsmissiona02enge/page/454; Francis J. Weber, *Encyclopedia of California's Catholic Heritage* (Mission Hills, CA: Arthur H. Clark, 2000), 60–61; Hoover et al., *Historic Spots in California*, 555–57; "Fort Tejon Earthquake," Southern California Earthquake Data Center, California Institute of Technology, http://scedc.caltech.edu/significant/forttejon1857.html; Duncan Carr Agnew, "Reports of the Great California Earthquake of 1857," (La Jolla, CA: Institute of Geophysics and Planetary Physics, Scripps Institution of Oceanography, 2006), esp. 54, https://escholarship.org/uc/item/6zn4b4jv.
166. The word used by Justo for a wooden shingle is *tajamanil*, derived from Nahuatl *tla*, "thing," and *xamani-manilli*, "broken." "Tajamanil," in Santamaría, *Diccionario de mejicanismos*, 7th ed.
167. Justo intends a skeptical metaphor here, wondering if these promises of easy profits will prove as elusive as the riches he had expected to gain by prospecting for gold.

168. Justo says *el día que salí de este pueblo*, "on the day I left this town"; he evidently wrote this diary entry after returning to San José, which is the town meant. The name has been supplied for clarity. The ranch referred to is, again, Rinconada de los Gatos.

169. Although gray wolves (*Canis lupus*) were reported in California in the eighteenth century, they were already rare by 1827, and found almost exclusively in the northernmost part of the state and in the Sierra Nevada range. It is therefore highly unlikely that the howls Justo Veytia heard in the Santa Cruz Mountains came from anything but coyotes (*Canis latrans*). Roger Schlickeisen, Mark Shaffer, Robert M. Ferris, and William J. Snape, "Northern California/Southwestern Oregon Gray Wolf Designated Population Segment," petition to the US Fish and Wildlife Service, United States Department of the Interior, April 30. 2001. Washington, DC:Defenders of Wildlife, accessed April 14, 2022 (dead link), http://www.defenders.org/resources/publications/programs_and_policy/wildlife_conservation/imperiled_species/wolf/pacific_west_wolves/northern_california-southwestern_oregon_gray_wolf_dps.pdf.

170. The term used is *intratables*, which can mean "unsociable," perhaps even with undertones of "poorly socialized." Yet this was the hardly the impression gleaned by most Atlantic American and European visitors to early California, who wrote at length about the Californios' hospitality and fondness for dances and parties.

171. Unfamiliar with local flora and fauna, Justo at first calls these immense trees "pitch pines" (*Pinus rigida*) but then gives as an alternative their correct name, redwoods (*Sequoia sempervirens*).

172. The phrase used is *y que creo sabe tanto como yo*, literally "and who, I believe, knows as much as I do." The context, however, clearly indicates a note of negative criticism on Justo's part.

173. Franciscan missionaries brought European modes of music to California, beginning in 1769, and the Indians who joined the missions learned choral singing and to play both secular and sacred music, on organs, stringed instruments, woodwinds, brass, and percussion. Their orchestras and choirs performed at Mass and also at festivals in towns near the missions. Most visitors to California who witnessed their performances thought rather more highly of them than Justo Veytia did. William John Summers, "California Mission Music," http://californiamissionsfoundation.org/articles/californiamissionmusic.

174. Monterey was founded in 1770 as both a mission and a *presidio* (fortress). It was the effective capital of Alta California during the Spanish colonial period and for much of the Mexican Republic period. A portion of the state's

first constitutional convention was held in Monterey, from September 1 to October 13, 1849. Hoover et al., *Historic Spots in California*, 264–66, 277.
175. A feminine word indicating travel, perhaps *jornada*, "day's journey," accidentally has been omitted by Matilde after *nuestra*, "our."
176. Underlining in the original, for sarcastic emphasis.
177. Matilde wrote over the initial letter of this word, making it difficult to decipher. A transcription of Justo Veytia's diary prepared by Salvador Villanueva Veytia in 2000 under the auspices of the Instituto Nacional de Antropología e Historia gives the word as *lóbrega*, "murky." Justo Veytia, *Viaje a la Alta California, 1849–1850*, ed. Cuauhtémoc Avila (Mexico City: Insituto Nacional de Antropología e Historia, 2000), 59.
178. Marcos Arana was married in Santa Cruz in January 1849, to Dolores Leyva. He and his brother Felipe, with their wives and Felipe's children, are listed in the 1850 US Census for Santa Cruz County as living in a joint household not far from that of their father, José Sr. According to the baptismal records of their sons Epifanio Genovevo (born 1847) and José Ygnacio (born 1848), Felipe's wife was Esperanza Guadalupe Amaya; these sons must have been the "damned boys" who so annoyed Justo. The census misstates the names of Felipe's wife and eldest son as "María" and "Juan," respectively, instead of Esperanza and Genovevo, although it correctly names the second son as Ygnacio. Huntington Library, Early California Population Project Database (2006), Santa Cruz Mission marriage record 00885 and baptism records 02770 and 02795.
179. The sense of *Hace poco mas de ocho dias*, literally, "a little over eight days," is more like "a little over a week." This traditional expression *ocho días* to mean a week is used several times in the diary and has been translated consistently as "a week."
180. The literal "nearest ranch" would have been Rancho Arroyo del Rodeo, but it was not owned by a woman; since 1845, it had been the property of John Daubenbiss and John Hames. The next rancho to the south, however, Rancho Soquel, was owned by Martina Castro de Cota de Lodge de Depeaux (1807–1890), who, according to her granddaughter's oral history, was a woman of decided character; so she may be the well-intentioned neighbor mentioned here. Carrie Lodge, "The Martina Castro Lodge Family," oral history, interview by Elizabeth Spedding Calciano (Santa Cruz: Regional History Project, University of California, Santa Cruz, Library, 1965), 4–17, 21–34; Hoover et al., *Historic Spots in California*, 566–67.
181. Again, the original has *Hace ocho dias*; see note 179, above.

182. While the phrase *del pais* referred to someone or something native to California, *paisano* was used in Spanish to indicate someone from one's own native country who was living in California.
183. Justo's syntax at this point—at least as rendered by his daughter, who obviously had trouble with it—is rather tortured: *El bramido continuo de las irritadas ondas que chocando contra las peñas las carcome y las destruye, formando en algunas partes, arcos-paredes ó piramides que se mantienen aisladas en medio de las aguas, son atacadas sin cesar por las olas que se estrellan* [crossed-out word] *y gimiendo contra ellas, caen espumosas y blancas cual si fuesen de plata.* The translation is an approximation of what seems to be his meaning, which nevertheless amounts to a lengthy sentence fragment.
184. Justo here recounts events that had occurred a week earlier, around December 1, 1849.
185. The original has *sin poder apartarse de un lado á otro aquel cuadro*, "without being able to tear itself away from one side to another that scene," with *de un lado á otro* subsequently crossed out.
186. Around December 2–3, 1849.
187. Justo here uses the word *pesuña* for "hoof," even though this normally means a cloven hoof, such as a cow's or goat's; *casco* is the proper word for a horse's uncloven hoof.
188. Gary Griggs identifies the site of this nearly fatal misadventure as the beach below Waddell Bluffs, south of Año Nuevo Point in San Mateo County. According to Griggs, normally "early travelers, whether on horseback, stagecoach, or Stanley Steamer, waited for low tide and then raced across the beach as fast as they could" on this section of the coast route of Alta California. Not until the 1940s was a road, State Highway 1, successfully constructed along the length of the coast route, including Waddell Bluffs; but even today, Waddell Bluffs is one of the sections of that highway notoriously prone to rock- and mudslides during rainy winters. "Coastal Cliffs and Rolling Rocks," *Santa Cruz Sentinel*, December 18, 2010, https://www.santacruzsentinel.com/2010/12/18/gary-griggs-our-ocean-backyard-coastal-cliffs-and-rolling-rocks/.
189. The diary uses the term *armas de montar*, which were flaps of leather attached to the saddle that the rider placed over their legs to protect them against harsh weather, brush, and so on. By the 1870s this protective gear had been modified into the cowboy's iconic chaps (from Spanish *chaparreras*) worn on the rider's legs instead of on the saddle. But during the 1840s and 1850s, *armas de montar* still were part of the saddle and so that term cannot really be translated as "chaps." Fay E. Ward, *The Cowboy at Work* (New York: Hastings House, rpt. 1958; Mineola, NY: Dover, 2003), chap. 25, esp. 225–27. Subsequently

in this passage, however, Justo uses the word *chaparreras* apparently to refer to the same piece of equipment. Because he specifies that the bolting stallion "had thrown off" these chaparreras, these could not have been gear worn by the rider. The latter term, therefore, was already in use in 1849–1850, albeit to mean rain leathers rather than chaps.

190. See previous note.
191. Matilde inadvertently has omitted a noun, writing *que yo traia en la de la chaqueta*; from context, the missing word must mean "pocket."
192. That is, at Rancho Buri Buri. See note 70, above.
193. Originally built in New York in 1840 for Mexico as a trading vessel, later that year the *Malek Adel* was seized by the USS *Enterprise* at Bahia, Brazil, and brought into Baltimore, after reports that her crew had engaged in piracy against other merchant ships along the US Atlantic Coast, in the course of a voyage from New York to Guaymas. The court found that Captain José Núñez had engaged in piracy without the ship owners' knowledge, so the brig was impounded but the cargo was returned to its owners. During the Mexican-American War, *Malek Adel* was fitted out as a ten-gun brig for Mexican naval forces. On September 7, 1846, she was captured at Mazatlán by the USS *Warren* and taken into the United States Navy. After the war ended, she was sold in 1848 and thereafter was a civilian merchant ship. In the December 6, 1849, issue of the *Alta California* appeared an advertisement for the "fast-sailing clipper brig" *Malek Adel*, scheduled to leave San Francisco "For Monterey, Santa Barbara, San Pedro, San Diego, and the Sandwich Islands" on December 15. This is the voyage Justo and his companions hoped to join as passengers. There is no mention in the advertised itinerary of Santa Cruz—a very minor port—but either they were verbally assured that a stop would be made there, or else they planned to disembark in Monterey and travel overland to Santa Cruz. The ship actually arrived in San Francisco from Monterey, however, only on December 10. Justo and his companions would have put their belongings aboard on the 14th. As Justo's diary makes clear, though, she did not leave on schedule, or for some time thereafter. United States *v.* the Brig Malek Adhel, 43 US 210 (1844), http://supreme.justia.com/cases/federal/us/43/210/case.html; *Dictionary of American Naval Fighting Ships*, 8 vols., vol. 4, L–M, ed. James L. Mooney (Washington, DC: Navy Department, Office of the Chief of Naval Operations, Naval History Division, 1959–1981), 206; "Marine Journal," (San Francisco) *Alta California*, December 15, 1849, 3.
194. Matilde has written *llevarian gente á apagar*, "they would bring people to put it out," with no logical antecedent for "they," instead of *llegaría gente á apagar*, "people would come to put it out." In this passage about the fire,

Justo's verb tenses change back and forth repeatedly between past and historical present tenses, reflecting the urgency and immediacy of the experience.
195. Justo used a singular form, *cual si fuese pieza de artilleria*, "as if it were an artillery piece," when he actually had a plural antecedent, *las pipas de aguardiente*, "the barrels of liquor." This is the common grammatical error of taking the object of the adjective phrase, *aguardiente*, as the antecedent, as it is in closer proximity to the dependent clause *cual si fuese pieza de artilleria* than is the actual subject, *las pipas*. In translation, this sentence has been corrected to use the plural.
196. From the description, these men were applying one of the few effective urban firefighting techniques of the time, creating a firebreak by demolishing a swathe of unburned buildings across the fire's path so that the fire would not be able to reach the rest of the city on the other side of the firebreak.
197. A detailed account of the fire appeared in the San Francisco newspaper *Alta California*, December 26, 1849, 2, under the title "Appalling and Destructive Conflagration!!" This article confirms Justo's report of the methods used to fight the fire, including the fire engine, and estimates the damages sustained as a result at between $1 million and $1.5 million. In the paper's next issue, on December 28, appeared both a diagram of the burned areas (p. 3) and an editorial about San Francisco's urgent need for a fire department (p. 2).
198. Pine trees, of course, are evergreens and would not lose their foliage in winter. But Justo might have had in mind the fact that many ships' masts were made from pine trees.
199. The Americans mentioned here may have been John Daubenbiss (1816–1896)—actually a Bavarian immigrant—and John Hames (1811–1894), who built a sawmill on Soquel Creek in the 1840s, which was the boundary between their Rancho Arroyo del Rodeo and Martina Castro de Cota de Lodge de Depeaux's Rancho Soquel (see note 180, above). Purchased by Daubenbiss and Hames in 1845 from original grantee Francisco Rodríguez, Rancho Arroyo del Rodeo neighbored José Arana's Rancho Potrero y Rincón de San Pedro Regalado on the south. Hoover et al., *Historic Spots in California*, 572–73; *Decisions of the Department of the Interior and General Land Office in Cases Relating to the Public Lands, from July, 1881, to June, 1883*, ed. S. V. Proudfit, rev. ed., vol. 1 (Washington, DC: Government Printing Office, 1887), 260; "Soquel Pioneer John Hames," *Santa Cruz Sentinel*, December 28, 1947, 9; Edward Martin, *History of Santa Cruz County, California* (Los Angeles: Historic Record Co., 1911), 48, https://archive.org/details/historyofsantac00mart/page/n5; E. S. Harrison, *History of Santa Cruz County* (San Francisco: Pacific, 1892), 301, https://books.google.com/books?id=unAUAAAAYAAJ&pg=PA289&lpg=

PA289&dq=John+Daubenbis&source=bl&ots=7NnPstetf9&sig=
43GzQSetlMQVf6wZow9q8N_dy6I&hl=en&sa=X&ved=2ahUKEwiu6aamobbe
AhWqJTQIHfSXAD0Q6AEwDHoECAQQAQ#v=onepage&q=John%
20Daubenbis&f=false.

200. Justo uses a monetary abbreviation transcribed in the 2000 edition of the diary as *12 reales*, which was equivalent to $1.50. Veytia, *Viaje*, ed. Cuauhtémoc Avila, 71.

201. Justo has *dos cuadras*, literally "two quarters," of a mile, which has been translated as the more idiomatic "half a mile."

202. Either Justo or Matilde has written *y*, "and," but from context it should be *de*, "from."

203. Underlining in original.

204. Underlining in original.

205. Justo uses the term *albardón*, which ordinarily means an English-style saddle and lacks a prominent horn. The context, however, makes it clear that there was no actual saddle involved here, only a makeshift pad that Ygnacio fashioned out of folded blankets. "Albardón," in Santamaría, *Diccionario de mejicanismos*, 7th ed.

206. An advertisement in the San Francisco *Alta California* on December 6, 1849 (3) announced that, on December 15, 1849, the *Malek Adel* would sail from San Francisco for Monterey, Santa Barbara, San Pedro, San Diego, and then the Sandwich Islands (i.e., Hawaii), to return "early in the spring" (see n. 182, above). The *Malek Adel* then is recorded as having duly arrived back in San Francisco on March 22, 1850. On March 25–28 and April 2, advertisements in the *Alta California* announced that the *Malek Adel* soon would depart for Santa Cruz, Monterey, and Santa Barbara. The advertisement of April 4, declared that she "will positively sail for the above ports on Thursday, 4th April." According to the "Shipping Intelligence" column of April 6, however, she did not clear San Francisco Bay till the 5th. Either Justo's clothing and saddle never were put on board in San Francisco in the first place, or they did not make it ashore during the abortive unloading at Santa Cruz. "Shipping Intelligence," (San Francisco) *Alta California*, March 23, 1850, 2, and advertisements of March 25, 1850, 3; March 26, 1850, 1; March 27, 1850, 1; March 28, 1850, 1; April 2, 1850, 3; April 4, 1850, 1; "Shipping Intelligence," April 6, 1850, 3.

207. The "lady who owns the ravine" probably was Martina Castro de Cota de Lodge de Depeaux of Rancho Soquel; see notes 180, 199, above.

208. The diary has *todas han sido adversas*, literally "all have been adverse," the antecedent being *aventuras*, "adventures." The sense, then, is that all Justo's adventures have really been misadventures.

209. Gabriel Moraga used the plural form, Las Mariposas ("the butterflies"), to refer to a place in what is now Merced County. Juan Bautista Alvarado named his ranch in that area Las Mariposas in 1844. The singular form, Mariposa, was used to name a creek, a town, and a mine in the foothills, in what is now Mariposa County. Justo Veytia calls the mine Las Mariposas, which does not seem to correspond any of these places; he probably meant the Mariposa Mine, along present-day Route 49. Hoover et al., *Historic Spots in* California, 108; Gudde, *California Place Names*, 228; Metsker's Map of Mariposa County.

210. The diary speaks of crossing the immense "San José Valley." There is no such place in the part of California Justo was traversing on his way to the mine he calls Mariposas. As his mention of the San Joaquin and Merced Rivers makes clear, he actually was crossing the San Joaquin Valley; so either he or Matilde wrote down the wrong geographical name.

211. In 1806, Gabriel Moraga named the Río de Nuestra Señora de la Merced (River of Our Lady of Mercy). Originating in the Yosemite Valley, the Merced River joins the San Joaquin about fifty miles south of Stockton. Hoover et al., *Historic Spots in California*, 112; DeLorme Mapping Company, *Northern California Atlas*, 108–11, 117–18.

212. A Canadian, William Perkins, described the mining town of Sonora during the summer of 1849: "The habitations were constructed of canvas, cotton cloth or of upright unhewn sticks with green branches and leaves and vines interwoven, and decorated with gaudy hangings of silks, fancy cottons, flags, brilliant goods of every description; the many-tinted Mexican *Zarape*, the rich *manga*, with its gold embroidery, chinese [*sic*] scarfs and shawls of the most costly quality; gold and silver plated saddles, bridles and spurs were strewn about in all directions. . . . But what article was too costly for men who could pay for it with handfuls of gold dust, the product of a few hours labor!" Traveling Mexican circuses and performers not infrequently visited Alta California during the Gold Rush and subsequent decades, and at least one troupe of native Californio performers is known. William Perkins, *Three Years in California: William Perkins' Journal of Life at Sonora, 1849–1852*, ed. Dale L. Morgan and James R. Scobie (Berkeley & Los Angeles: University of California Press, 1964), 101; "Letter from Los Angeles," (San Francisco) *Alta California*, February 28, 1858, 1; "Noticias Sueltas del Pacífico," (Los Angeles) *La Crónica*, April 9, 1873, 3.

213. Agua Fria, Spanish for "cold water," was the county seat of the original county of Mariposa. It is on the banks of Agua Fria Creek, a tributary of the Merced River, near the intersection of Routes 140 and 49; Metsker's Map of Mariposa County.

214. The "Don Juan Smith and his siblings" mentioned here were most of the sons and daughters of Thomas Smith and his wife María Meza, of Baja California. In Spanish, *hermanos* can mean either specifically "brothers" or more generally "siblings" of both sexes; and documentation indicates that the siblings Juan, Manuel, José María, Juan Bautista (aka Washington), Salvadora, Nieves, and Antonio Felix Smith were in California around this time. Juan (b. 1810) was the eldest of the siblings. Donna Przecha, "Smith Family of Baja California," http://docplayer.net/32077214-Smith-family-of-baja-california-donna-przecha.html.

215. "An Act for the better regulation of the Mines and the government of foreign Miners" was passed by the California State Legislature on April 13, 1850. It stipulated that persons who were not citizens of the United States and were not eligible to "have become citizens under the treaty of Guadalupe Hidalgo"—that is, Indians and Blacks—were not allowed to mine in California unless they had first obtained a license, which cost $20 a month. The license had to be renewed every month. Although the language of the act merely referred vaguely to "foreign Miners," without specifying any country or countries of origin, in practice it was aimed at discouraging miners from Mexico and other Spanish-speaking countries, as well as Chinese miners. This was made explicit in a later version of the act, which was revised to exempt any "free white person" from the tax, regardless of national origin. *The Statutes of California passed at the First Session of the Legislature, Begun the 15th Day of Dec, 1849 and ended the 22nd day of April, 1850, at the city of Pueblo de San Jose* (San José: J. Winchester, 1850), 221–23; Jean Pfaelzer, *Driven Out: The Forgotten War Against Chinese Americans* (New York: Random House, 2007), 50.

216. The diary incorrectly has the plural form of the verb, *eran*, "were," but the subject is singular, *El otro*, "The other."

217. The diary has *donde no nos viesen, lo que no sucedio*, "on which they might not see us, which didn't happen." From the context, however, it is clear that the Indians did *not* see them. Possibly Matilde accidentally inserted the negative *no*, or else wrote *no* for *nos* after *lo que*, with the meaning "which [is what] happened to us." Or it may be that Justo's syntax got a bit tangled here, as occasionally it did in the diary, and he meant that the thing that didn't happen was the Indians catching sight of him and his companions. In any case, the sense seems to be that taking that particular road enabled them to escape the Indians' notice, as they had hoped; hence the translation "which went according to plan."

218. For the Smith family from Baja California, see note 214, above.

219. Estanislao, an Indian neophyte, ran away from Mission San José to the

Central Valley in the 1820s and fomented a rebellion against Mexican rule that was not put down until 1829. The river along whose banks his forces finally were defeated came to be known by the 1830s as the Río Estanislao. John C. Frémont called the area by the English translation of Estanislao's name, Stanislaus. Stanislaus City was founded in 1849 but renamed Ripon in 1879. Gudde, *California Place Names*, 318, 373.

220. Antonio Felix Smith (b. 1831) was the youngest of the Smith siblings from Baja California; see note 214, above.

221. The word is heavily abbreviated: *que tiene casa de como*. This would seem to be *casa de comercio*, "a commercial establishment." In fact, his cousin Ybarra was running a cantina and gambling house.

222. Six reales would have been worth about 75 cents.

223. Under the terms of the Treaty of Guadalupe-Hidalgo, all Californios who remained in California had become citizens of the United States in 1848, and as such theoretically they were exempt from the Foreign Miners' Tax. See note 215, above.

224. This is Antonio Smith; see notes 214, 220, above.

225. Underlining in original.

226. Silvano Valencia has not been identified.

227. Los Melones lies along the banks of the Stanislaus River in Calaveras County. The name is Spanish for "melons" and may have come from Latino miners' description of the placer gold found there as resembling melon seeds, although this etymology has been contested. Olaf P. Jenkins, dir. ed., *The Mother Lode County*, Centennial ed. Geologic Guidebook along Highway 49—Sierran Gold Belt, Bulletin 141 (San Francisco: California Department of Natural Resources, Division of Mines, 1948), 55; Hoover et al., *Historic Spots in California*, 78; Gudde, *California Place Names*, 233.

228. "Dr. Rodgers" may be Samuel Josiah Smith Rogers (1824–1904), born in Massachusetts, who had only just arrived in San Francisco in 1850. He eventually settled in Marysville, California. J. M. Guinn, *History of the State of California and Biographical Record of the Sacramento Valley, California: An Historical Story of the State's Marvelous Growth from Its Earliest Settlement to the Present Time* (Chicago: Chapman, 1906), 1618; https://www.findagrave.com/memorial/132029864.

229. The text has *con* "with," instead of *sin*, "without," most likely a copying error by Matilde.

230. Although Justo does not name the ship on which he returned to Mexico, the *Panama*, of the Pacific Mail Steamship Company, left San Francisco at 5:00 p.m.

on August 1, 1850, bound for Panama, with unspecified intermediate stops, probably much the same as an earlier Pacific Mail steamship that called in at Mazatlán, San Blas, Acapulco, and Panama. As the *Panama* was the only steamship scheduled to leave San Francisco that day, Justo Veytia most likely was aboard her. (San Francisco) *Alta California*, July 29, 1850, 1, and April 5, 1849, 1.

231. Roque Delgado has not been identified.
232. The slight incoherence of Justo's prose here reflects the confusion and frustration he obviously felt at the time.
233. That is, July 9.

Epilogue

1. In the introduction to the 1975 facsimile edition of Justo Veytia's diary, albeit without indicating his sources, Ricardo Lancaster-Jones states that Justo was born on August 9, 1822, at 4:00 in the morning (5). Most genealogical sources agree with this date, which appears to originate with a Veytia family tree made by Petra Veytia Villaseñor de Remus in 1905. On the other hand, a label affixed to the back of Justo's portrait, in the possession of Luis Jaime Veytia Orozco in Guadalajara, gives Justo's birthdate as September 26, 1820. This portrait, however, was not painted until 1953. For the 1905 family tree, see https://veytiafamilytree.wordpress.com/un-recuerdo-2/, accessed November 1, 2018 (dead link).
2. That Justo and Ygnacio were cousins, and that Ygnacio's surname was Arana, is stated by Lancaster-Jones, without further explanation, in his introduction (11).
3. As evidenced, for example, by the theft of the group's hard-earned gold on their journey from Santa Cruz to San Francisco (fol. 46r.), and the theft of Justo's silver watch while he slept aboard the steamship taking him home (fol. 58rv.).
4. In his diary, Veytia mentioned that his companion Ygnacio and Marcos Arana of Santa Cruz went to look for Richard [Maddox] Jones at a place Justo calls Arroyo Seco (fol. 32r.) to see if he could find them employment in the business Dr. Jones planned to start, of mining riverbeds for gold by using a diving bell; see notes 132–133 to the translation, above.
5. In his introduction, Ricardo Lancaster-Jones—a great-grandson of Richard Maddox Jones and Elizabeth Lancaster—gives this summary of his forefathers' experiences in the California Gold Rush (9): "In the family of the person writing

this is the example of Professor Richard [Maddox] Jones, mentioned by Señor Veytia as the maker of a diving bell, surely for searching for gold at the bottom of some lake or deep river. He left Guadalajara, together with three of his sons and the Irishman Don José Mary [*sic*], assayer of the Guadalajara Mint. After having collected a significant amount of gold, they lost it upon their return to Mazatlán, on account of having entrusted it to a person from Guadalajara who had joined their group in California—apparently contributing funds towards constructing the diving bell—who disappeared upon disembarking in the port of Mazatlán, carrying the whole group's funds away with him. In this way, the group of people headed by Professor Jones arrived in Guadalajara poorer than when they left, despite their technical knowledge and perfect organization."

6. Some members of the Orendáin family stayed in California after the Gold Rush. Hipólita Orendáin, born in Guadalajara in the mid-1840s, was taken to San Francisco by her wealthy widowed mother, Francisca Tejeda de Orendáin in the late 1850s. During the US Civil War, Hipólita was an active member of the Junta Patriótica Mejicana in San Francisco, and later was known for her poetry. She married Emigdio (or Emilio) Medina, a journalist for a San Francisco Spanish-language newspaper, *La República*, in 1869. Between 1867 and 1870, she visited Guadalajara and brought back to San Francisco photographs of relatives, taken in Guadalajara: Antonia, Carmen, Cipriana, Denón, Felix, Joaquín, Luisa, Micaela, and Miguel Orendáin. She and her husband had four children but separated in 1880. She died in 1922 and was buried in Los Angeles. (California Historical Society, Hipólita Orendáin de Medina Correspondence and Miscellany, MSP 1441.)

7. Fols. 46r., 51r.–53v.

8. Acatlán was founded in 1509, a little over a decade before Cortés's arrival in Mexico. The town was mapped in 1550 and later given the name Santa Ana Acatlán. In 1858, during the War of the Reform, Benito Juárez was nearly captured here by Conservative forces, but parish priest Francisco Melitón Vargas Gutiérrez led a group of townsfolk to achieve his release. In 1906, the town's name was officially changed to Santa Ana Acatlán de Juárez. (Gobierno del Estado de Jalisco, Municipios de Jalisco, Acatlán de Juárez, https://www.jalisco.gob.mx/es/jalisco/municipios/acatlan-de-juarez.)

9. According to Lancaster-Jones's introduction, the couple married on April 15, 1863, and Matilde was born on March 19, 1865.

10. There seems to be no documentation available regarding Justo Veytia's educational background. In the introduction to the 1975 facsimile edition, Lancaster-Jones draws a few general conclusions based on the diary itself:

"Young Justo surely had undertaken the study of mathematics and grammar, as well as religion; for in his good handwriting, the excellent drafting displayed by the telling of his journey, together with his moral concepts—to say nothing of his kind feelings—one notices a good literary education and well-developed imagination" (6). Lancaster-Jones, however, was mistaken in at least one respect. The good handwriting belongs not to Justo but to his daughter Matilde; and it is possible that some share of the editing of the diary, in the form we now have it, was hers as well. It can also be argued that Justo's "kind feelings" were somewhat selective, as attested by his disdainful comments on Indians, rural Mexican culture, small children, and most Californios (the Aranas excepted).

11. The 1975 facsimile edition features a sort of title page preceding the first folio of the diary; on it is drawn a three-masted sailing ship—presumably meant to represent the *Volante*, although as a brigantine the *Volante* would have had only two masts—from whose stern flies a square banner bearing the partially obscured words VIAGE ALA [*sic*] ALTA CALIFORNIA AÑO 1849. Below this image is written, in the same hand as the rest of the manuscript, *Propiedad de Matilde V. de Veytia* (Property of Matilde V. de Veytia), with a large, confident flourish below. Contrary to Luis Jaime Veytia's surmise above, that Matilde wrote this statement of ownership of the diary when she lived at the Cabañas Hospice, the form of her surname, *V. de Veytia*—with the V. standing for either *Veytia* or *viuda* (widow)—indicates that she must have done so after she married her cousin Luis Veytia Villaseñor in 1890. She must have already been a married woman, possibly even a widow, at the time she made the fair copy of her father's diary. It is possible, therefore, that Matilde did not possess the diary while she was at the Cabañas Hospice, but it came into her hands at some point after her marriage. See the introduction, n. 89, above.

12. Jesús González Gallo was governor of the state of Jalisco from 1947 to 1953. "Jesús González Gallo, Gobernador de Jalisco," Secretaría de Cultura, Instituto Nacional de Antropología e Historia, Mediateca, colecciones, https://mediateca.inah.gob.mx/islandora_74/islandora/object/fotografia:37439.

13. Tomás de Híjar Ornelas, Héctor Antonio Martínez González, Eduardo Salcedo Becerra, Fernando Luna Aguilar, Gerardo Ramírez Martínez, and Héctor Ramírez. *Arte sacro, arte nuestro. Tomad y comed. Tomad y bebed* (Mexico City: Landucci, 2004).

Index

Page numbers in *italic* text refer to text and notes in Spanish. Page numbers in **boldface** text refer to figures.

Alta California (geographical designation), xix, 1, 3–4, **5**, 48, 55, 113, 190, 196, 201–2n26, *223n9, 226n27, 229n52, 229n54, 230n62, 233n78, 233–34n80, 235–36n92, 240n124, 246–47n172, 251n194,* 255n9, 256n12, 258n27, 262n54, 262n56, 263n62, 280n188, 284n212

Alta California (San Francisco newspaper), 10, 12, 29, 34, 43–44, **175**, 203n25, *248n176, 248–49n181, 250n190,* 281n193, 282n197, 283n206. See also Gilbert, Edward

Amador County, *223n23, 240n123,* 257n23, 273n138

Amador, José María, 11, *225n23,* 257n23

Arana family of Santa Cruz, 4, 40–42, 86, *91–92, 104–5,* **132**, 145, 155, 161, 162–63, 166, **167**, 179, 190–91, *235n89, 238–39n109,* 268n96, 271–72n121, 279n178, 289n10; Feliciana Alderete de, 41, *238–39n109,* 271–72n121; Felipe, 41–42, *91, 93,* 162, 164, 166, 169, 217–18n131, 217n121, *238–39n109,* 271–72n121; Florencia, 41, 271–72n121, *238–39n109,* 271–72n121; José Jr., 41, 217n121, *238–39n109,* 271–72n121; José Sr., 40–41, *82, 84, 87, 91–92, 95, 104–5,* 145, 151–52, 156, 161, **161**, 162–63, 178–79, *238–39n109, 239n113, 241n128, 242n134, 245–46n161, 249n185,* 271–72n121, 272n126, 274–75n142, 275n148, 282–83n199; Marcos, 41, *85, 97–98, 100–1, 104,* 154, 166, 169–74, 178, *238–39n109, 245–46n161,* 271–72n121, 279n178, 287n4. See also Rancho Potrero y Rincón de San Pedro Regalado

Arana, Ygnacio (Justo Veytia's cousin), *58, 60, 62, 68, 73, 84–86, 88–89, 95, 105, 108–9, 111,* 118, 120, 128, 130, 133, 136, 138–39, 142, 144–48, 152–58, 166, 170, 172–74, 176, 179, 182–83, 185, 188–90, *243n143, 250n189,* 276n157, 283n205, 287n2, 287n4

Asians: in Gold Rush California, 208n86, *251–52n197*, 285n215

Atlantic Americans, xiii, xv–xvii, 1–2, 8–9, 13–14, 17–18, 29–39, **31**, 43, 46, *68*, *71*, 88–89, *102*, *104*, *107*, *109–10*, 176, 182, 199n5, 200n13, 208nn85–86, 213nn106–7, 228–29n47, 230n62, 257–58n23, 261n49, 276n154, 278n170; attitudes to Asians, xiii, 208n86, 218n133, *251–52n197*, 285n215; attitudes to Blacks, xiii, 33–38, 209nn87–88, 211n99, 212n101, 212n103, 213nn106–7, 214–16nn111–19; attitudes to Latinos, xiii, 18, 29–30, 33, 45, 199n5, 213n107, 278n170; definition of term, xv–xvi, 201–2nn19–28; ethnic terminology for in nineteenth century, xv, *68*, *71*, 200n13, 219–20n154, 228–29n47, 230n62, 261n49; immigration to California, xv–xvi, 1, 43, 213n107; Justo Veytia's interactions with, *73*, *88–89*, *104*, *109–10*, 139, 157–58, 177, 183, 185–87, 276nn154–56, 282–83n199. *See also* negrophobia; United States racial binary

California: as state of Mexico (Alta California), xiii, 1, 3, 17, 19, 22, 29, 33–35, 40–42, *223n9*, *224n13*, *226n27*, *230n62*, *233n78*, *235n89*, *238n109*, *245n157*, 255n9, 256n12, 258n27, 268n96, 271n121, 278n174, 284n212; as US state, xiii, xvii, 3, 6–12, 15–16, 19–22, 27–29, 33–46, 208n86

California Constitutional Convention (1849), 18, 32–39, 208nn84–85, 209nn87–88, 209n92, 209–13nn93–106, 213–17nn110–22, 217n124, 217n126, 218n133, 278–79n174; adopts Hispanic tradition of married women's property rights, 38–39, 217n124; Atlantic American delegates to, 32–39, 41, 208n83, 209–11nn92–97, 211–13nn99–106, 213–17nn110–21, 217n124; attempts to define whiteness, 34–36, 211nn97–98, 212–13nn104–5; English transcription of minutes, 32, 208nn84–85, 209nn87–88, 209n92, 209–13nn93–106, 213–17nn110–22, 217n124, 217n126, 218n133; Latino delegates to, 32, 34–39, 208n83, 211–12nn98–100; mandates bilingual publication of laws, 39, 217n126; prohibits slavery, 36–38; Spanish translation of minutes, xviii, 32, 208nn84–85, 209nn87–88, 209n92, 209–13nn93–106, 213–17nn110–22, 217n124, 217n126, 218n133; voting rights decided by, 35–36, 38, 41, 210nn94–95, 213n106, 216–17n120, 218n133. *See also* de la Guerra y Noriega, Pablo; Gilbert, Edward; Gwin, William McKendree; Hartnell, William E. P.; Wozencraft, Oliver M.

California Gold Rush, xiii–xvii, 2, 4, 13–15, 19, 21, 27–28, 42, **129**, 213n107, *228n46*, *229n50*, *236n94*, *240n124*, 261n48; high prices during, *68–69*, *83*, 130, 133, 151, *229n48*, 261n50; Justo Veytia's hardships during, *68–72*, *74–83*, *85–92*,

INDEX

94–110, 130–33, 135–36, 140–51, 154–58, 160–66, 168–74, 176–83, 185–87; Latino accounts of, xvii, 4, 5, 10–13, 47; Latinos in, xiii–xv, xvii, 2, 4–5, 11–15, 27–32, 39–40, 44, 204n41, 225n23, 233n78, 237n100, 251n194, 257n23, 266n84, 270n110
Californios, xiv, 11–13, 19, 22, 27, 32, 40, 42, 45, 68, 71, 73–74, 79, 92, 95–96, 107, 130, 163, 181, 190, 199nn4–6, 200n11, 204n43, 217n121, 219–20n154, 225n23, 230n62, 233n74, 245n154, 246n164, 252n204, 257n23, 263n66, 264–65n72, 266n80, 278n170, 280n182, 284n212, 286n223, 288–89n10; definition of term, xiv, 19, 206n80; Justo Veytia and companions pretend to be, 42, 106–7, 182, 252n204, 286n223; Justo Veytia's opinions of, 40, 73–74, 92, 95–96, 107, 138–40, 163–65, 181, 245n154, 278n170, 288–89n10; marriage patterns of, 30, 30; terms for, xiv, 13, 71, 79, 200n11, 204n43, 207n80, 217n121, 230n62, 246n164, 263n66, 280n182; traditional historical narratives of, 6–8, 11. *See also* Latinos de Estados Unidos; Treaty of Guadalupe Hidalgo Castro de Cota de Lodge de Depeaux, Martina, 179, 246n163, 249n185, 250n191, 279n180, 282–83n199, 283n207
Ceboruco (volcano), 57, 116, 222–23n7, 255n7
Center for the Study of Latino Health and Culture (CESLAC), UCLA, xvii, 17–19, 22–31, 203n25, 207n73
Chamberlin, Cynthia L., xviii–xix, 52

Corpus Christi holiday, 82, 149, **150**, *237–38n105*, 271n117

Dana family, 8, 17, 20, 33
de Anza, Juan Bautista, *226n32*, *228n44*, 259n33, 260n46
de la Guerra y Noriega, Pablo, 18, 34–35, 38, 44, 208n83, 211n98, 211–12n100

El Clamor Público (Los Angeles newspaper), 10, 44–45, 52, **114**, 203n25
El Nuevo Mundo (San Francisco newspaper), 10, 23–24
English-language press: advertisements in, 14, **129**, **131**, **172**, **186**, *226n27*, *247–48n176*, *250n190*, 258n27, 281n193, 283n206; as historical source, 11, *248–49n181*, 282n197; depictions of Atlantic Americans in, xv–xvi; depictions of Latinos in, xiv, 9–15, 29, 43–44; in nineteenth-century California, xiv–xvi, 10–11; in twenty-first-century California, 6, 9–10; use of Spanish in, 14, **131**, *226n27*, 258n27. *See also Alta California* (newspaper)

flora and fauna, 282n198; of California, 72–73, 76–79, 91–92, 94–95, 136–39, 143–46, 162–63, 165–66, **167fig 23**, *232n68*, *232n70*, *233–34n80*, *234n87*, 265n73, 265n75, 266–67n86, 267n94, 268–69nn98–99, 269n103, 277n164, 278n169, 278n171; of Mexico, 56, 59, 61, 65, 115, 118–19, 121–22, 125, *227nn35–37*, 260nn38–40 food and drink, 43, *55–56, 59–60, 62, 64–68, 70–74, 76, 78, 80–82, 84–85, 87–89, 92, 94, 96, 101, 104–6,* 113, 115, 119, 124–28, **129**, 130, **131**, 133, 135–40, 143–44, 149–50, **150**, 153–54, 156–59, 168, 174, 178–81, 189–90, *221–22n2, 223n9, 230n55, 230n64, 238n107,* 254n2, 259n34, 262n58, 263nn68–69, 271n119

Forbes, Alexander, 14, *223n9,* 255n9

Forbes, James Alexander, *87,* 156, *223n9, 242nn135–36,* 255n9, 275nn149–50

Foreign Miners' Tax, 7, 11, 41–42, 45, *106–7,* 180, **181**, 182, 218n136, *251–52n197, 252n204,* 285n215, 286n223; Latino resistance to, 42, *106–7,* 180, 218n136, *252n204,* 286n223

French Camp (town), 4, *77,* 143, *234n81,* 267n87

French Intervention in Mexico (Second), 3, 22–23, 45–46

Gil Navarro, Ramón, 11–12, *225n23,* 257n23

Gilbert, Edward, 34–35, 209n92, 212–13n105

Gostin, Ted, xviii, **31**

Gray, Paul Bryan, xix, 52–53

Green, Thomas Jefferson, 41–42

Guadalajara, iii, xiv, xix, 3–4, 40–41, 47–48, 50, **51**, 52–53, *87, 109, 111,* **114, 117,** 125–26, **150**, 155–56, 183, 187–88, **188**, 189–96, **196**, *222–23n7, 223n9, 224n16, 225n21, 227n38, 229n50, 229n54, 233n80,* 235n89, 240n124, 255n7, 255n9, 256n15, 257nn21–22, 260n41, 262n52, 262n56, 266–67n86, 268n96, 273–74n139, 287n1, 287–78nn5–6

Gwin, William McKendree, 34–35, 209–10n93, 211–12nn99–100

Hartnell, William E. P., 32, 208n83, 215n116

Hayes-Bautista, David E., xix, 4–11, 15–16, 40, 47–48, 52–53, 194–95; author of *La Nueva California: Latinos in the Golden State,* 6, 202n8

Hayes-Bautista, Maria Teodocia, xix, 8, 48

Hijar-Padrés colonizing expedition, *78,* 145, 268n96

Hospicio Cabañas, 50, **51**, 53, 191–92, 195

indigenous peoples: communications with, *80, 84–85,* 147, 153–55, *239–40n122,* 273n137; in 1849 California Constitution, 34–36, 38, 211–12nn99–100, 213n106, 216–17n120, 218n133, *251–52n197;* in other US states, xv, 33, 40, 212n103, 218n133, 286n215; of California, 6, 29, 33–36, 38, *71, 74, 79–80, 84–86, 93, 106–7,* 135, 140, 146–47, 151, 153–55, 164, 180–82, *230nn61–63, 230–31n65, 239n112, 239–40n122, 242n140, 245m156, 252n199, 252n210,* 263nn65–67, 264n70, 272n124, 273n137, 276n154, 278n173, 285n217, 286–87n219; of Mexico, 33–35, 40, *56,* 116, 196, *221–22nn1–3,*

INDEX

222nn5–6, 223n9, 225n20, 226n32, 229n54, 235–36n92, 237–38n105, 254nn1–3, 254–55nn5–6, 255n9, 257n20, 259n33, 262n56, 269n99, 271n117, 277n166; under Mexican constitution, 34–36, 211–12nn99–100, 213n106, 218n133; Veytia's opinions of, *71, 79–80, 83–84, 93, 107,* 135, 140, 146–47, 151–53, 164, 181–82, *230n63,* 263n67, 278n173, 289. See also Polo Jones, Ricardo (Richard Maddox Jones), *85,* 154, *240n124,* 273–74n139, 287–88nn4–5

Juárez, Benito, 3, 22–23, 46, 191, 288n8
Juntas Patrióticas Mejicanas (Mexican Patriotic Assemblies), 22–23; donation lists as data source, xvii, 22–28, **23**

La Crónica (Los Angeles newspaper), 10, 12, 203n25
Lancaster-Jones family, 190, 273–74n139, 287–78n5; and Lancasterian system of education, 273–74n139; Ricardo, 194, *240–41n124,* 287nn1–2, 287–88nn5, 288–89nn9–10. *See also* Jones, Ricardo
Latina women, 13, 24–25, 38–39, 41, 47, 52, *57, 59–60, 71, 93–96,* 116, 119–20, 135, 164–66, 168, 179, 191–92, 196, 200n10, 207n73, 207n81, 217n124, 220nn158–59, *231–32n67, 246n163, 250n191,* 264–65n72, 271–72n121, 275n149, 276n156, 279n178, 279n180,

283n207, 285n214, 289n11. *See also* Castro de Cota de Lodge de Depeaux, Martina; Veytia y Reyes de Veytia, Matilde
"Latino Big Bang," xiii–xiv, 1–4, 8, 15, 19–20, 39–41, 43–46
Latino entertainment in California, 43–45, *106,* 180, 219n151, *245n156, 251n194,* 278n173, 284n212
Latinos: definition of term, xiv–xv; ethnic terminology for in nineteenth century, xiv–xv, 17, 44, 199–201nn7–18, 204n41, 204n43, 207n80, *230n62, 233n78,* 263n66, 266n84; ethnic terminology for in twenty-first century, xv, 1. *See also* United States Census Latinos de Estados Unidos (US Latinos), xiii–xv, 1, 3–4, 19, 39–40, 42–46, 48, 199n3, 199n7, 219–20n154, *228–29n47,* 242nn135–36, 275nn149–50; biculturalism of, xiii, 1, 3, 39–40, 42–46, *242n136,* 275n150; bilingualism of, xiii, 1, 3, 39–40, 42–44, 48, 52, **131,** *242n136,* 261n49, 275n150
Latinos in California: endogamous marriages of, 9, 29–32, **30;** 207–8n81, 279n178, 288n6; immigration to California, xiii–xiv, 2–3, 6–7, 10, 13, 19, 31, 27, 30–32, 39–40, 42, 45, 48, 195–96, 204n41, 219n152, *228–29n47, 230n62, 233n78,* 259n33, 261n49, 263n66, 266n84; intermarriage with non-Latinos, 12, 29–31, **30,** 46, 207–8n81, 208n83, *242nn135–36,* 275nn149–50; mixed-race, xv, 3, 33–36, 40, 196,

295

Latinos in California (*continued*)
212n102; oppose slavery, 36, 38, 213–14n110, 217n121; originally settle in Alta California, 40–41, *78*, *83*, 145, *235n89*, 268n96; quantifying population of, xiii–xv, 1–32, 44, 46, **27**, **28**, **31**, 39, 197–98, 207n73, 207n79, 213n107, 261n49; social institutions of, 43–45, *243n142*, 276m156; support Juárez during French Intervention, 3, 22–23, 45–46; support Union during US Civil War, 3, 22, 45–46; traditional narrative of in California history, 6–8, 11, 28–29, 32, 43; voting rights of, 33–36, 38, 45, 200n11, 209n92, 211n98, 213n107, 216–17n120, 218n133. *See also* California, as state of Mexico; Californios; *Juntas Patrióticas Mejicanas*; Latinos de Estados Unidos; Latinos, ethnic terminology for; United States Census

Latin-Yanquís, 12, 17, 29–30; definition of term, 17

La Voz de Méjico (San Francisco newspaper), 10, 13–14, 23–24

Librería Madero (Madero Bookstore), 4, 47, 50, 194

Lompoc (town), 8; Latinos in, 8–9, 16

Los Angeles (city), 8–10, 12–13, 19–20, 33, 36, 44–45, **114**, 205n47, 288n6

Los Angeles County, xvii–xviii, 27, 29–31, **30**, **31**, 52, 197–98, 207–8n81, 213n107

Malek Adel (sailing ship), *100*, *105*,

172, **172**, 174, 179, *247–48n176*, *250n190*, 281n193, 283n206; fails to unload Veytia's belongings, *105*, **172**, 179, *247–48n176*, *250n190*, 281n193, 283n206

Mariposa, *106*, 180, *250nn192–93*, *251n195*, 284nn209–10, 284n213

Merced County, *250n192*, 284n209

Merced River, *106–8*, 180–83, *250–51n193*, *251n195*, 284nn210–11, 284n213

Mexican-American War, 33, 36, 40–41, 44, *88*, 218n133, *243n141*, *247–48n176*, 276n155, 281n193. *See also* Treaty of Guadalupe-Hidalgo Mexican Constitution, xiv, 2–3, 29, 32, 39, 41; abolition of slavery under, xiv, 3, 32, 36, 38–39; racial equality in citizenship, xiv, 3, 32, 34–35, 38–39, 41, 209n92, 211–12nn99–100

Mexican mining technology in Gold Rush, 12–14, *81–83*, *85*, *105*, 148–51, 154, *228n46*, *237nn100–101*, 261n48, *270nn110–12*

Mexico City, xix, 4, 13, 40, 45, 194, 217–18n131, *235n89*, *237n100*, *238n109*, 268n96, 270nn110–12, 271n121

miners, 13–14, 42–43, *83*, *88*, *106–7*, 148, 151, 157, 180, **181**, *234n82*, *238n107*, *242n138*, *251n194*, *251–52n197*, *252n204*, 267n88, 271n119, 276n152; Atlantic American, 4, 37, 42–43, *107*, 182, *225n23*, *240–41n124*, 257n23; companies of, 12–13, 42, *61*, *67*, *69*, *77–78*, *80–83*, *85*, *88*, *91*, *97–100*,

INDEX

121, 127, 131, **131**, **132**, **134**, **141**, 143, 145, 147, 151, 157, 162, 169–71, 173, 181–83, 190, *225n23*, *238–39n109*, 257n23, 273–74n139, 287–88n5; Latino, xiv, xvii, 1, 3–5, 7, 9–15, 20, 40, 42–43, 47, **114**, *106*, *108*, 145, 151–52, 154, 189, *225n23*, *238n107*, *251–52n197*, *252n204*, *253n209*, 257n23, 261n48, 270nn110–12, 271n119, 285n215, 286n223, 286n227

missions in California, 6–8, *74*, *87*, 140, 156, *224n13*, *233n74*, *235n89*, *245nn156–57*, 256n12, 266n80, 268n96, 278n173, 278–79n174; Mission Dolores, xvi, *69–71*, *97*, *99–102*, 133–35, **136**, 140, 169, 172–74, 176, 202n27, *228n44*, *230n58*, *230n61*, *230–31n65*, 260–61n46, 263nn61–62, 263n65, 264n70; Mission San José, *74*, 140, **141**, *232n71*, *252n201*, 265n76, 285–86n219; Mission Santa Cruz, *91–97*, *106*, 162–66, 168–69, 179–80, *238–39n109*, *244n149*, *245–46n161*, 272n121, 277n165, 279n178

Mokelumne, *79*, *86–87*, 146, 155–56, *236n93*, *241n131*, 269n101, 275n145

Monterey (town in California), 12–14, 35, 165–66, **172**, 210–11n96, *224n13*, *231n66*, *241n128*, *245n157*, *248n176*, *250n190*, 256n12, 264n71, 274n142, 278–79n174, 281n193, 283n206

Mora, Jo, 8–9

Moraga, Gabriel, *233n77*, *234n88*, *239n120*, *250–51nn192–93*, 266n83, 268n95, 273n134, 284n209, 284n211

negrophobia, 36–38, 214–16nn112–19

niña bien ("posh girl"), 220n158

Orendáin family, 190, 288n6

oxcarts, 4, *69–79*, *81*, *85–86*, 131, 133, **134**, 135–39, **136**, 141–46, 149, 153–55

Panama (steamship), 43, 185, **186**, *253n212*, 286–87n230

Polo, indigenous leader in California's Gold Country, *83*, 151, *239n112*, *239–40n122*, 272n124, 273n137

prices of goods and services in 1849–1850: boards, *104–5*, 178–79; feathers, *83*, 151; food, *68*, 130; gold, 12, *81*, *83–84*, *86*, *108*, 148, 151–52, 155, 183; gold pans (*bateas*), *86*, *105*, 155, 179; horses, *87*, *111*, 156, 187; land, *234n81*, 267n87; mining shares, 13; oxcarts, *69*, *72–73*, 131, 133, 138; oxen, *69*, *72*, 131, 137; rental of horses, *97*, 169–70; rental of storage space, *97*, 169; saddles, *111*, 187; saddle repairs, *87*, 156; shingles, *105*, 179; ship's passages, *58*, *62*, *109–10*, 118, 122, 185, 187; stagecoach fares, *109*, 185; wages, *104*, *108*, 178, 183

Puga, Pepe (José), *58*, *61*, *68–69*, *72*, *83*, *85–87*, *110*, 118, 121, 130–31, 136–37, 151, 154–57, 186–87, *224n16*, *229n49*, *241n132*, 256n15, 262n51, 275n146

Ramírez, Francisco P., editor of
El Clamor Público, 44–45, 52,
219–20n154
ranchos in California, xvii, 7–9, 21–22,
24, 26–27, *71–72*, *74*, *88–89*, *97–98*,
102, 138–40, 157–58, 170–71, 176,
207n73, *232n69*, *242n140*, 265,
266n80, 276n154; Agua Caliente,
74, 139, *231–32n67*, *232n71*, 264–
65n72, 265n76; Alisal, 13; Arroyo
del Rodeo, *246n163*, *249n185*,
279n180, 282–83n199; Buri Buri
(Sánchez), *72*, 99, *102*, 136–37, **137**,
171–72, 176, *230–31n65*, *247n175*,
264n70, 281n192; La Purísima, 8;
Las Mariposas, *250n192*, 284n209;
Las Positas, *74*, 139, *233n73*, 265–
66n78; Lompoc, 8; Potrero y Rincón
de San Pedro Regalado, 4–5, **132**,
135–36, **161**, 163–66, **167**, 177–79,
241n128, *249n185*, 274–75n142,
282–83n199; Rinconada de los
Gatos, *91–92*, 161–62, *243–44n148*,
244n152, 277n164, 278n168;
Rincón de los Esteros (Cantúa),
72–73, 138–39, *232–32n67*,
264–65n72; San Antonio, *74*, 139,
232n72, 265n77; San Francisquito,
72, 138, *231–32nn66–67*, 264n71,
264–65n72; San Julián, 9; Soquel,
95–96, 166–68, *246n163*, *249n185*,
250n191, 279n180, 282–83n199,
283n207
records as data sources, *224n13*; parish
records, 29, 207n79, 271–72n121,
279n178; public records, xvii,
21–25, 29–31, **31**, 207–8n81,
271–72n121. *See also Juntas*

Patrióticas Mejicanas donation lists;
United States Census. redwoods,
92–94, *104–5*, 163, 165, **167**,
245n155, 278n171
Republicano (sailing ship), *58*, *62*, 118,
122, *225n25*, 258n25
Reyes y Delgado de Veytia, Mercedes,
wife of Justo Veytia, 47–48, **49**, 50,
51, 191, 288n9
Rico (member of Justo Veytia's
company), *78*, *85–86*, *88–89*, 144,
154–58
Rodgers, Dr., *109–10*, 183, 185, 187,
253n210, 286n228

Sacramento, 4–5, 35, 52, *84*, 152,
236n93, *239n120*, *243n142*,
269n101, 273n134, 276n156
San Blas (city in Mexico), 4, *57–59*, *61*,
87, *109–10*, **117**, 118–19, 121–22,
129, 156, 185, 187, 189, *223n9*,
224nn13–14, *226n33*, *235n89*,
253n212, 255n9, 256nn12–13,
259n35, 268n96, 286–87n230
San Joaquin River, *75*, *106*, 141–42,
180, *233n77*, *235n88*, *240n124*,
250–51n193, 266n83, 268n95,
274n139, 284n210
San Joaquin Valley, 41, *106*, 180,
250n193, 284n210
San José (city in California), 4–5,
14, 20, 38, 42, *87*, *90–92*, *94–95*,
132, 156, 160–63, 165–66, *223n9*,
231n65, *232n71*, *242n136*, *243n148*,
244n152, 255n9, 254n70, 275n150,
277n164, 278n168
San Francisco (city and county), 4–5,
10–11, 19–20, 22, 27, 29, 34, 41, 44,

86–87, 91, 97, 99–100, 105–6, 109–10,
117, **129**, **131**, **132**, **134**, **136**,
137, 155–56, 161, 169–70, 172–73,
179–80, 185, **186**, 187, 190–91, 197,
225–26nn25–27, 227n42, 228n44,
229n50, 230–31n65, 231–32nn66–67,
233n77, 247–48n176, 250n190,
253n210, 253n212, 258nn25–27,
260n44, 260–61n46, 262nn52–54,
264–65nn70–72, 266n83, 281n193,
283n206, 282n198, 283n206,
286n228, 286–87n230, 287n3,
288n6; descriptions of in 1849–1850,
67–69, 102, 128–31, **129**, 155–56,
169, 171–76, 191, 197, 201n23,
225–26n26, 229nn50–52, 249n182,
262nn52–54; fire in, 44, *100–1,*
132, 173–74, *175, 229nn50–52,*
248–49nn180–81, 281–82nn194–97;
Latino communities in, 44–45,
131, *228–29n47, 243n142,* 261n49,
276n156, 288n6
San Luis Obispo County, xvii, 8–9,
19–27, **23**, **27**, 44, 197
Santa Clara County, 14, 197, *225n23,*
231–32n67, 257n23, 254–55n72
Santa Cruz (town in California), 4–5,
42–44, *57, 94, 97, 99–100, 105–6,*
132, 155, 161–62, **161**, 165, **167**,
169, 171–72, **172**, 174, 176,
179–80, 190–91, *235n89, 238n109,*
241n128, 243n148, 244n149,
244n153, 245n161, 248n176,
250n190, 268n96, 271n121,
274–75n142, 277nn164–65,
278n169, 279n178, 281n193,
283n206, 287nn3–4
Sierra Nevada, 2, 4, 12, *82, 106,* 148–51,
180, *233n77, 238n108, 244n153,*
266n83, 271n120, 278n169
Smith family, *106–8,* 180–82, *251n196,*
252n202, 285n214, 285n218,
286n220; Antonio, *107–8,* 182,
251n196, 252n202, 253n205, 286n214,
286n220, 286n224; Juan, *106,*
180–81, *251n196,* 285n214, 285n218
Sonora (state of Mexico), xiv, 7, 12, 40,
204n41, *233n78,* 266n84
Sonora (town in California), *251n194,*
284n212
Sonorenses (Sonorans), xiv, 12, *75, 90,*
100, 142, 159, 173, 199n8, 200n15;
definition of term, xiv, 204n41,
233n78, 266n84; Spanish-language
press: advertisements in, 10, 12,
184; as historical source, xvii, 10–12,
15–16, 22, 50, 203n25; depictions
of Atlantic Americans in, *228–29n47,*
261n49; depictions of Latinos in, xiv,
9–12, 15–16, 50, 199–200nn6–13,
243n142, 276n156; in nineteenth-century California, xiv, xvii,
10–12, 15, 22, 44–45, **114**, 288n6;
in twenty-first-century California,
9–10; survival of issues of, 203n25.
See also El Clamor Público, El Nuevo
Mundo, La Crónica, La Voz de Méjico
stagecoaches, *109,* **132**, **184**, 185,
231n65, 246–47n172, 260n45,
280n188
Stanislaus, 4, 13, *107–9,* 182, 185,
197, *227n43, 252n201, 253n209,*
285–86n219, 286n227
states' rights doctrine and voting rights,
34–36, 210nn93–95, 212nn102–3,
213n106

Stockton (city in California), 4, *77*,
86–88, *90*, *109*, 143, 155–57, 160,
185, *233n73*, *233n75*, *234nn81–82*,
234–35n88, *236n93*, *240n124*,
251n193, 266n78, 266n81,
267nn87–88, 268n95, 269n101,
274n139, 284n211
St. John of God, *65*, *80*, 125–26, 148;
order of, *227n38*, 260n41

Tapia family, *111*, 187; Carlos, *58*, 118,
224n15, 256n14; Ygnacio, *109*, 185,
224n15, 256n14
Tepic, 4, *57–9*, *102*, *111*, 116–19,
177, 156, 176, 187, *222n7*, *223n9*,
224n14, *224n19*, *235n89*, 255n7,
255n9, 256n13, 257n18, 268n96;
Carnival in, *59–61*, 119–21, *225n20*,
257n20, 257n22
Tequila (town), 4, *56*, 115, **177**,
189–90, *221–22n2*, 254n2
Treaty of Guadalupe Hidalgo, 2–3, 33–
36, 42, 45, 209–10n93, 219n153,
243n141, *251–52n197*, *252n204*,
276n155, 285n215, 286n223
Tuolumne County, xvii, 12, 27, 197,
218n136

United States Census, 205n60; 1890
returns destroyed, 205–6n61; as data
source, xvii, 6, 15–20, 206–7n69,
279n178; ethnic terminology in,
xv, 15, 17; Hispanic names in,
17–18, 279n178; Latinos in, xv,
xvii, 6, 8, 15–22, **23**, 24–29, 197;
methodology of, xv, 15–16, 18, 21;
undercounts in, 21–28
United States Civil War, xiv, xvii, 2–4,
11, 15–16, 22–23, 27, 32, 34,
41–42, 45–46, 207n73, 207–8n81,
288n6
United States Constitution, xiv,
2–3, 29, 32, 38–39, 41, 210n95,
214n111; full citizenship denied to
nonwhites (before 1868), xiv, 3, 32,
38–39, 214n111; permitted slavery
(before 1865), xiv, 3, 32, 38–39;
rights of citizenship, 34, 41; voting
rights denied to nonwhites (before
1870), xiv, 34–36, 41, 213n106
United States racial binary, xv, 33–36,
38, 208nn84–86, 209nn87–88,
210–11nn96–98, 212–13nn104–6;
considers Latinos racially inferior
to whites, 33; Latino rejection of,
34–35, 38, 211–12nn97–100

vaqueros (cowboys), 8–9, 16, 22; gear
and equipment, *229n54*, *247n173*,
262n57, 280–1n189, 283n205
Veytia Orozco, Luis Jaime, iii, xix, **5**,
47–48, **49**, 50, **51**, 53, 189, 194–96,
196, 287n1, 289n11
Veytia y Reyes de Veytia, Matilde,
5, 47–48, **49**, 50, **51**, 191–95,
220n159, *226n31*, *227n40*, *229n52*,
229n54, *230nn59–60*, *232n70*,
234n87, *235n90*, *236nn94–96*,
237n98, *237n104*, *239n110*,
241n129, *242n135*, *242n137*,
243n147, *245n158*, *245n160*,
246n168, *247n174*, *248n177*,
249n183, *249n187*, *250n193*,
252n199, *253n211*, 259n32, 260n42,
262n54, 262n56, 263nn63–64,
265n75, 267n94, 268n97, 269n103,

INDEX

270nn105–6, 270n108, 270n115, 272n122, 275n143, 275n149, 275n151, 277n163, 279n175, 279n177, 281n191, 281n194, 283n202, 284n210, 285n217, 286n229, 288–89nn9–11

Veytia y Valencia, Justo, 40, 189; after return to Mexico, 47–48, 191; arrives in California, 41, *67–68*, 127–28; birthdate, 287n1; death of, 47, 50, 189, 191; leaves Guadalajara for California, 55, 113, **114**; mishaps with horses, *82–83, 87–88, 90–92, 95, 98,* 152, 156, 160, 162–63, 170–71, *239n118, 243n147, 247n173,* 272–73nn131–32, 280–81n189; portrait of, **iii**, 287n1; returns to Mexico, 43, *108–11*, 183–87; route from Guadalajara to San Blas, *55–59, 61–62,* 113, 115–19, 121–22, **117**; routes in California, **132**; victim of theft, *99, 110,* 171, 186–87, 191, 287n3; views on music, 56, *93–94,* 115–16, 165, *245n156,* 278n173. *See also* Atlantic Americans; Arana family; California Gold Rush; Californios; indigenous peoples; Reyes y Delgado de Veytia, Mercedes; Veytia y Reyes de Veytia, Matilde; Veytia y Valencia, Justo, diary of

Veytia y Valencia, Justo, diary of, **iii**, xiv, xvii–xix, 3–4, **5**, 40–43, 46–48, 50, **51**, 52–53, 55, *75–76, 78–79, 95,* 113, 140, 143–44, 146, 166, 168, **175**, 189–90, 192, 194–96, 217n127, 220n159, *223n11, 227n40, 227n43, 229n52, 230nn62–63, 236nn95–96, 238–39n109, 239n117, 240–41n124, 241nn127–29, 242n134, 242n138, 243n142, 243n147, 244n150, 244n152, 245n160, 246n162, 246n165, 246n169, 247n173, 247–48n176, 249n184, 249n187, 250–51n193, 252nn198–200, 253n217,* 255n10, 259n32, 259n36, 260n42, 260n45, 263nn66–67, 268n97, 270nn105–6, 270–71n116, 271–72n121, 272n130, 273–74n139, 274–75nn142–43, 275n148, 276n152, 276n156, 277n163, 278n168, 279n177, 279n179, 280–81n189, 281n193, 281–82n194, 283nn200–202, 283n208, 284n210, 285nn216–17, 287n1, 287n4; cites *Don Quixote*, 83, *90–92,* 152, 160, 163, *239n117, 243n147,* 272n130, 277n163; copying errors in, 50, *226n31, 227n40, 229n52, 230nn59–60, 236n94, 242n137, 245n158, 246n168, 247n174, 248n177, 249–50nn187–89,* 259n32, 260n42, 262n54, 263nn63–64, 267n94, 268n97, 269n103, 270n106, 270n108, 270n115, 271n122, 272n122, 275n151, 276n152, 279n175, 281n191, 283nn202–4, 285n217, 286n229; facsimile edition, 4, **5fig. 2**, 47, 194, 273–74n139, 287n1, 287–88n5, 288–89nn10–11; handwriting of, 4, 47–48, 50, 194, 288–89nn10–11; UNAM edition, 50, 220n160, *245n160, 249n186,* 279n177, 283n200; rights to, 47, 50, 279n177. *See also* Veytia y Reyes de Veytia, Matilde

Veytia y Veytia, Salvador, **5**, 47–48, 50, 193–94
Veytia Villaseñor, Luis, 50, **51**, 192, 220n159, 289n11
Volante (sailing ship), 4, 41, *58*, *62–67*, **117**, 118, 122–27, **129**, *224n16*, *227n34*, 256n15, 259–60n37, 289n11; description of, *62–63*, 122–23; hardships of travel in, *63–67*, 122, 124–27

Waddell Bluffs, *98*, 170, *246–47n172*, 280n188
weights, measures, and money, 47, 57, *62–63*, *69–70*, *73*, *75*, *77–78*, *80–81*, *83–85*, *98–99*, *105*, 116, 123, 131, 133, 139, 142, 144, 148, 154, 178, 182, *223–24n12*, *224n13*, *226nn27–28*, *229n48*, *229n53*, *232n69*, *237n99*, *237n102*, *239n119*, *241n125*, *241n130*, *249n186*, 255–56n11, 258nn27–28, 261n50, 262n55, 265n74, 270n109, 270n113, 273n133, 274n140, 275n144, 283nn200–201, 286n222
Welch, Guillermo ("Wester"), *87*, 156, *242n135*, 275n149
Wozencraft, Oliver M., 37, 215n116

Ybarra, José María, *67–69*, *107–8*, 128, 131, 182, *227n43*, *252n203*, 260n45, 286n221